# A CARTOON COLLECTION
# BY PHIL DUNLAP

WITH A FOREWORD BY PAUL "POOCH CAFÉ" GILLIGAN

D1557746

Chamblin Bookmine
Jax, FL 904-384-1685
March 07

**Andrews McMeel Publishing, LLC**
Kansas City

**Ink Pen** is distributed internationally by Universal Press Syndicate.



09 10 11 12 13 TEN 10 9 8 7 6 5 4 3 2 1

ISBN-13: 978-0-7407-8095-0
ISBN-10: 0-7407-8095-6

Library of Congress Control Number: 2008936251

www.andrewsmcmeel.com

# Foreword
## by Paul Gilligan

Growing up, I always wanted my family to be funnier. When I watched families on television shows, they always cracked jokes and got lots of laughs from an invisible audience. Wow, how great would that be? I thought. I tried to get that kind of shtick going in my family, but it didn't work even when I used the exact same jokes that were causing a riot around the Brady household.

For cartoonists, stealing jokes is taboo, of course. But sometimes we see concepts that are so bang-on that we wish they were ours. I think that's the holy grail of cartoonist compliments: "Dammit, why didn't *I* think of that? Dammit." Those sentences apply to the whole *Ink Pen* world.

I met Phil years ago in L.A. in the bar of a boutique hotel owned by Gregory Peck (no, not *the* Gregory Peck), and I think I kept the "dammits" to a minimum. I don't know if it was our shared love of *Bloom County*, Looney Tunes, *The Simpsons*, Jack Kirby, and Will Eisner, or if it was the whiskey sours, but we got along famously. I'd been doing my comic strip for a while, letting my influences trickle and drip in here and there like a toothless sap. It had never occurred to me to create a world where they could all frolic together undiluted! I mean, who hasn't wondered what it would be like for Captain America and Porky Pig to share drinks together at a bar? Well, maybe lots of people, but nobody at the table that day. Phil has got Opus's desk at the *Bloom Picayune*, Thor's hammer, and Oscar the Grouch's garbage can all within spit-take distance of each other. He's got sidekicks, aliens, sound effects, and pie gags all mixed together like gumballs in a machine at the supermarket beside a rack of tabloids. In my strip, I've got a bunch of dogs. Dammit.

And Phil has done something more with his cast of barely employable misfits; he's given them *character*. Each one represents people I'm sure you see around you every day, your own friends, your own family. And what makes them so watchable, so real, and so hilarious is that they don't even know they're funny. They're grumpy, fussy, demanding, and oblivious. That's comedy.

Hmm, maybe my family *was* funny. *Ink Pen*'s is, and magically so. Turn the handle, and in every strip you get a new mittfull of influences celebrating cartooning at its finest.

*Paul Gilligan is the creator of the comic strip* Pooch Café. *Visit his Web site at poochcafe.com.*

# FOR DANIELLE

WHO NEVER LETS ME GET
STUCK IN A RUT...

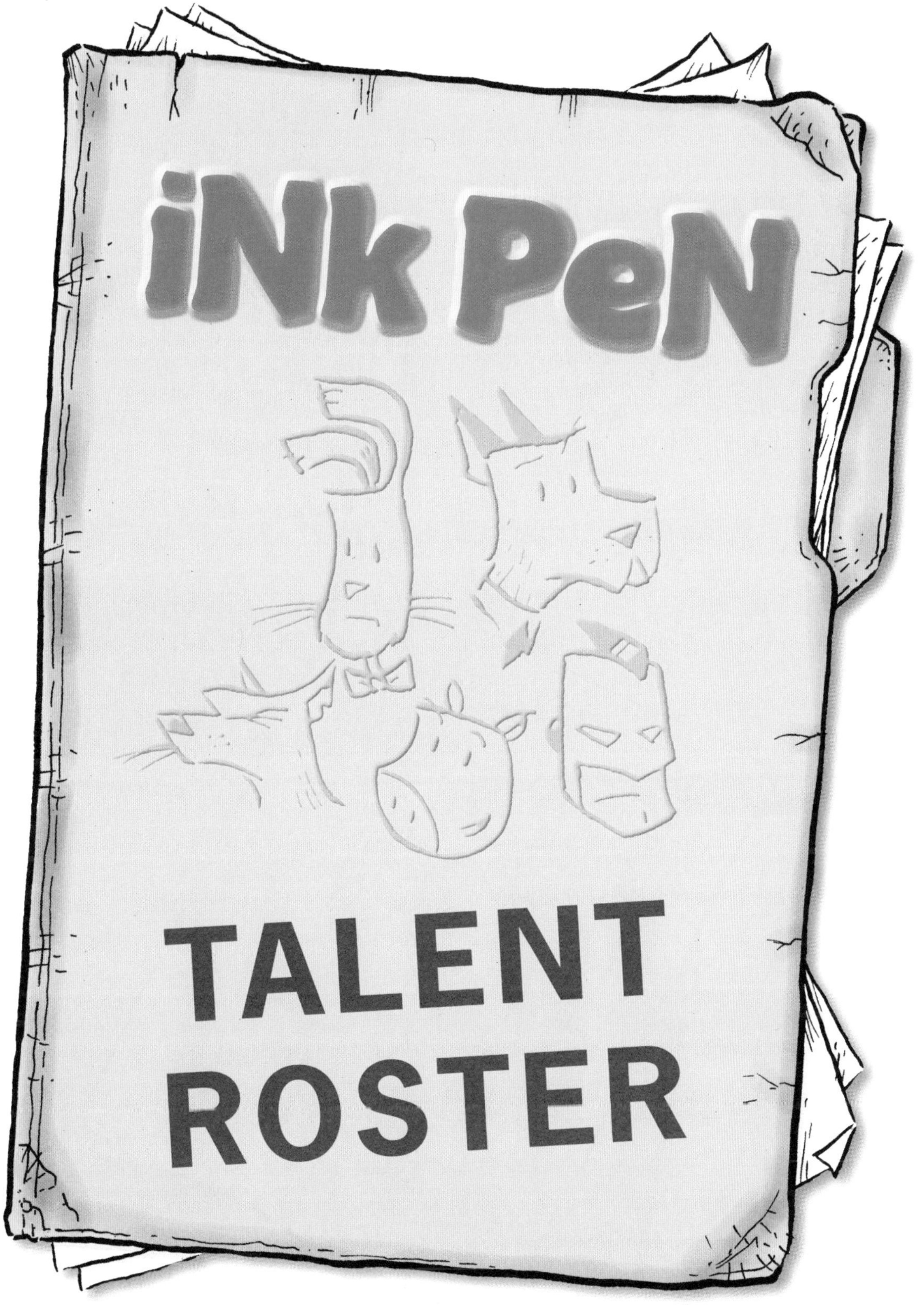
iNk PeN
TALENT ROSTER

## Bixby

A former obnoxious child star, Bixby grew into a dirty, ugly rat unable to attract work or the love of children. Bixby is now the talent coordinator for *Ink Pen*, placing other cartoon characters in degrading jobs while showing no sympathy for their plight.

**Assets:** Lack of conscience allows him to crush the dreams of starry-eyed hopefuls on a daily basis.

**Drawbacks:** Bathes infrequently at best: "I eat garbage and live in my own filth. Self-esteem isn't really a priority for me."

## Fritz

After unionizing the extras during a guest stint in *Marmaduke*, Fritz decided he could make more of a difference behind the scenes.

**Assets:** Convinced that every company should have an adorable cartoon mascot.

**Drawbacks:** Can't understand why the American Heart Association wouldn't want its corporate image represented by a chubby, gravy-sweating pig: "If you don't capitalize on the youth market now, you'll be missing out on profits well into the future!"

## Hamhock

Willing to endure almost any amount of humiliation for a life in the limelight, Hamhock hungers for his big break, while others hunger for his apple-smoked belly and tender ribs.

**Assets:** Virtually no pride.

**Drawbacks:** Virtually no talent: "I see the stares! At my rump, my loins, my chops! And the baloney fans! I can't even repeat what they stare at!"

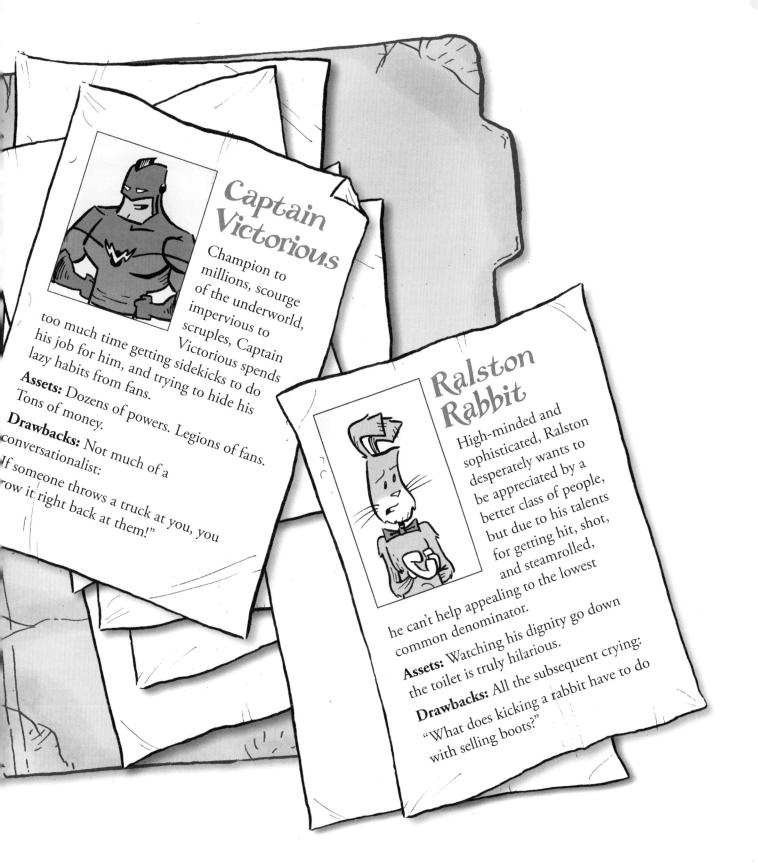

## Captain Victorious

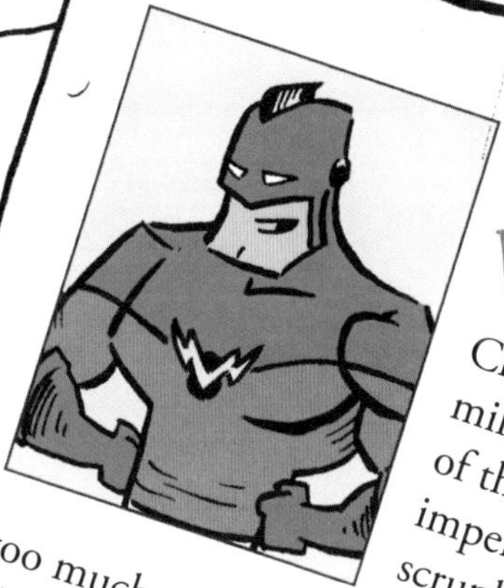

Champion to millions, scourge of the underworld, impervious to scruples, Captain Victorious spends too much time getting sidekicks to do his job for him, and trying to hide his lazy habits from fans.

**Assets:** Dozens of powers. Legions of fans. Tons of money.

**Drawbacks:** Not much of a conversationalist:

“If someone throws a truck at you, you row it right back at them!”

## Ralston Rabbit

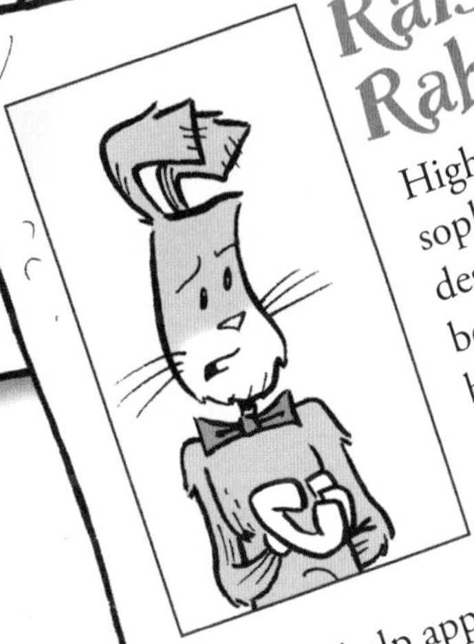

High-minded and sophisticated, Ralston desperately wants to be appreciated by a better class of people, but due to his talents for getting hit, shot, and steamrolled, he can’t help appealing to the lowest common denominator.

**Assets:** Watching his dignity go down the toilet is truly hilarious.

**Drawbacks:** All the subsequent crying:

“What does kicking a rabbit have to do with selling boots?”

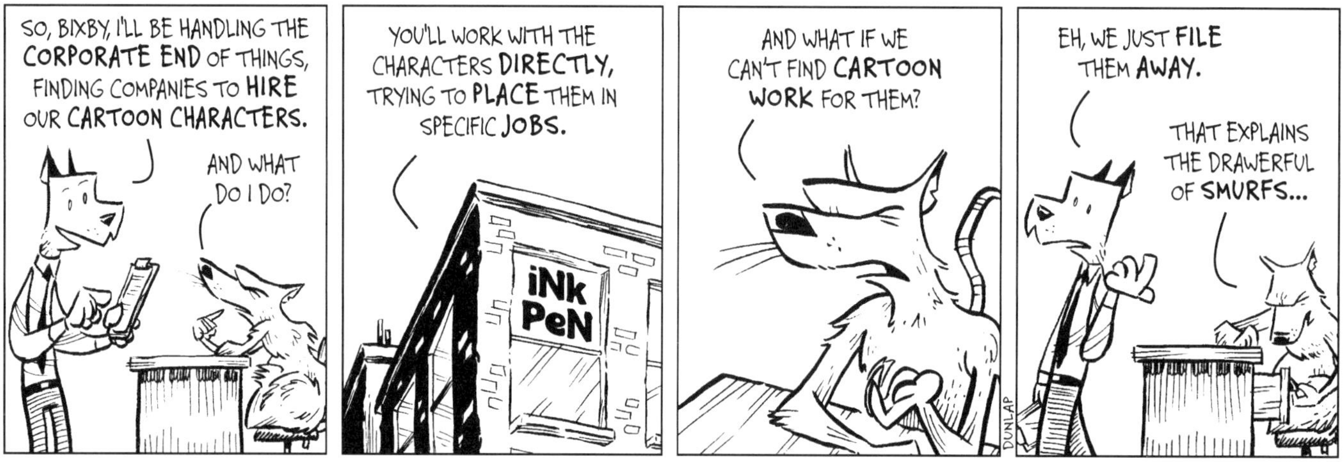
SO, BIXBY, I'LL BE HANDLING THE CORPORATE END OF THINGS, FINDING COMPANIES TO HIRE OUR CARTOON CHARACTERS.
AND WHAT DO I DO?
YOU'LL WORK WITH THE CHARACTERS DIRECTLY, TRYING TO PLACE THEM IN SPECIFIC JOBS.
iNk PeN
AND WHAT IF WE CAN'T FIND CARTOON WORK FOR THEM?
EH, WE JUST FILE THEM AWAY.
THAT EXPLAINS THE DRAWERFUL OF SMURFS...
DUNLAP

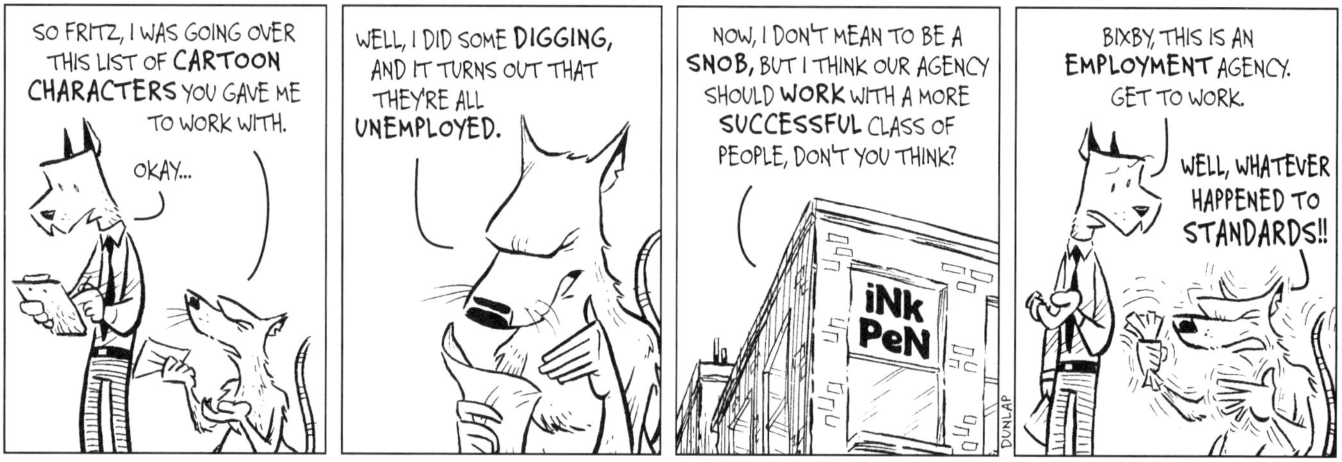
SO FRITZ, I WAS GOING OVER THIS LIST OF CARTOON CHARACTERS YOU GAVE ME TO WORK WITH.
OKAY...
WELL, I DID SOME DIGGING, AND IT TURNS OUT THAT THEY'RE ALL UNEMPLOYED.
NOW, I DON'T MEAN TO BE A SNOB, BUT I THINK OUR AGENCY SHOULD WORK WITH A MORE SUCCESSFUL CLASS OF PEOPLE, DON'T YOU THINK?
iNk PeN
DUNLAP
BIXBY, THIS IS AN EMPLOYMENT AGENCY. GET TO WORK.
WELL, WHATEVER HAPPENED TO STANDARDS!!

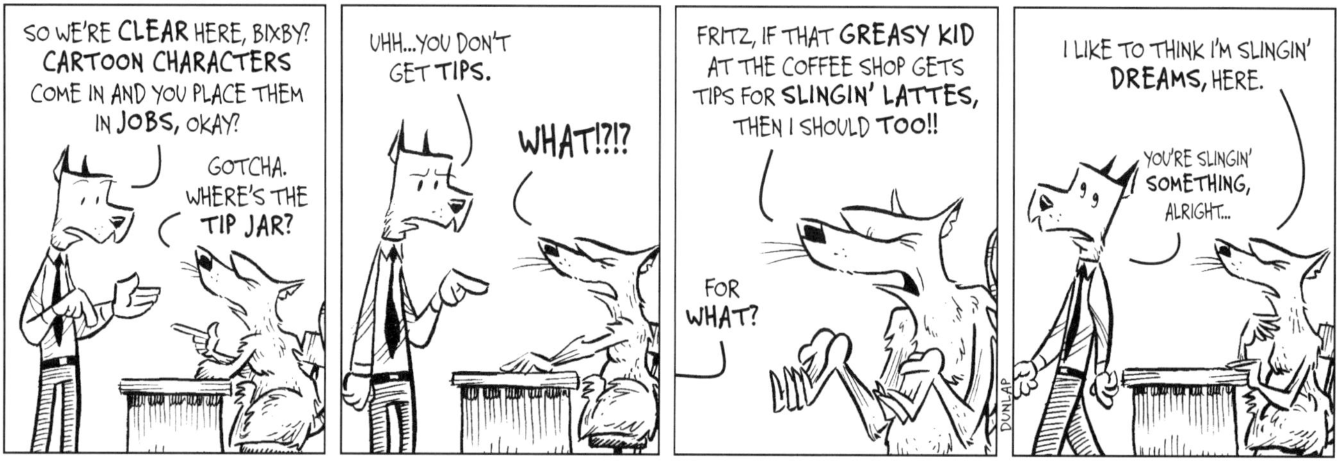
SO WE'RE CLEAR HERE, BIXBY? CARTOON CHARACTERS COME IN AND YOU PLACE THEM IN JOBS, OKAY?
GOTCHA. WHERE'S THE TIP JAR?
UHH...YOU DON'T GET TIPS.
WHAT!?!?
FRITZ, IF THAT GREASY KID AT THE COFFEE SHOP GETS TIPS FOR SLINGIN' LATTES, THEN I SHOULD TOO!!
FOR WHAT?
DUNLAP
I LIKE TO THINK I'M SLINGIN' DREAMS, HERE.
YOU'RE SLINGIN' SOMETHING, ALRIGHT...

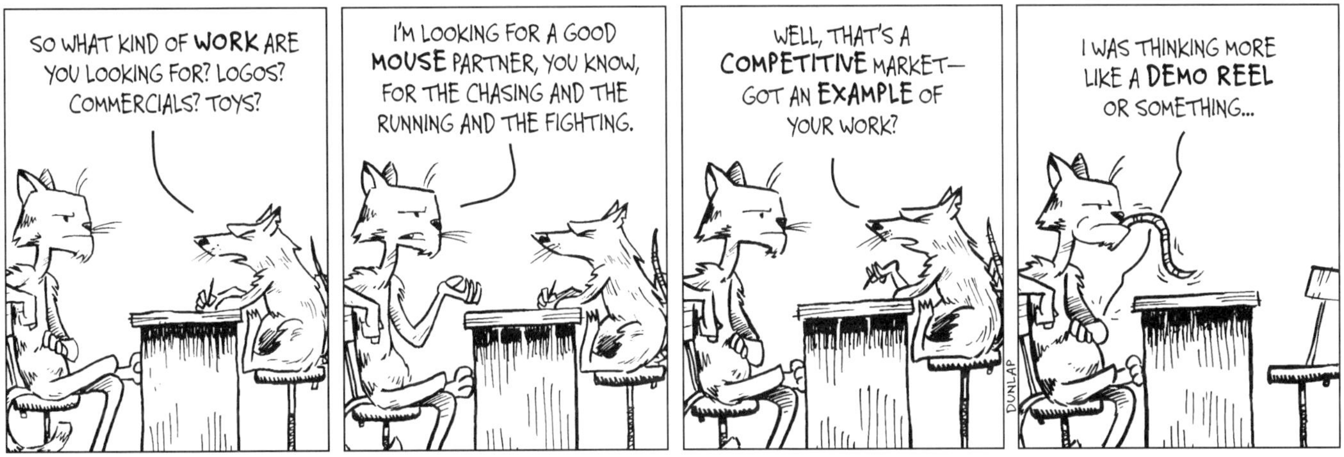
SO WHAT KIND OF **WORK** ARE YOU LOOKING FOR? LOGOS? COMMERCIALS? TOYS?
I'M LOOKING FOR A GOOD **MOUSE** PARTNER, YOU KNOW, FOR THE CHASING AND THE RUNNING AND THE FIGHTING.
WELL, THAT'S A **COMPETITIVE** MARKET— GOT AN **EXAMPLE** OF YOUR WORK?
I WAS THINKING MORE LIKE A **DEMO REEL** OR SOMETHING...
DUNLAP

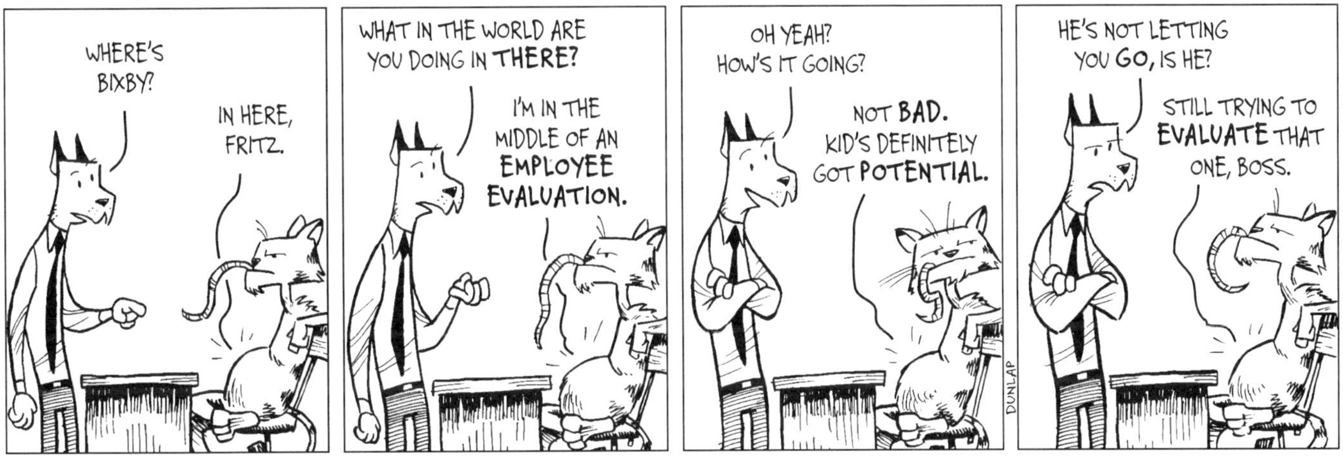
WHERE'S BIXBY?
IN HERE, FRITZ.
WHAT IN THE WORLD ARE YOU DOING IN **THERE?**
I'M IN THE MIDDLE OF AN **EMPLOYEE EVALUATION.**
OH YEAH? HOW'S IT GOING?
NOT **BAD.** KID'S DEFINITELY GOT **POTENTIAL.**
HE'S NOT LETTING YOU **GO,** IS HE?
STILL TRYING TO **EVALUATE** THAT ONE, BOSS.
DUNLAP

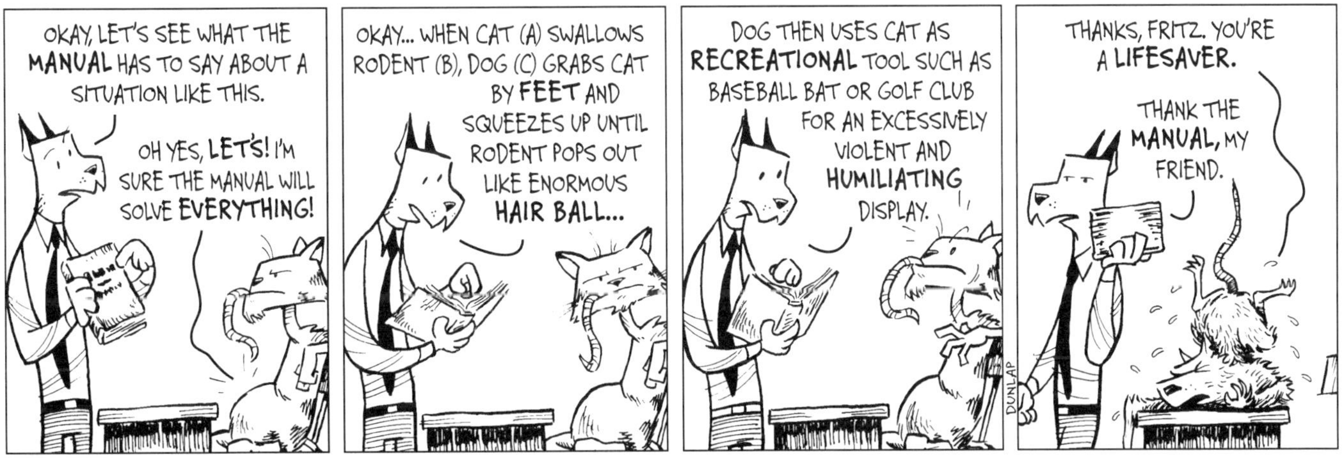
OKAY, LET'S SEE WHAT THE **MANUAL** HAS TO SAY ABOUT A SITUATION LIKE THIS.
OH YES, **LET'S!** I'M SURE THE MANUAL WILL SOLVE **EVERYTHING!**
OKAY... WHEN CAT (A) SWALLOWS RODENT (B), DOG (C) GRABS CAT BY **FEET** AND SQUEEZES UP UNTIL RODENT POPS OUT LIKE ENORMOUS **HAIR BALL...**
DOG THEN USES CAT AS **RECREATIONAL** TOOL SUCH AS BASEBALL BAT OR GOLF CLUB FOR AN EXCESSIVELY VIOLENT AND **HUMILIATING** DISPLAY.
THANKS, FRITZ. YOU'RE A **LIFESAVER.**
THANK THE **MANUAL,** MY FRIEND.
DUNLAP

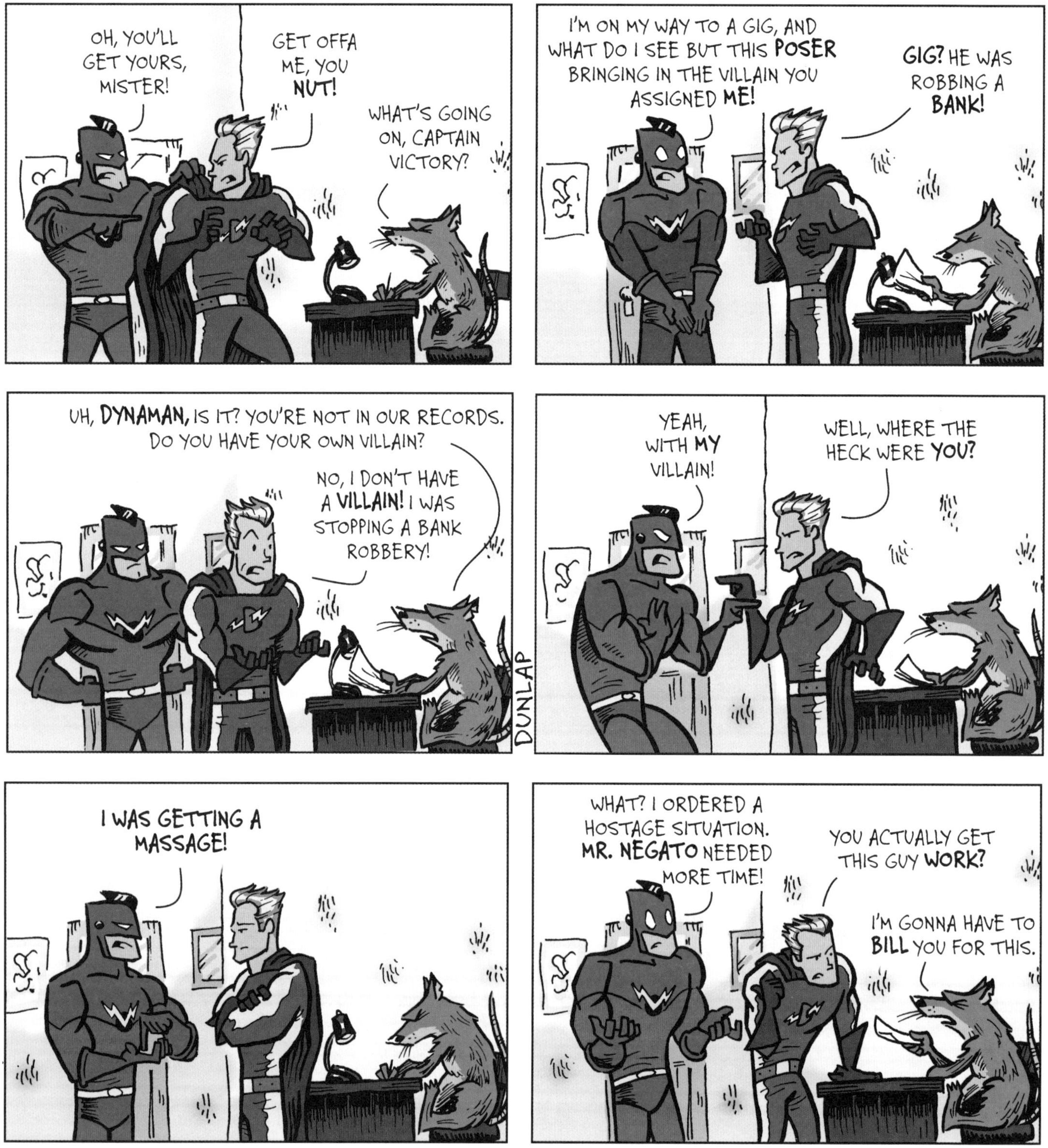
OH, YOU'LL GET YOURS, MISTER!
GET OFFA ME, YOU NUT!
WHAT'S GOING ON, CAPTAIN VICTORY?
I'M ON MY WAY TO A GIG, AND WHAT DO I SEE BUT THIS POSER BRINGING IN THE VILLAIN YOU ASSIGNED ME!
GIG? HE WAS ROBBING A BANK!
UH, DYNAMAN, IS IT? YOU'RE NOT IN OUR RECORDS. DO YOU HAVE YOUR OWN VILLAIN?
NO, I DON'T HAVE A VILLAIN! I WAS STOPPING A BANK ROBBERY!
DUNLAP
YEAH, WITH MY VILLAIN!
WELL, WHERE THE HECK WERE YOU?
I WAS GETTING A MASSAGE!
WHAT? I ORDERED A HOSTAGE SITUATION. MR. NEGATO NEEDED MORE TIME!
YOU ACTUALLY GET THIS GUY WORK?
I'M GONNA HAVE TO BILL YOU FOR THIS.

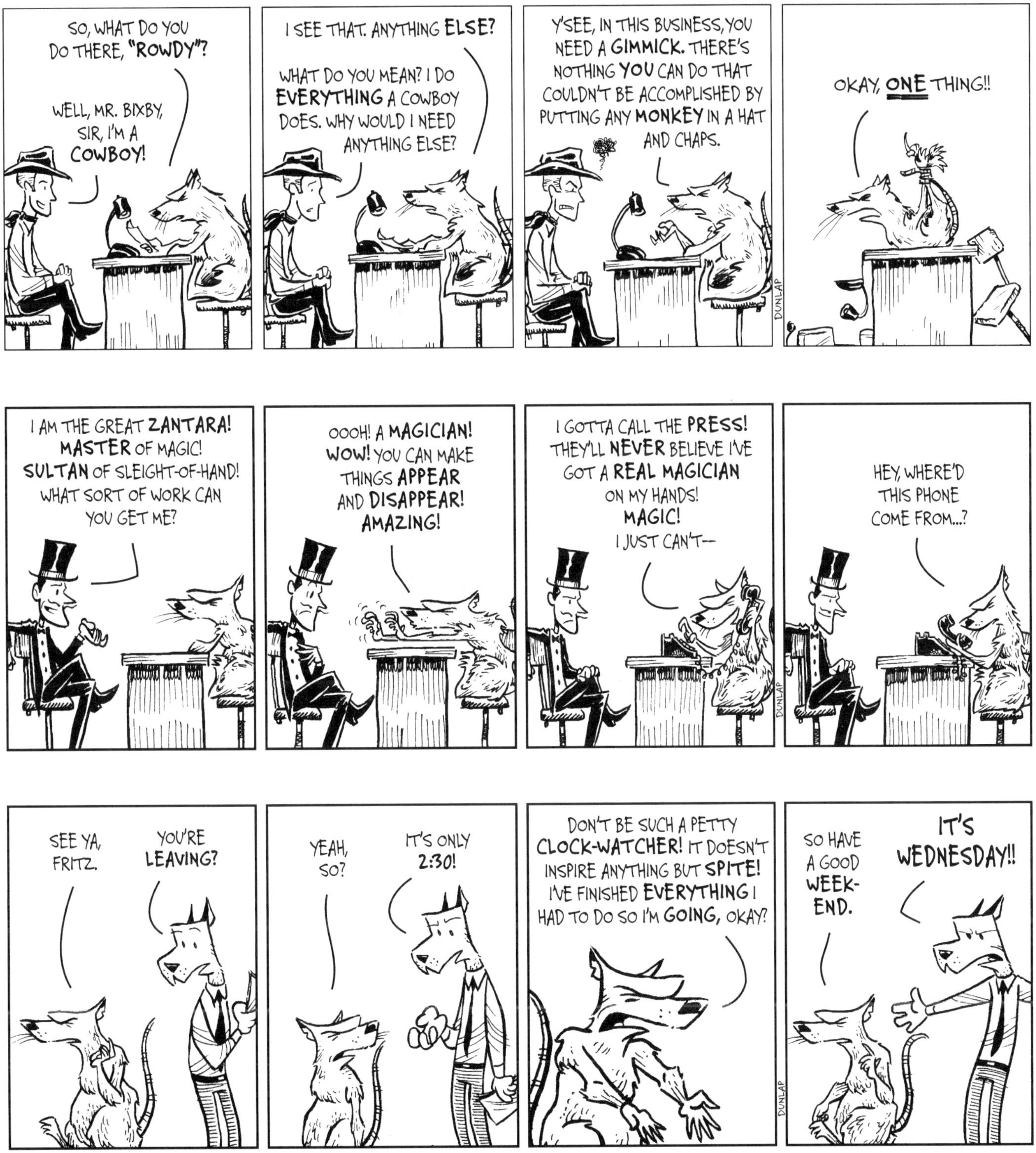
SO, WHAT DO YOU DO THERE, "ROWDY"?
WELL, MR. BIXBY, SIR, I'M A COWBOY!
I SEE THAT. ANYTHING ELSE?
WHAT DO YOU MEAN? I DO EVERYTHING A COWBOY DOES. WHY WOULD I NEED ANYTHING ELSE?
Y'SEE, IN THIS BUSINESS, YOU NEED A GIMMICK. THERE'S NOTHING YOU CAN DO THAT COULDN'T BE ACCOMPLISHED BY PUTTING ANY MONKEY IN A HAT AND CHAPS.
OKAY, ONE THING!!
DUNLAP
I AM THE GREAT ZANTARA! MASTER OF MAGIC! SULTAN OF SLEIGHT-OF-HAND! WHAT SORT OF WORK CAN YOU GET ME?
OOOH! A MAGICIAN! WOW! YOU CAN MAKE THINGS APPEAR AND DISAPPEAR! AMAZING!
I GOTTA CALL THE PRESS! THEY'LL NEVER BELIEVE I'VE GOT A REAL MAGICIAN ON MY HANDS! MAGIC! I JUST CAN'T—
HEY, WHERE'D THIS PHONE COME FROM...?
DUNLAP
SEE YA, FRITZ.
YOU'RE LEAVING?
YEAH, SO?
IT'S ONLY 2:30!
DON'T BE SUCH A PETTY CLOCK-WATCHER! IT DOESN'T INSPIRE ANYTHING BUT SPITE! I'VE FINISHED EVERYTHING I HAD TO DO SO I'M GOING, OKAY?
SO HAVE A GOOD WEEK-END.
IT'S WEDNESDAY!!
DUNLAP

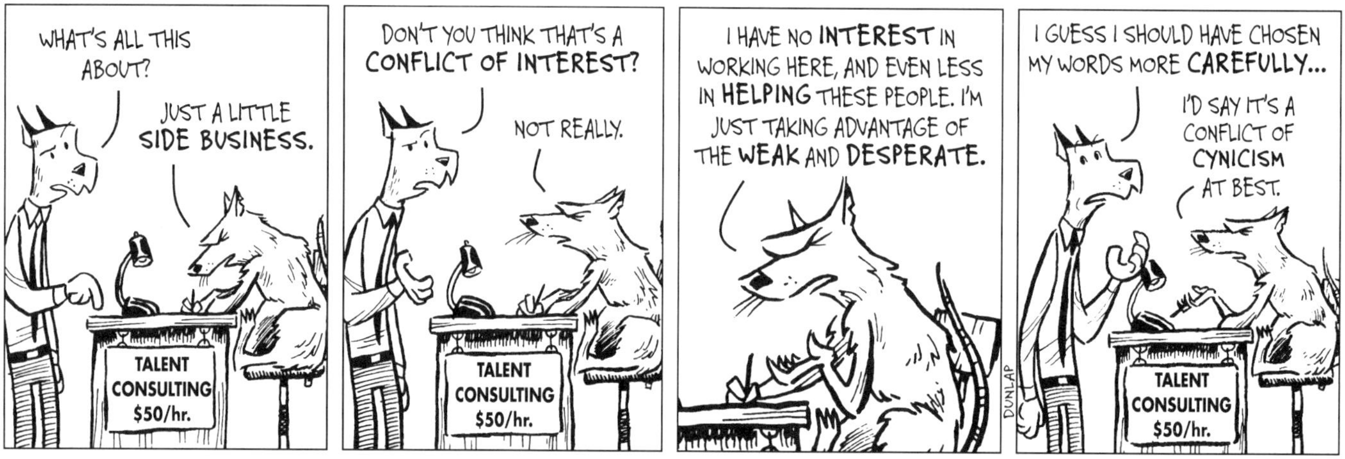
WHAT'S ALL THIS ABOUT?
JUST A LITTLE SIDE BUSINESS.
TALENT CONSULTING $50/hr.
DON'T YOU THINK THAT'S A CONFLICT OF INTEREST?
NOT REALLY.
I HAVE NO INTEREST IN WORKING HERE, AND EVEN LESS IN HELPING THESE PEOPLE. I'M JUST TAKING ADVANTAGE OF THE WEAK AND DESPERATE.
DUNLAP
I GUESS I SHOULD HAVE CHOSEN MY WORDS MORE CAREFULLY...
I'D SAY IT'S A CONFLICT OF CYNICISM AT BEST.

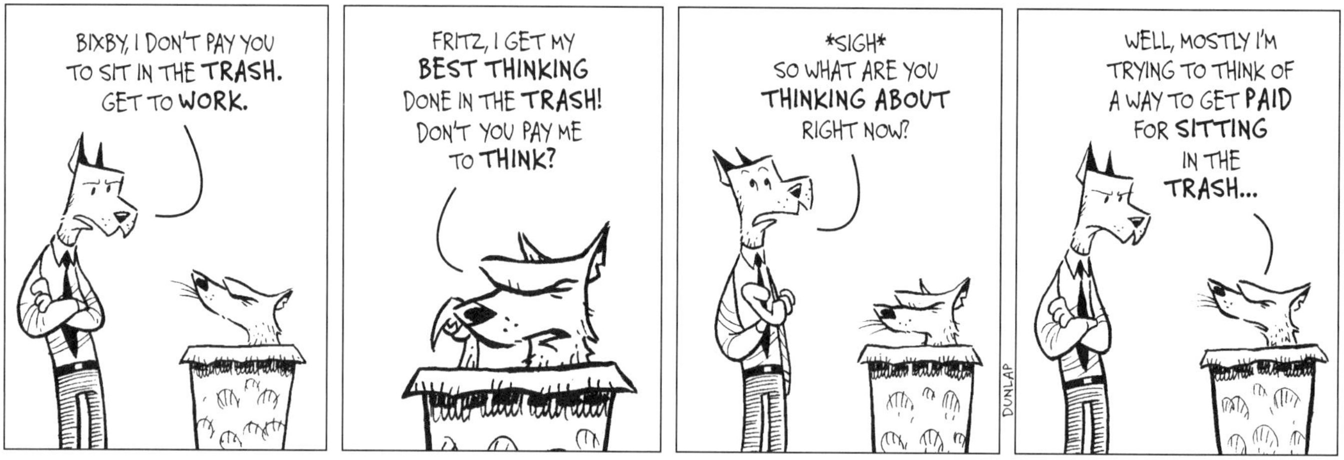
BIXBY, I DON'T PAY YOU TO SIT IN THE TRASH. GET TO WORK.
FRITZ, I GET MY BEST THINKING DONE IN THE TRASH! DON'T YOU PAY ME TO THINK?
*SIGH* SO WHAT ARE YOU THINKING ABOUT RIGHT NOW?
DUNLAP
WELL, MOSTLY I'M TRYING TO THINK OF A WAY TO GET PAID FOR SITTING IN THE TRASH...

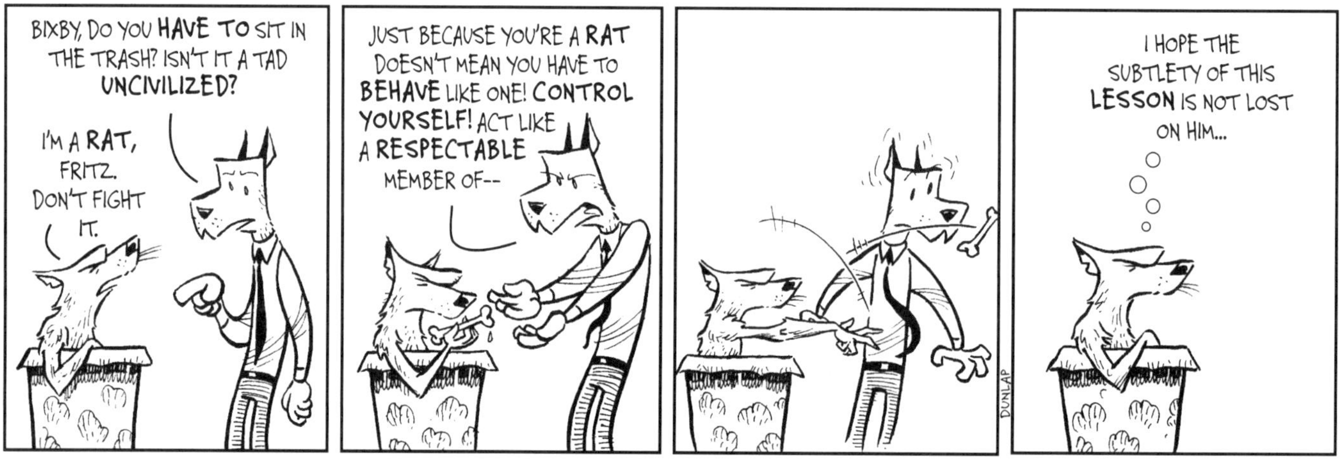
BIXBY, DO YOU HAVE TO SIT IN THE TRASH? ISN'T IT A TAD UNCIVILIZED?
I'M A RAT, FRITZ. DON'T FIGHT IT.
JUST BECAUSE YOU'RE A RAT DOESN'T MEAN YOU HAVE TO BEHAVE LIKE ONE! CONTROL YOURSELF! ACT LIKE A RESPECTABLE MEMBER OF--
DUNLAP
I HOPE THE SUBTLETY OF THIS LESSON IS NOT LOST ON HIM...

HEY, LOOK...
SOMEONE DROPPED SOME KRYPTONITE.
AAAAA!!!
N-NOOO!
DUNLAP
AAAGH!!
HACKK!!
HCCHH!!
HKKKK---!!
CAP, FOR THE LAST TIME, YOU'RE NOT VULNERABLE TO KRYPTONITE.
I'M STILL DATING LOIS LANE THOUGH, RIGHT?

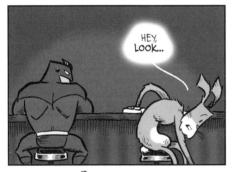

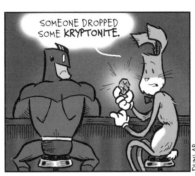

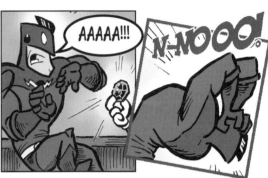

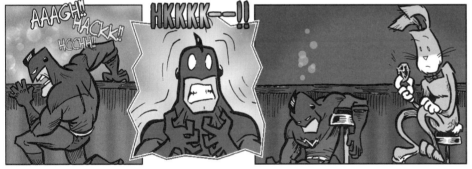

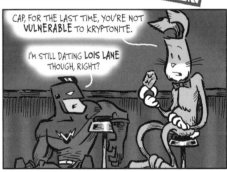

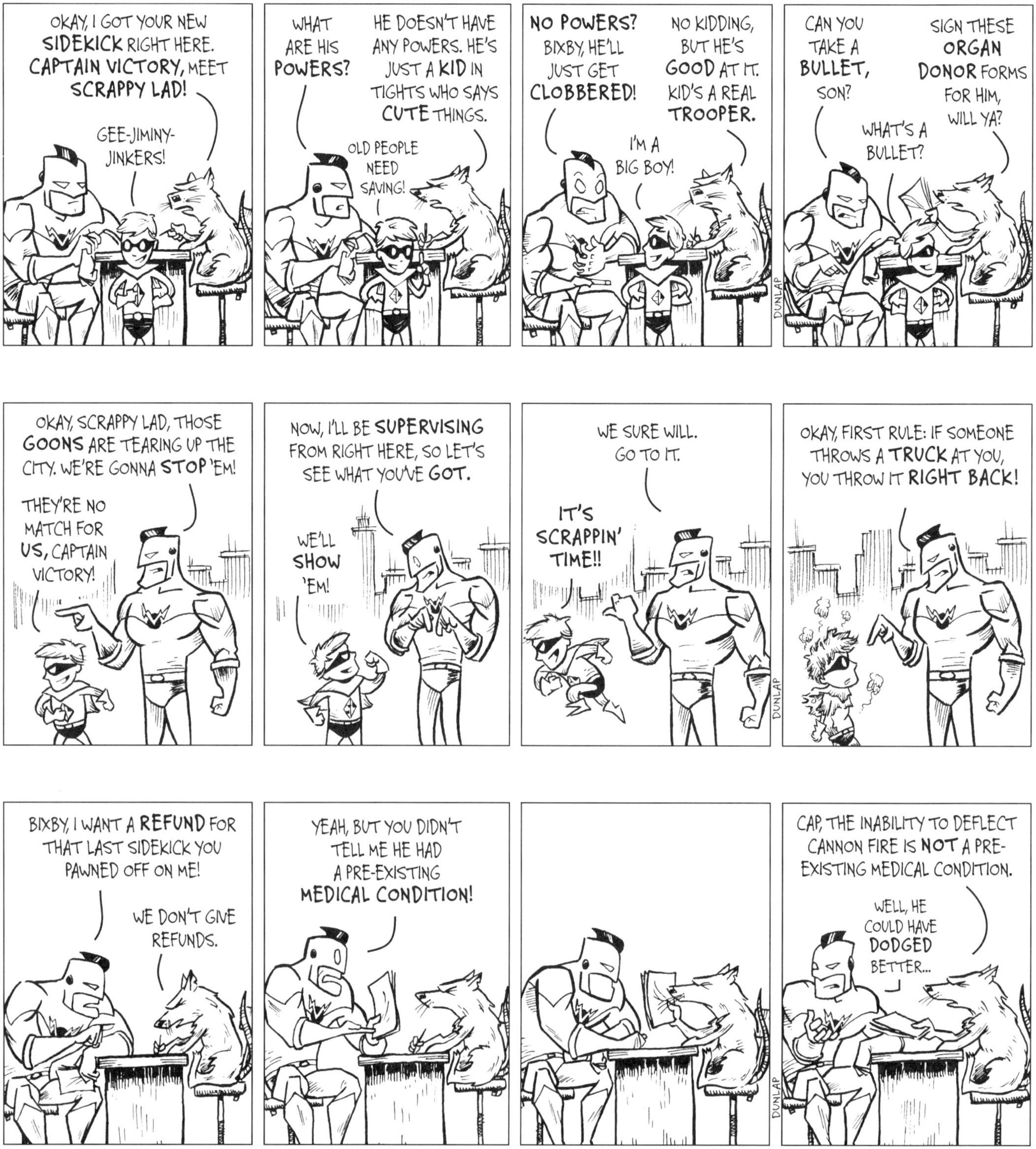
OKAY, I GOT YOUR NEW SIDEKICK RIGHT HERE. CAPTAIN VICTORY, MEET SCRAPPY LAD!
GEE-JIMINY-JINKERS!
WHAT ARE HIS POWERS?
HE DOESN'T HAVE ANY POWERS. HE'S JUST A KID IN TIGHTS WHO SAYS CUTE THINGS.
OLD PEOPLE NEED SAVING!
NO POWERS? BIXBY, HE'LL JUST GET CLOBBERED!
NO KIDDING, BUT HE'S GOOD AT IT. KID'S A REAL TROOPER.
I'M A BIG BOY!
CAN YOU TAKE A BULLET, SON?
SIGN THESE ORGAN DONOR FORMS FOR HIM, WILL YA?
WHAT'S A BULLET?
DUNLAP
OKAY, SCRAPPY LAD, THOSE GOONS ARE TEARING UP THE CITY. WE'RE GONNA STOP 'EM!
THEY'RE NO MATCH FOR US, CAPTAIN VICTORY!
NOW, I'LL BE SUPERVISING FROM RIGHT HERE, SO LET'S SEE WHAT YOU'VE GOT.
WE'LL SHOW 'EM!
WE SURE WILL. GO TO IT.
IT'S SCRAPPIN' TIME!!
DUNLAP
OKAY, FIRST RULE: IF SOMEONE THROWS A TRUCK AT YOU, YOU THROW IT RIGHT BACK!
BIXBY, I WANT A REFUND FOR THAT LAST SIDEKICK YOU PAWNED OFF ON ME!
WE DON'T GIVE REFUNDS.
YEAH, BUT YOU DIDN'T TELL ME HE HAD A PRE-EXISTING MEDICAL CONDITION!
DUNLAP
CAP, THE INABILITY TO DEFLECT CANNON FIRE IS NOT A PRE-EXISTING MEDICAL CONDITION.
WELL, HE COULD HAVE DODGED BETTER...

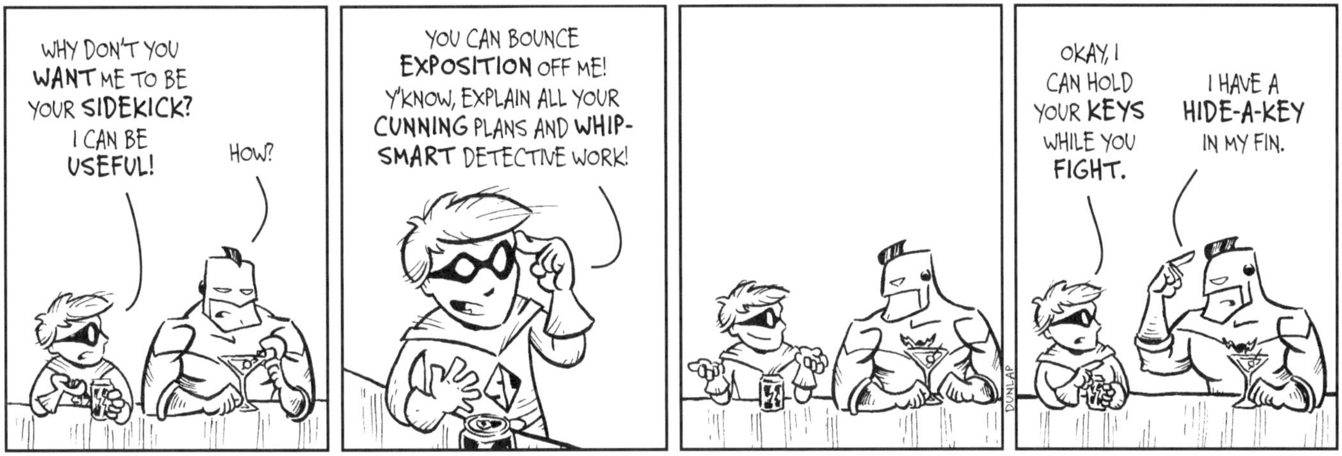
WHY DON'T YOU WANT ME TO BE YOUR SIDEKICK? I CAN BE USEFUL!
HOW?
YOU CAN BOUNCE EXPOSITION OFF ME! Y'KNOW, EXPLAIN ALL YOUR CUNNING PLANS AND WHIP-SMART DETECTIVE WORK!
OKAY, I CAN HOLD YOUR KEYS WHILE YOU FIGHT.
I HAVE A HIDE-A-KEY IN MY FIN.
DUNLAP

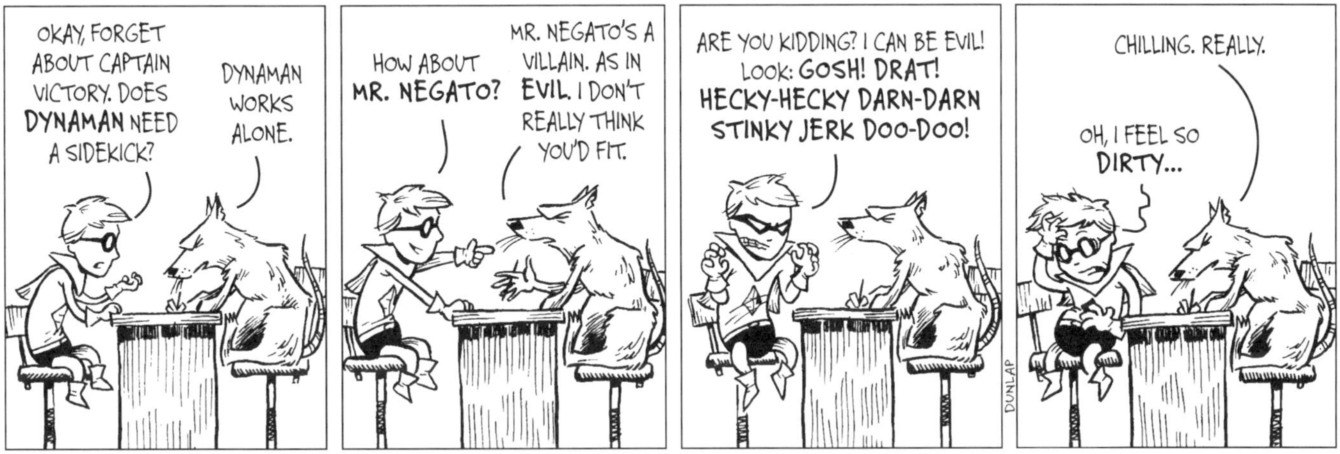
OKAY, FORGET ABOUT CAPTAIN VICTORY. DOES DYNAMAN NEED A SIDEKICK?
DYNAMAN WORKS ALONE.
HOW ABOUT MR. NEGATO?
MR. NEGATO'S A VILLAIN. AS IN EVIL. I DON'T REALLY THINK YOU'D FIT.
ARE YOU KIDDING? I CAN BE EVIL! LOOK: GOSH! DRAT! HECKY-HECKY DARN-DARN STINKY JERK DOO-DOO!
CHILLING. REALLY.
OH, I FEEL SO DIRTY...
DUNLAP

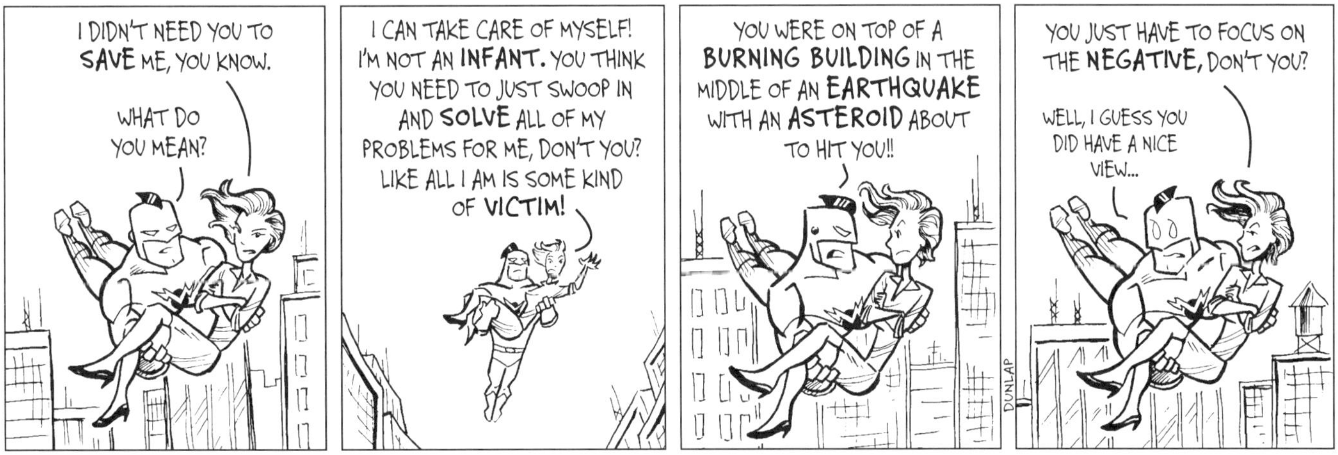
I DIDN'T NEED YOU TO SAVE ME, YOU KNOW.
WHAT DO YOU MEAN?
I CAN TAKE CARE OF MYSELF! I'M NOT AN INFANT. YOU THINK YOU NEED TO JUST SWOOP IN AND SOLVE ALL OF MY PROBLEMS FOR ME, DON'T YOU? LIKE ALL I AM IS SOME KIND OF VICTIM!
YOU WERE ON TOP OF A BURNING BUILDING IN THE MIDDLE OF AN EARTHQUAKE WITH AN ASTEROID ABOUT TO HIT YOU!!
YOU JUST HAVE TO FOCUS ON THE NEGATIVE, DON'T YOU?
WELL, I GUESS YOU DID HAVE A NICE VIEW...
DUNLAP

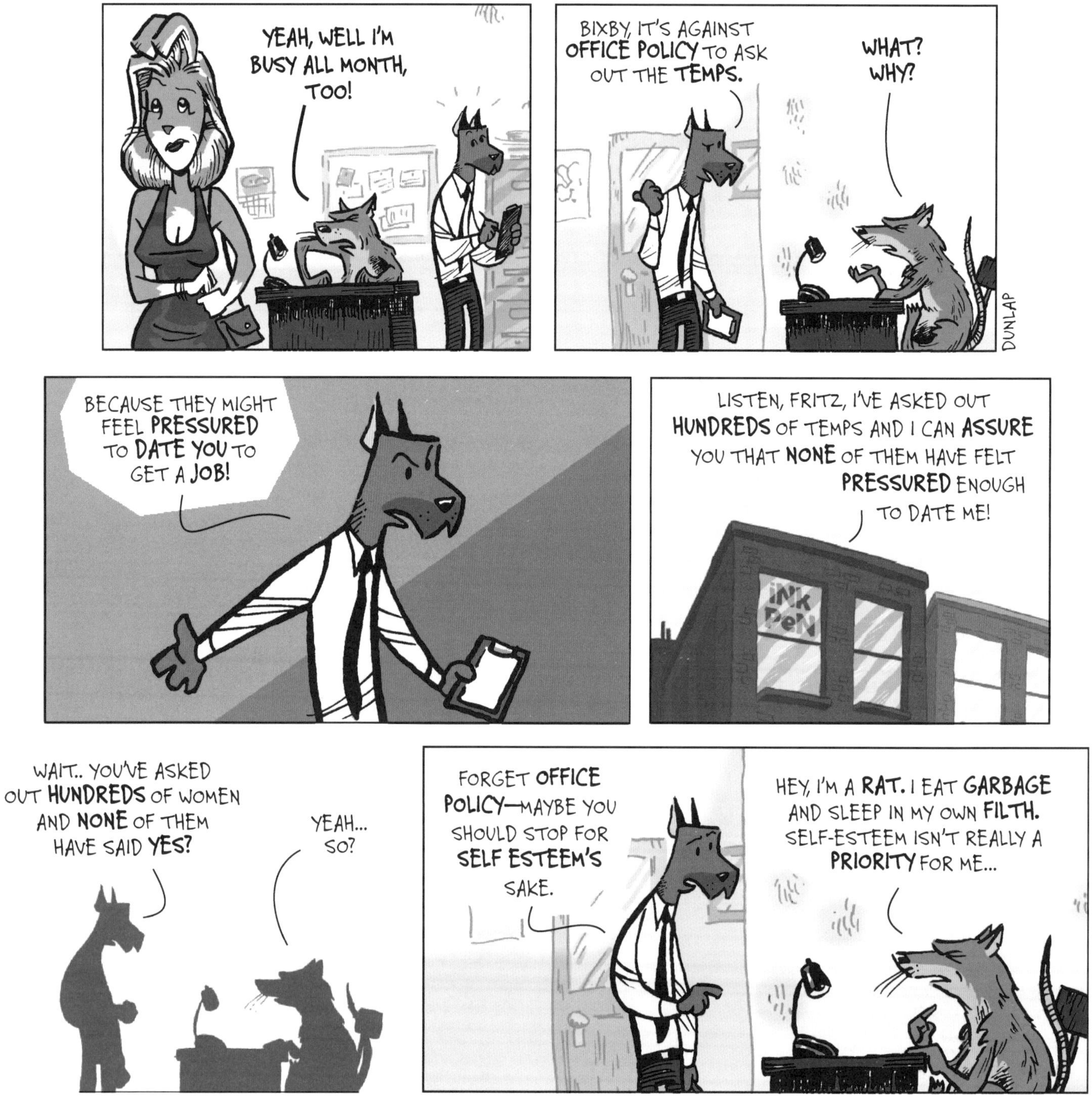
YEAH, WELL I'M BUSY ALL MONTH, TOO!
BIXBY, IT'S AGAINST OFFICE POLICY TO ASK OUT THE TEMPS.
WHAT? WHY?
DUNLAP
BECAUSE THEY MIGHT FEEL PRESSURED TO DATE YOU TO GET A JOB!
LISTEN, FRITZ, I'VE ASKED OUT HUNDREDS OF TEMPS AND I CAN ASSURE YOU THAT NONE OF THEM HAVE FELT PRESSURED ENOUGH TO DATE ME!
INK PEN
WAIT.. YOU'VE ASKED OUT HUNDREDS OF WOMEN AND NONE OF THEM HAVE SAID YES?
YEAH... SO?
FORGET OFFICE POLICY—MAYBE YOU SHOULD STOP FOR SELF ESTEEM'S SAKE.
HEY, I'M A RAT. I EAT GARBAGE AND SLEEP IN MY OWN FILTH. SELF-ESTEEM ISN'T REALLY A PRIORITY FOR ME...

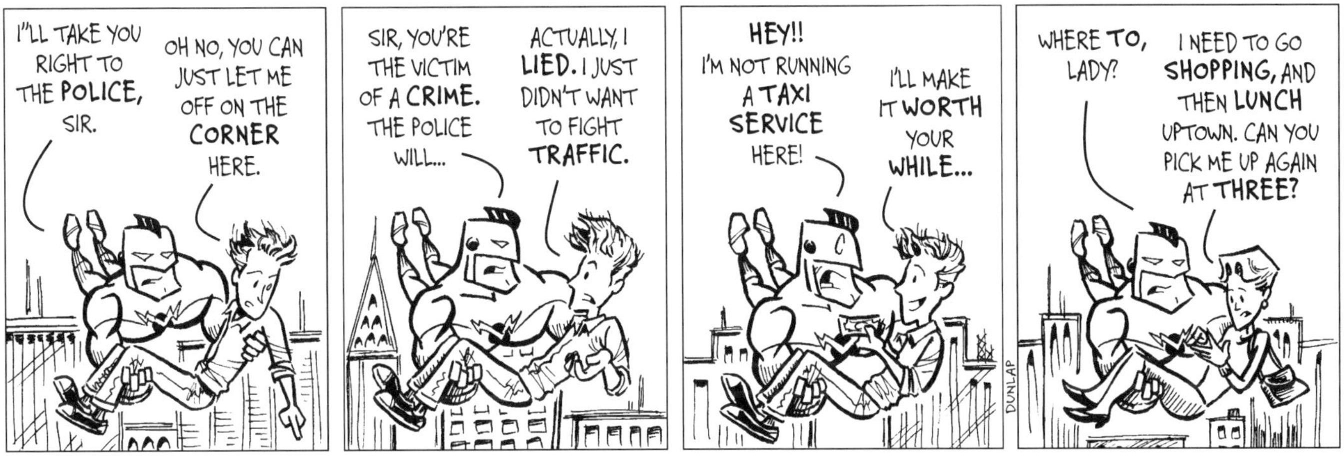
I'LL TAKE YOU RIGHT TO THE POLICE, SIR.
OH NO, YOU CAN JUST LET ME OFF ON THE CORNER HERE.
SIR, YOU'RE THE VICTIM OF A CRIME. THE POLICE WILL...
ACTUALLY, I LIED. I JUST DIDN'T WANT TO FIGHT TRAFFIC.
HEY!! I'M NOT RUNNING A TAXI SERVICE HERE!
I'LL MAKE IT WORTH YOUR WHILE...
DUNLAP
WHERE TO, LADY?
I NEED TO GO SHOPPING, AND THEN LUNCH UPTOWN. CAN YOU PICK ME UP AGAIN AT THREE?

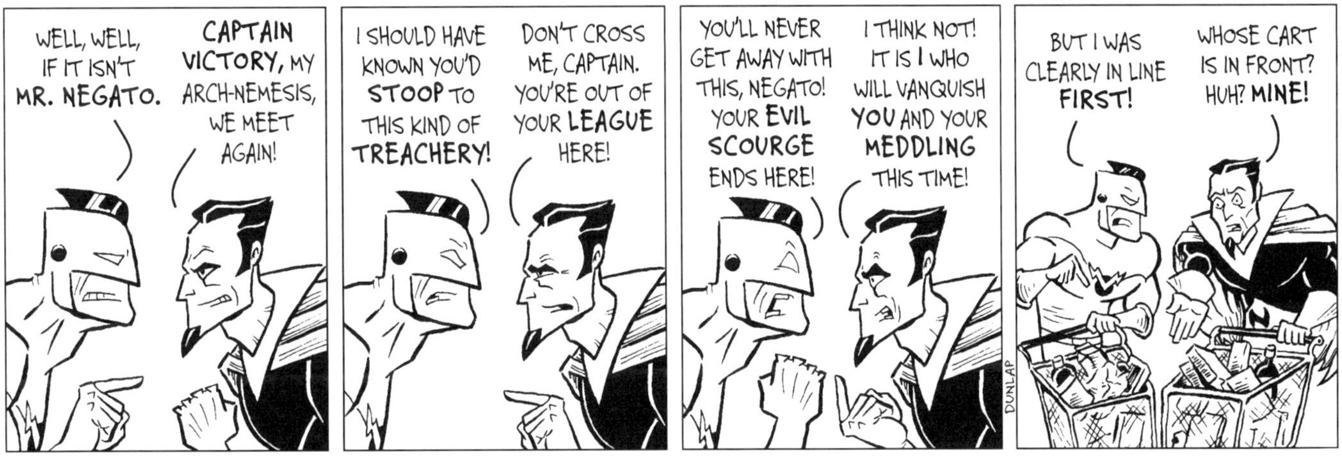
WELL, WELL, IF IT ISN'T MR. NEGATO.
CAPTAIN VICTORY, MY ARCH-NEMESIS, WE MEET AGAIN!
I SHOULD HAVE KNOWN YOU'D STOOP TO THIS KIND OF TREACHERY!
DON'T CROSS ME, CAPTAIN. YOU'RE OUT OF YOUR LEAGUE HERE!
YOU'LL NEVER GET AWAY WITH THIS, NEGATO! YOUR EVIL SCOURGE ENDS HERE!
I THINK NOT! IT IS I WHO WILL VANQUISH YOU AND YOUR MEDDLING THIS TIME!
DUNLAP
BUT I WAS CLEARLY IN LINE FIRST!
WHOSE CART IS IN FRONT? HUH? MINE!

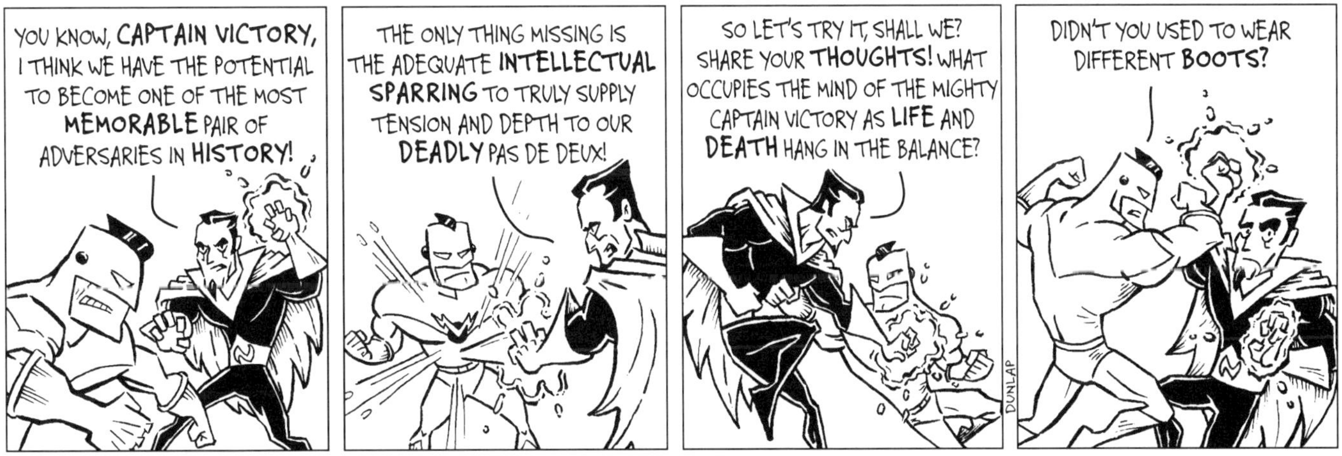
YOU KNOW, CAPTAIN VICTORY, I THINK WE HAVE THE POTENTIAL TO BECOME ONE OF THE MOST MEMORABLE PAIR OF ADVERSARIES IN HISTORY!
THE ONLY THING MISSING IS THE ADEQUATE INTELLECTUAL SPARRING TO TRULY SUPPLY TENSION AND DEPTH TO OUR DEADLY PAS DE DEUX!
SO LET'S TRY IT, SHALL WE? SHARE YOUR THOUGHTS! WHAT OCCUPIES THE MIND OF THE MIGHTY CAPTAIN VICTORY AS LIFE AND DEATH HANG IN THE BALANCE?
DUNLAP
DIDN'T YOU USED TO WEAR DIFFERENT BOOTS?

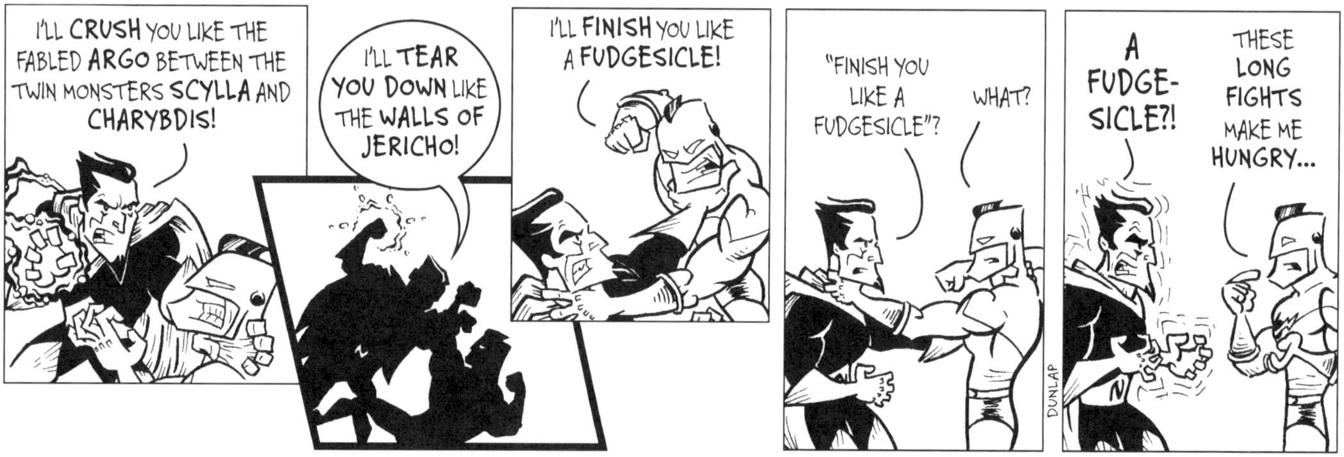
I'LL CRUSH YOU LIKE THE FABLED ARGO BETWEEN THE TWIN MONSTERS SCYLLA AND CHARYBDIS!
I'LL TEAR YOU DOWN LIKE THE WALLS OF JERICHO!
I'LL FINISH YOU LIKE A FUDGESICLE!
"FINISH YOU LIKE A FUDGESICLE"?
WHAT?
DUNLAP
A FUDGE-SICLE?!
THESE LONG FIGHTS MAKE ME HUNGRY...

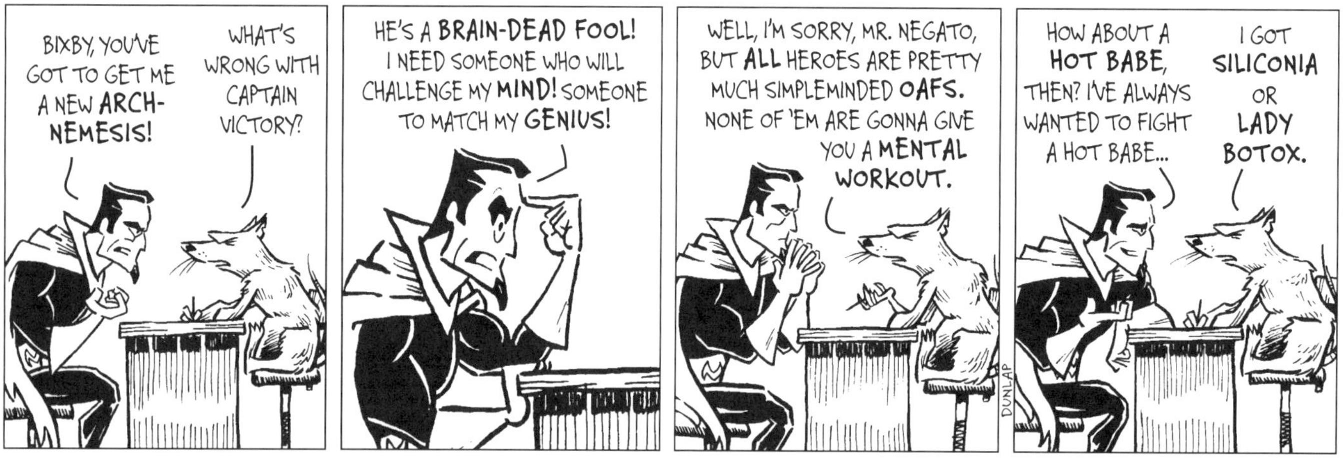
BIXBY, YOU'VE GOT TO GET ME A NEW ARCH-NEMESIS!
WHAT'S WRONG WITH CAPTAIN VICTORY?
HE'S A BRAIN-DEAD FOOL! I NEED SOMEONE WHO WILL CHALLENGE MY MIND! SOMEONE TO MATCH MY GENIUS!
WELL, I'M SORRY, MR. NEGATO, BUT ALL HEROES ARE PRETTY MUCH SIMPLEMINDED OAFS. NONE OF 'EM ARE GONNA GIVE YOU A MENTAL WORKOUT.
DUNLAP
HOW ABOUT A HOT BABE, THEN? I'VE ALWAYS WANTED TO FIGHT A HOT BABE...
I GOT SILICONIA OR LADY BOTOX.

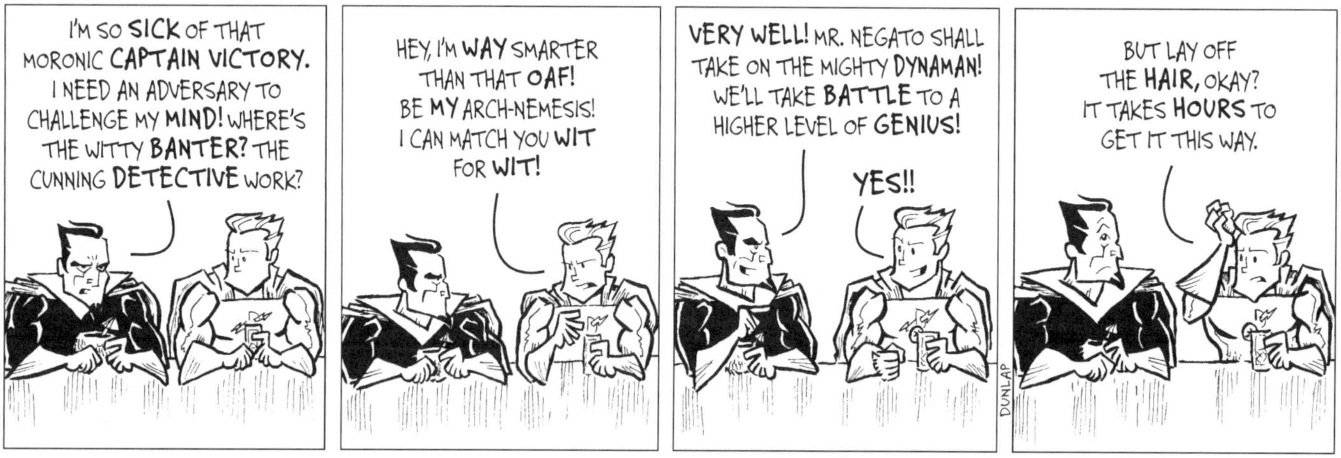
I'M SO SICK OF THAT MORONIC CAPTAIN VICTORY. I NEED AN ADVERSARY TO CHALLENGE MY MIND! WHERE'S THE WITTY BANTER? THE CUNNING DETECTIVE WORK?
HEY, I'M WAY SMARTER THAN THAT OAF! BE MY ARCH-NEMESIS! I CAN MATCH YOU WIT FOR WIT!
VERY WELL! MR. NEGATO SHALL TAKE ON THE MIGHTY DYNAMAN! WE'LL TAKE BATTLE TO A HIGHER LEVEL OF GENIUS!
YES!!
DUNLAP
BUT LAY OFF THE HAIR, OKAY? IT TAKES HOURS TO GET IT THIS WAY.

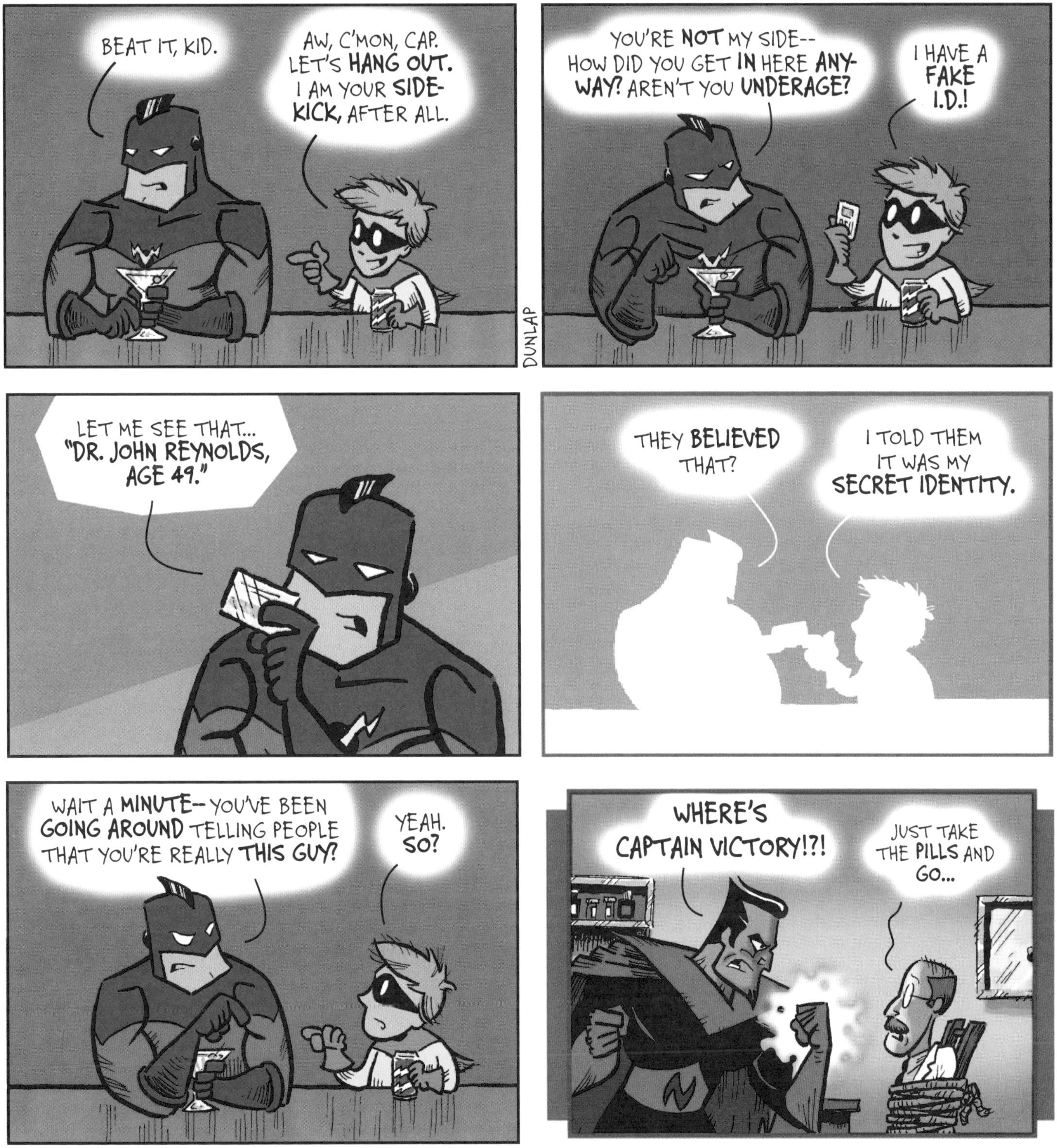
BEAT IT, KID.
AW, C'MON, CAP. LET'S HANG OUT. I AM YOUR SIDE-KICK, AFTER ALL.
DUNLAP
YOU'RE NOT MY SIDE-- HOW DID YOU GET IN HERE ANY-WAY? AREN'T YOU UNDERAGE?
I HAVE A FAKE I.D.!
LET ME SEE THAT... "DR. JOHN REYNOLDS, AGE 49."
THEY BELIEVED THAT?
I TOLD THEM IT WAS MY SECRET IDENTITY.
WAIT A MINUTE-- YOU'VE BEEN GOING AROUND TELLING PEOPLE THAT YOU'RE REALLY THIS GUY?
YEAH. SO?
WHERE'S CAPTAIN VICTORY!?!
JUST TAKE THE PILLS AND GO...

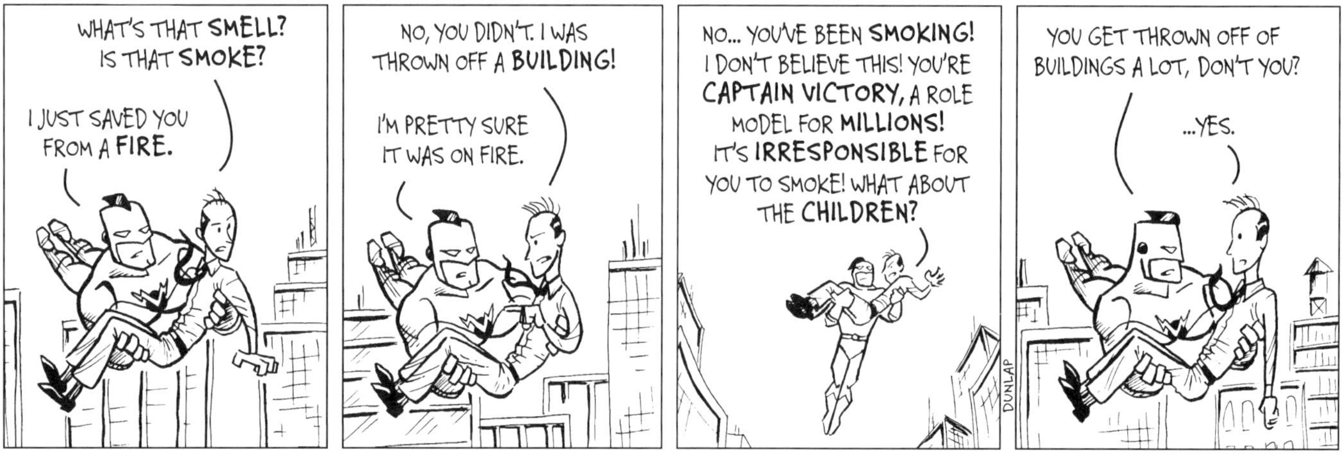
WHAT'S THAT SMELL? IS THAT SMOKE?
I JUST SAVED YOU FROM A FIRE.
NO, YOU DIDN'T. I WAS THROWN OFF A BUILDING!
I'M PRETTY SURE IT WAS ON FIRE.
NO... YOU'VE BEEN SMOKING! I DON'T BELIEVE THIS! YOU'RE CAPTAIN VICTORY, A ROLE MODEL FOR MILLIONS! IT'S IRRESPONSIBLE FOR YOU TO SMOKE! WHAT ABOUT THE CHILDREN?
DUNLAP
YOU GET THROWN OFF OF BUILDINGS A LOT, DON'T YOU?
...YES.

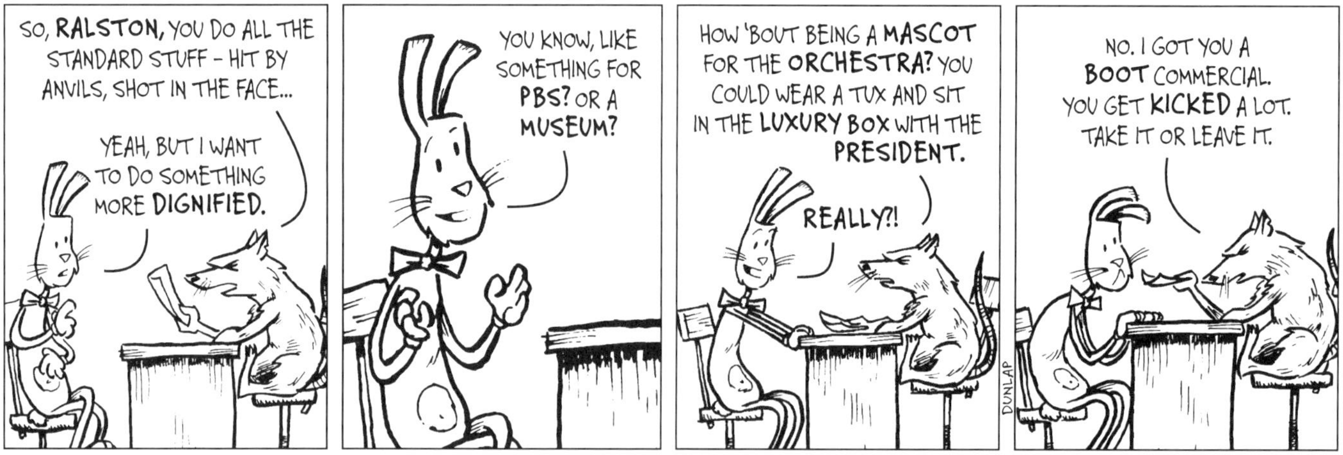
SO, RALSTON, YOU DO ALL THE STANDARD STUFF - HIT BY ANVILS, SHOT IN THE FACE...
YEAH, BUT I WANT TO DO SOMETHING MORE DIGNIFIED.
YOU KNOW, LIKE SOMETHING FOR PBS? OR A MUSEUM?
HOW 'BOUT BEING A MASCOT FOR THE ORCHESTRA? YOU COULD WEAR A TUX AND SIT IN THE LUXURY BOX WITH THE PRESIDENT.
REALLY?!
DUNLAP
NO. I GOT YOU A BOOT COMMERCIAL. YOU GET KICKED A LOT. TAKE IT OR LEAVE IT.

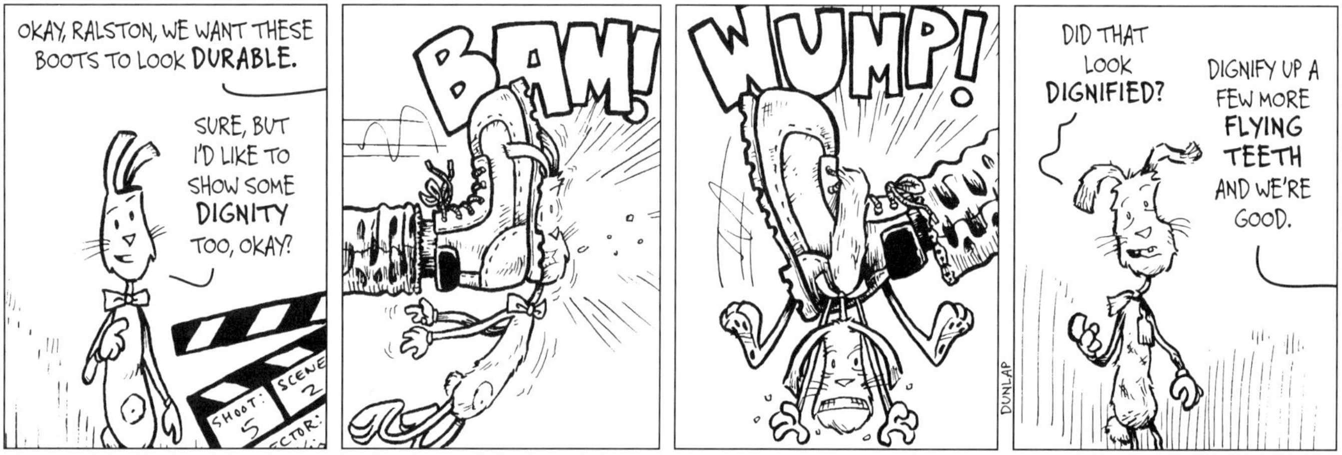
OKAY, RALSTON, WE WANT THESE BOOTS TO LOOK DURABLE.
SURE, BUT I'D LIKE TO SHOW SOME DIGNITY TOO, OKAY?
SHOOT: 5
SCENE 2
BAM!
WUMP!
DUNLAP
DID THAT LOOK DIGNIFIED?
DIGNIFY UP A FEW MORE FLYING TEETH AND WE'RE GOOD.

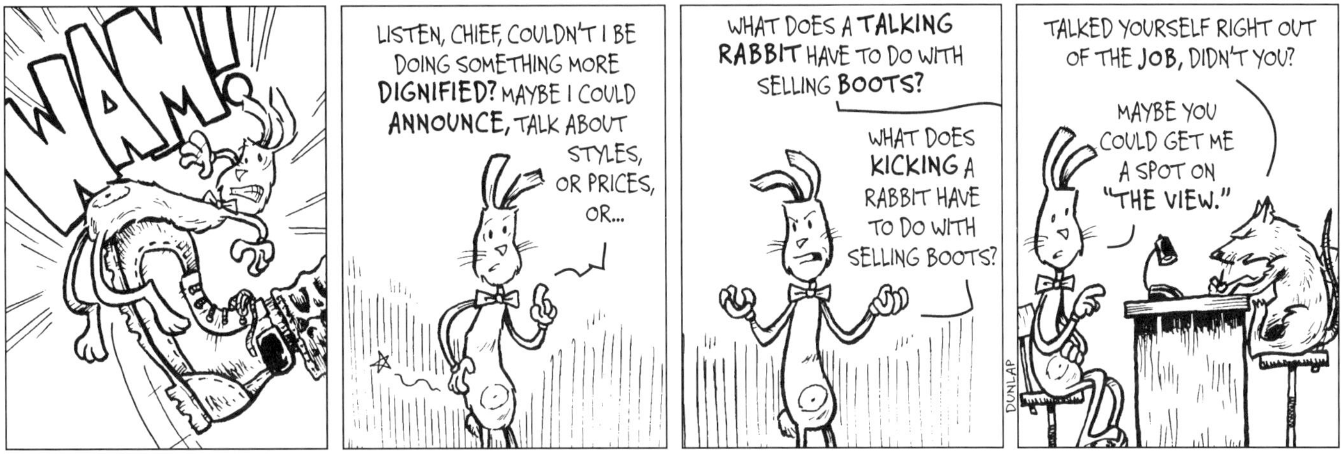
WAM!
LISTEN, CHIEF, COULDN'T I BE DOING SOMETHING MORE DIGNIFIED? MAYBE I COULD ANNOUNCE, TALK ABOUT STYLES, OR PRICES, OR...
WHAT DOES A TALKING RABBIT HAVE TO DO WITH SELLING BOOTS?
WHAT DOES KICKING A RABBIT HAVE TO DO WITH SELLING BOOTS?
TALKED YOURSELF RIGHT OUT OF THE JOB, DIDN'T YOU?
MAYBE YOU COULD GET ME A SPOT ON "THE VIEW."
DUNLAP

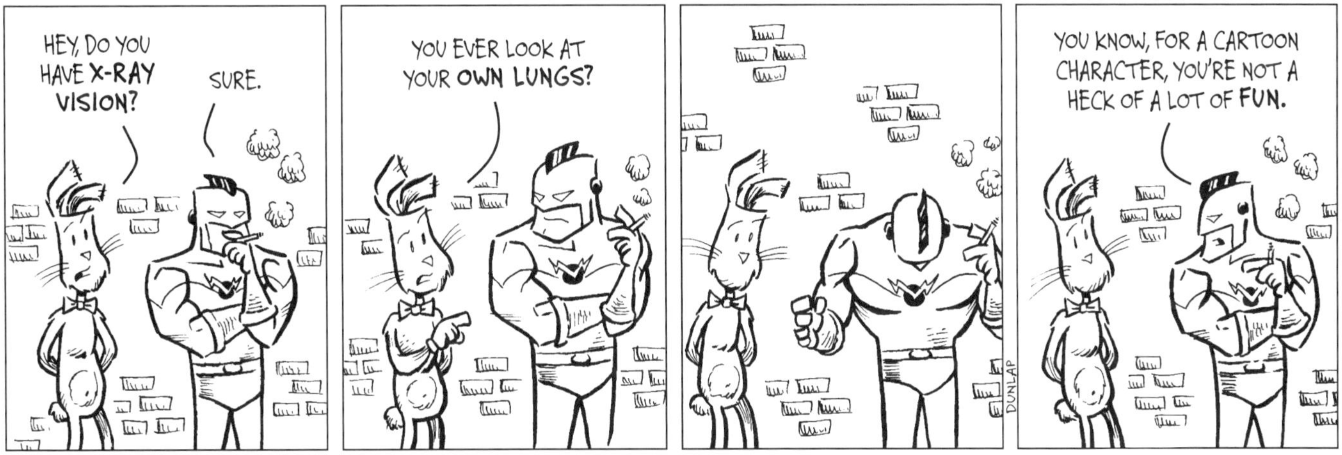
HEY, DO YOU HAVE X-RAY VISION?
SURE.
YOU EVER LOOK AT YOUR OWN LUNGS?
YOU KNOW, FOR A CARTOON CHARACTER, YOU'RE NOT A HECK OF A LOT OF FUN.
DUNLAP

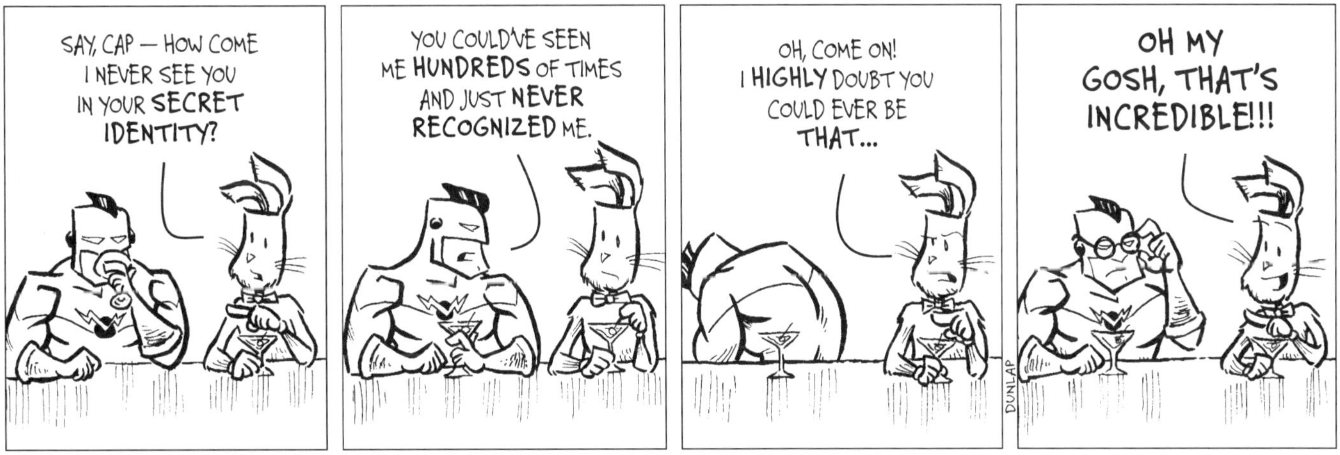
SAY, CAP — HOW COME I NEVER SEE YOU IN YOUR SECRET IDENTITY?
YOU COULD'VE SEEN ME HUNDREDS OF TIMES AND JUST NEVER RECOGNIZED ME.
OH, COME ON! I HIGHLY DOUBT YOU COULD EVER BE THAT...
OH MY GOSH, THAT'S INCREDIBLE!!!
DUNLAP

BOW, CAPTAIN VICTORY!! BOW BEFORE MY UNRIVALED GENIUS!
DUNLAP
HEY MR. NEGATO — IF YOU'RE SO MUCH SMARTER THAN ME, HOW COME I ALWAYS BEAT YOU?
AH, I'M GLAD YOU ASKED, CAPTAIN!
YOU SEE, YOUR MIND IS UNCLUTTERED BY DOUBT, REGRET OR REMORSE. WHERE I SECOND-GUESS, RATIONALIZE AND PROCRASTINATE, YOU JUST BLINDLY PLOD FORWARD.
I OBSESS OVER EVERY DETAIL WHILE YOU JUST LET THINGS GO. I ANALYZE, THEORIZE AND HYPOTHESIZE, BUT YOU JUST ACCEPT WHATEVER EXPLANATION IS EASIEST.
I MUST FORGE MY OWN UNDERSTANDING OF THE WORLD, WHILE YOU ARE PLACATED BY THE MOST BANAL CLICHÉS.
I'M HAMSTRUNG BY MY OWN GENIUS, AND THAT IS WHY I ALWAYS FAIL TO YOUR LESSER INTELLECT.
PLUS I CAN, LIKE, BEAT YOU UP AND STUFF.
WELL, YES, THERE'S THAT TOO...

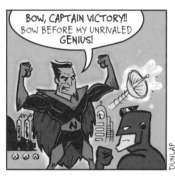

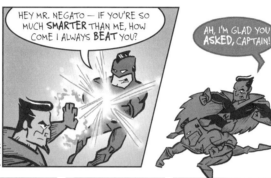

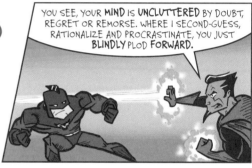

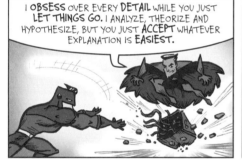

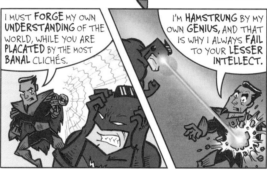

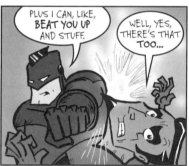

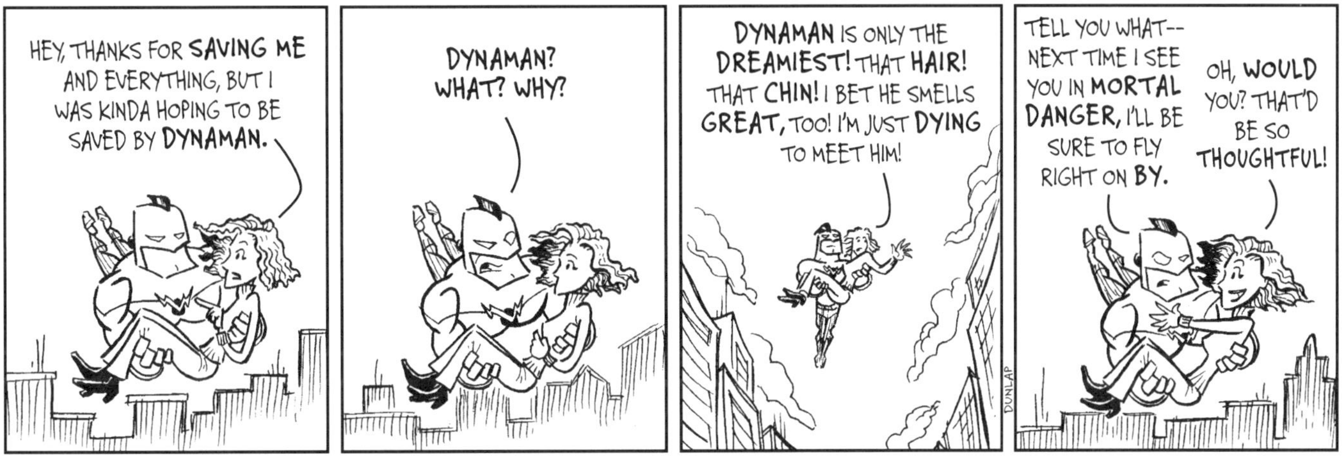
HEY, THANKS FOR SAVING ME AND EVERYTHING, BUT I WAS KINDA HOPING TO BE SAVED BY DYNAMAN.
DYNAMAN? WHAT? WHY?
DYNAMAN IS ONLY THE DREAMIEST! THAT HAIR! THAT CHIN! I BET HE SMELLS GREAT, TOO! I'M JUST DYING TO MEET HIM!
DUNLAP
TELL YOU WHAT-- NEXT TIME I SEE YOU IN MORTAL DANGER, I'LL BE SURE TO FLY RIGHT ON BY.
OH, WOULD YOU? THAT'D BE SO THOUGHTFUL!

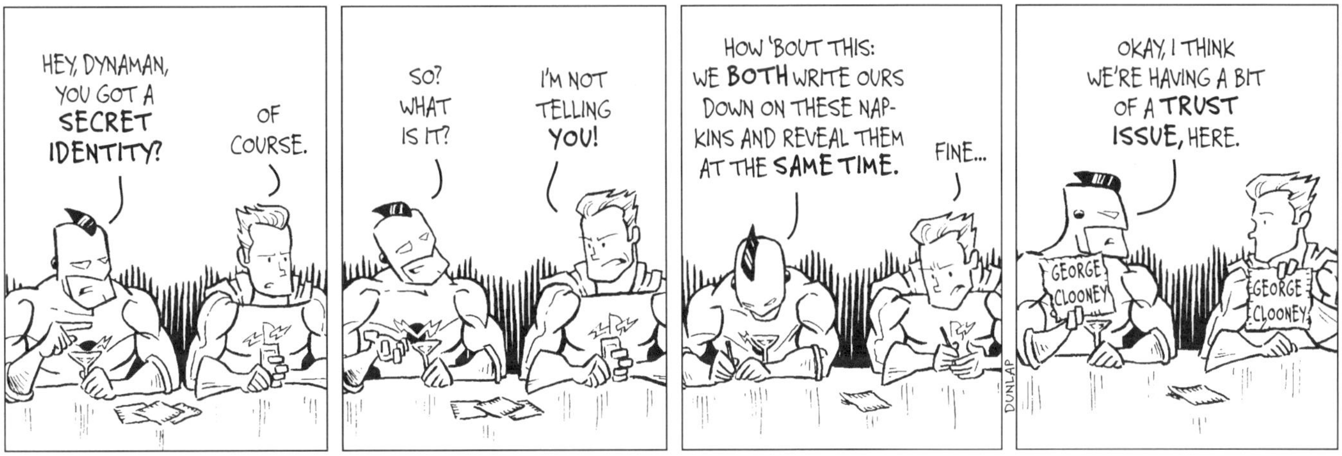
HEY, DYNAMAN, YOU GOT A SECRET IDENTITY?
OF COURSE.
SO? WHAT IS IT?
I'M NOT TELLING YOU!
HOW 'BOUT THIS: WE BOTH WRITE OURS DOWN ON THESE NAPKINS AND REVEAL THEM AT THE SAME TIME.
FINE...
DUNLAP
OKAY, I THINK WE'RE HAVING A BIT OF A TRUST ISSUE, HERE.
GEORGE CLOONEY
GEORGE CLOONEY

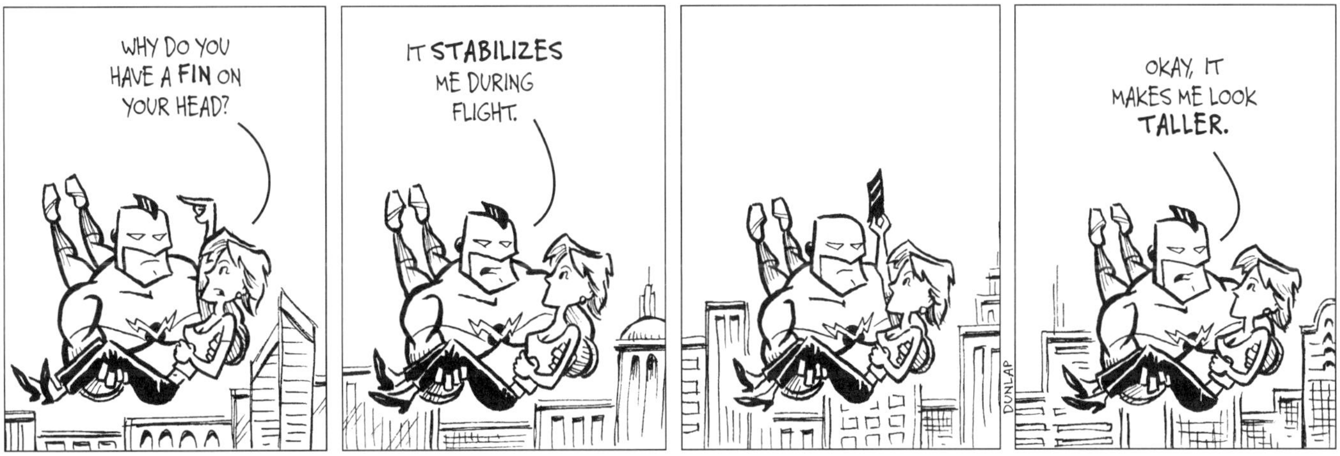
WHY DO YOU HAVE A FIN ON YOUR HEAD?
IT STABILIZES ME DURING FLIGHT.
DUNLAP
OKAY, IT MAKES ME LOOK TALLER.

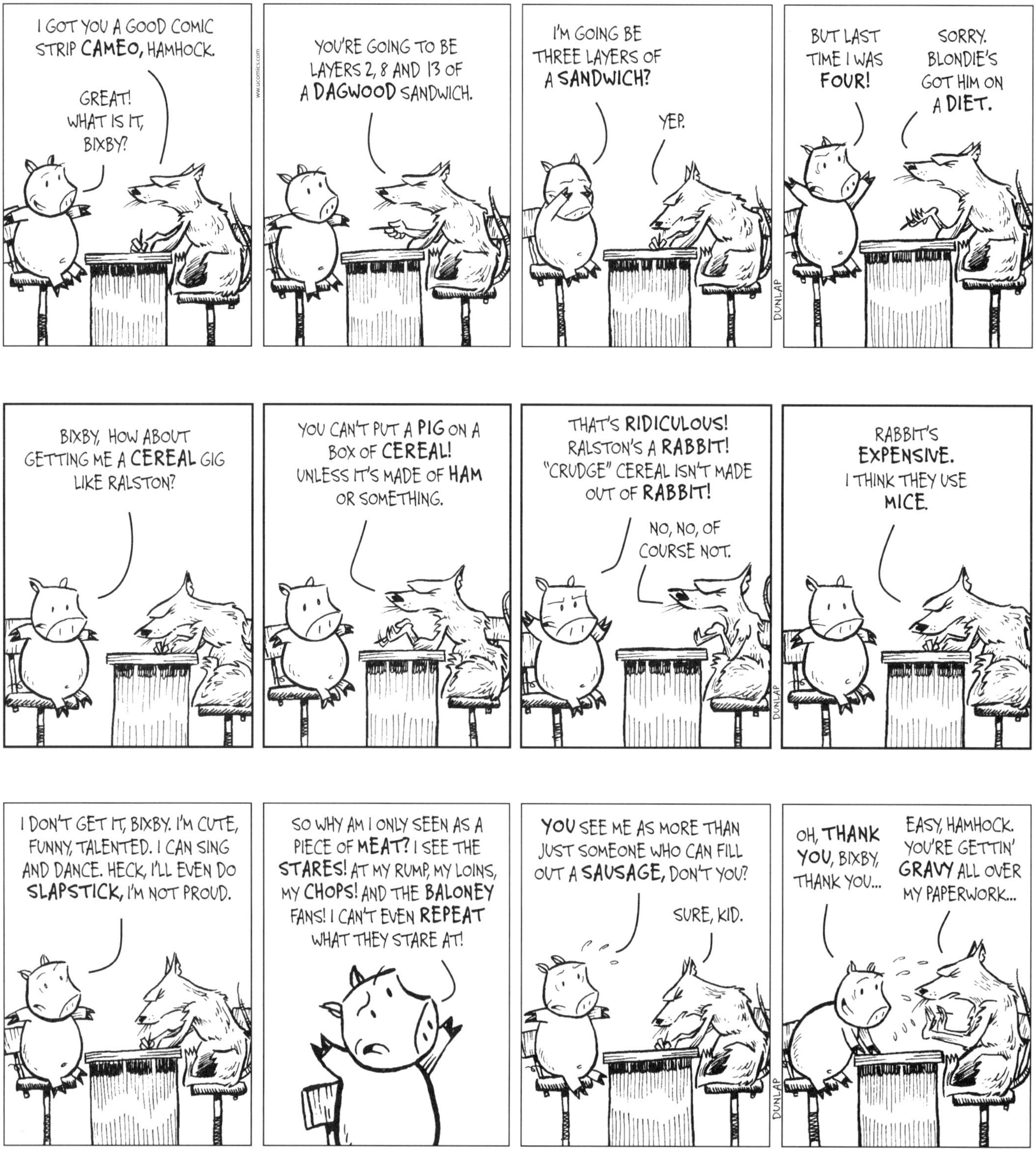
I GOT YOU A GOOD COMIC STRIP CAMEO, HAMHOCK.
GREAT! WHAT IS IT, BIXBY?
YOU'RE GOING TO BE LAYERS 2, 8 AND 13 OF A DAGWOOD SANDWICH.
I'M GOING BE THREE LAYERS OF A SANDWICH?
YEP.
BUT LAST TIME I WAS FOUR!
SORRY. BLONDIE'S GOT HIM ON A DIET.
DUNLAP
BIXBY, HOW ABOUT GETTING ME A CEREAL GIG LIKE RALSTON?
YOU CAN'T PUT A PIG ON A BOX OF CEREAL! UNLESS IT'S MADE OF HAM OR SOMETHING.
THAT'S RIDICULOUS! RALSTON'S A RABBIT! "CRUDGE" CEREAL ISN'T MADE OUT OF RABBIT!
NO, NO, OF COURSE NOT.
RABBIT'S EXPENSIVE. I THINK THEY USE MICE.
DUNLAP
I DON'T GET IT, BIXBY. I'M CUTE, FUNNY, TALENTED. I CAN SING AND DANCE. HECK, I'LL EVEN DO SLAPSTICK, I'M NOT PROUD.
SO WHY AM I ONLY SEEN AS A PIECE OF MEAT? I SEE THE STARES! AT MY RUMP, MY LOINS, MY CHOPS! AND THE BALONEY FANS! I CAN'T EVEN REPEAT WHAT THEY STARE AT!
YOU SEE ME AS MORE THAN JUST SOMEONE WHO CAN FILL OUT A SAUSAGE, DON'T YOU?
SURE, KID.
OH, THANK YOU, BIXBY, THANK YOU...
EASY, HAMHOCK. YOU'RE GETTIN' GRAVY ALL OVER MY PAPERWORK...
DUNLAP

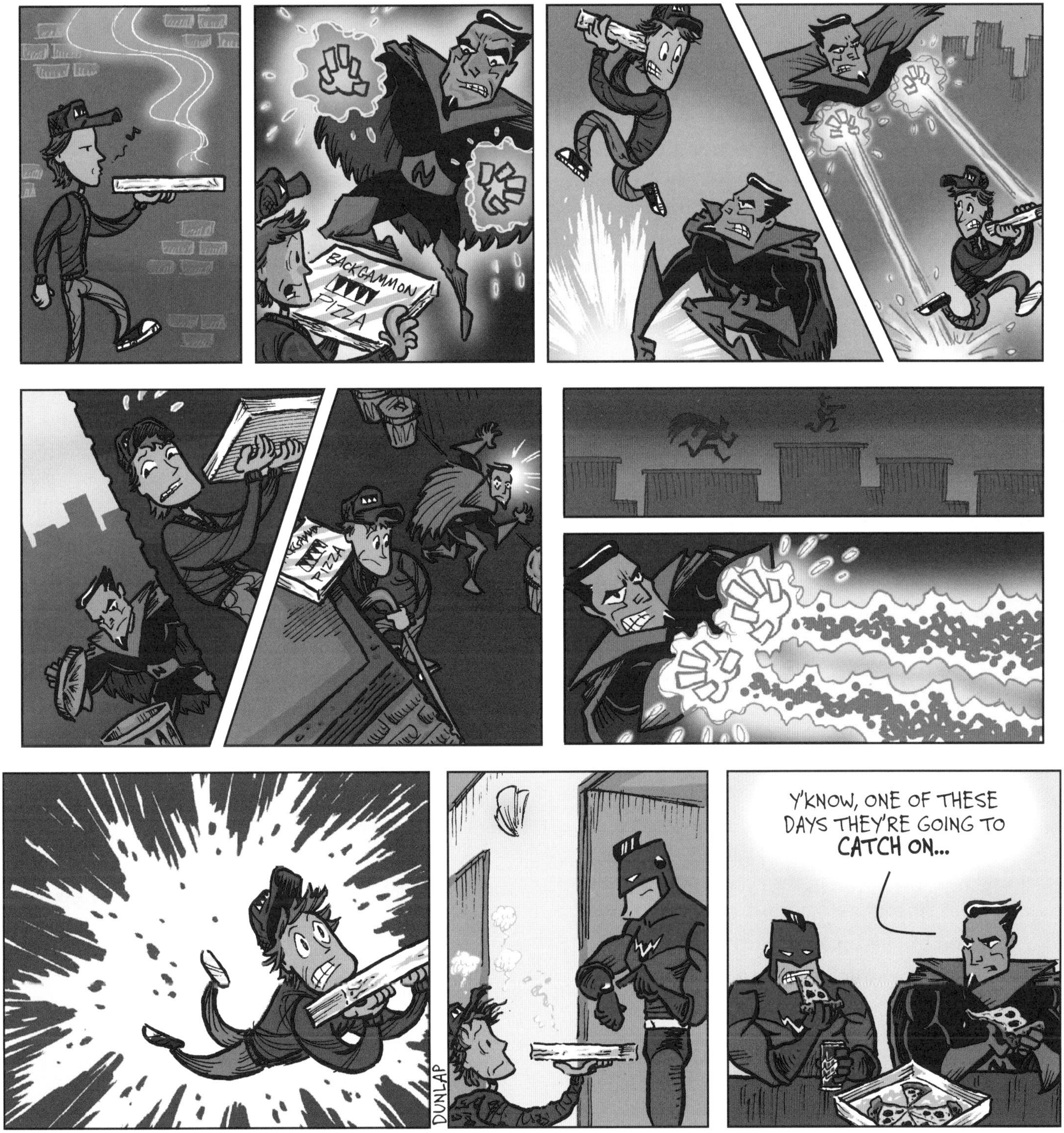
BACKGAMMON
PIZZA
DUNLAP
Y'KNOW, ONE OF THESE DAYS THEY'RE GOING TO CATCH ON...

## Will the Real Captain Victory Please Stand Up?

The following week of strips were drawn in response to a real-life event that occurred early in the syndicated life of *Ink Pen*. I had been developing the strip for nearly four years, and Captain Victory had emerged to become a central character. So it was quite a shock when, not two weeks after the strip debuted, we received an e-mail from Lisa Kirby, the daughter of the late comic book legend Jack Kirby, informing us that he had already created a character named "Captain Victory." My first response was, of course, "Man, is there anything that guy *didn't* create?" But my second was far more sobering: "What the heck do I do now?"

CAPTAIN VICTORY
AND THE GALACTIC RANGERS
"CAPTAIN VICTORY" TM and © The Jack Kirby Estate 2008, all rights reserved.

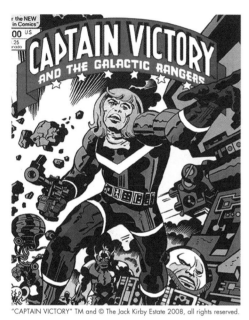

The thought of changing his name was devastating and I worried about the confusion it would cause. But then my editor had an idea: write it into the strip. After all, matters of media, public relations, and branding were all working themes in *Ink Pen*, as were actual cartoon and comic book characters. Suddenly, it seemed less absurd to have a character change his name if I could mention the real-life Jack Kirby and his previous creation, and to depict the ensuing professional dilemma. My Captain Victory was no mental giant, so it was easy enough to depict him as the kind of witless oaf who'd have committed such a faux pas (with the obvious subtext being that I had also been such an oaf).

I ran this idea by Lisa and she graciously agreed to let me work the whole thing into the strip, paying respectful homage to her father along the way. After all, Kirby had always been a huge influence on me and it was embarrassing enough to have inadvertently stepped on his toes, much less to have missed out completely on some of his work. The results, I think, were positive, except for the fact that I now have to cram three extra letters into each utterance of his name—no small feat considering the limited space of the comics page.

So there you have it—the true story behind the fictional story of Captain Victorious's name change. Once again, I'd like to thank Lisa Kirby for being so understanding of a young cartoonist's folly and give one last shout-out to Jack "King" Kirby for his extraordinary contribution to comics in general and to my growth in particular. Long live the King.

Phil Dunlap
Brooklyn, 2008

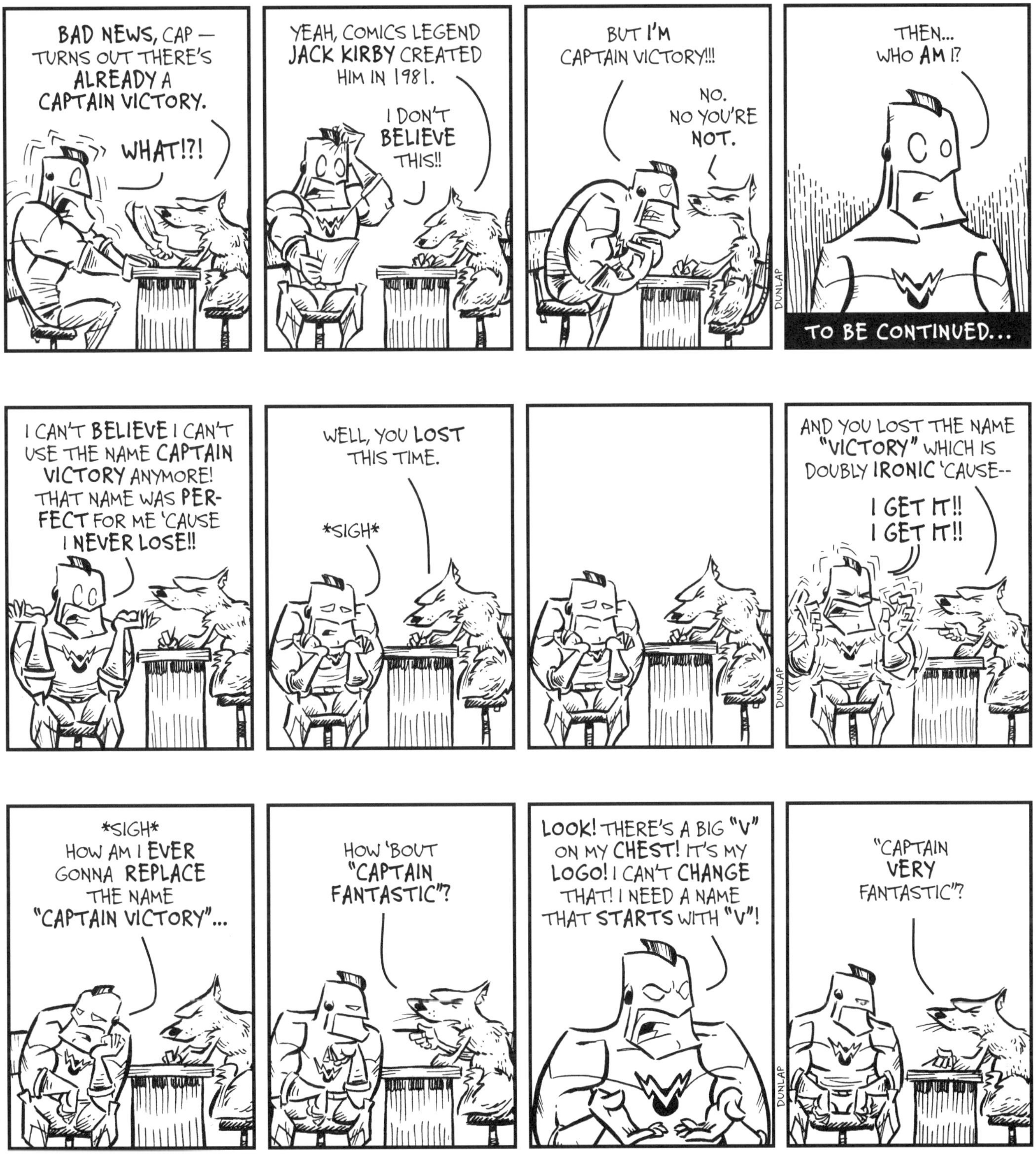
BAD NEWS, CAP — TURNS OUT THERE'S ALREADY A CAPTAIN VICTORY.
WHAT!?!
YEAH, COMICS LEGEND JACK KIRBY CREATED HIM IN 1981.
I DON'T BELIEVE THIS!!
BUT I'M CAPTAIN VICTORY!!!
NO. NO YOU'RE NOT.
THEN... WHO AM I?
DUNLAP
TO BE CONTINUED...
I CAN'T BELIEVE I CAN'T USE THE NAME CAPTAIN VICTORY ANYMORE! THAT NAME WAS PERFECT FOR ME 'CAUSE I NEVER LOSE!!
WELL, YOU LOST THIS TIME.
*SIGH*
DUNLAP
AND YOU LOST THE NAME "VICTORY" WHICH IS DOUBLY IRONIC 'CAUSE--
I GET IT!! I GET IT!!
*SIGH* HOW AM I EVER GONNA REPLACE THE NAME "CAPTAIN VICTORY"...
HOW 'BOUT "CAPTAIN FANTASTIC"?
LOOK! THERE'S A BIG "V" ON MY CHEST! IT'S MY LOGO! I CAN'T CHANGE THAT! I NEED A NAME THAT STARTS WITH "V"!
DUNLAP
"CAPTAIN VERY FANTASTIC"?

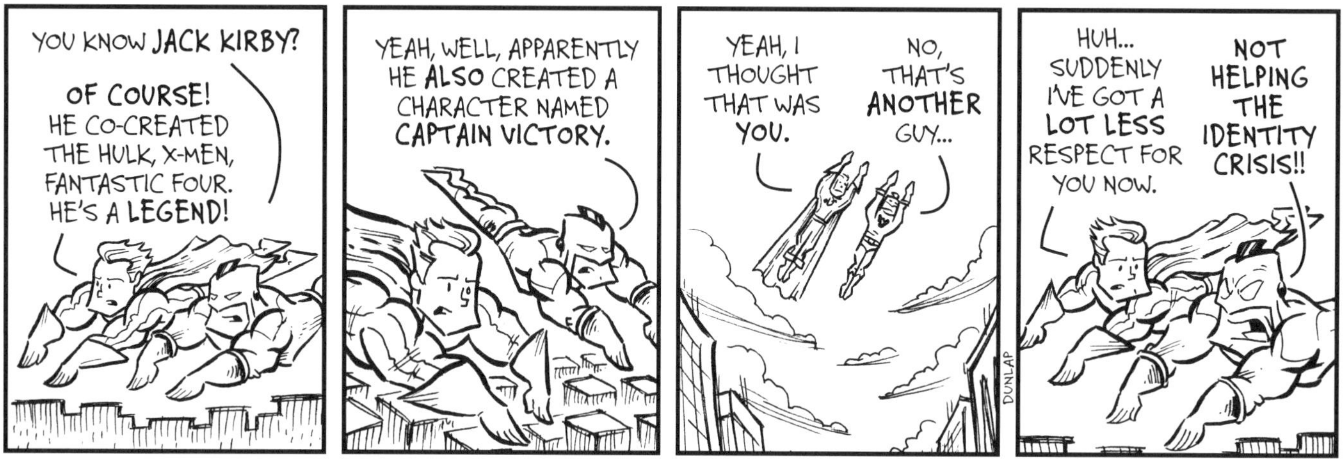
YOU KNOW JACK KIRBY?
OF COURSE! HE CO-CREATED THE HULK, X-MEN, FANTASTIC FOUR. HE'S A LEGEND!
YEAH, WELL, APPARENTLY HE ALSO CREATED A CHARACTER NAMED CAPTAIN VICTORY.
YEAH, I THOUGHT THAT WAS YOU.
NO, THAT'S ANOTHER GUY...
DUNLAP
HUH... SUDDENLY I'VE GOT A LOT LESS RESPECT FOR YOU NOW.
NOT HELPING THE IDENTITY CRISIS!!

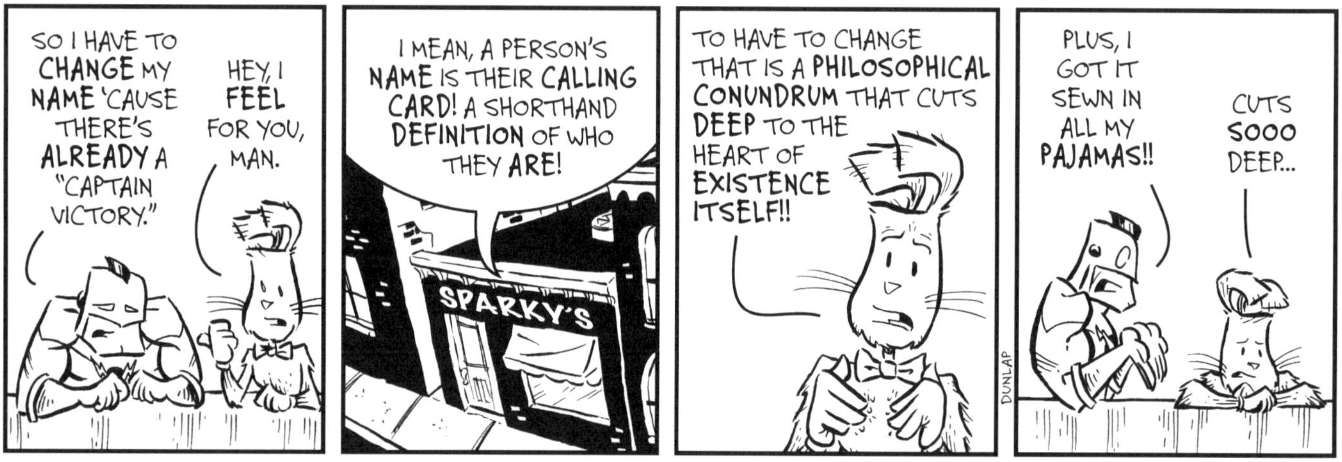
SO I HAVE TO CHANGE MY NAME 'CAUSE THERE'S ALREADY A "CAPTAIN VICTORY."
HEY, I FEEL FOR YOU, MAN.
I MEAN, A PERSON'S NAME IS THEIR CALLING CARD! A SHORTHAND DEFINITION OF WHO THEY ARE!
SPARKY'S
TO HAVE TO CHANGE THAT IS A PHILOSOPHICAL CONUNDRUM THAT CUTS DEEP TO THE HEART OF EXISTENCE ITSELF!!
DUNLAP
PLUS, I GOT IT SEWN IN ALL MY PAJAMAS!!
CUTS SOOO DEEP...

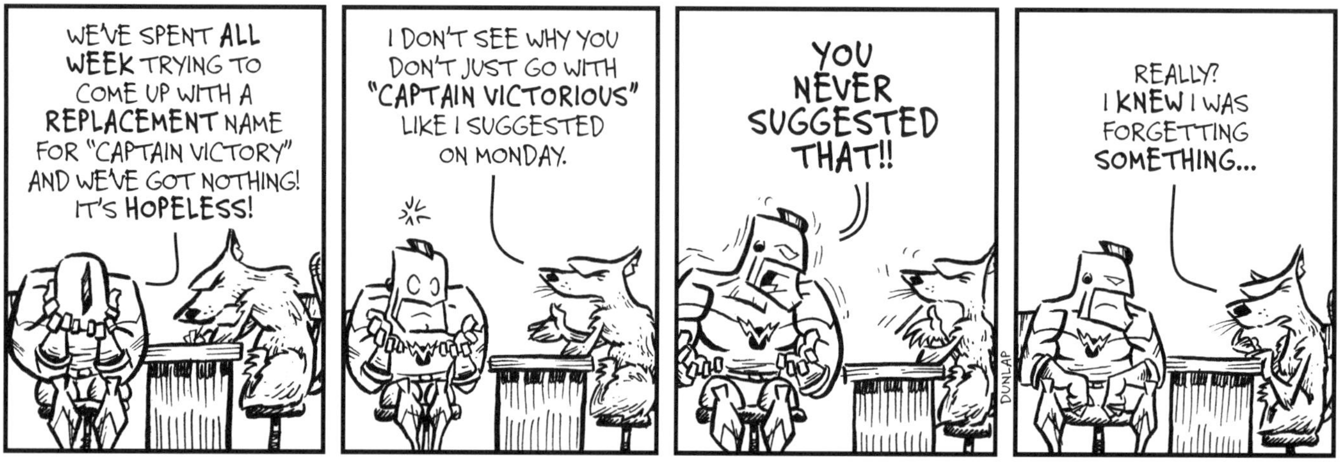
WE'VE SPENT ALL WEEK TRYING TO COME UP WITH A REPLACEMENT NAME FOR "CAPTAIN VICTORY" AND WE'VE GOT NOTHING! IT'S HOPELESS!
I DON'T SEE WHY YOU DON'T JUST GO WITH "CAPTAIN VICTORIOUS" LIKE I SUGGESTED ON MONDAY.
YOU NEVER SUGGESTED THAT!!
DUNLAP
REALLY? I KNEW I WAS FORGETTING SOMETHING...

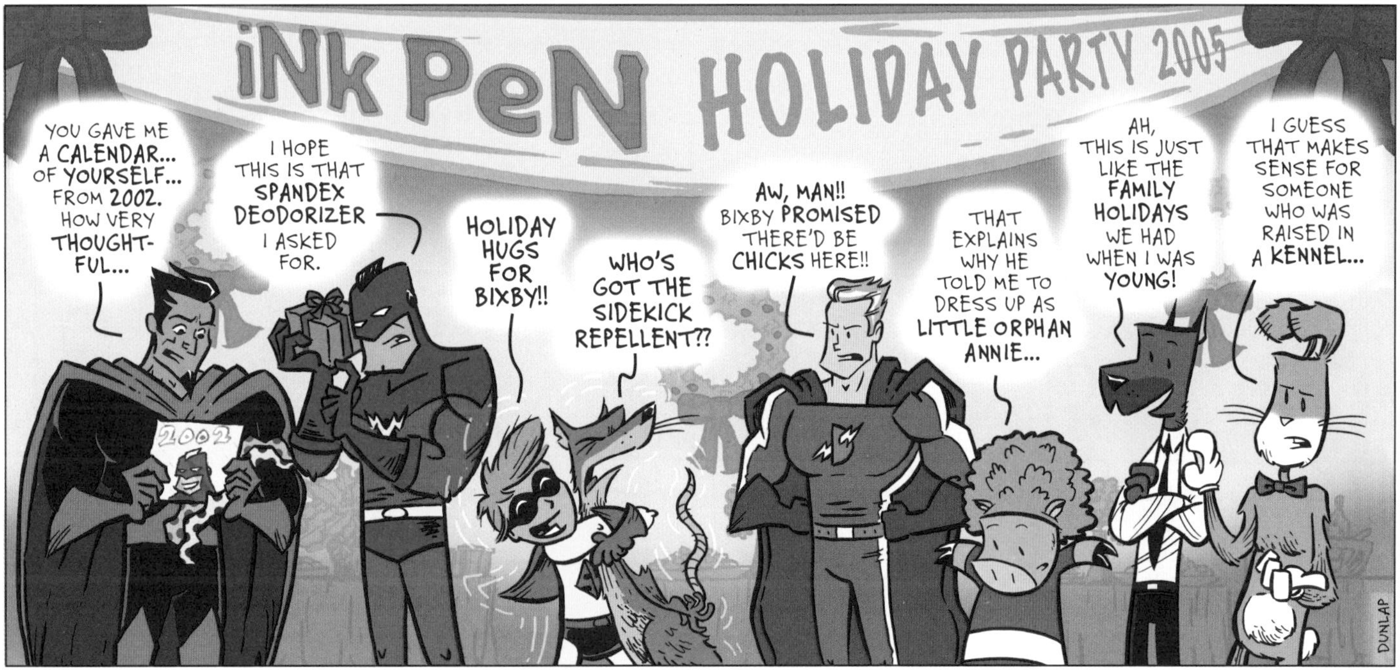
iNk PeN HOLIDAY PARTY 2005
YOU GAVE ME A CALENDAR... OF YOURSELF... FROM 2002. HOW VERY THOUGHT-FUL...
I HOPE THIS IS THAT SPANDEX DEODORIZER I ASKED FOR.
HOLIDAY HUGS FOR BIXBY!!
WHO'S GOT THE SIDEKICK REPELLENT??
AW, MAN!! BIXBY PROMISED THERE'D BE CHICKS HERE!!
THAT EXPLAINS WHY HE TOLD ME TO DRESS UP AS LITTLE ORPHAN ANNIE...
AH, THIS IS JUST LIKE THE FAMILY HOLIDAYS WE HAD WHEN I WAS YOUNG!
I GUESS THAT MAKES SENSE FOR SOMEONE WHO WAS RAISED IN A KENNEL...
2002
DUNLAP

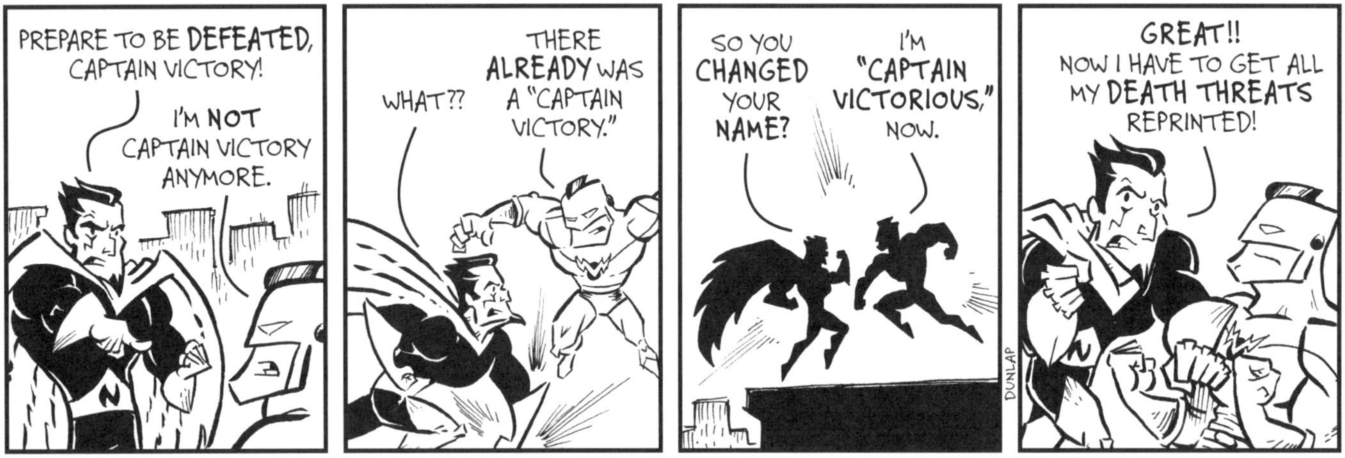
PREPARE TO BE DEFEATED, CAPTAIN VICTORY!
I'M NOT CAPTAIN VICTORY ANYMORE.
WHAT??
THERE ALREADY WAS A "CAPTAIN VICTORY."
SO YOU CHANGED YOUR NAME?
I'M "CAPTAIN VICTORIOUS," NOW.
DUNLAP
GREAT!! NOW I HAVE TO GET ALL MY DEATH THREATS REPRINTED!

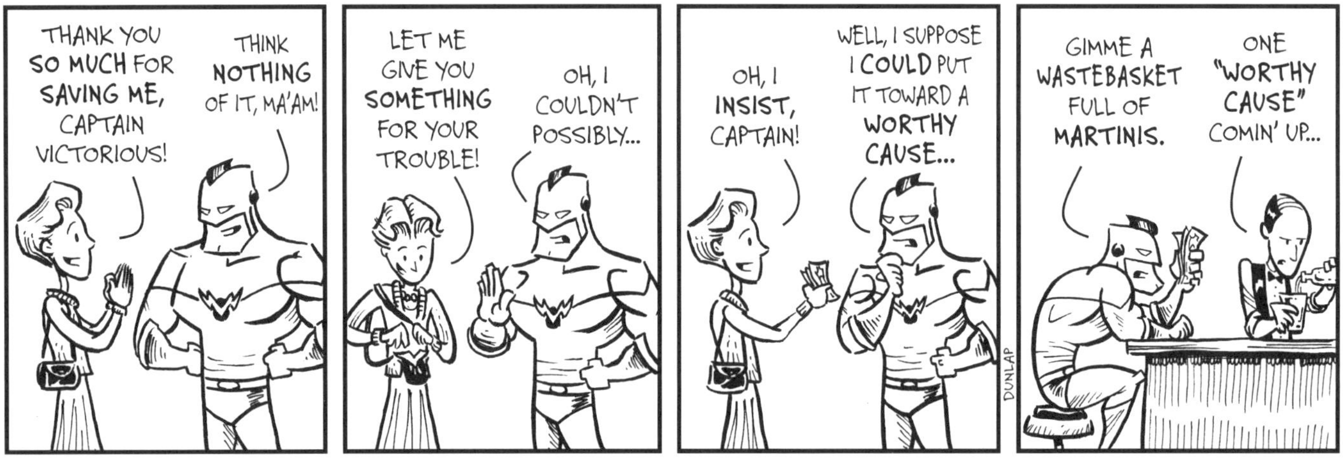
THANK YOU SO MUCH FOR SAVING ME, CAPTAIN VICTORIOUS!
THINK NOTHING OF IT, MA'AM!
LET ME GIVE YOU SOMETHING FOR YOUR TROUBLE!
OH, I COULDN'T POSSIBLY...
OH, I INSIST, CAPTAIN!
WELL, I SUPPOSE I COULD PUT IT TOWARD A WORTHY CAUSE...
DUNLAP
GIMME A WASTEBASKET FULL OF MARTINIS.
ONE "WORTHY CAUSE" COMIN' UP...

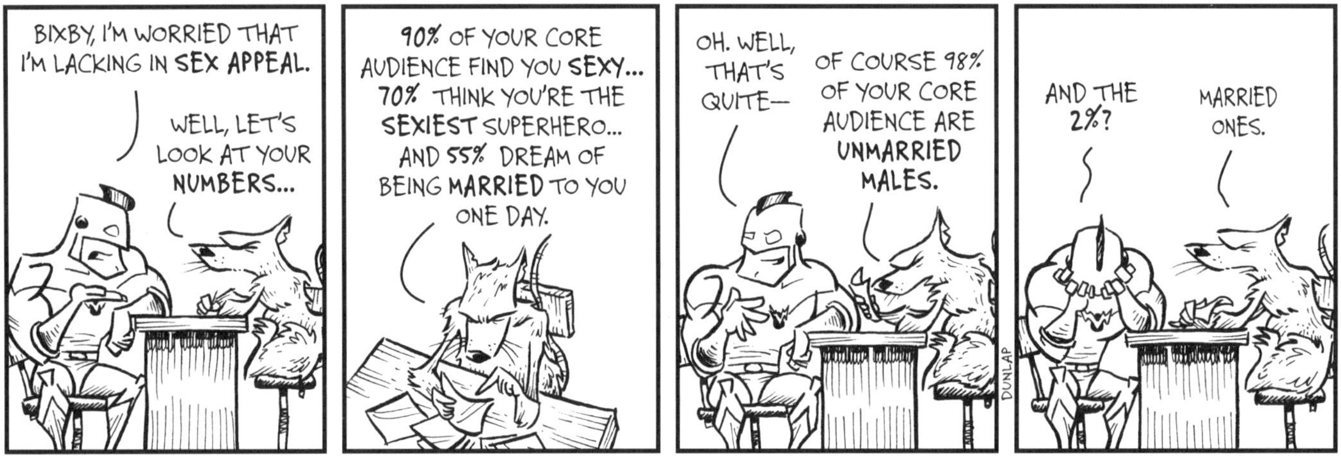
BIXBY, I'M WORRIED THAT I'M LACKING IN SEX APPEAL.
WELL, LET'S LOOK AT YOUR NUMBERS...
90% OF YOUR CORE AUDIENCE FIND YOU SEXY... 70% THINK YOU'RE THE SEXIEST SUPERHERO... AND 55% DREAM OF BEING MARRIED TO YOU ONE DAY.
OH. WELL, THAT'S QUITE—
OF COURSE 98% OF YOUR CORE AUDIENCE ARE UNMARRIED MALES.
DUNLAP
AND THE 2%?
MARRIED ONES.

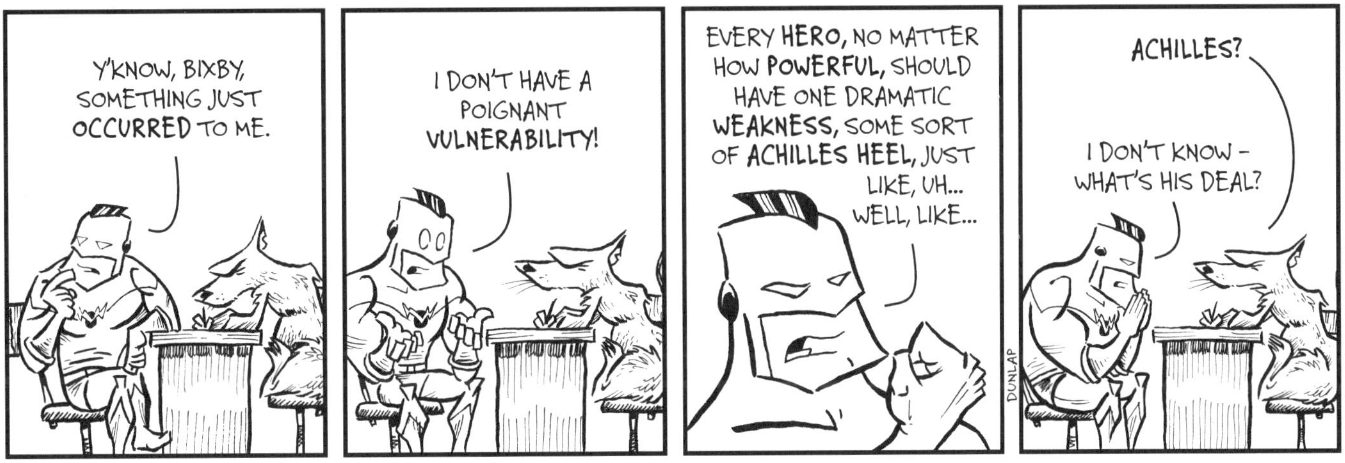
Y'KNOW, BIXBY, SOMETHING JUST OCCURRED TO ME.
I DON'T HAVE A POIGNANT VULNERABILITY!
EVERY HERO, NO MATTER HOW POWERFUL, SHOULD HAVE ONE DRAMATIC WEAKNESS, SOME SORT OF ACHILLES HEEL, JUST LIKE, UH... WELL, LIKE...
DUNLAP
ACHILLES?
I DON'T KNOW - WHAT'S HIS DEAL?

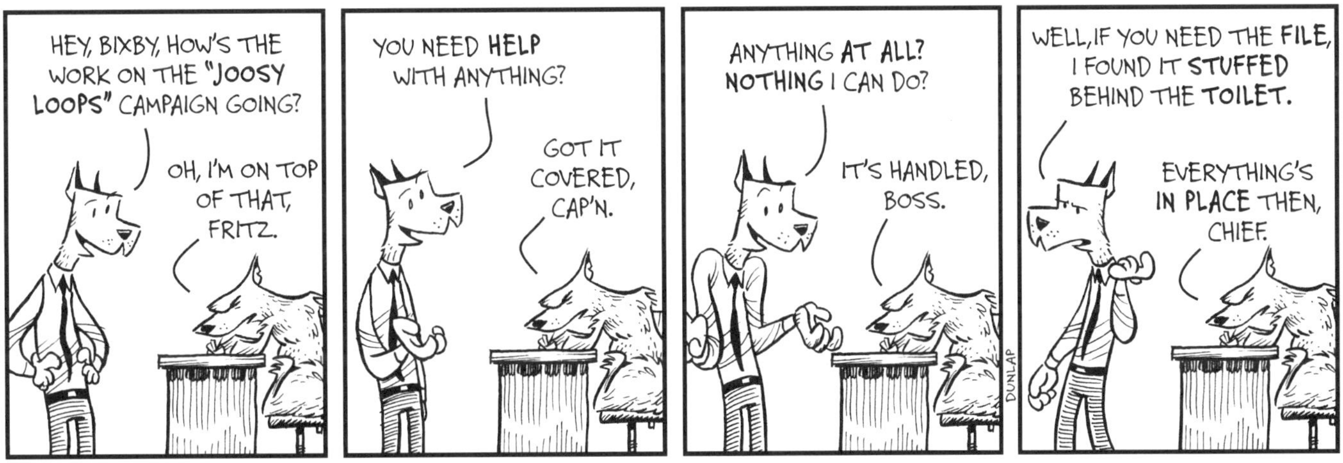
HEY, BIXBY, HOW'S THE WORK ON THE "JOOSY LOOPS" CAMPAIGN GOING?
OH, I'M ON TOP OF THAT, FRITZ.
YOU NEED HELP WITH ANYTHING?
GOT IT COVERED, CAP'N.
ANYTHING AT ALL? NOTHING I CAN DO?
IT'S HANDLED, BOSS.
DUNLAP
WELL, IF YOU NEED THE FILE, I FOUND IT STUFFED BEHIND THE TOILET.
EVERYTHING'S IN PLACE THEN, CHIEF.

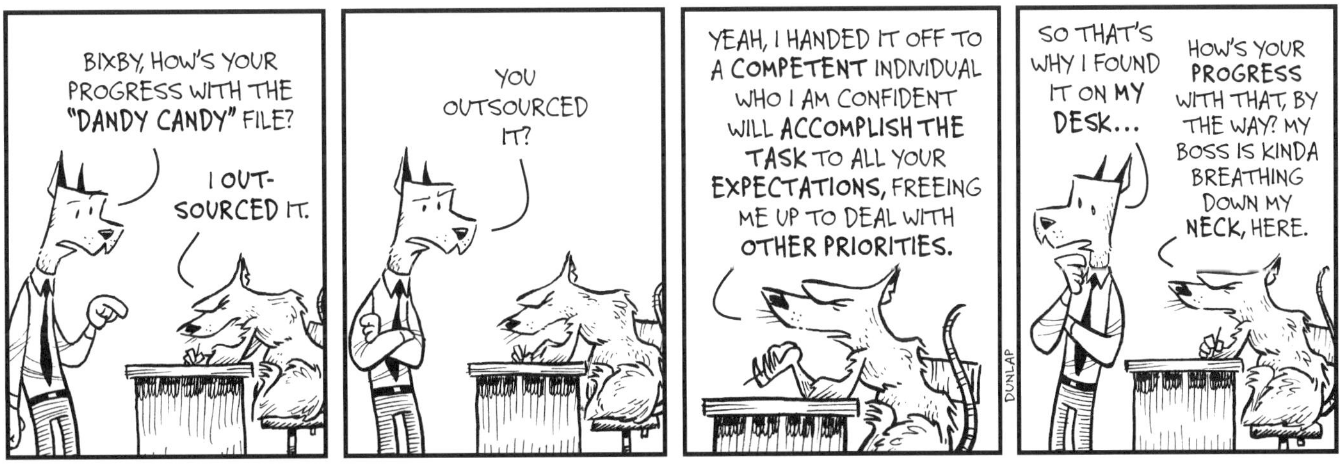
BIXBY, HOW'S YOUR PROGRESS WITH THE "DANDY CANDY" FILE?
I OUT-SOURCED IT.
YOU OUTSOURCED IT?
YEAH, I HANDED IT OFF TO A COMPETENT INDIVIDUAL WHO I AM CONFIDENT WILL ACCOMPLISH THE TASK TO ALL YOUR EXPECTATIONS, FREEING ME UP TO DEAL WITH OTHER PRIORITIES.
DUNLAP
SO THAT'S WHY I FOUND IT ON MY DESK...
HOW'S YOUR PROGRESS WITH THAT, BY THE WAY? MY BOSS IS KINDA BREATHING DOWN MY NECK, HERE.

IN THE OLD DAYS, YOU COULD GRAB A CROOK OFF THE STREET AND THROW HIM IN JAIL YOURSELF!
BUT NOWADAYS IT'S ALL "DUE PROCESS" THIS, AND "HABEAS CORPUS" THAT! I'VE GOT TO READ PEOPLE THEIR RIGHTS? IT'S RIDICULOUS!
WELL, HOW WOULD YOU FEEL IF SOMEONE SWOOPED YOU UP AND THREW YOU IN JAIL WITHOUT THE CHANCE TO DEFEND YOURSELF?
I'D JUST BEND OPEN THE BARS!
WELL, WHAT IF THEY WERE... NUCLEOTRONIC OR SOMETHING, AND YOU COULDN'T?
HMMM... I THINK I SEE WHAT YOU'RE SAYING...
SPARKY'S
AS LONG AS I CAN STAY AWAY FROM THESE "NUCLEOTRONIC BARS," I CAN ESCAPE ACCOUNTABILITY!
I THINK YOU'RE MISSING THE POINT OF THIS WHOLE "JUSTICE SYSTEM" CONCEPT HERE...
"DON'T GET CAUGHT"! I GET IT!! I GET IT!!
DUNLAP

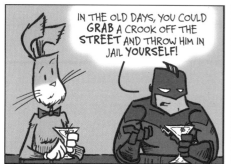

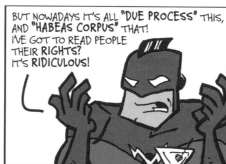

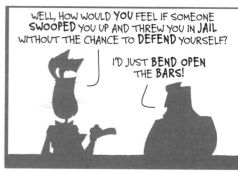

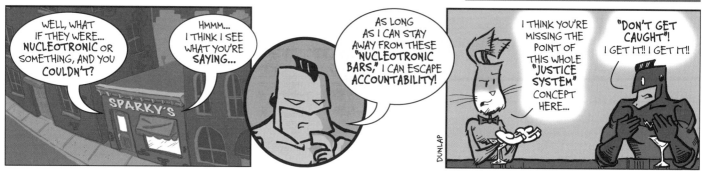

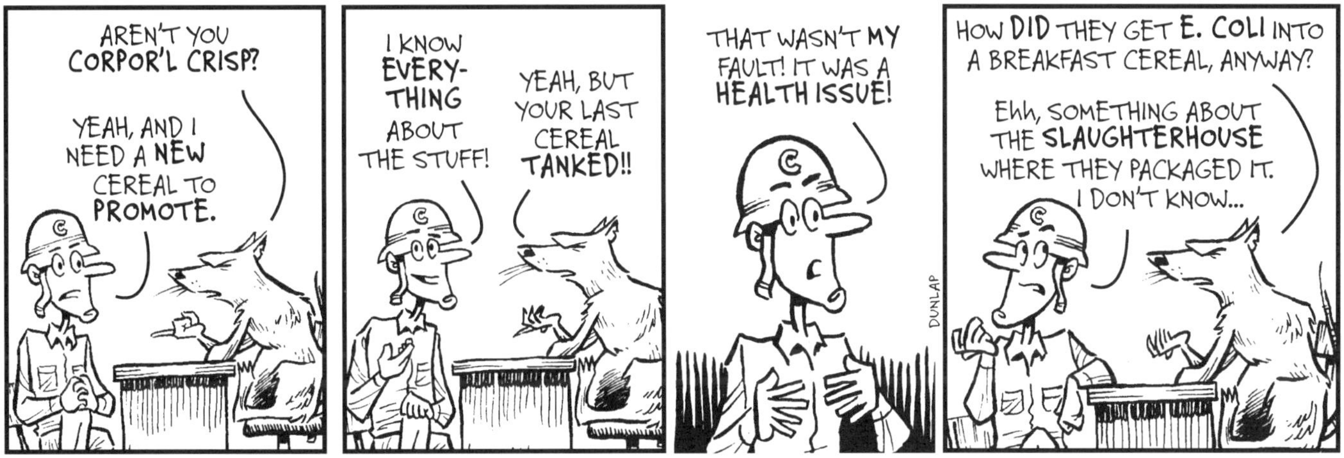
AREN'T YOU CORPOR'L CRISP?
YEAH, AND I NEED A NEW CEREAL TO PROMOTE.
I KNOW EVERY-THING ABOUT THE STUFF!
YEAH, BUT YOUR LAST CEREAL TANKED!!
THAT WASN'T MY FAULT! IT WAS A HEALTH ISSUE!
DUNLAP
HOW DID THEY GET E. COLI INTO A BREAKFAST CEREAL, ANYWAY?
Ehh, SOMETHING ABOUT THE SLAUGHTERHOUSE WHERE THEY PACKAGED IT. I DON'T KNOW...

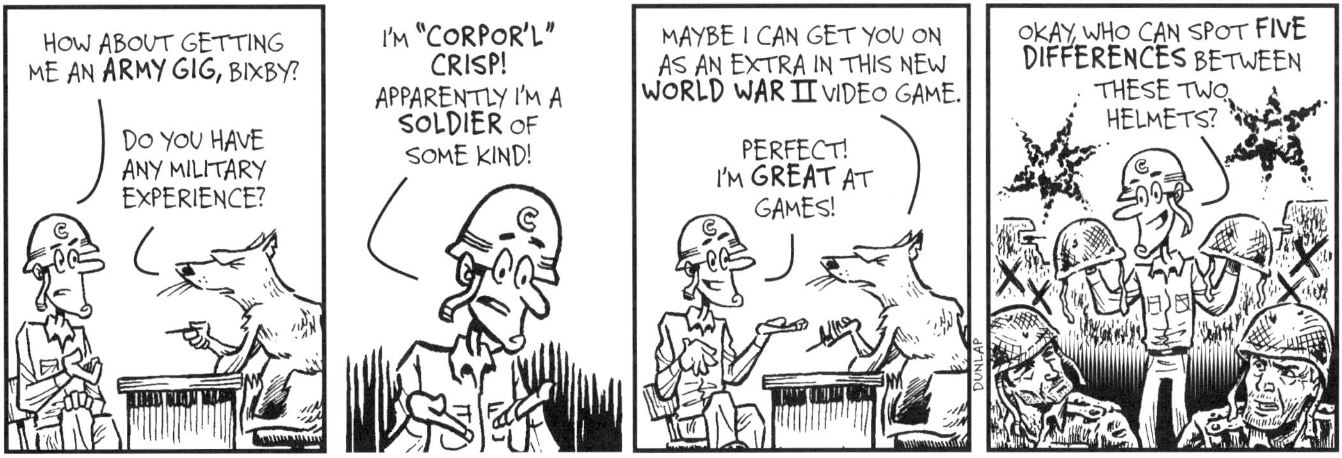
HOW ABOUT GETTING ME AN ARMY GIG, BIXBY?
DO YOU HAVE ANY MILITARY EXPERIENCE?
I'M "CORPOR'L" CRISP! APPARENTLY I'M A SOLDIER OF SOME KIND!
MAYBE I CAN GET YOU ON AS AN EXTRA IN THIS NEW WORLD WAR II VIDEO GAME.
PERFECT! I'M GREAT AT GAMES!
DUNLAP
OKAY, WHO CAN SPOT FIVE DIFFERENCES BETWEEN THESE TWO HELMETS?

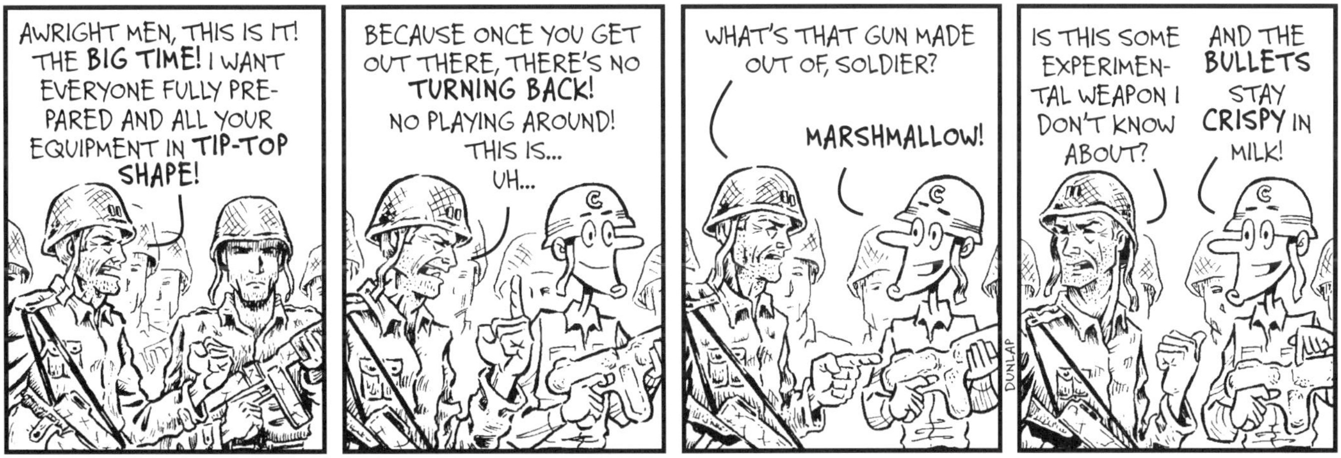
AWRIGHT MEN, THIS IS IT! THE BIG TIME! I WANT EVERYONE FULLY PRE-PARED AND ALL YOUR EQUIPMENT IN TIP-TOP SHAPE!
BECAUSE ONCE YOU GET OUT THERE, THERE'S NO TURNING BACK! NO PLAYING AROUND! THIS IS... UH...
WHAT'S THAT GUN MADE OUT OF, SOLDIER?
MARSHMALLOW!
DUNLAP
IS THIS SOME EXPERIMEN-TAL WEAPON I DON'T KNOW ABOUT?
AND THE BULLETS STAY CRISPY IN MILK!

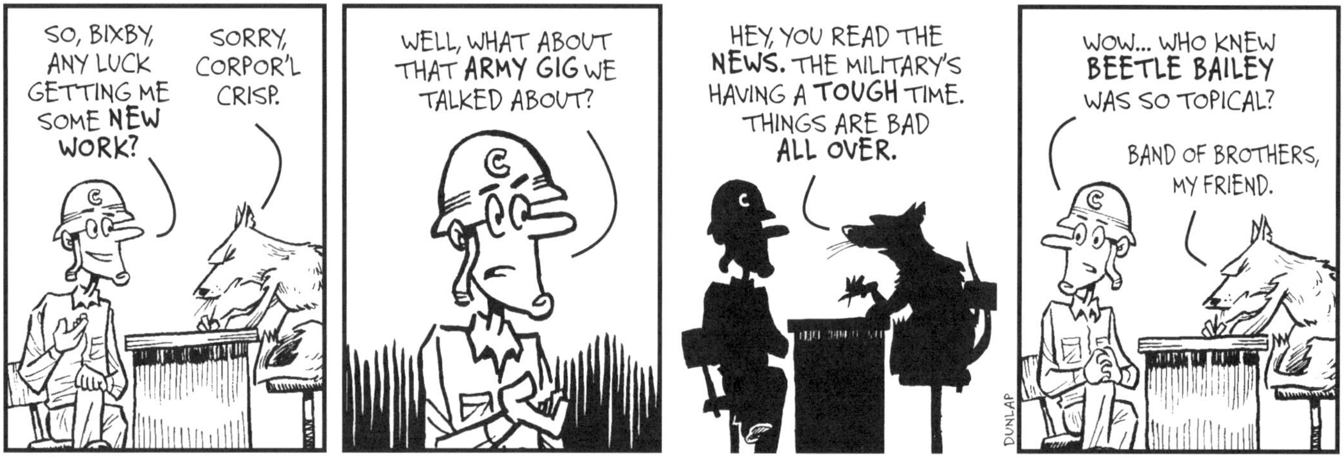
SO, BIXBY, ANY LUCK GETTING ME SOME NEW WORK?
SORRY, CORPOR'L CRISP.
WELL, WHAT ABOUT THAT ARMY GIG WE TALKED ABOUT?
HEY, YOU READ THE NEWS. THE MILITARY'S HAVING A TOUGH TIME. THINGS ARE BAD ALL OVER.
WOW... WHO KNEW BEETLE BAILEY WAS SO TOPICAL?
BAND OF BROTHERS, MY FRIEND.
DUNLAP

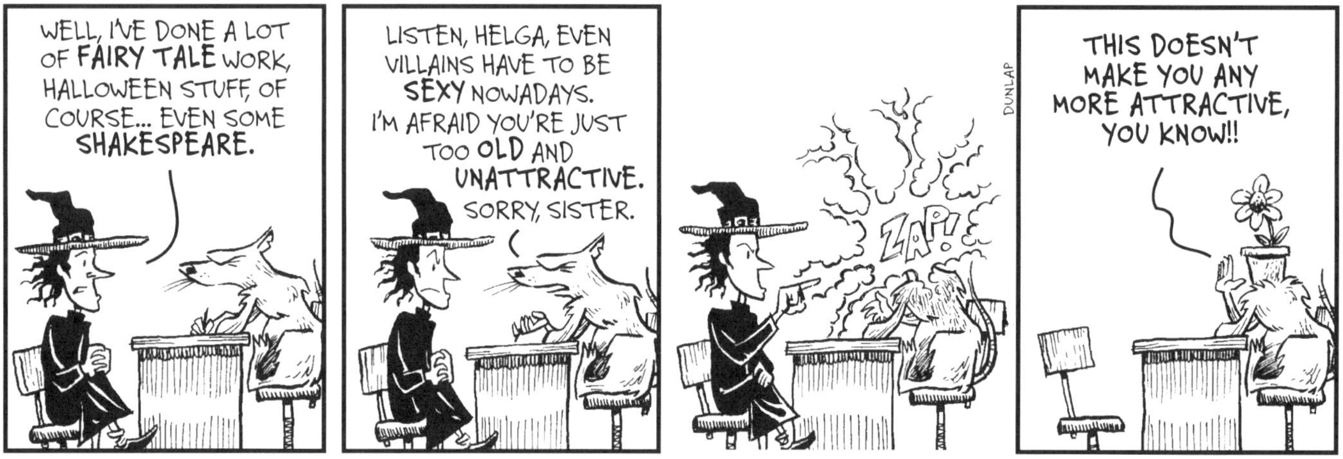
WELL, I'VE DONE A LOT OF FAIRY TALE WORK, HALLOWEEN STUFF, OF COURSE... EVEN SOME SHAKESPEARE.
LISTEN, HELGA, EVEN VILLAINS HAVE TO BE SEXY NOWADAYS. I'M AFRAID YOU'RE JUST TOO OLD AND UNATTRACTIVE.
SORRY, SISTER.
ZAP!
THIS DOESN'T MAKE YOU ANY MORE ATTRACTIVE, YOU KNOW!!
DUNLAP

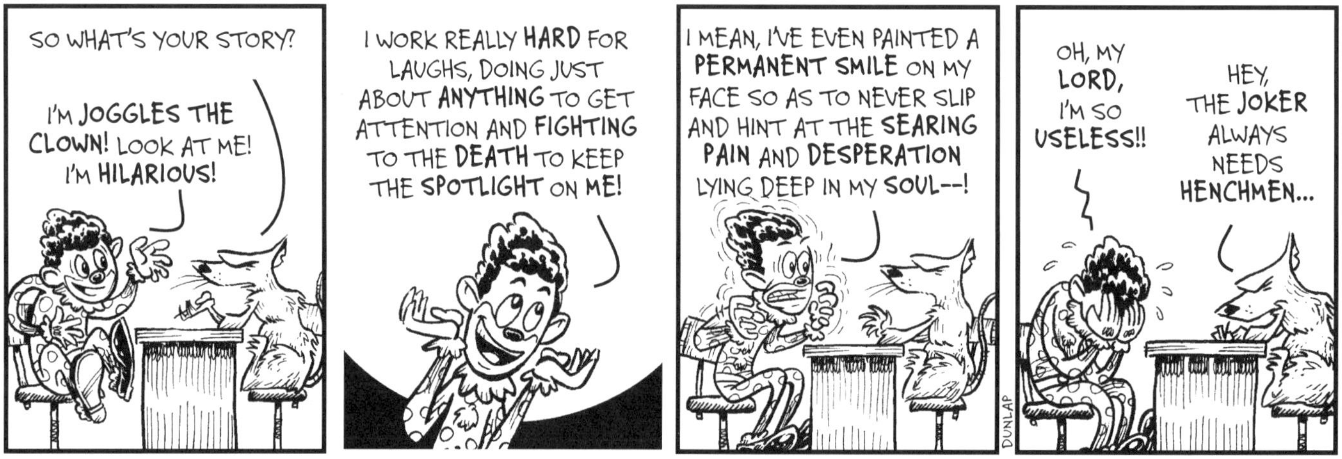
SO WHAT'S YOUR STORY?
I'M JOGGLES THE CLOWN! LOOK AT ME! I'M HILARIOUS!
I WORK REALLY HARD FOR LAUGHS, DOING JUST ABOUT ANYTHING TO GET ATTENTION AND FIGHTING TO THE DEATH TO KEEP THE SPOTLIGHT ON ME!
I MEAN, I'VE EVEN PAINTED A PERMANENT SMILE ON MY FACE SO AS TO NEVER SLIP AND HINT AT THE SEARING PAIN AND DESPERATION LYING DEEP IN MY SOUL--!
OH, MY LORD, I'M SO USELESS!!
HEY, THE JOKER ALWAYS NEEDS HENCHMEN...
DUNLAP

LOOK AT SOME OF THESE ACTION FIGURES THEY MADE OF ME, BIXBY!
WHAT ABOUT 'EM?
"ALPINE CAP WITH ACTION TOBOGGAN"?? "JUNGLE CAP WITH ACTION MOSQUITO NET"??
ALL THEY DO IS REPAINT THE FIGURE AND THEN PACKAGE IT WITH SOME LEFTOVER FROM ANOTHER TOY! A KAYAK?? WHY WOULD I NEED A KAYAK? I CAN FLY!!
WHITEWATER CAP W/ ACTION KAYAK!
CAPTAIN VICTORIOUS' ACTION PALS!
DUNLAP
WHY DON'T THEY MAKE SOMETHING MORE IN KEEPING WITH WHAT I'D ACTUALLY DO?
LIKE WHAT?
INK PEN
HOW 'BOUT "CRAFT SHOW CAP WITH ACTION SEQUIN GUN"?
YOU KNOW SPIDER-MAN'S AGENT NEVER HAS TO GO THROUGH THIS...

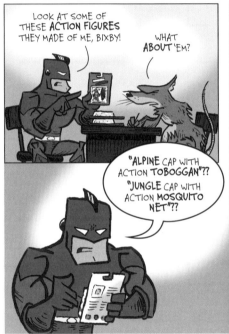

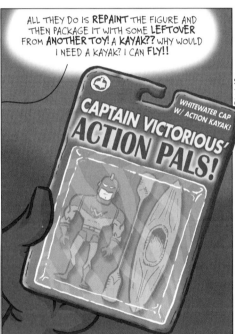

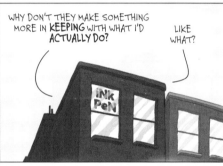

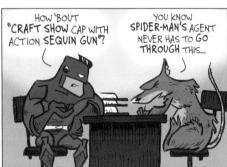

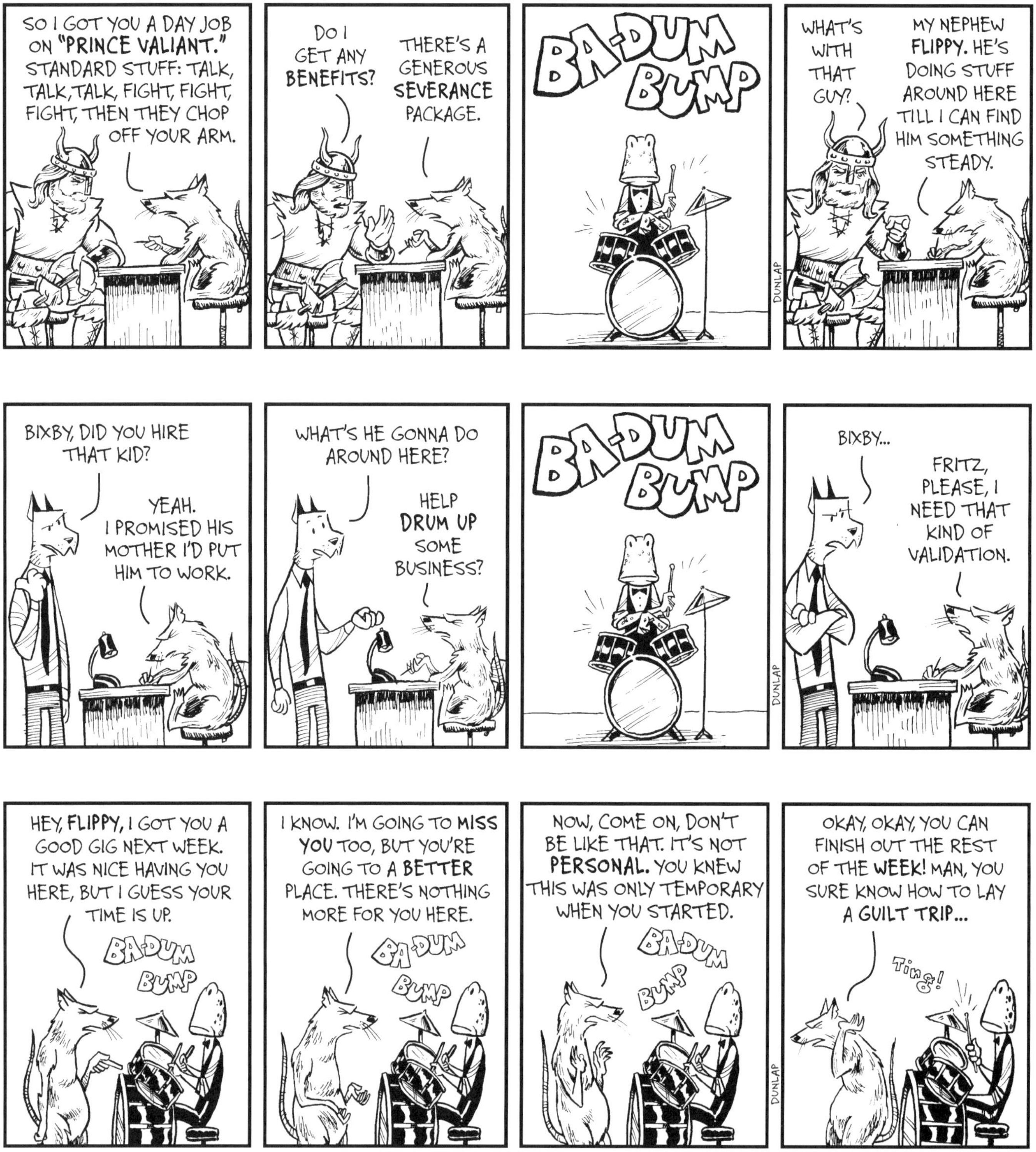
SO I GOT YOU A DAY JOB ON "PRINCE VALIANT." STANDARD STUFF: TALK, TALK, TALK, FIGHT, FIGHT, FIGHT, THEN THEY CHOP OFF YOUR ARM.
DO I GET ANY BENEFITS?
THERE'S A GENEROUS SEVERANCE PACKAGE.
BA-DUM BUMP
WHAT'S WITH THAT GUY?
MY NEPHEW FLIPPY. HE'S DOING STUFF AROUND HERE TILL I CAN FIND HIM SOMETHING STEADY.
DUNLAP
BIXBY, DID YOU HIRE THAT KID?
YEAH. I PROMISED HIS MOTHER I'D PUT HIM TO WORK.
WHAT'S HE GONNA DO AROUND HERE?
HELP DRUM UP SOME BUSINESS?
BA-DUM BUMP
BIXBY...
FRITZ, PLEASE, I NEED THAT KIND OF VALIDATION.
DUNLAP
HEY, FLIPPY, I GOT YOU A GOOD GIG NEXT WEEK. IT WAS NICE HAVING YOU HERE, BUT I GUESS YOUR TIME IS UP.
BA-DUM BUMP
I KNOW. I'M GOING TO MISS YOU TOO, BUT YOU'RE GOING TO A BETTER PLACE. THERE'S NOTHING MORE FOR YOU HERE.
BA-DUM BUMP
NOW, COME ON, DON'T BE LIKE THAT. IT'S NOT PERSONAL. YOU KNEW THIS WAS ONLY TEMPORARY WHEN YOU STARTED.
BA-DUM BUMP
DUNLAP
OKAY, OKAY, YOU CAN FINISH OUT THE REST OF THE WEEK! MAN, YOU SURE KNOW HOW TO LAY A GUILT TRIP...
Ting!

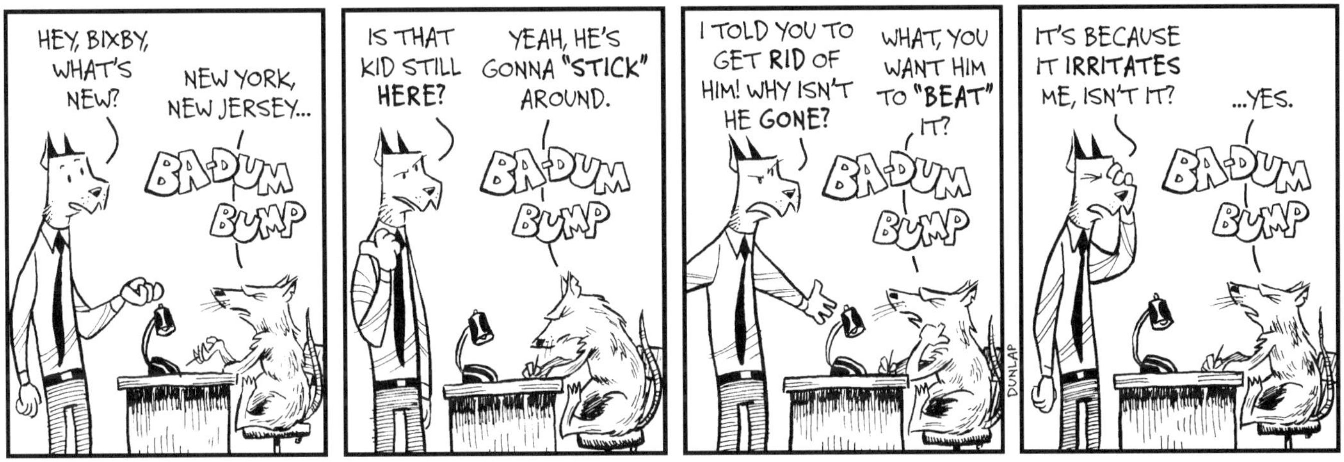
HEY, BIXBY, WHAT'S NEW?
NEW YORK, NEW JERSEY...
BA-DUM BUMP
IS THAT KID STILL HERE?
YEAH, HE'S GONNA "STICK" AROUND.
BA-DUM BUMP
I TOLD YOU TO GET RID OF HIM! WHY ISN'T HE GONE?
WHAT, YOU WANT HIM TO "BEAT" IT?
BA-DUM BUMP
DUNLAP
IT'S BECAUSE IT IRRITATES ME, ISN'T IT?
...YES.
BA-DUM BUMP

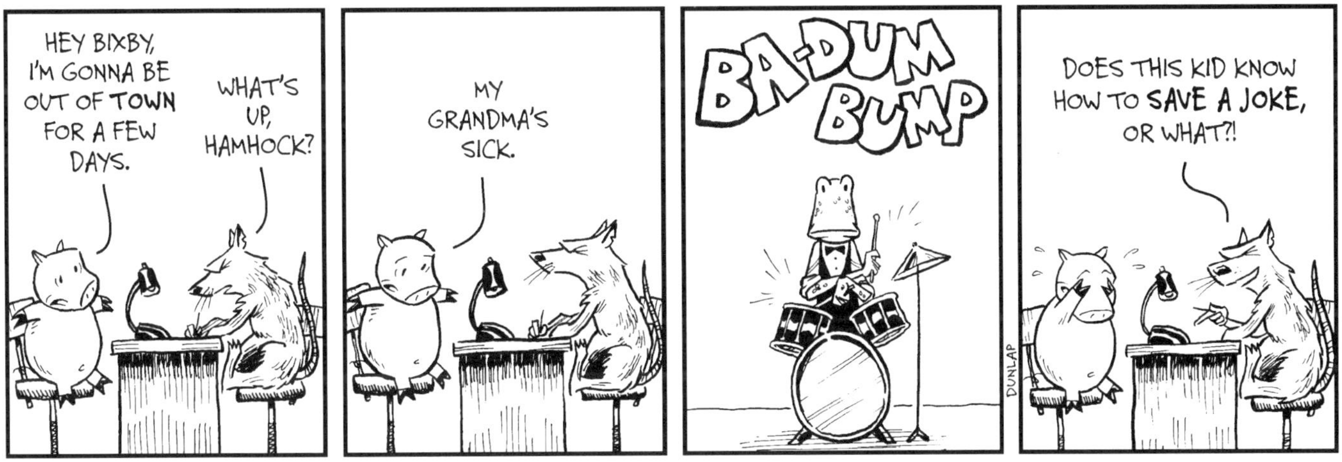
HEY BIXBY, I'M GONNA BE OUT OF TOWN FOR A FEW DAYS.
WHAT'S UP, HAMHOCK?
MY GRANDMA'S SICK.
BA-DUM BUMP
DUNLAP
DOES THIS KID KNOW HOW TO SAVE A JOKE, OR WHAT?!

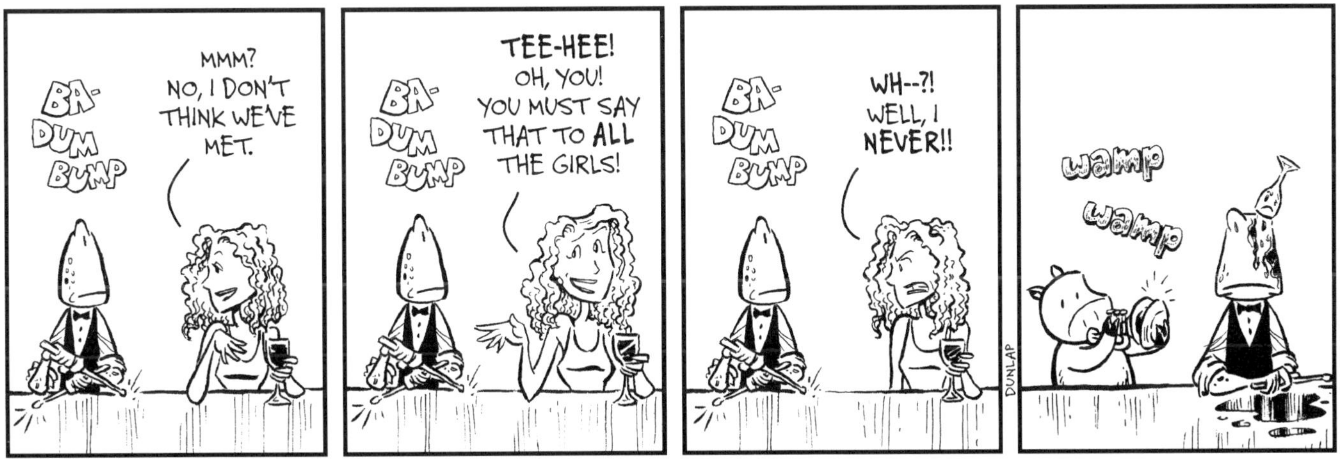
BA-DUM BUMP
MMM? NO, I DON'T THINK WE'VE MET.
BA-DUM BUMP
TEE-HEE! OH, YOU! YOU MUST SAY THAT TO ALL THE GIRLS!
BA-DUM BUMP
WH--?! WELL, I NEVER!!
DUNLAP
wamp
wamp

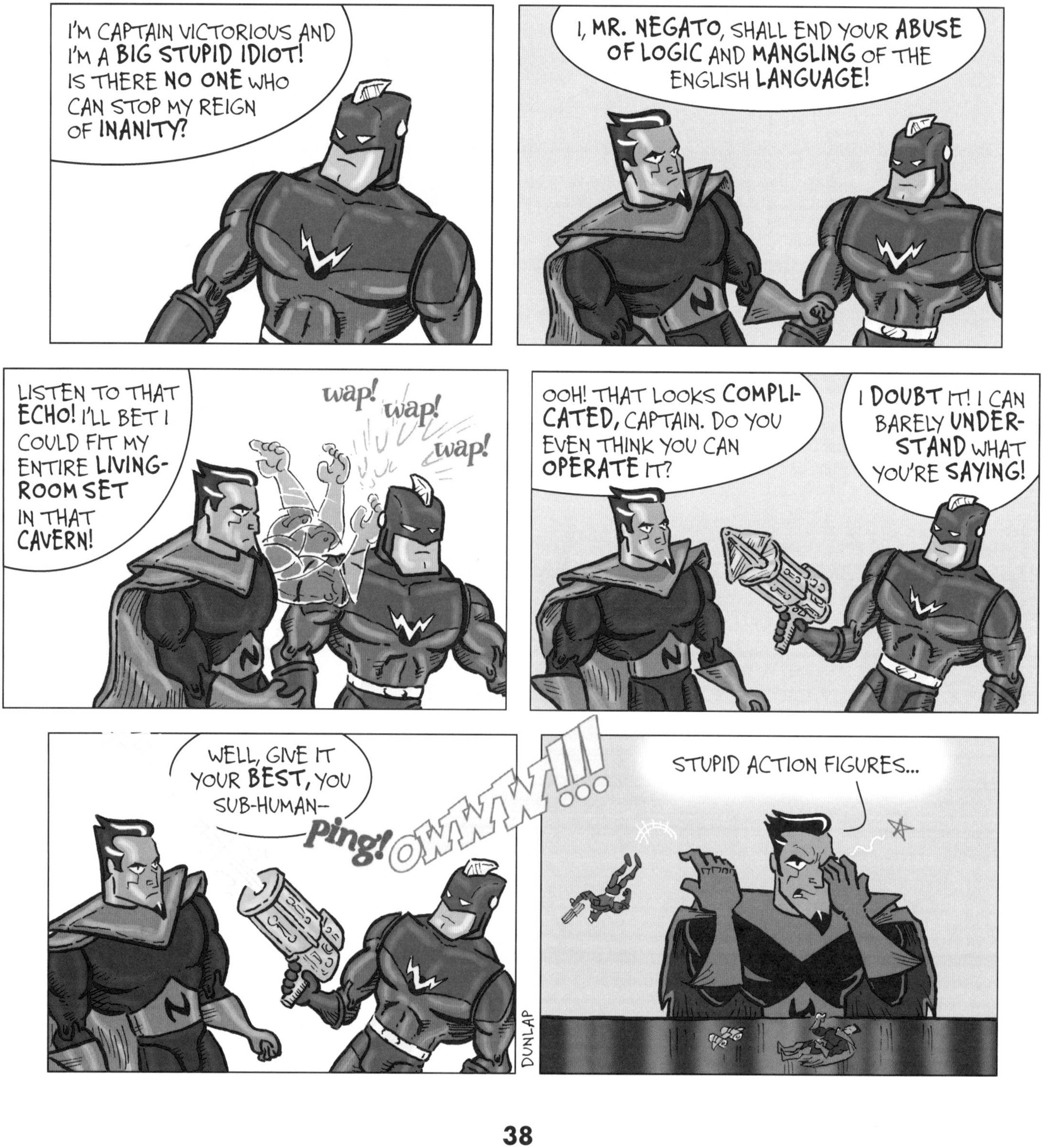
I'M CAPTAIN VICTORIOUS AND I'M A BIG STUPID IDIOT! IS THERE NO ONE WHO CAN STOP MY REIGN OF INANITY?
I, MR. NEGATO, SHALL END YOUR ABUSE OF LOGIC AND MANGLING OF THE ENGLISH LANGUAGE!
LISTEN TO THAT ECHO! I'LL BET I COULD FIT MY ENTIRE LIVING-ROOM SET IN THAT CAVERN!
wap! wap! wap!
OOH! THAT LOOKS COMPLICATED, CAPTAIN. DO YOU EVEN THINK YOU CAN OPERATE IT?
I DOUBT IT! I CAN BARELY UNDERSTAND WHAT YOU'RE SAYING!
WELL, GIVE IT YOUR BEST, YOU SUB-HUMAN–
ping!
OWWW!!!
DUNLAP
STUPID ACTION FIGURES...

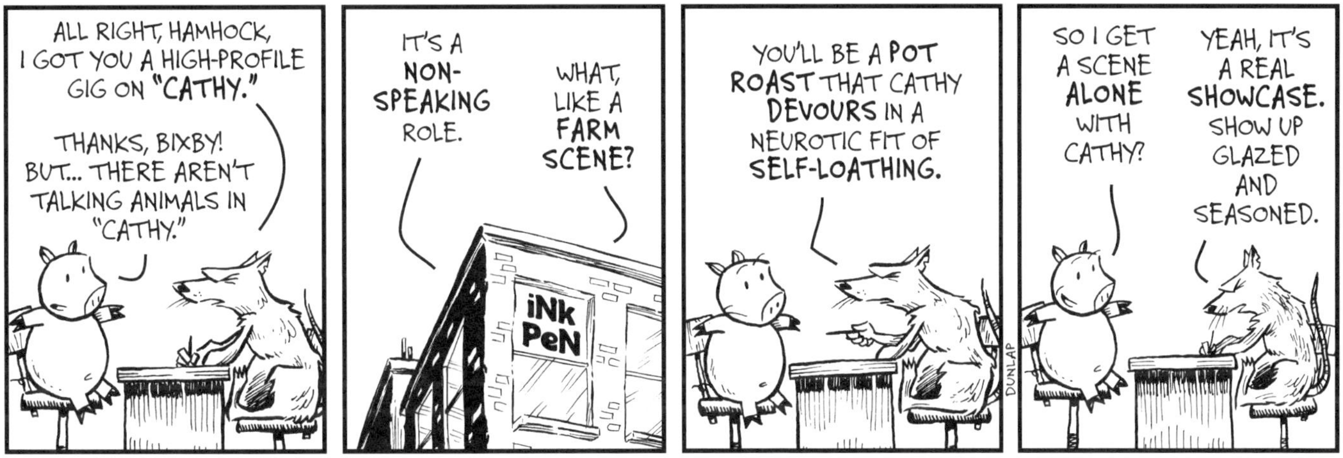
ALL RIGHT, HAMHOCK, I GOT YOU A HIGH-PROFILE GIG ON "CATHY."
THANKS, BIXBY! BUT... THERE AREN'T TALKING ANIMALS IN "CATHY."
IT'S A NON-SPEAKING ROLE.
WHAT, LIKE A FARM SCENE?
iNk PeN
YOU'LL BE A POT ROAST THAT CATHY DEVOURS IN A NEUROTIC FIT OF SELF-LOATHING.
SO I GET A SCENE ALONE WITH CATHY?
YEAH, IT'S A REAL SHOWCASE. SHOW UP GLAZED AND SEASONED.
DUNLAP

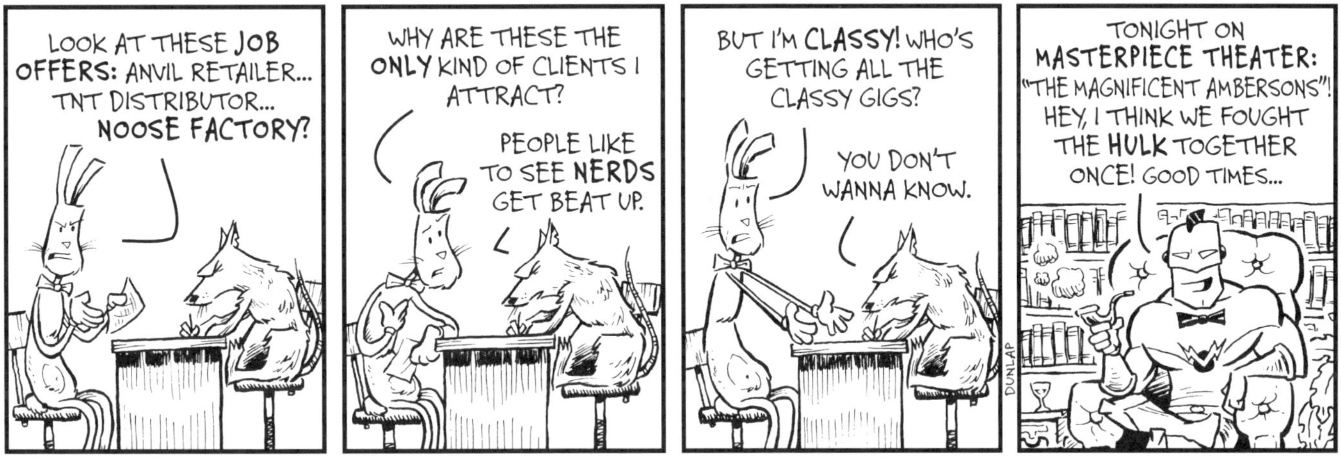
LOOK AT THESE JOB OFFERS: ANVIL RETAILER... TNT DISTRIBUTOR... NOOSE FACTORY?
WHY ARE THESE THE ONLY KIND OF CLIENTS I ATTRACT?
PEOPLE LIKE TO SEE NERDS GET BEAT UP.
BUT I'M CLASSY! WHO'S GETTING ALL THE CLASSY GIGS?
YOU DON'T WANNA KNOW.
DUNLAP
TONIGHT ON MASTERPIECE THEATER: "THE MAGNIFICENT AMBERSONS"! HEY, I THINK WE FOUGHT THE HULK TOGETHER ONCE! GOOD TIMES...

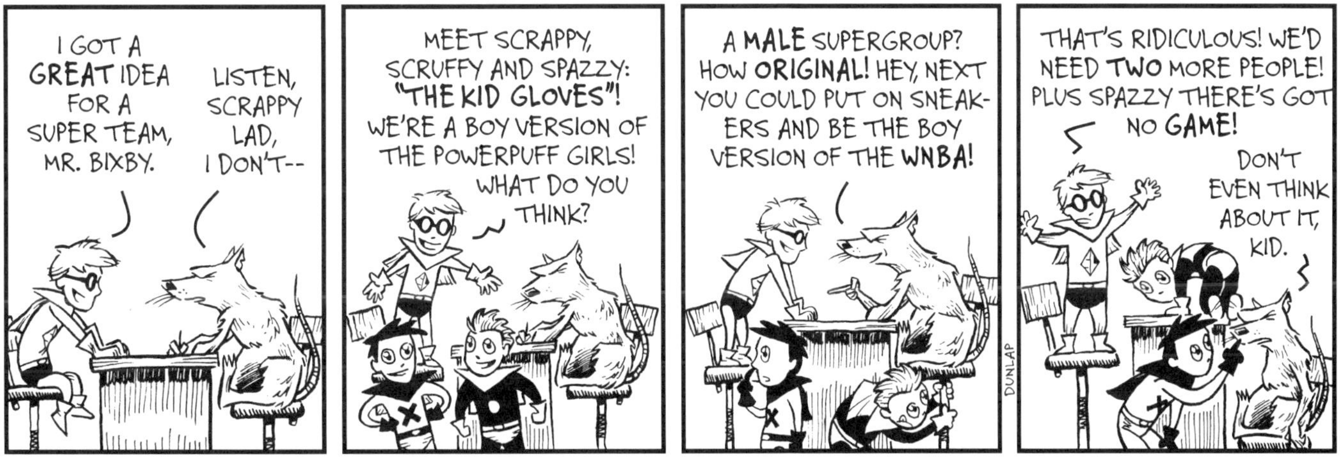
I GOT A GREAT IDEA FOR A SUPER TEAM, MR. BIXBY.
LISTEN, SCRAPPY LAD, I DON'T--
MEET SCRAPPY, SCRUFFY AND SPAZZY: "THE KID GLOVES"! WE'RE A BOY VERSION OF THE POWERPUFF GIRLS!
WHAT DO YOU THINK?
A MALE SUPERGROUP? HOW ORIGINAL! HEY, NEXT YOU COULD PUT ON SNEAK-ERS AND BE THE BOY VERSION OF THE WNBA!
DUNLAP
THAT'S RIDICULOUS! WE'D NEED TWO MORE PEOPLE! PLUS SPAZZY THERE'S GOT NO GAME!
DON'T EVEN THINK ABOUT IT, KID.

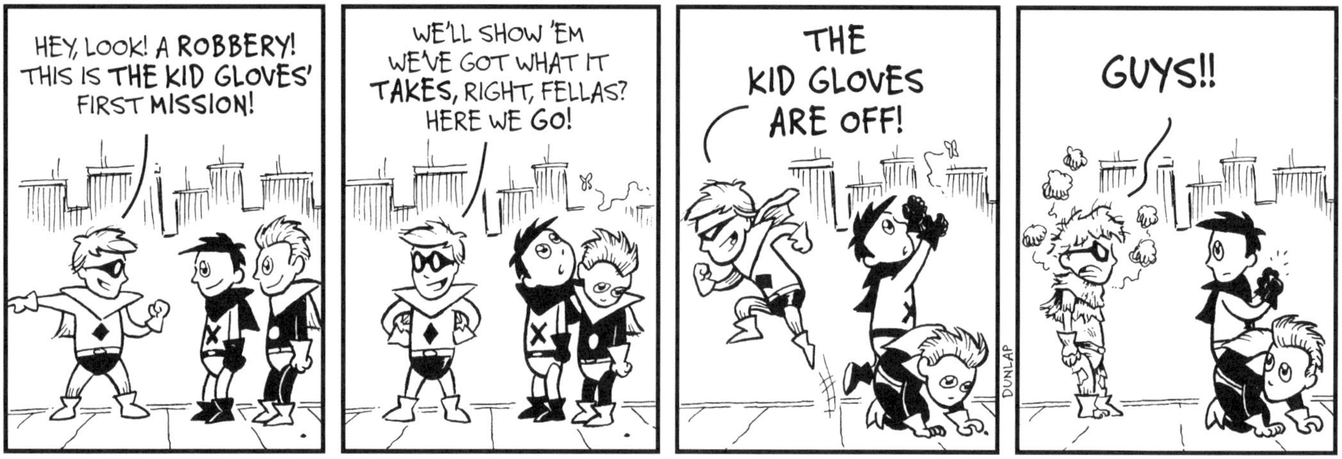

HEY, LOOK! A **ROBBERY!** THIS IS **THE KID GLOVES'** FIRST **MISSION!**
WE'LL SHOW 'EM WE'VE GOT WHAT IT **TAKES,** RIGHT, FELLAS? HERE WE **GO!**
THE KID GLOVES ARE OFF!
GUYS!!
DUNLAP


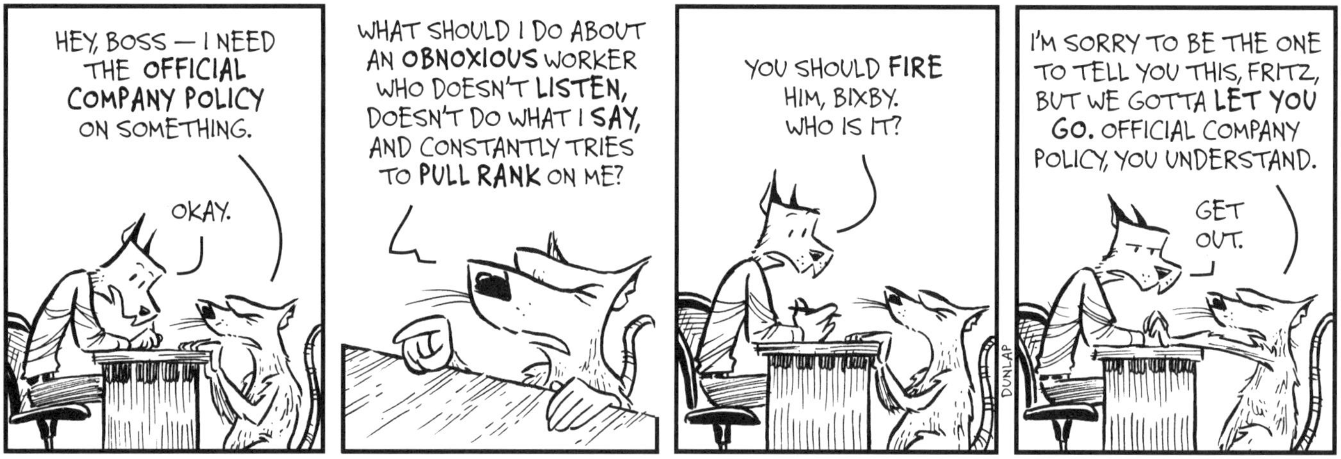

HEY, BOSS — I NEED THE **OFFICIAL COMPANY POLICY** ON SOMETHING.
OKAY.
WHAT SHOULD I DO ABOUT AN **OBNOXIOUS** WORKER WHO DOESN'T **LISTEN,** DOESN'T DO WHAT I **SAY,** AND CONSTANTLY TRIES TO **PULL RANK** ON ME?
YOU SHOULD **FIRE** HIM, BIXBY. WHO IS IT?
I'M SORRY TO BE THE ONE TO TELL YOU THIS, FRITZ, BUT WE GOTTA **LET YOU GO.** OFFICIAL COMPANY POLICY, YOU UNDERSTAND.
GET OUT.
DUNLAP


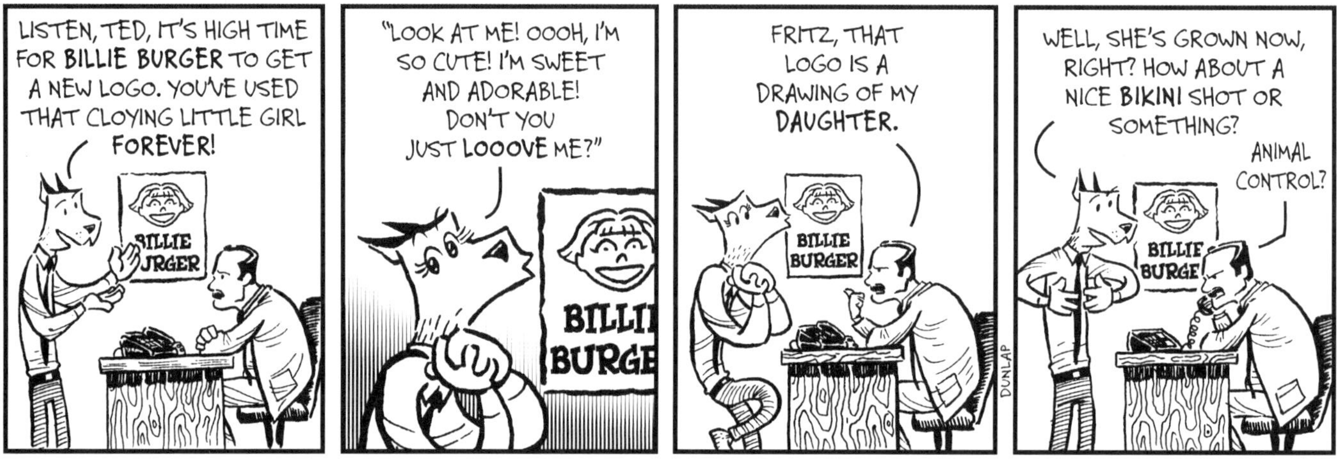

LISTEN, TED, IT'S HIGH TIME FOR **BILLIE BURGER** TO GET A NEW LOGO. YOU'VE USED THAT CLOYING LITTLE GIRL **FOREVER!**
"LOOK AT ME! OOOH, I'M SO CUTE! I'M SWEET AND ADORABLE! DON'T YOU JUST **LOOOVE** ME?"
FRITZ, THAT LOGO IS A DRAWING OF MY **DAUGHTER.**
BILLIE BURGER
WELL, SHE'S GROWN NOW, RIGHT? HOW ABOUT A NICE **BIKINI** SHOT OR SOMETHING?
ANIMAL CONTROL?
DUNLAP

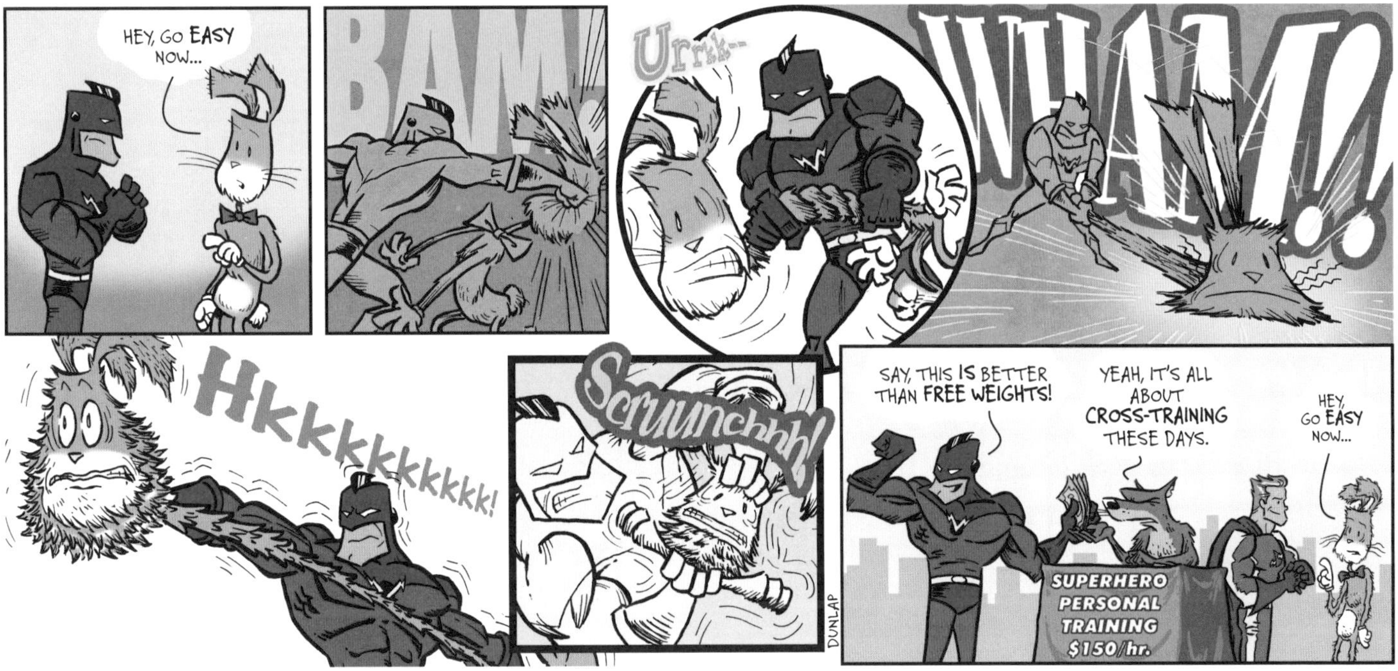
HEY, GO EASY NOW...
BAM!
Urrk--
WHAM!!
Hkkkkkkkkkk!
Scruunchhh!
DUNLAP
SAY, THIS IS BETTER THAN FREE WEIGHTS!
YEAH, IT'S ALL ABOUT CROSS-TRAINING THESE DAYS.
HEY, GO EASY NOW...
SUPERHERO PERSONAL TRAINING $150/hr.

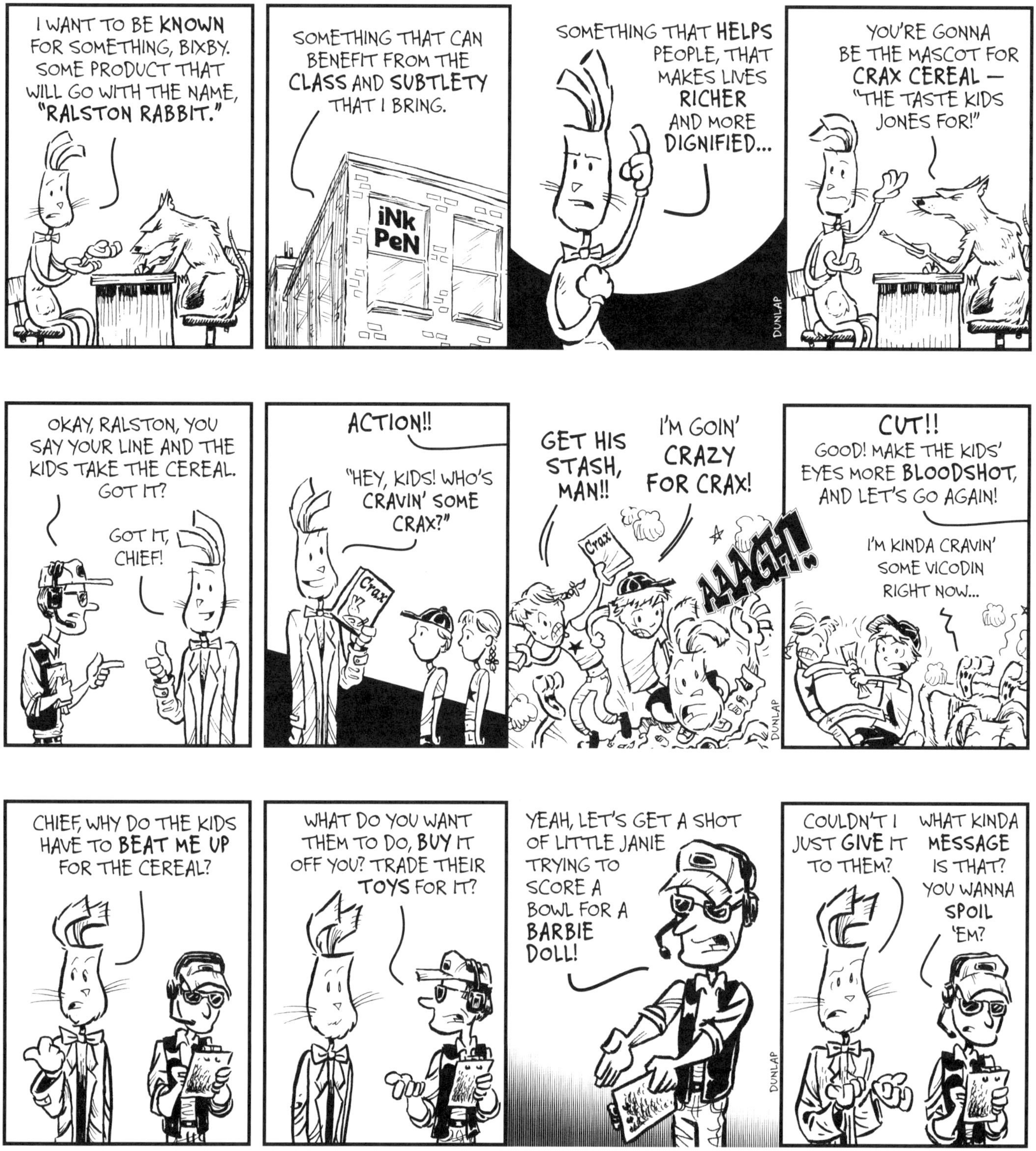
I WANT TO BE KNOWN FOR SOMETHING, BIXBY. SOME PRODUCT THAT WILL GO WITH THE NAME, "RALSTON RABBIT."
SOMETHING THAT CAN BENEFIT FROM THE CLASS AND SUBTLETY THAT I BRING.
iNk PeN
SOMETHING THAT HELPS PEOPLE, THAT MAKES LIVES RICHER AND MORE DIGNIFIED...
DUNLAP
YOU'RE GONNA BE THE MASCOT FOR CRAX CEREAL — "THE TASTE KIDS JONES FOR!"
OKAY, RALSTON, YOU SAY YOUR LINE AND THE KIDS TAKE THE CEREAL. GOT IT?
GOT IT, CHIEF!
ACTION!!
"HEY, KIDS! WHO'S CRAVIN' SOME CRAX?"
Crax
GET HIS STASH, MAN!!
I'M GOIN' CRAZY FOR CRAX!
Crax
AAAGH!!
DUNLAP
CUT!! GOOD! MAKE THE KIDS' EYES MORE BLOODSHOT, AND LET'S GO AGAIN!
I'M KINDA CRAVIN' SOME VICODIN RIGHT NOW...
CHIEF, WHY DO THE KIDS HAVE TO BEAT ME UP FOR THE CEREAL?
WHAT DO YOU WANT THEM TO DO, BUY IT OFF YOU? TRADE THEIR TOYS FOR IT?
YEAH, LET'S GET A SHOT OF LITTLE JANIE TRYING TO SCORE A BOWL FOR A BARBIE DOLL!
DUNLAP
COULDN'T I JUST GIVE IT TO THEM?
WHAT KINDA MESSAGE IS THAT? YOU WANNA SPOIL 'EM?

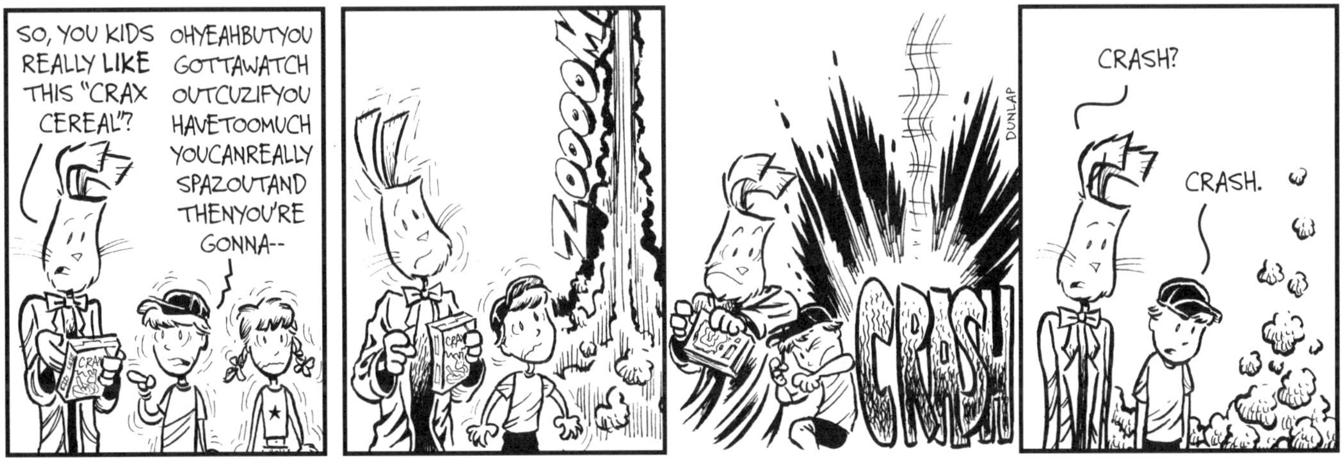
SO, YOU KIDS REALLY LIKE THIS "CRAX CEREAL"?
OHYEAHBUTYOU GOTTAWATCH OUTCUZIFYOU HAVETOOMUCH YOUCANREALLY SPAZOUTAND THENYOU'RE GONNA--
ZOOOOOM
CRASH
DUNLAP
CRASH?
CRASH.

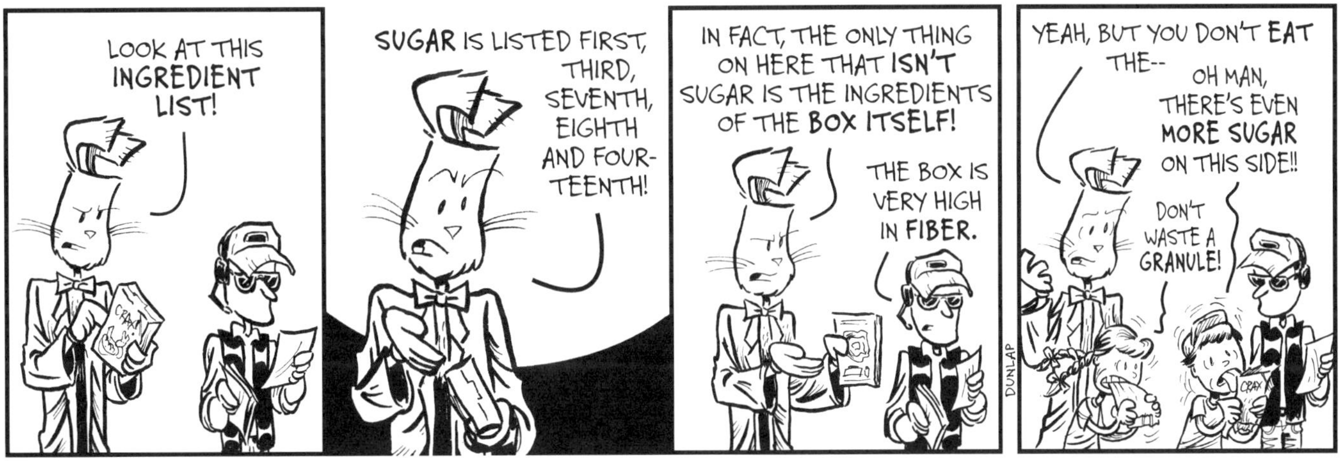
LOOK AT THIS INGREDIENT LIST!
SUGAR IS LISTED FIRST, THIRD, SEVENTH, EIGHTH AND FOURTEENTH!
IN FACT, THE ONLY THING ON HERE THAT ISN'T SUGAR IS THE INGREDIENTS OF THE BOX ITSELF!
THE BOX IS VERY HIGH IN FIBER.
DUNLAP
YEAH, BUT YOU DON'T EAT THE--
OH MAN, THERE'S EVEN MORE SUGAR ON THIS SIDE!!
DON'T WASTE A GRANULE!

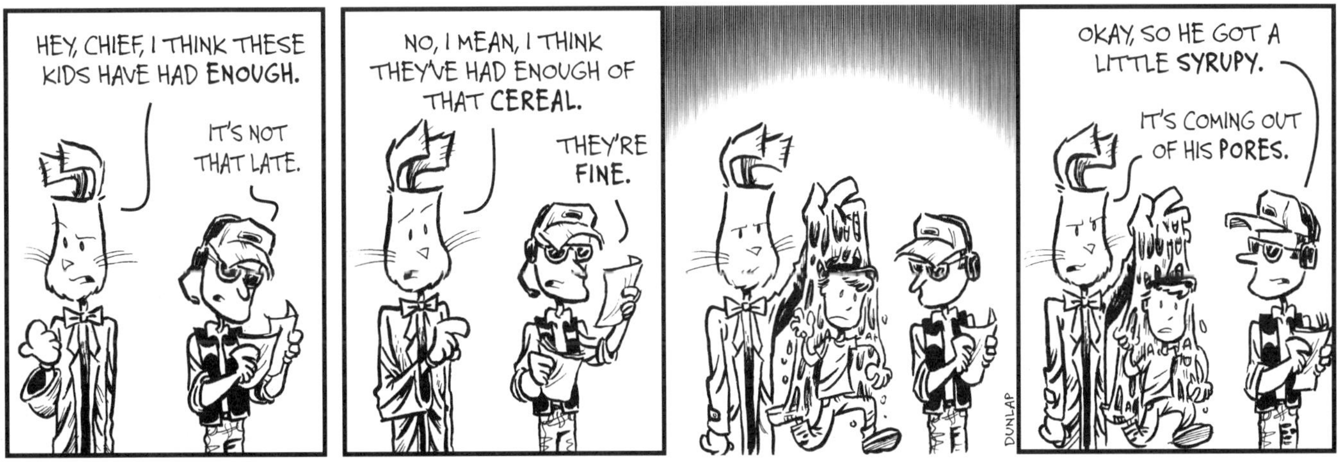
HEY, CHIEF, I THINK THESE KIDS HAVE HAD ENOUGH.
IT'S NOT THAT LATE.
NO, I MEAN, I THINK THEY'VE HAD ENOUGH OF THAT CEREAL.
THEY'RE FINE.
DUNLAP
OKAY, SO HE GOT A LITTLE SYRUPY.
IT'S COMING OUT OF HIS PORES.

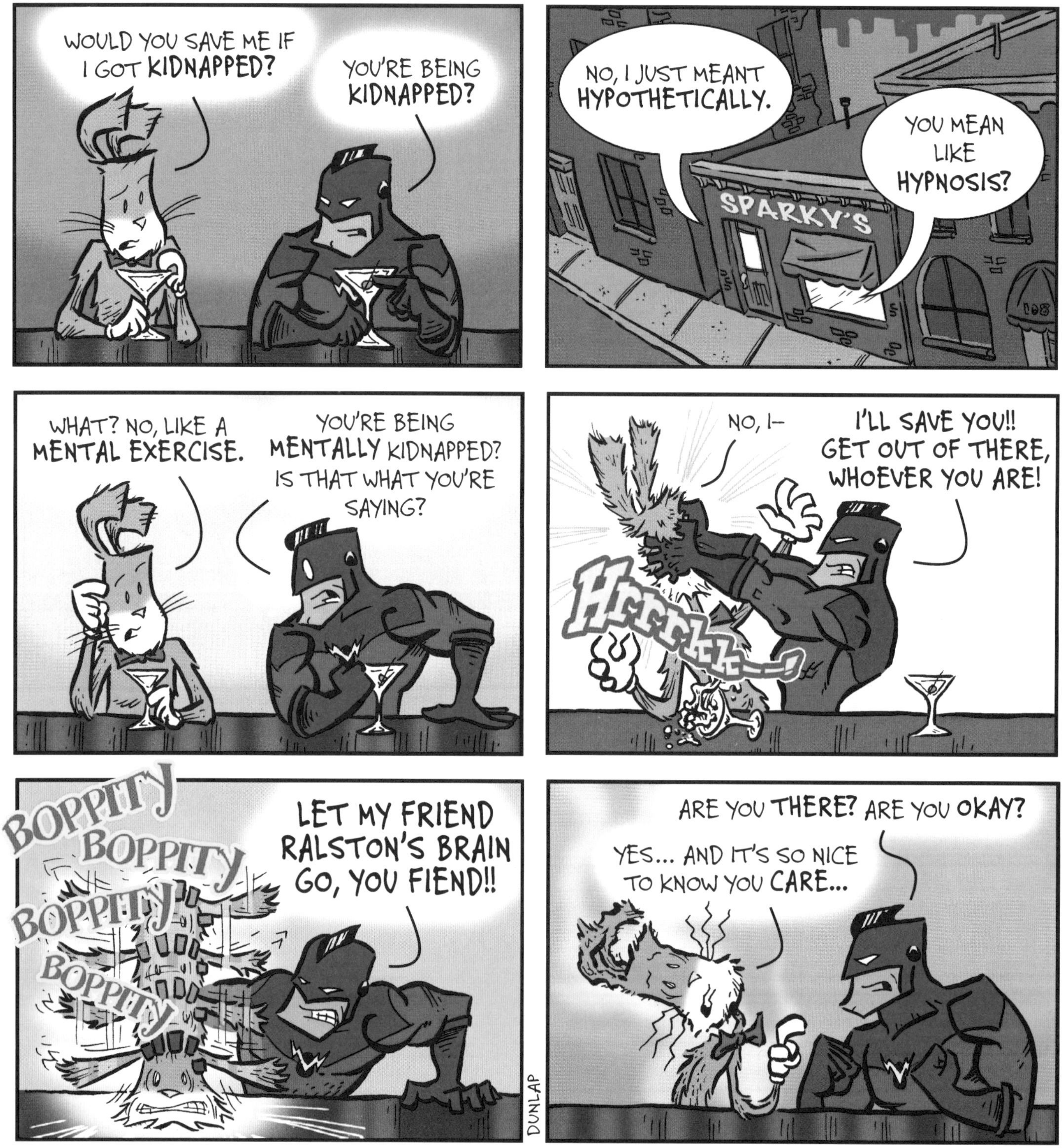
WOULD YOU SAVE ME IF I GOT KIDNAPPED?
YOU'RE BEING KIDNAPPED?
NO, I JUST MEANT HYPOTHETICALLY.
SPARKY'S
YOU MEAN LIKE HYPNOSIS?
WHAT? NO, LIKE A MENTAL EXERCISE.
YOU'RE BEING MENTALLY KIDNAPPED? IS THAT WHAT YOU'RE SAYING?
NO, I–
I'LL SAVE YOU!! GET OUT OF THERE, WHOEVER YOU ARE!
Hrrrkkk–!
BOPPITY BOPPITY BOPPITY BOPPITY
LET MY FRIEND RALSTON'S BRAIN GO, YOU FIEND!!
DUNLAP
ARE YOU THERE? ARE YOU OKAY?
YES... AND IT'S SO NICE TO KNOW YOU CARE...

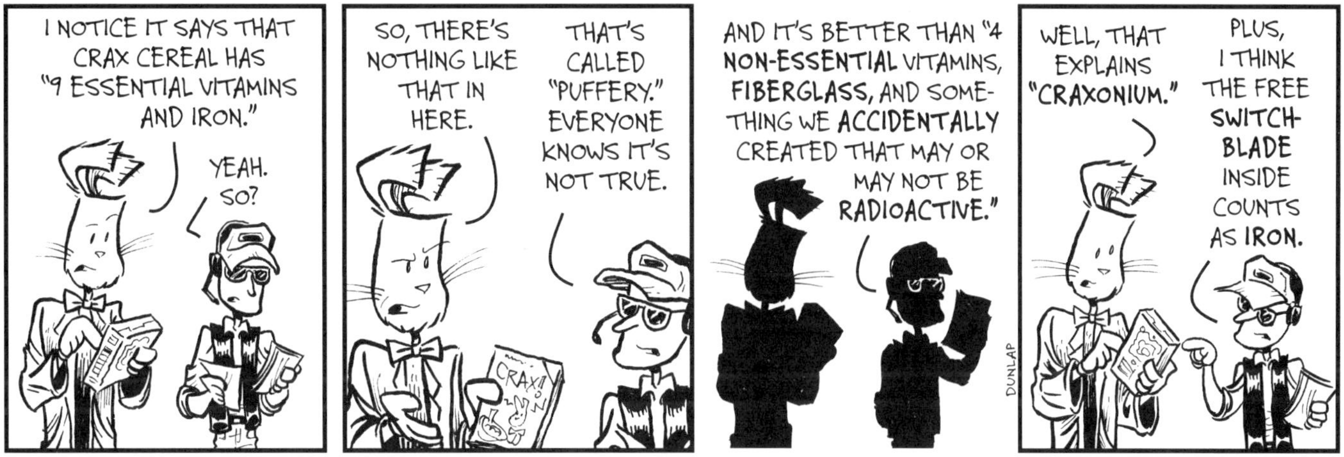
I NOTICE IT SAYS THAT CRAX CEREAL HAS "9 ESSENTIAL VITAMINS AND IRON."
YEAH. SO?
SO, THERE'S NOTHING LIKE THAT IN HERE.
THAT'S CALLED "PUFFERY." EVERYONE KNOWS IT'S NOT TRUE.
CRAX!!
AND IT'S BETTER THAN "4 NON-ESSENTIAL VITAMINS, FIBERGLASS, AND SOMETHING WE ACCIDENTALLY CREATED THAT MAY OR MAY NOT BE RADIOACTIVE."
DUNLAP
WELL, THAT EXPLAINS "CRAXONIUM."
PLUS, I THINK THE FREE SWITCHBLADE INSIDE COUNTS AS IRON.

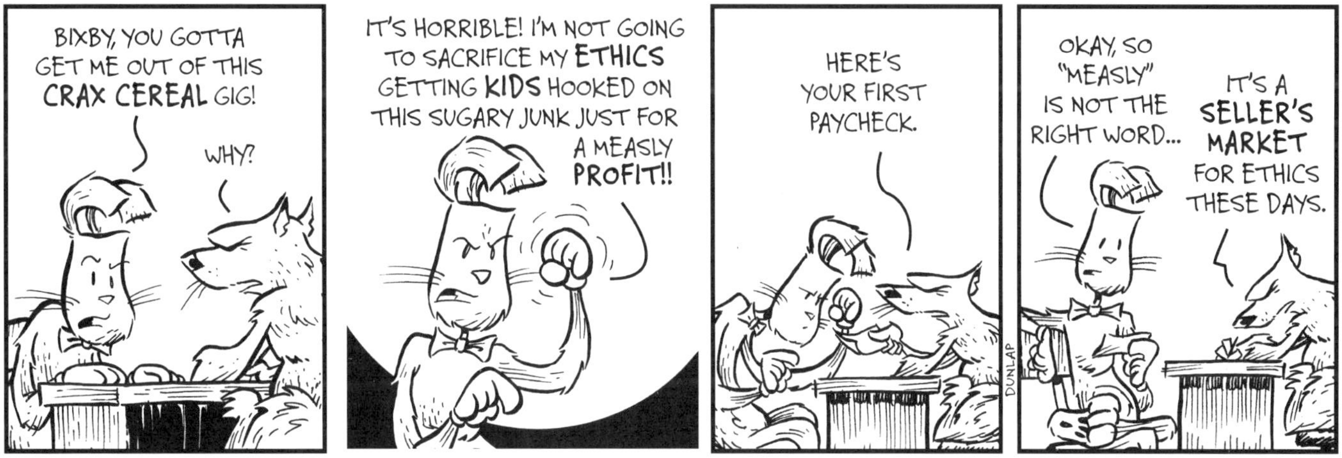
BIXBY, YOU GOTTA GET ME OUT OF THIS CRAX CEREAL GIG!
WHY?
IT'S HORRIBLE! I'M NOT GOING TO SACRIFICE MY ETHICS GETTING KIDS HOOKED ON THIS SUGARY JUNK JUST FOR A MEASLY PROFIT!!
HERE'S YOUR FIRST PAYCHECK.
DUNLAP
OKAY, SO "MEASLY" IS NOT THE RIGHT WORD...
IT'S A SELLER'S MARKET FOR ETHICS THESE DAYS.

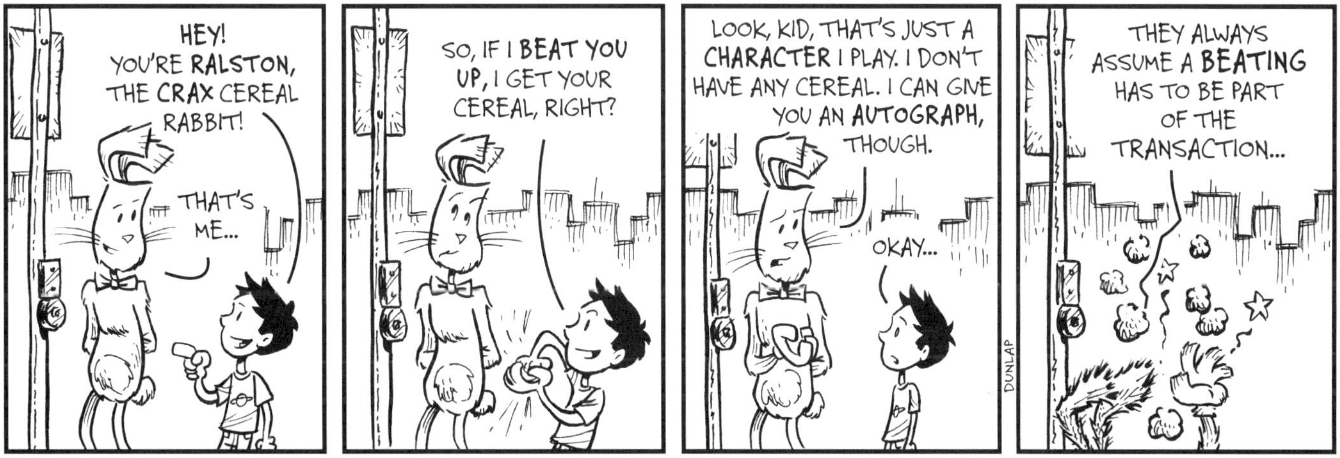
HEY! YOU'RE RALSTON, THE CRAX CEREAL RABBIT!
THAT'S ME...
SO, IF I BEAT YOU UP, I GET YOUR CEREAL, RIGHT?
LOOK, KID, THAT'S JUST A CHARACTER I PLAY. I DON'T HAVE ANY CEREAL. I CAN GIVE YOU AN AUTOGRAPH, THOUGH.
OKAY...
DUNLAP
THEY ALWAYS ASSUME A BEATING HAS TO BE PART OF THE TRANSACTION...

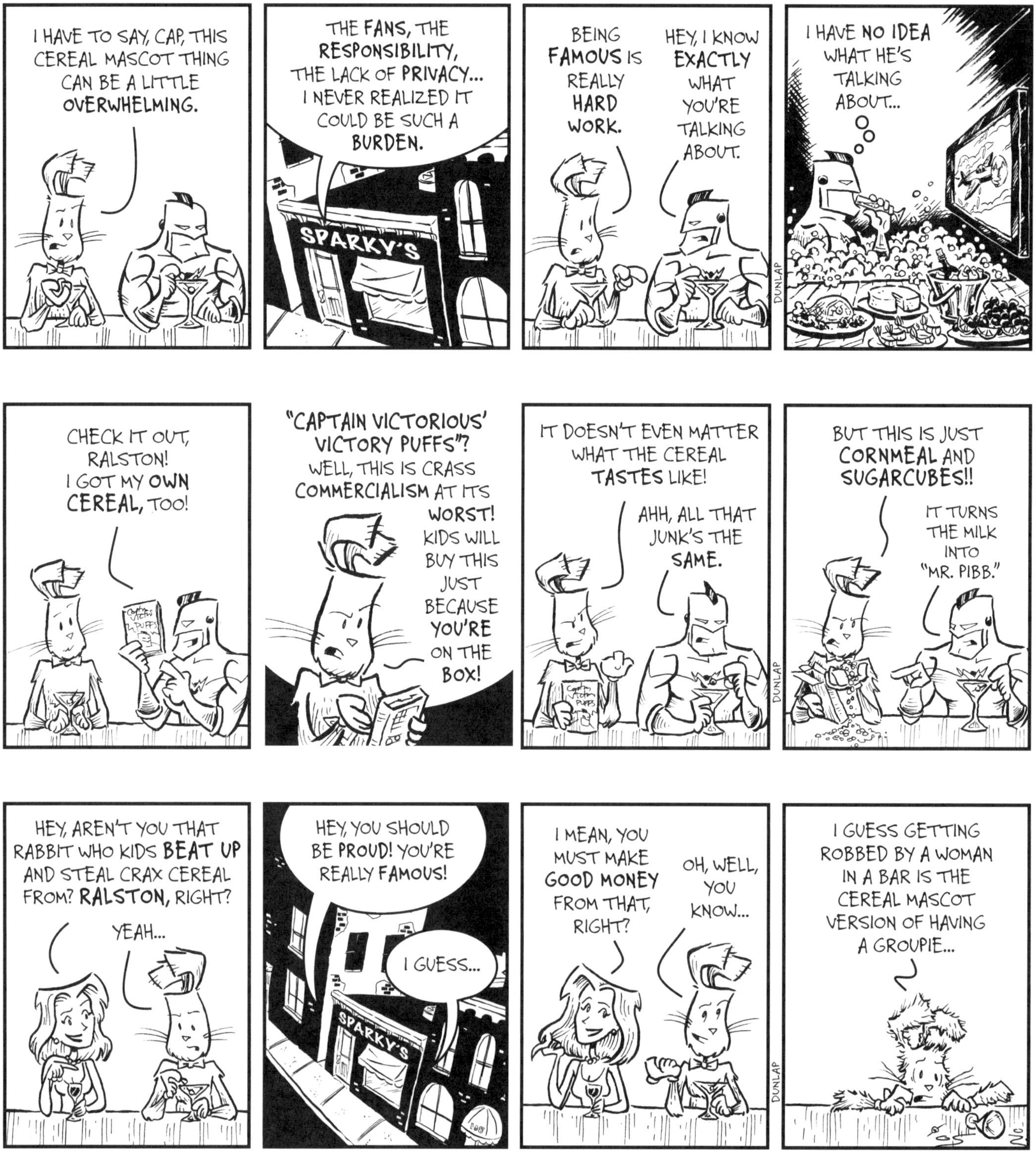
I HAVE TO SAY, CAP, THIS CEREAL MASCOT THING CAN BE A LITTLE OVERWHELMING.
THE FANS, THE RESPONSIBILITY, THE LACK OF PRIVACY... I NEVER REALIZED IT COULD BE SUCH A BURDEN.
SPARKY'S
BEING FAMOUS IS REALLY HARD WORK.
HEY, I KNOW EXACTLY WHAT YOU'RE TALKING ABOUT.
DUNLAP
I HAVE NO IDEA WHAT HE'S TALKING ABOUT...
CHECK IT OUT, RALSTON! I GOT MY OWN CEREAL, TOO!
"CAPTAIN VICTORIOUS' VICTORY PUFFS"? WELL, THIS IS CRASS COMMERCIALISM AT ITS WORST! KIDS WILL BUY THIS JUST BECAUSE YOU'RE ON THE BOX!
IT DOESN'T EVEN MATTER WHAT THE CEREAL TASTES LIKE!
AHH, ALL THAT JUNK'S THE SAME.
DUNLAP
BUT THIS IS JUST CORNMEAL AND SUGARCUBES!!
IT TURNS THE MILK INTO "MR. PIBB."
HEY, AREN'T YOU THAT RABBIT WHO KIDS BEAT UP AND STEAL CRAX CEREAL FROM? RALSTON, RIGHT?
YEAH...
HEY, YOU SHOULD BE PROUD! YOU'RE REALLY FAMOUS!
I GUESS...
SPARKY'S
I MEAN, YOU MUST MAKE GOOD MONEY FROM THAT, RIGHT?
OH, WELL, YOU KNOW...
DUNLAP
I GUESS GETTING ROBBED BY A WOMAN IN A BAR IS THE CEREAL MASCOT VERSION OF HAVING A GROUPIE...

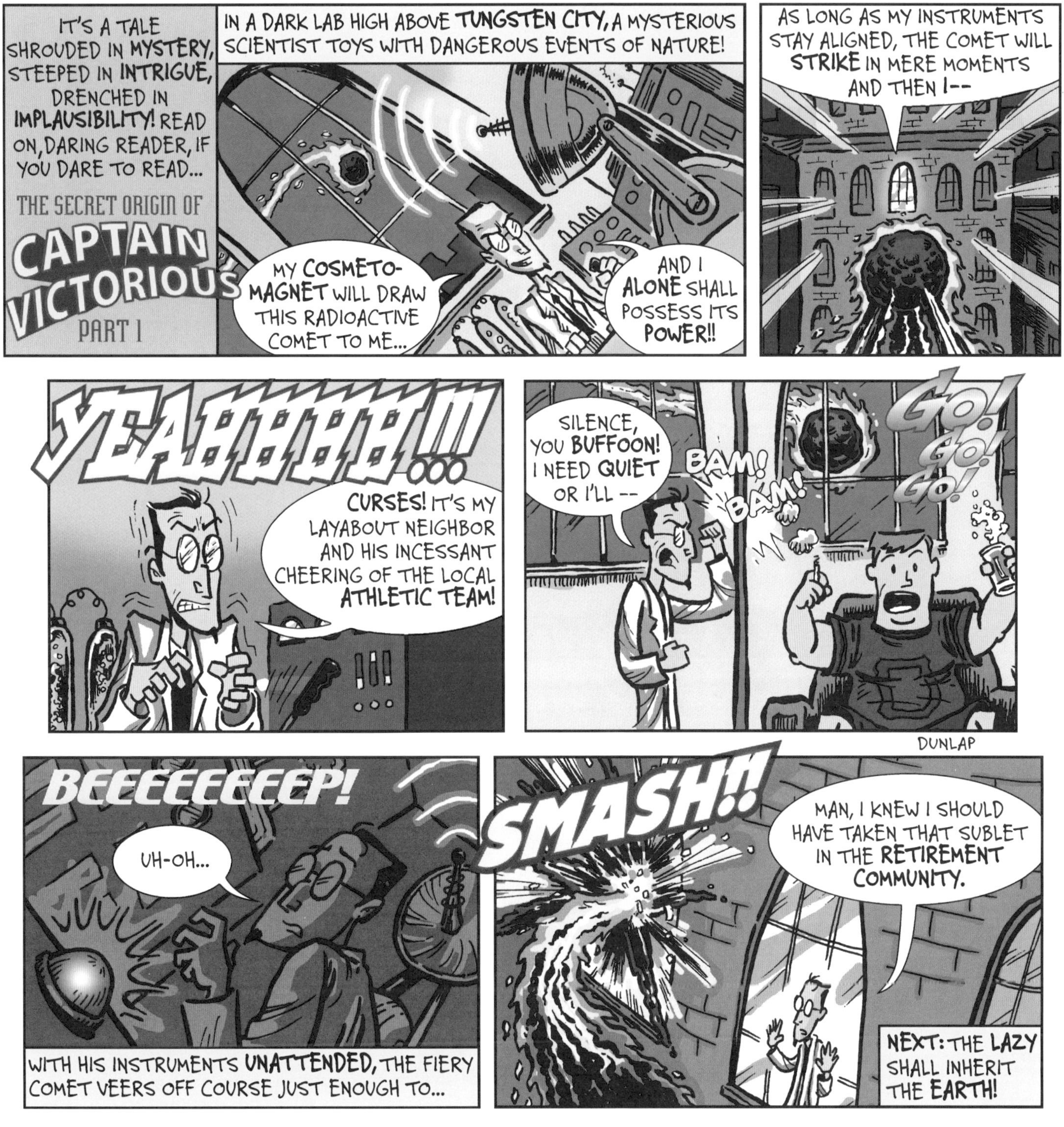
IT'S A TALE SHROUDED IN MYSTERY, STEEPED IN INTRIGUE, DRENCHED IN IMPLAUSIBILITY! READ ON, DARING READER, IF YOU DARE TO READ...
THE SECRET ORIGIN OF
CAPTAIN VICTORIOUS
PART 1
IN A DARK LAB HIGH ABOVE TUNGSTEN CITY, A MYSTERIOUS SCIENTIST TOYS WITH DANGEROUS EVENTS OF NATURE!
MY COSMETO-MAGNET WILL DRAW THIS RADIOACTIVE COMET TO ME...
AND I ALONE SHALL POSSESS ITS POWER!!
AS LONG AS MY INSTRUMENTS STAY ALIGNED, THE COMET WILL STRIKE IN MERE MOMENTS AND THEN I--
YEAHHHHH!!!...
CURSES! IT'S MY LAYABOUT NEIGHBOR AND HIS INCESSANT CHEERING OF THE LOCAL ATHLETIC TEAM!
SILENCE, YOU BUFFOON! I NEED QUIET OR I'LL --
BAM!
BAM!
GO! GO! GO!
DUNLAP
BEEEEEEEEEP!
UH-OH...
WITH HIS INSTRUMENTS UNATTENDED, THE FIERY COMET VEERS OFF COURSE JUST ENOUGH TO...
SMASH!!
MAN, I KNEW I SHOULD HAVE TAKEN THAT SUBLET IN THE RETIREMENT COMMUNITY.
NEXT: THE LAZY SHALL INHERIT THE EARTH!

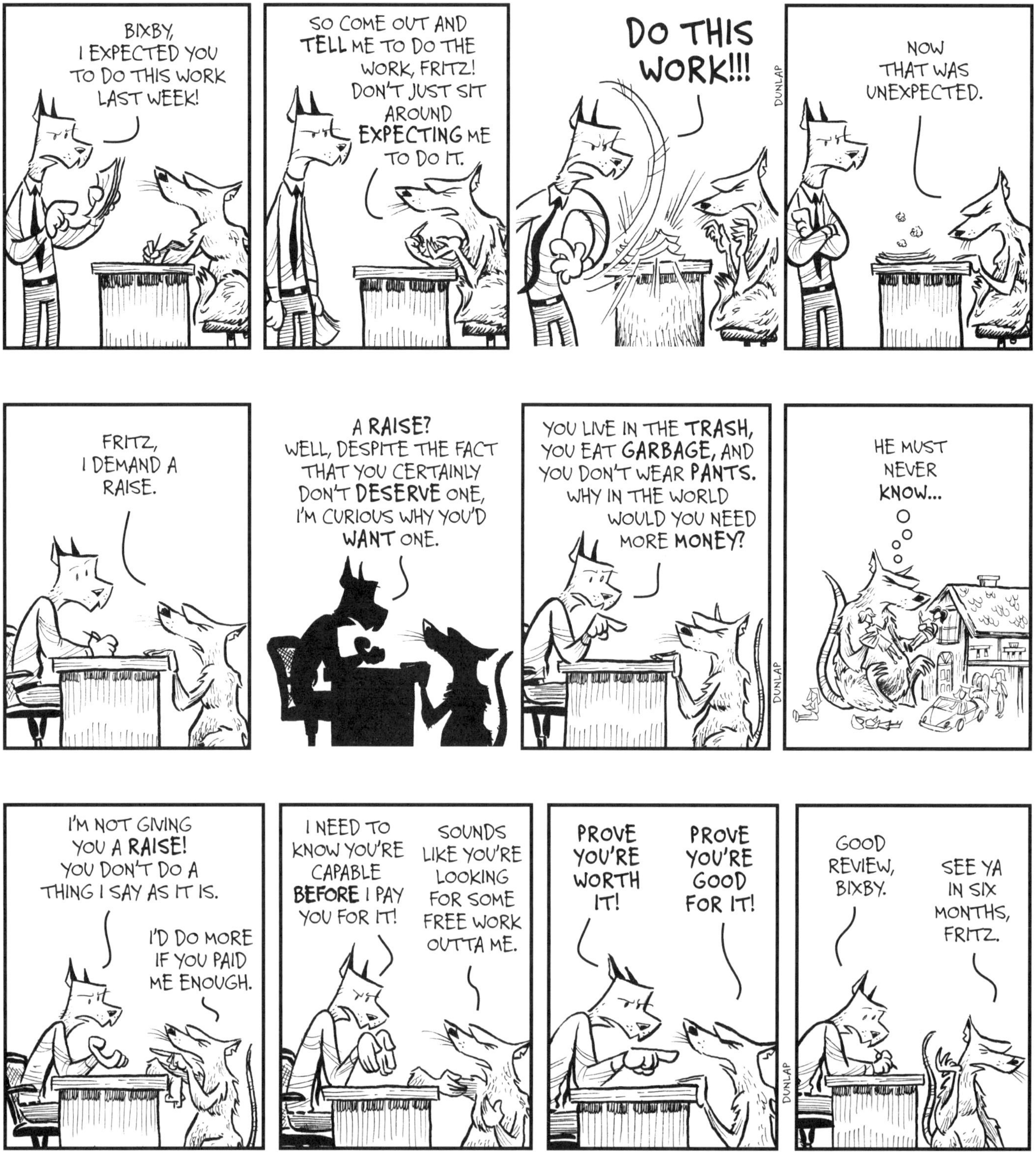
BIXBY, I EXPECTED YOU TO DO THIS WORK LAST WEEK!
SO COME OUT AND TELL ME TO DO THE WORK, FRITZ! DON'T JUST SIT AROUND EXPECTING ME TO DO IT.
DO THIS WORK!!!
DUNLAP
NOW THAT WAS UNEXPECTED.
FRITZ, I DEMAND A RAISE.
A RAISE? WELL, DESPITE THE FACT THAT YOU CERTAINLY DON'T DESERVE ONE, I'M CURIOUS WHY YOU'D WANT ONE.
YOU LIVE IN THE TRASH, YOU EAT GARBAGE, AND YOU DON'T WEAR PANTS. WHY IN THE WORLD WOULD YOU NEED MORE MONEY?
DUNLAP
HE MUST NEVER KNOW...
I'M NOT GIVING YOU A RAISE! YOU DON'T DO A THING I SAY AS IT IS.
I'D DO MORE IF YOU PAID ME ENOUGH.
I NEED TO KNOW YOU'RE CAPABLE BEFORE I PAY YOU FOR IT!
SOUNDS LIKE YOU'RE LOOKING FOR SOME FREE WORK OUTTA ME.
PROVE YOU'RE WORTH IT!
PROVE YOU'RE GOOD FOR IT!
DUNLAP
GOOD REVIEW, BIXBY.
SEE YA IN SIX MONTHS, FRITZ.

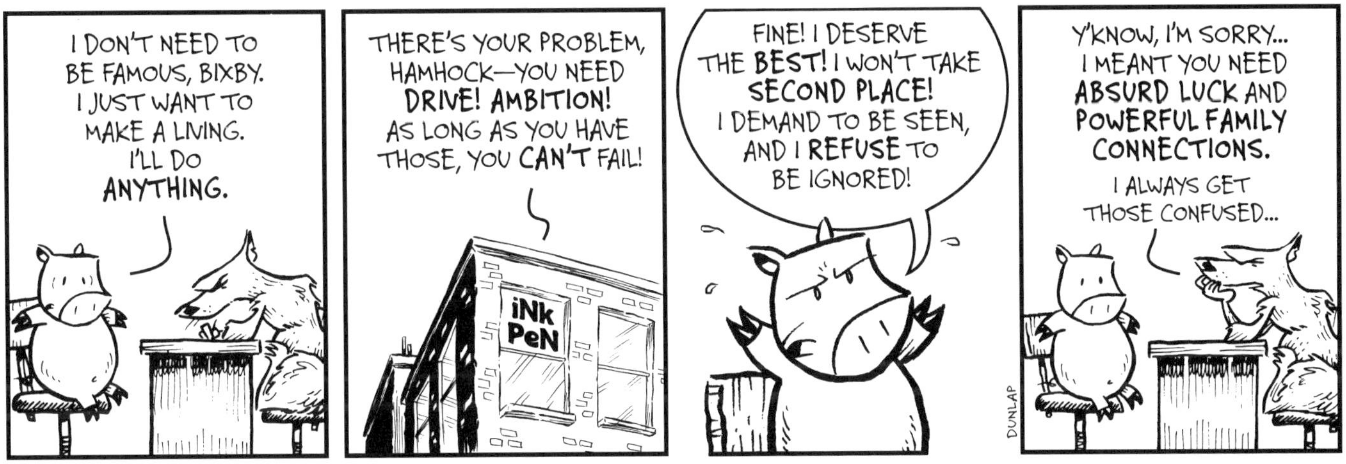
I DON'T NEED TO BE FAMOUS, BIXBY. I JUST WANT TO MAKE A LIVING. I'LL DO ANYTHING.
THERE'S YOUR PROBLEM, HAMHOCK—YOU NEED DRIVE! AMBITION! AS LONG AS YOU HAVE THOSE, YOU CAN'T FAIL!
iNk PeN
FINE! I DESERVE THE BEST! I WON'T TAKE SECOND PLACE! I DEMAND TO BE SEEN, AND I REFUSE TO BE IGNORED!
Y'KNOW, I'M SORRY... I MEANT YOU NEED ABSURD LUCK AND POWERFUL FAMILY CONNECTIONS.
I ALWAYS GET THOSE CONFUSED...
DUNLAP

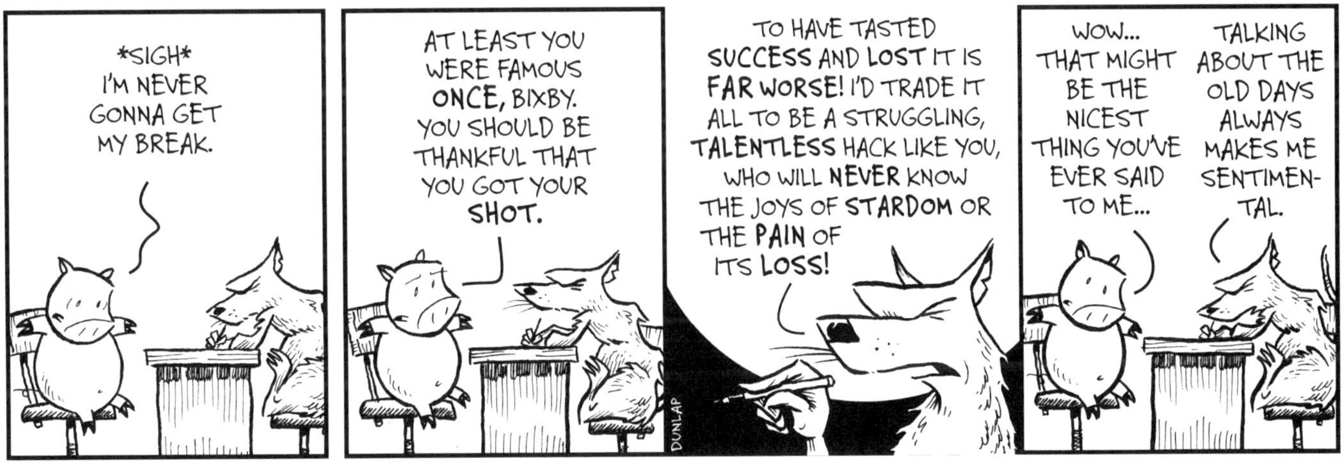
*SIGH* I'M NEVER GONNA GET MY BREAK.
AT LEAST YOU WERE FAMOUS ONCE, BIXBY. YOU SHOULD BE THANKFUL THAT YOU GOT YOUR SHOT.
TO HAVE TASTED SUCCESS AND LOST IT IS FAR WORSE! I'D TRADE IT ALL TO BE A STRUGGLING, TALENTLESS HACK LIKE YOU, WHO WILL NEVER KNOW THE JOYS OF STARDOM OR THE PAIN OF ITS LOSS!
DUNLAP
WOW... THAT MIGHT BE THE NICEST THING YOU'VE EVER SAID TO ME...
TALKING ABOUT THE OLD DAYS ALWAYS MAKES ME SENTIMEN-TAL.

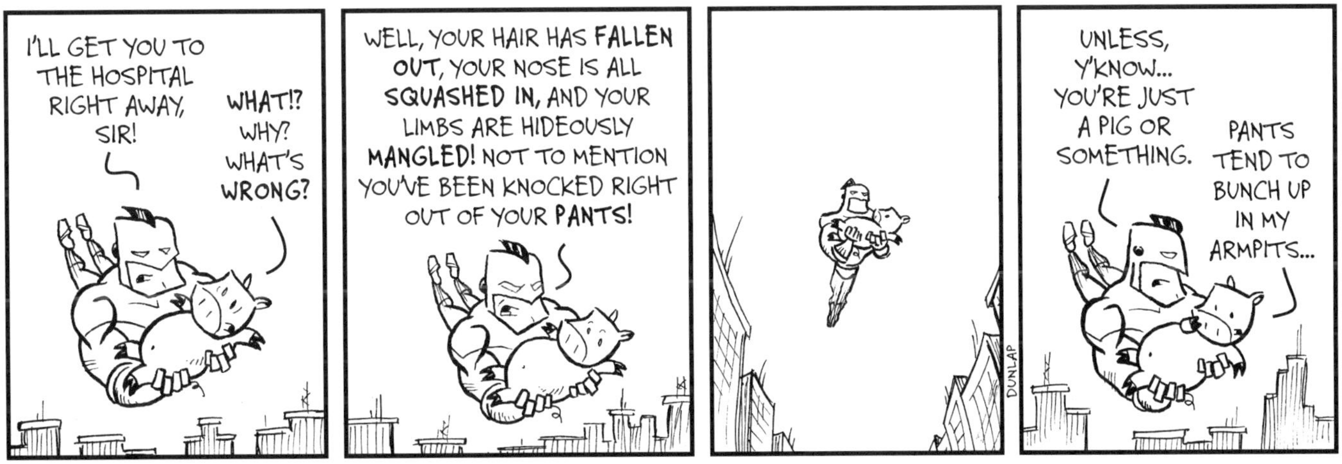
I'LL GET YOU TO THE HOSPITAL RIGHT AWAY, SIR!
WHAT!? WHY? WHAT'S WRONG?
WELL, YOUR HAIR HAS FALLEN OUT, YOUR NOSE IS ALL SQUASHED IN, AND YOUR LIMBS ARE HIDEOUSLY MANGLED! NOT TO MENTION YOU'VE BEEN KNOCKED RIGHT OUT OF YOUR PANTS!
DUNLAP
UNLESS, Y'KNOW... YOU'RE JUST A PIG OR SOMETHING.
PANTS TEND TO BUNCH UP IN MY ARMPITS...

A MYSTERIOUS **SCIENTIST** BECKONS A FIERY RADIOACTIVE **COMET** TO HIM WHEN A **DISTRACTION** RESULTS IN IT VEERING **OFF COURSE!**

THE SECRET ORIGIN OF

# CAPTAIN VICTORIOUS

PART 2

OH, POOH...

THE SCIENTIST'S BELLOWING NEIGHBOR BECOMES THE UNEXPECTED RECIPIENT OF THE COMET'S ATTENTIONS!

SMASH!

BUT FROM THE REMAINS OF THE CRASH, THE BEER-SWILLING SLOTH EMERGES...

...TRANSFORMED!

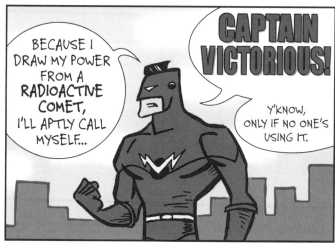

BECAUSE I DRAW MY POWER FROM A RADIOACTIVE COMET, I'LL APTLY CALL MYSELF...

CAPTAIN VICTORIOUS!

Y'KNOW, ONLY IF NO ONE'S USING IT.

DUNLAP

AND SO THIS CELESTIAL-POWERED **TITAN** WENT FORTH AND **PROTECTED** THE **INNOCENT** AND HELPED THE **HELPLESS,** WHEN THERE WAS NOTHING MUCH TO WATCH ON TV.

OH, HOLD ON A SEC... THIS IS A GOOD PART...

ELECTRONICS

AND OF COURSE, HE LEARNED THE MOST IMPORTANT LESSON A HERO CAN: WITH GREAT **POWER** COMES—

GREAT **RELAXATION!** LOOK AT THESE **ABS!** AND I DON'T EVEN HAVE TO **WORK OUT!**

**NEXT:** NEGATIVE EFFECT!

50

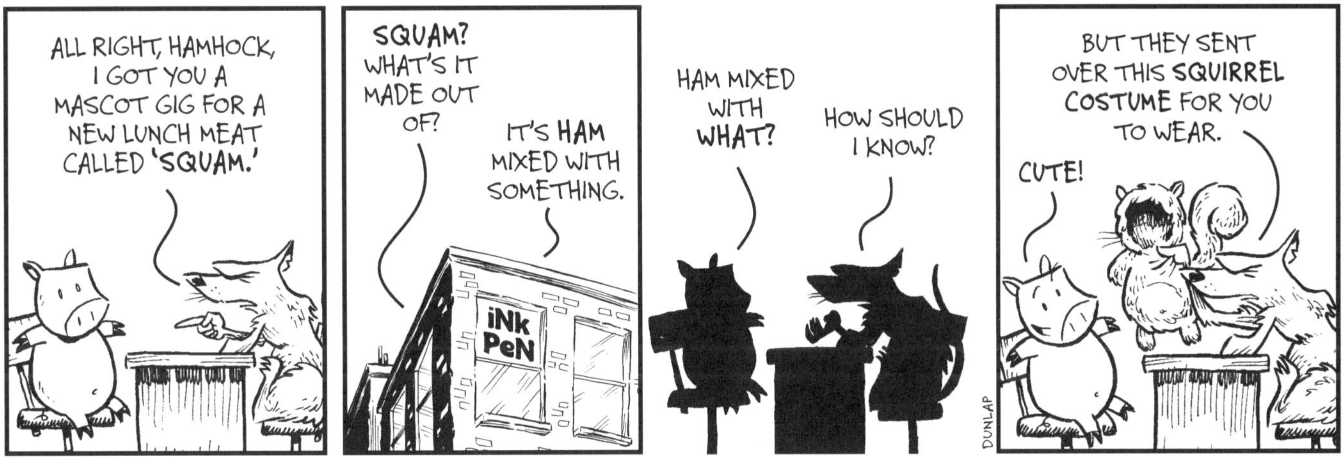
ALL RIGHT, HAMHOCK, I GOT YOU A MASCOT GIG FOR A NEW LUNCH MEAT CALLED 'SQUAM.'
SQUAM? WHAT'S IT MADE OUT OF?
IT'S HAM MIXED WITH SOMETHING.
iNk PeN
HAM MIXED WITH WHAT?
HOW SHOULD I KNOW?
BUT THEY SENT OVER THIS SQUIRREL COSTUME FOR YOU TO WEAR.
CUTE!
DUNLAP

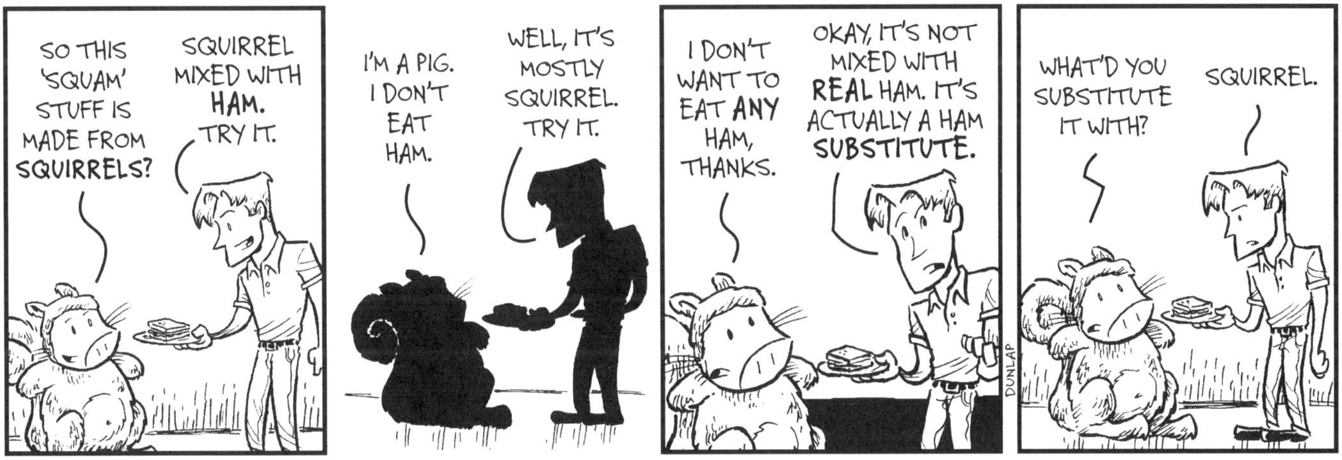
SO THIS 'SQUAM' STUFF IS MADE FROM SQUIRRELS?
SQUIRREL MIXED WITH HAM. TRY IT.
I'M A PIG. I DON'T EAT HAM.
WELL, IT'S MOSTLY SQUIRREL. TRY IT.
I DON'T WANT TO EAT ANY HAM, THANKS.
OKAY, IT'S NOT MIXED WITH REAL HAM. IT'S ACTUALLY A HAM SUBSTITUTE.
WHAT'D YOU SUBSTITUTE IT WITH?
SQUIRREL.
DUNLAP

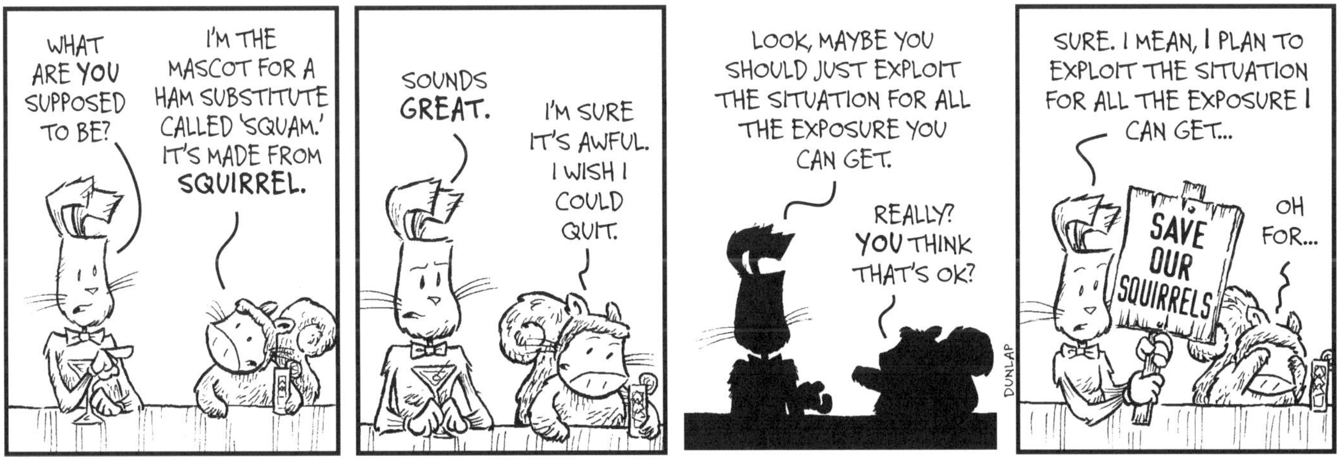
WHAT ARE YOU SUPPOSED TO BE?
I'M THE MASCOT FOR A HAM SUBSTITUTE CALLED 'SQUAM.' IT'S MADE FROM SQUIRREL.
SOUNDS GREAT.
I'M SURE IT'S AWFUL. I WISH I COULD QUIT.
LOOK, MAYBE YOU SHOULD JUST EXPLOIT THE SITUATION FOR ALL THE EXPOSURE YOU CAN GET.
REALLY? YOU THINK THAT'S OK?
SURE. I MEAN, I PLAN TO EXPLOIT THE SITUATION FOR ALL THE EXPOSURE I CAN GET...
SAVE OUR SQUIRRELS
OH FOR...
DUNLAP

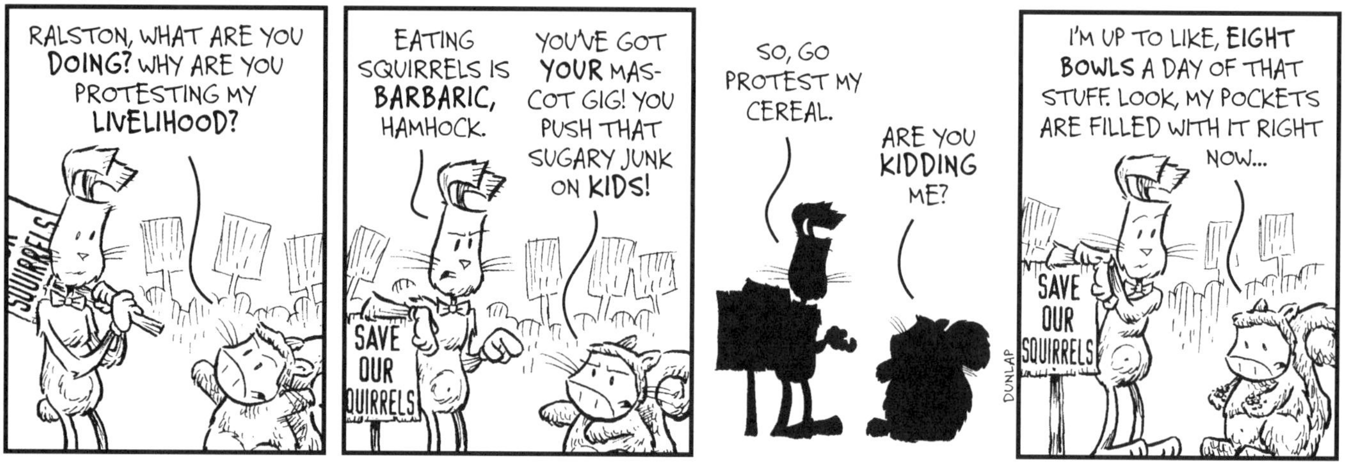
RALSTON, WHAT ARE YOU DOING? WHY ARE YOU PROTESTING MY LIVELIHOOD?
EATING SQUIRRELS IS BARBARIC, HAMHOCK.
YOU'VE GOT YOUR MAS-COT GIG! YOU PUSH THAT SUGARY JUNK ON KIDS!
SAVE OUR
SO, GO PROTEST MY CEREAL.
ARE YOU KIDDING ME?
DUNLAP
I'M UP TO LIKE, EIGHT BOWLS A DAY OF THAT STUFF. LOOK, MY POCKETS ARE FILLED WITH IT RIGHT NOW...
SAVE OUR SQUIRRELS

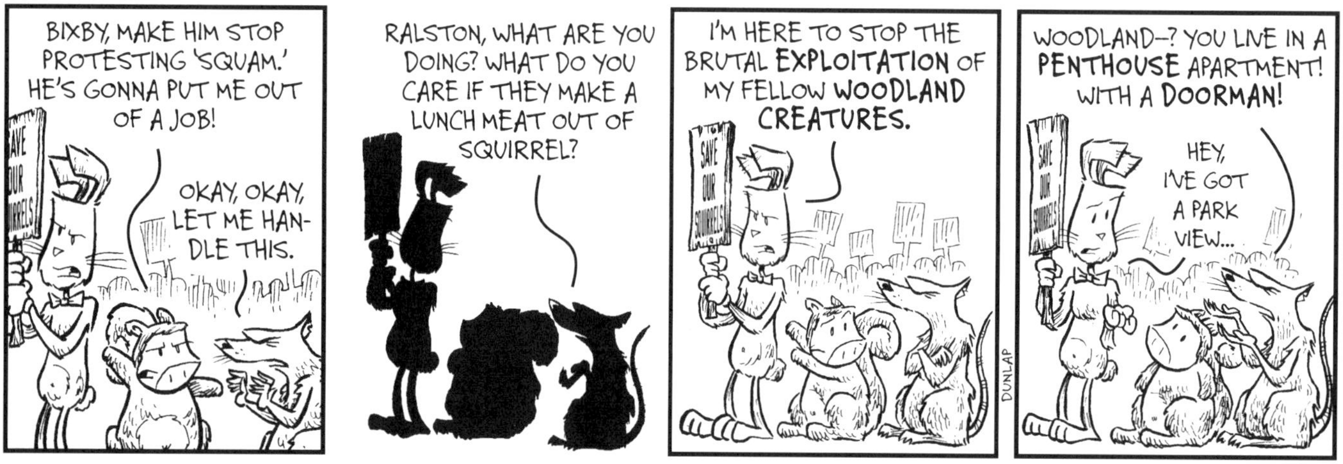
BIXBY, MAKE HIM STOP PROTESTING 'SQUAM.' HE'S GONNA PUT ME OUT OF A JOB!
OKAY, OKAY, LET ME HAN-DLE THIS.
RALSTON, WHAT ARE YOU DOING? WHAT DO YOU CARE IF THEY MAKE A LUNCH MEAT OUT OF SQUIRREL?
I'M HERE TO STOP THE BRUTAL EXPLOITATION OF MY FELLOW WOODLAND CREATURES.
DUNLAP
WOODLAND–? YOU LIVE IN A PENTHOUSE APARTMENT! WITH A DOORMAN!
HEY, I'VE GOT A PARK VIEW...

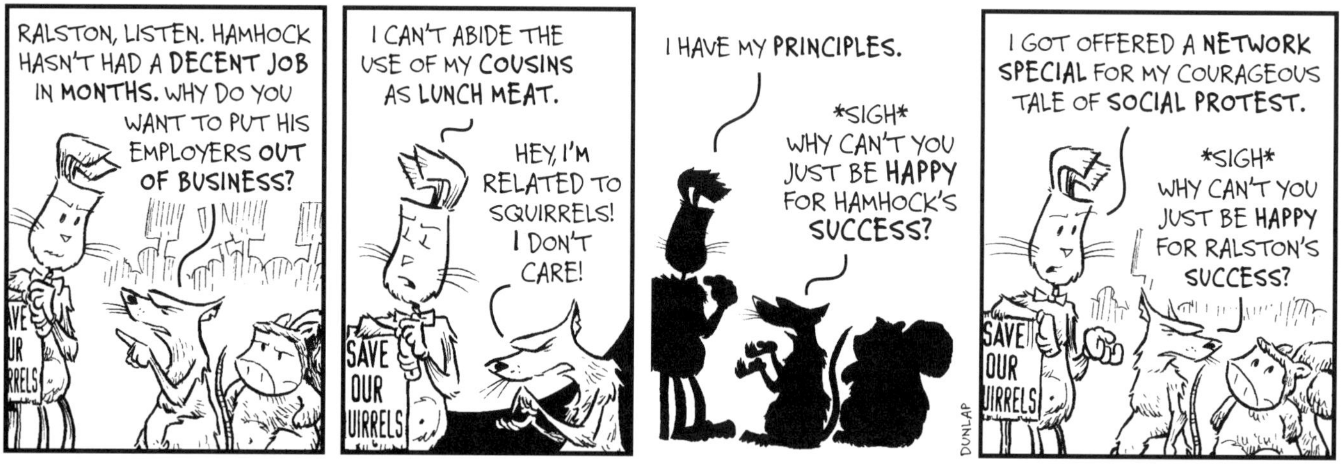
RALSTON, LISTEN. HAMHOCK HASN'T HAD A DECENT JOB IN MONTHS. WHY DO YOU WANT TO PUT HIS EMPLOYERS OUT OF BUSINESS?
I CAN'T ABIDE THE USE OF MY COUSINS AS LUNCH MEAT.
HEY, I'M RELATED TO SQUIRRELS! I DON'T CARE!
SAVE OUR
I HAVE MY PRINCIPLES.
*SIGH* WHY CAN'T YOU JUST BE HAPPY FOR HAMHOCK'S SUCCESS?
DUNLAP
I GOT OFFERED A NETWORK SPECIAL FOR MY COURAGEOUS TALE OF SOCIAL PROTEST.
*SIGH* WHY CAN'T YOU JUST BE HAPPY FOR RALSTON'S SUCCESS?
SAVE OUR

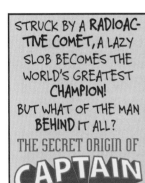

STRUCK BY A RADIOAC-TIVE COMET, A LAZY SLOB BECOMES THE WORLD'S GREATEST CHAMPION! BUT WHAT OF THE MAN BEHIND IT ALL?

THE SECRET ORIGIN OF

# CAPTAIN VICTORIOUS

PART 3

OH, DOES THAT **STING!**

THE SCIENTIST RESPONSIBLE IS LEFT **ALONE** AND **BRUISED** IN THE DEBRIS OF HIS RUINED LABORATORY...

CURSE THAT LOUDMOUTHED **COUCH-POTATO** AND HIS **SPORTS ENTHUSIASM!** HE GOT ALL THE POWERS, LEAVING ME COMPLETELY **UNAFFECTED!!**

BUT WAIT! THE **NEGATIVE COSMO-ION** GAUGE IS OFF THE CHART! I'M BEING BOMBARDED BY THE **NEGATIVE** EFFECT OF WHAT HIT THAT BABOON!

I'M **CHANGING!** CHANGING INTO...

DUNLAP

MR. NEGATO!

AND I'LL USE MY **NEGA-ACTIVE** POWERS TO GET **REVENGE...** REVENGE ON THE **WORLD!**

WHICH, FOR THE PURPOSES OF THIS **LUNATIC MANIFESTO**, IS SPECIFICALLY, BUT NOT LIMITED TO: THE **CO-OP BOARD** WHO REJECTED ME THAT TIME, THE **COLLEGE** WHO FELT THAT "EVIL GENIUS" WAS NOT AN APPROPRIATE **MAJOR**, UH, LET'S SEE... **GIRLS**... CATS OF COURSE, UMM...

AND SO FORTH...

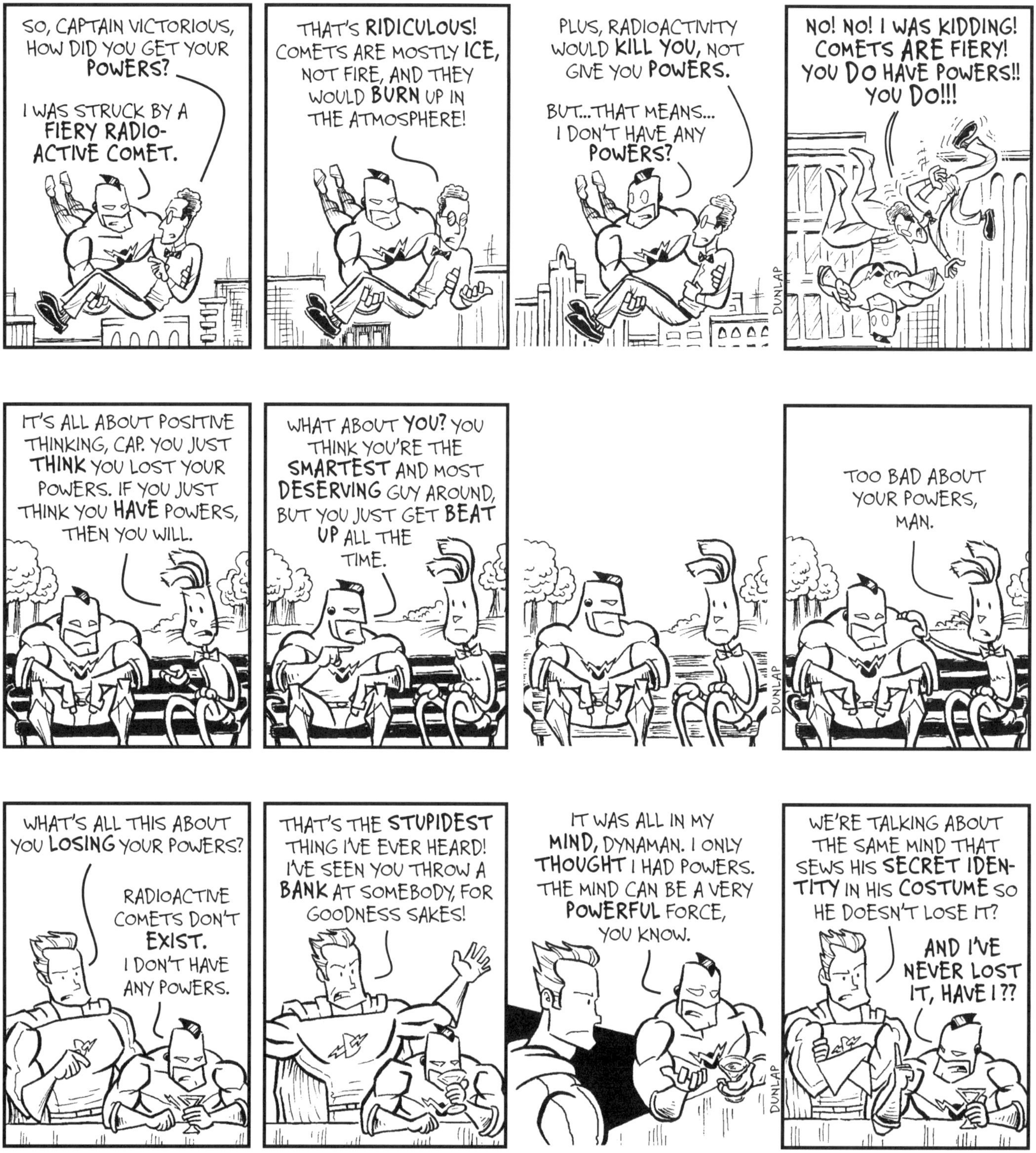
SO, CAPTAIN VICTORIOUS, HOW DID YOU GET YOUR POWERS?
I WAS STRUCK BY A FIERY RADIO-ACTIVE COMET.
THAT'S RIDICULOUS! COMETS ARE MOSTLY ICE, NOT FIRE, AND THEY WOULD BURN UP IN THE ATMOSPHERE!
PLUS, RADIOACTIVITY WOULD KILL YOU, NOT GIVE YOU POWERS.
BUT...THAT MEANS... I DON'T HAVE ANY POWERS?
DUNLAP
NO! NO! I WAS KIDDING! COMETS ARE FIERY! YOU DO HAVE POWERS!! YOU DO!!!
IT'S ALL ABOUT POSITIVE THINKING, CAP. YOU JUST THINK YOU LOST YOUR POWERS. IF YOU JUST THINK YOU HAVE POWERS, THEN YOU WILL.
WHAT ABOUT YOU? YOU THINK YOU'RE THE SMARTEST AND MOST DESERVING GUY AROUND, BUT YOU JUST GET BEAT UP ALL THE TIME.
DUNLAP
TOO BAD ABOUT YOUR POWERS, MAN.
WHAT'S ALL THIS ABOUT YOU LOSING YOUR POWERS?
RADIOACTIVE COMETS DON'T EXIST. I DON'T HAVE ANY POWERS.
THAT'S THE STUPIDEST THING I'VE EVER HEARD! I'VE SEEN YOU THROW A BANK AT SOMEBODY, FOR GOODNESS SAKES!
IT WAS ALL IN MY MIND, DYNAMAN. I ONLY THOUGHT I HAD POWERS. THE MIND CAN BE A VERY POWERFUL FORCE, YOU KNOW.
DUNLAP
WE'RE TALKING ABOUT THE SAME MIND THAT SEWS HIS SECRET IDENTITY IN HIS COSTUME SO HE DOESN'T LOSE IT?
AND I'VE NEVER LOST IT, HAVE I??

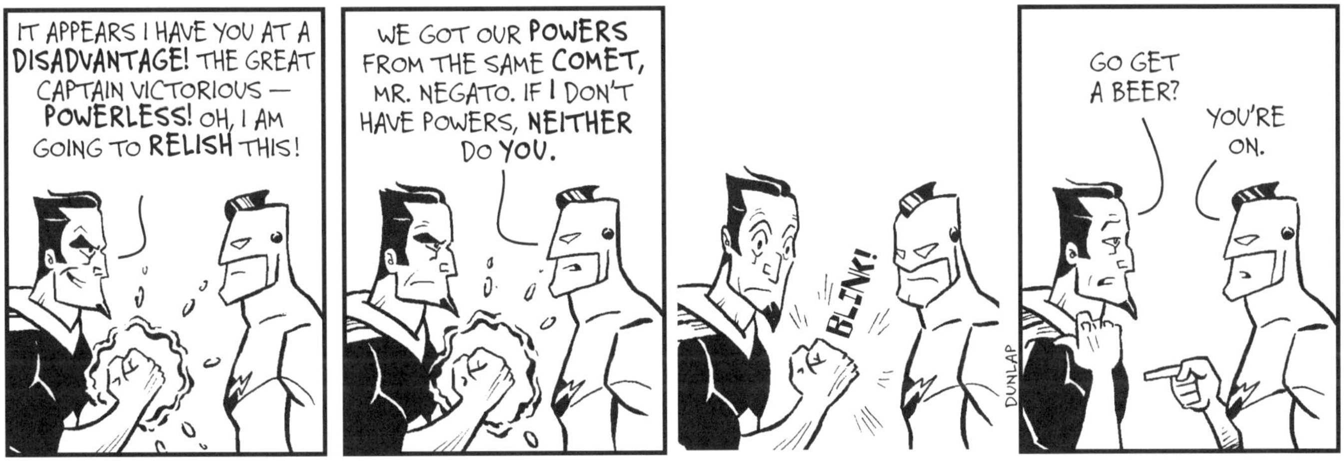
IT APPEARS I HAVE YOU AT A DISADVANTAGE! THE GREAT CAPTAIN VICTORIOUS — POWERLESS! OH, I AM GOING TO RELISH THIS!
WE GOT OUR POWERS FROM THE SAME COMET, MR. NEGATO. IF I DON'T HAVE POWERS, NEITHER DO YOU.
BLINK!
DUNLAP
GO GET A BEER?
YOU'RE ON.

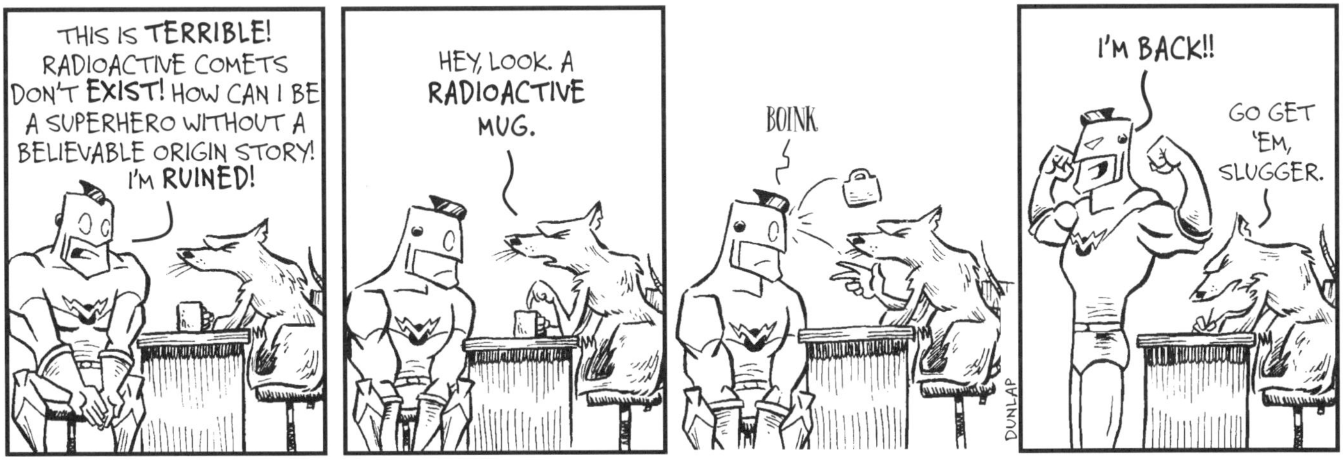
THIS IS TERRIBLE! RADIOACTIVE COMETS DON'T EXIST! HOW CAN I BE A SUPERHERO WITHOUT A BELIEVABLE ORIGIN STORY! I'M RUINED!
HEY, LOOK. A RADIOACTIVE MUG.
BOINK
DUNLAP
I'M BACK!!
GO GET 'EM, SLUGGER.

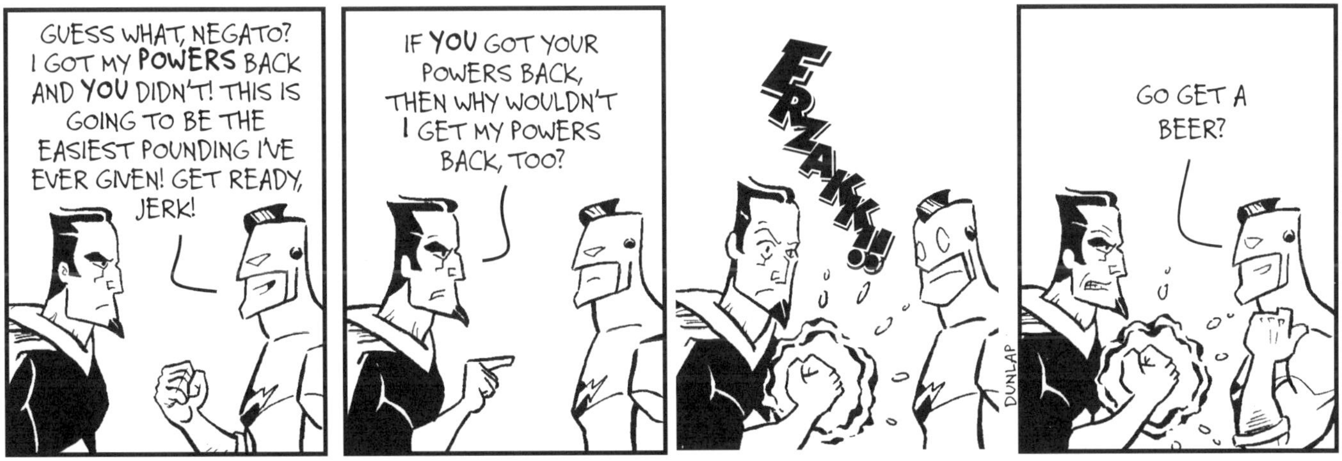
GUESS WHAT, NEGATO? I GOT MY POWERS BACK AND YOU DIDN'T! THIS IS GOING TO BE THE EASIEST POUNDING I'VE EVER GIVEN! GET READY, JERK!
IF YOU GOT YOUR POWERS BACK, THEN WHY WOULDN'T I GET MY POWERS BACK, TOO?
FRZAKK!!
DUNLAP
GO GET A BEER?

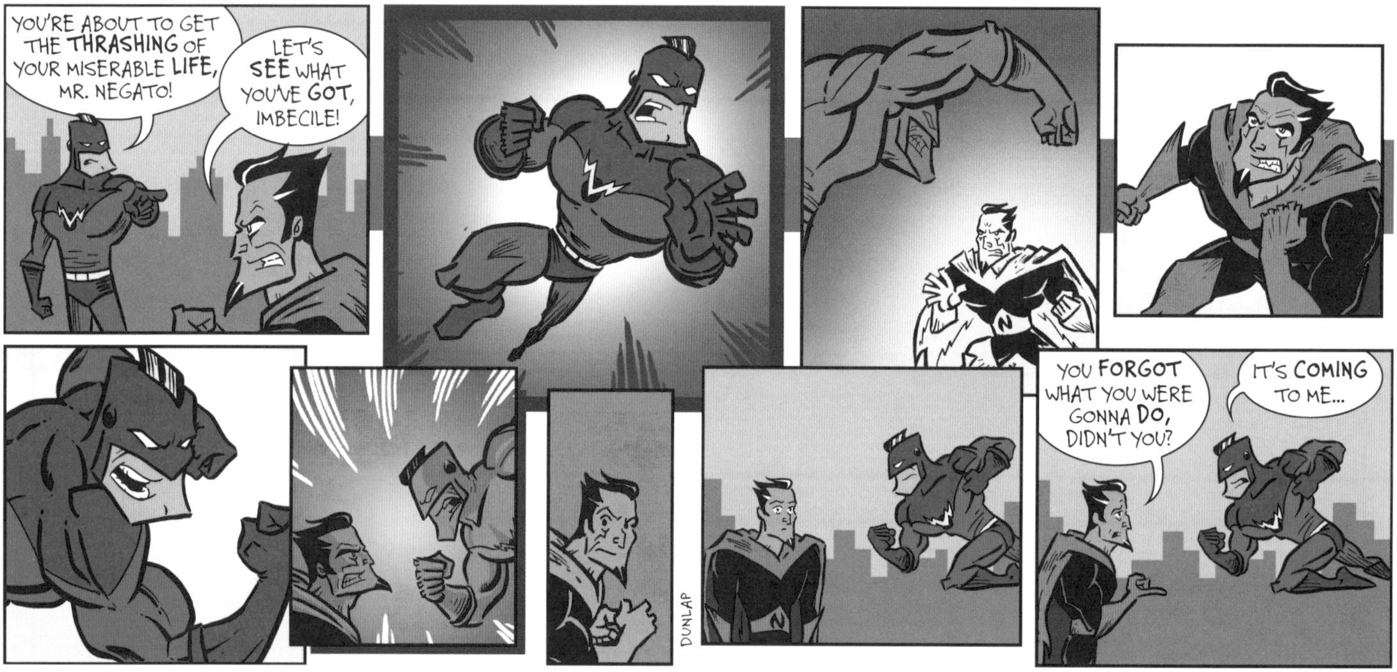
YOU'RE ABOUT TO GET THE THRASHING OF YOUR MISERABLE LIFE, MR. NEGATO!
LET'S SEE WHAT YOU'VE GOT, IMBECILE!
DUNLAP
YOU FORGOT WHAT YOU WERE GONNA DO, DIDN'T YOU?
IT'S COMING TO ME...

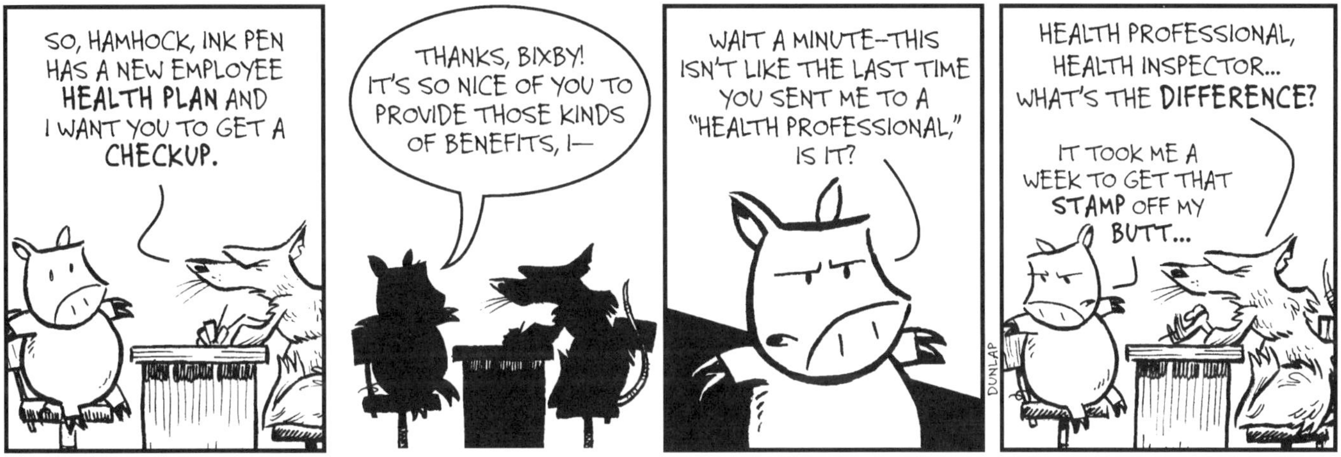
SO, HAMHOCK, INK PEN HAS A NEW EMPLOYEE HEALTH PLAN AND I WANT YOU TO GET A CHECKUP.
THANKS, BIXBY! IT'S SO NICE OF YOU TO PROVIDE THOSE KINDS OF BENEFITS, I—
WAIT A MINUTE—THIS ISN'T LIKE THE LAST TIME YOU SENT ME TO A "HEALTH PROFESSIONAL," IS IT?
HEALTH PROFESSIONAL, HEALTH INSPECTOR... WHAT'S THE DIFFERENCE?
IT TOOK ME A WEEK TO GET THAT STAMP OFF MY BUTT...
DUNLAP

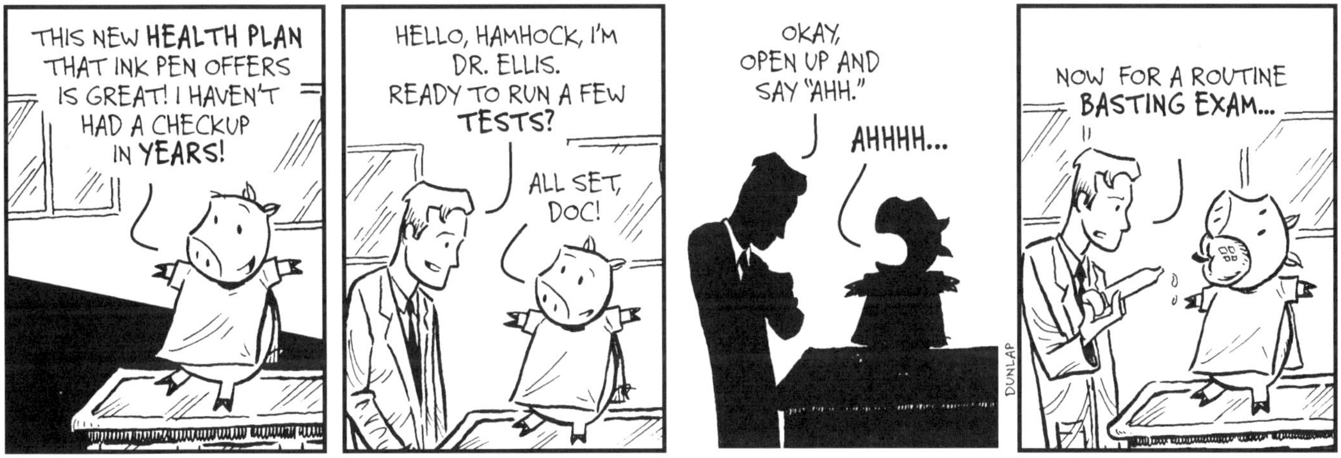
THIS NEW HEALTH PLAN THAT INK PEN OFFERS IS GREAT! I HAVEN'T HAD A CHECKUP IN YEARS!
HELLO, HAMHOCK, I'M DR. ELLIS. READY TO RUN A FEW TESTS?
ALL SET, DOC!
OKAY, OPEN UP AND SAY "AHH."
AHHHH...
NOW FOR A ROUTINE BASTING EXAM...
DUNLAP

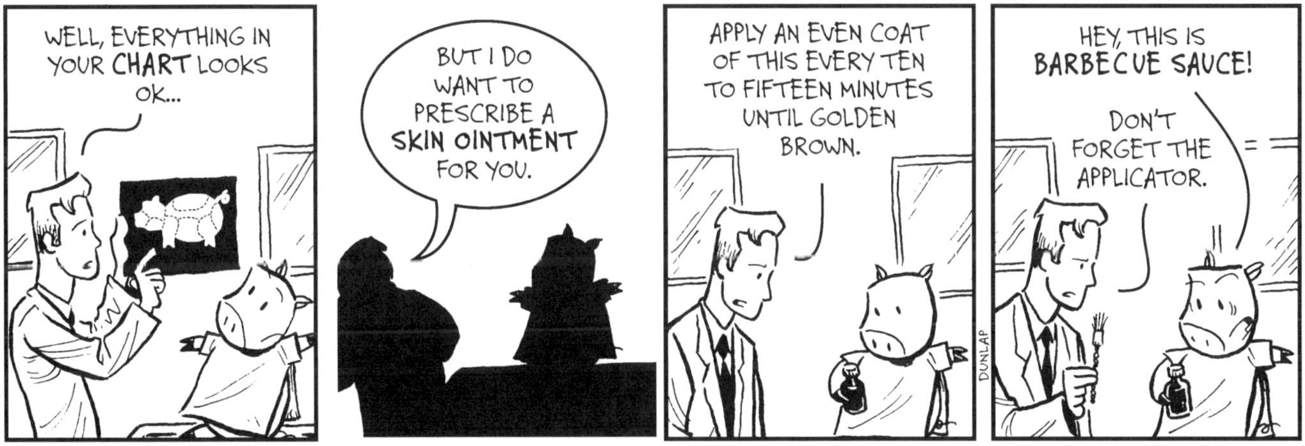
WELL, EVERYTHING IN YOUR CHART LOOKS OK...
BUT I DO WANT TO PRESCRIBE A SKIN OINTMENT FOR YOU.
APPLY AN EVEN COAT OF THIS EVERY TEN TO FIFTEEN MINUTES UNTIL GOLDEN BROWN.
HEY, THIS IS BARBECUE SAUCE!
DON'T FORGET THE APPLICATOR.
DUNLAP

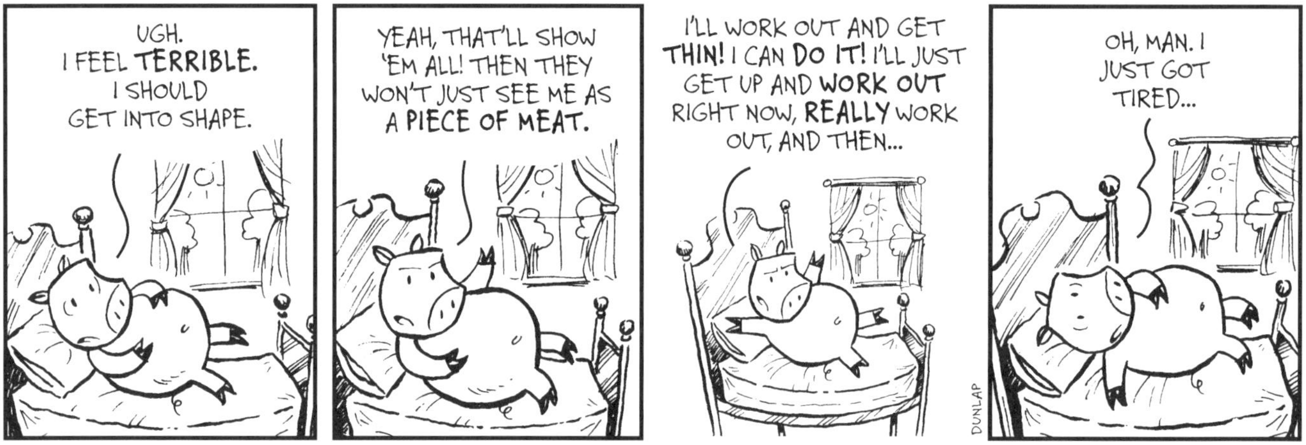
UGH.
I FEEL **TERRIBLE.** I SHOULD GET INTO SHAPE.
YEAH, THAT'LL SHOW 'EM ALL! THEN THEY WON'T JUST SEE ME AS A **PIECE OF MEAT.**
I'LL WORK OUT AND GET **THIN!** I CAN **DO IT!** I'LL JUST GET UP AND **WORK OUT** RIGHT NOW, **REALLY** WORK OUT, AND THEN...
OH, MAN. I JUST GOT TIRED...
DUNLAP

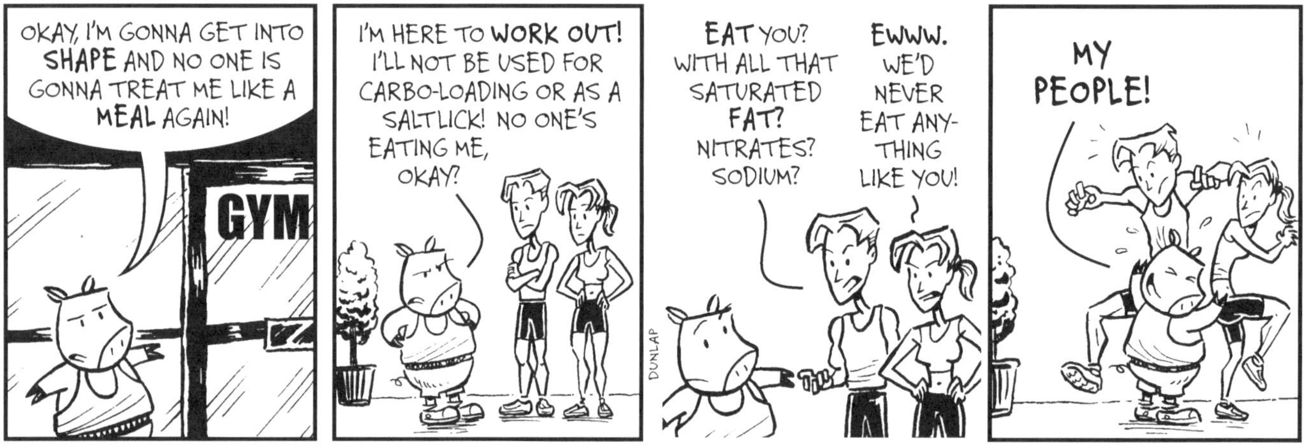
OKAY, I'M GONNA GET INTO **SHAPE** AND NO ONE IS GONNA TREAT ME LIKE A **MEAL** AGAIN!
GYM
I'M HERE TO **WORK OUT!** I'LL NOT BE USED FOR CARBO-LOADING OR AS A SALTLICK! NO ONE'S EATING ME, OKAY?
DUNLAP
**EAT** YOU? WITH ALL THAT SATURATED **FAT?** NITRATES? SODIUM?
**EWWW.** WE'D NEVER EAT ANYTHING LIKE YOU!
**MY PEOPLE!**

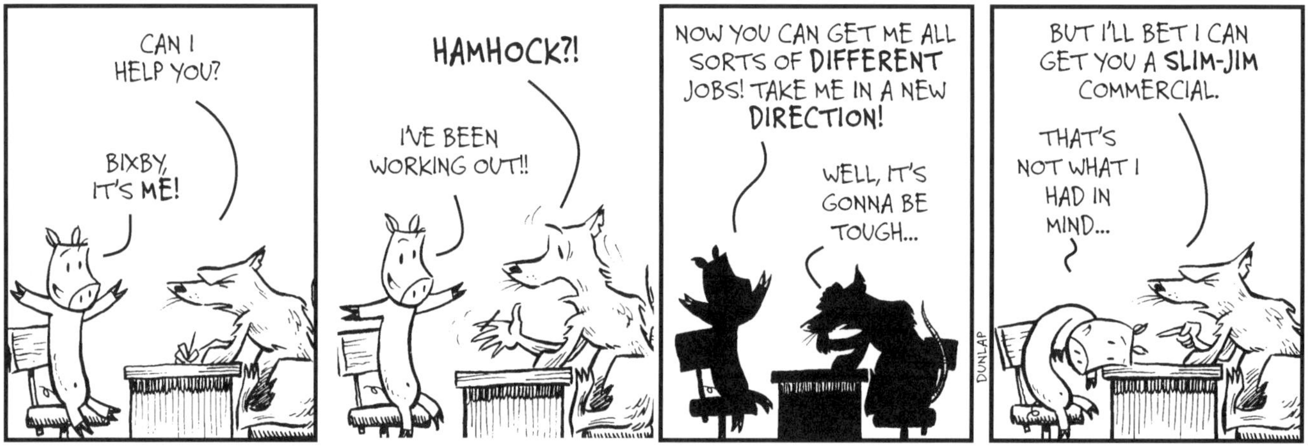
CAN I HELP YOU?
BIXBY, IT'S **ME!**
**HAMHOCK?!**
I'VE BEEN WORKING OUT!!
NOW YOU CAN GET ME ALL SORTS OF **DIFFERENT** JOBS! TAKE ME IN A NEW **DIRECTION!**
WELL, IT'S GONNA BE TOUGH...
DUNLAP
BUT I'LL BET I CAN GET YOU A **SLIM-JIM** COMMERCIAL.
THAT'S NOT WHAT I HAD IN MIND...

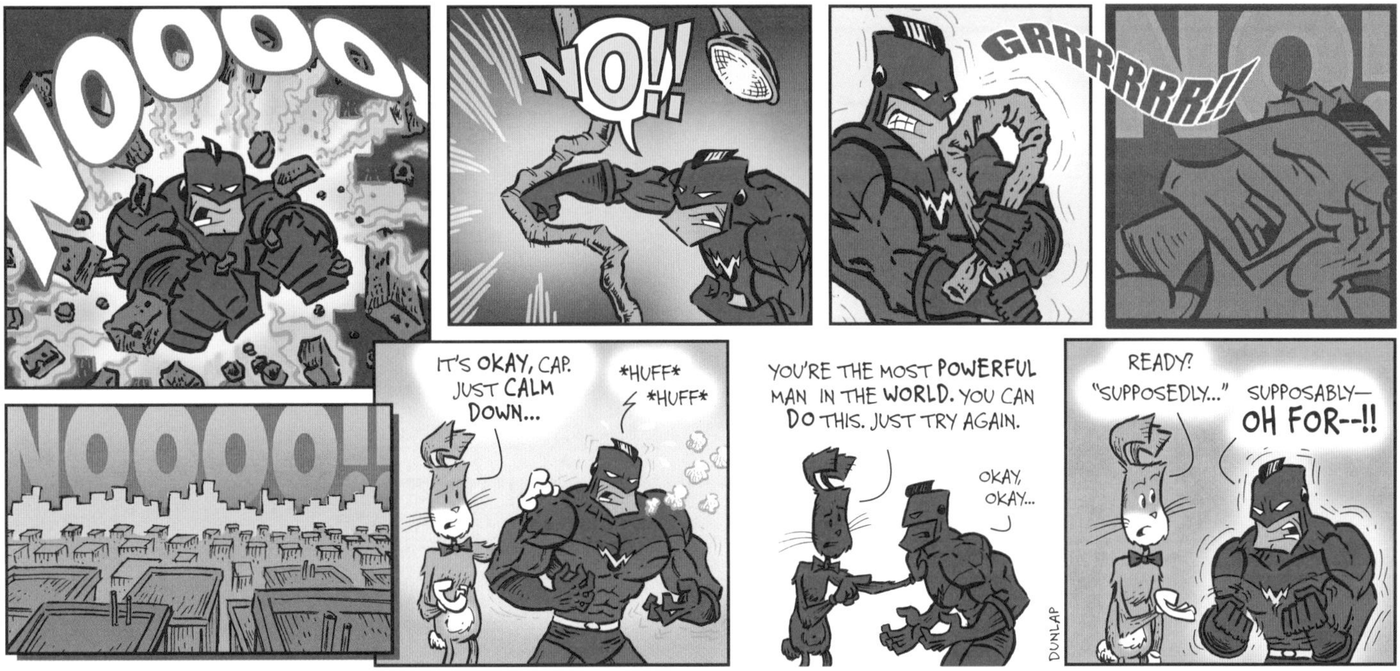
NOOOO
NO!!
GRRRRRRR!!
NO!
NOOOO!!
IT'S OKAY, CAP. JUST CALM DOWN...
*HUFF* *HUFF*
YOU'RE THE MOST POWERFUL MAN IN THE WORLD. YOU CAN DO THIS. JUST TRY AGAIN.
OKAY, OKAY...
DUNLAP
READY? "SUPPOSEDLY..."
SUPPOSABLY— OH FOR--!!

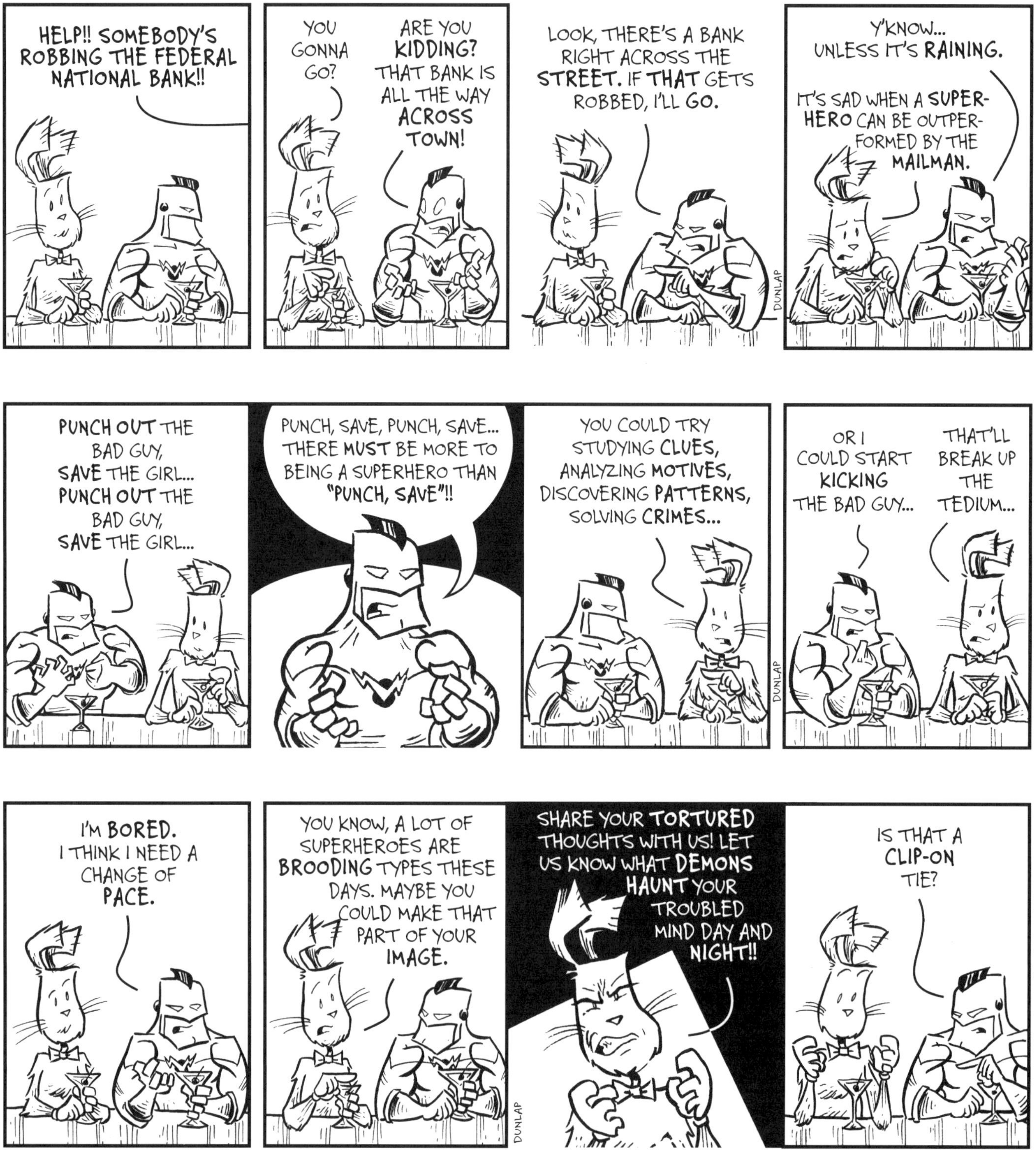
HELP!! SOMEBODY'S ROBBING THE FEDERAL NATIONAL BANK!!
YOU GONNA GO?
ARE YOU KIDDING? THAT BANK IS ALL THE WAY ACROSS TOWN!
LOOK, THERE'S A BANK RIGHT ACROSS THE STREET. IF THAT GETS ROBBED, I'LL GO.
DUNLAP
Y'KNOW... UNLESS IT'S RAINING.
IT'S SAD WHEN A SUPER-HERO CAN BE OUTPER-FORMED BY THE MAILMAN.
PUNCH OUT THE BAD GUY, SAVE THE GIRL... PUNCH OUT THE BAD GUY, SAVE THE GIRL...
PUNCH, SAVE, PUNCH, SAVE... THERE MUST BE MORE TO BEING A SUPERHERO THAN "PUNCH, SAVE"!!
YOU COULD TRY STUDYING CLUES, ANALYZING MOTIVES, DISCOVERING PATTERNS, SOLVING CRIMES...
DUNLAP
OR I COULD START KICKING THE BAD GUY...
THAT'LL BREAK UP THE TEDIUM...
I'M BORED. I THINK I NEED A CHANGE OF PACE.
YOU KNOW, A LOT OF SUPERHEROES ARE BROODING TYPES THESE DAYS. MAYBE YOU COULD MAKE THAT PART OF YOUR IMAGE.
DUNLAP
SHARE YOUR TORTURED THOUGHTS WITH US! LET US KNOW WHAT DEMONS HAUNT YOUR TROUBLED MIND DAY AND NIGHT!!
IS THAT A CLIP-ON TIE?

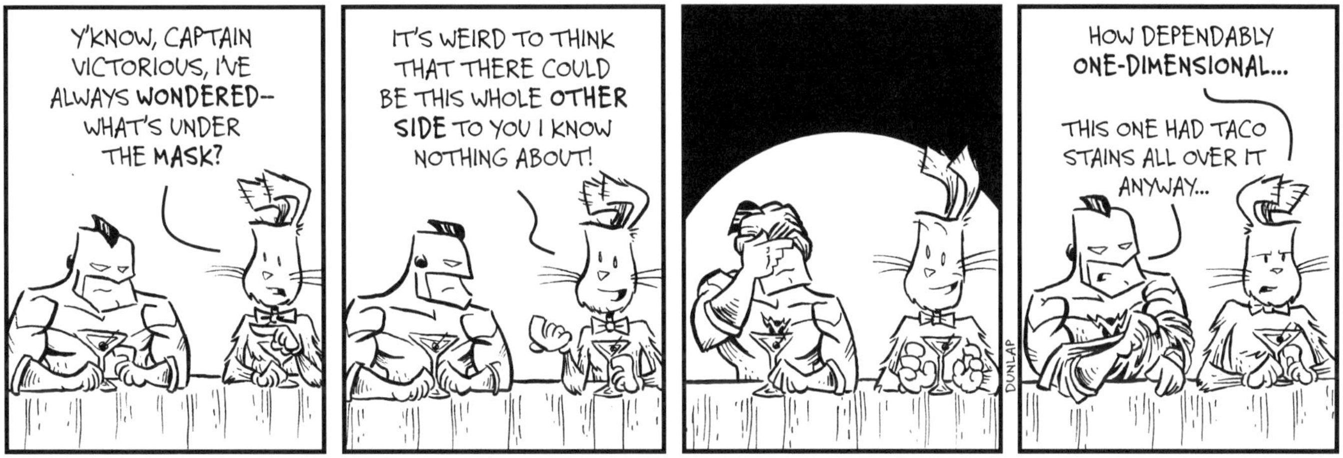
Y'KNOW, CAPTAIN VICTORIOUS, I'VE ALWAYS WONDERED-- WHAT'S UNDER THE MASK?
IT'S WEIRD TO THINK THAT THERE COULD BE THIS WHOLE OTHER SIDE TO YOU I KNOW NOTHING ABOUT!
DUNLAP
HOW DEPENDABLY ONE-DIMENSIONAL...
THIS ONE HAD TACO STAINS ALL OVER IT ANYWAY...

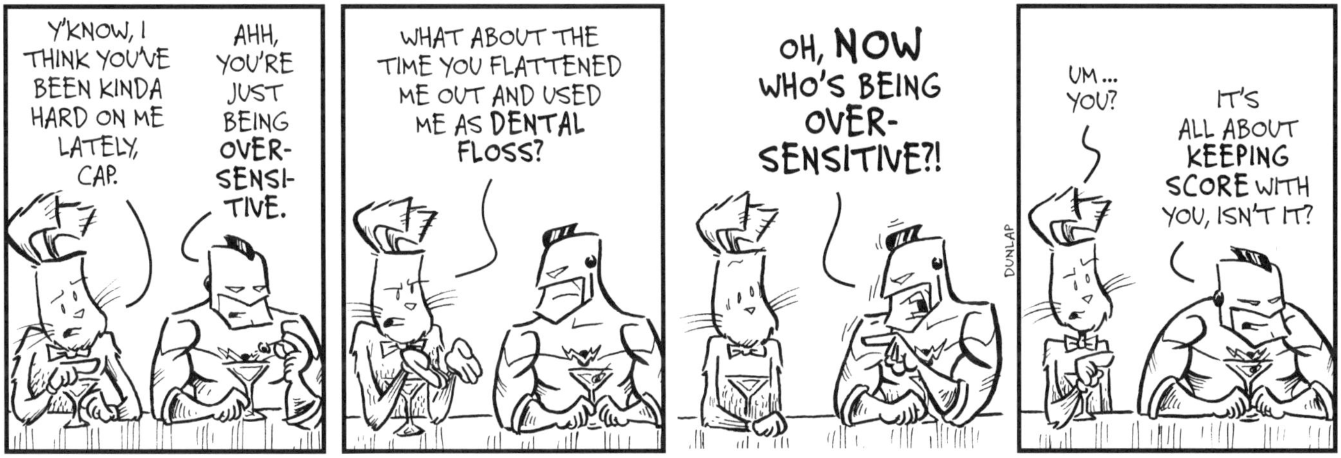
Y'KNOW, I THINK YOU'VE BEEN KINDA HARD ON ME LATELY, CAP.
AHH, YOU'RE JUST BEING OVER-SENSI-TIVE.
WHAT ABOUT THE TIME YOU FLATTENED ME OUT AND USED ME AS DENTAL FLOSS?
OH, NOW WHO'S BEING OVER-SENSITIVE?!
DUNLAP
UM... YOU?
IT'S ALL ABOUT KEEPING SCORE WITH YOU, ISN'T IT?

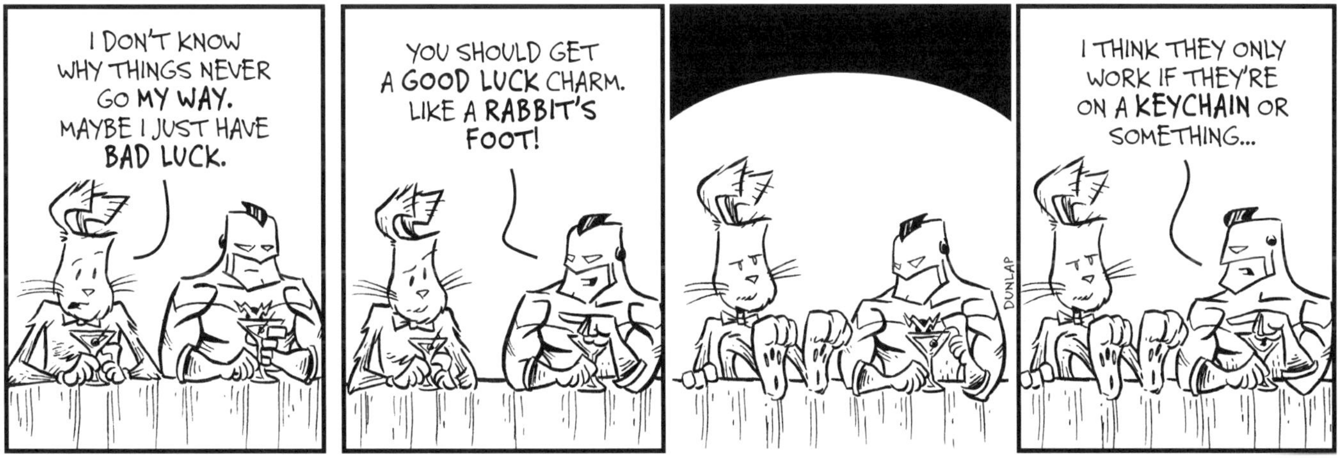
I DON'T KNOW WHY THINGS NEVER GO MY WAY. MAYBE I JUST HAVE BAD LUCK.
YOU SHOULD GET A GOOD LUCK CHARM. LIKE A RABBIT'S FOOT!
DUNLAP
I THINK THEY ONLY WORK IF THEY'RE ON A KEYCHAIN OR SOMETHING...

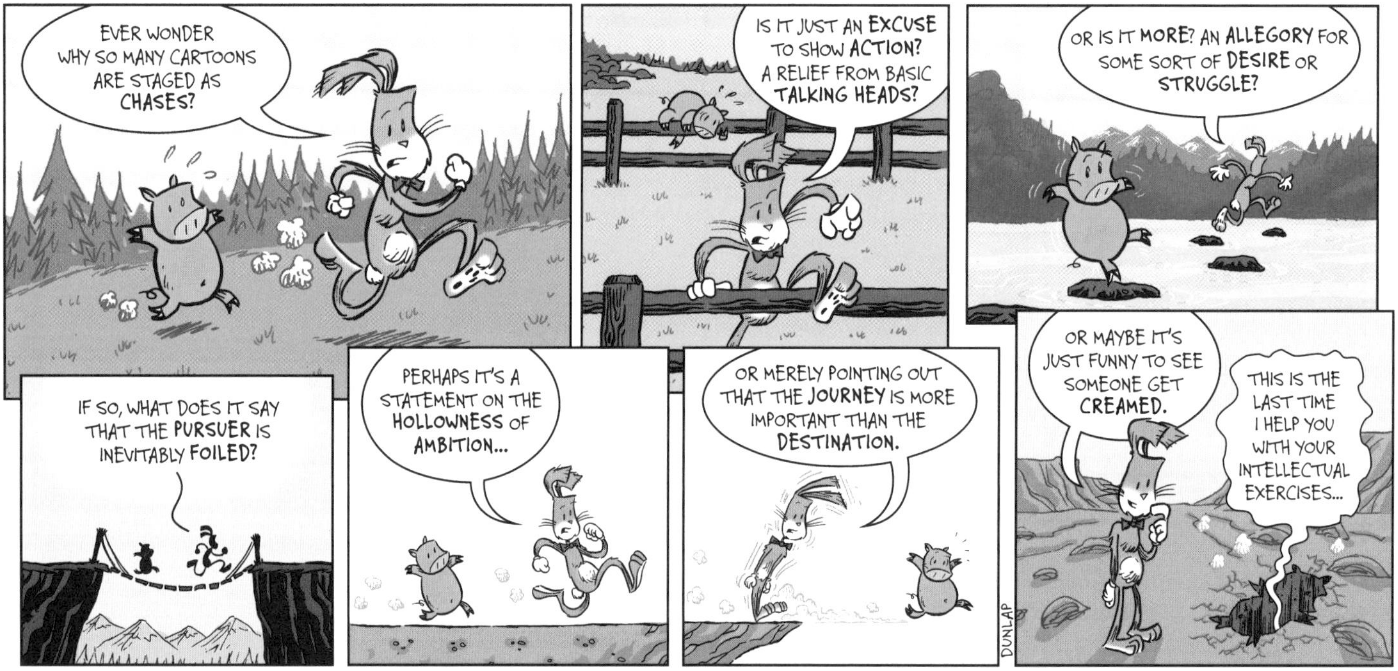
EVER WONDER WHY SO MANY CARTOONS ARE STAGED AS CHASES?
IS IT JUST AN EXCUSE TO SHOW ACTION? A RELIEF FROM BASIC TALKING HEADS?
OR IS IT MORE? AN ALLEGORY FOR SOME SORT OF DESIRE OR STRUGGLE?
IF SO, WHAT DOES IT SAY THAT THE PURSUER IS INEVITABLY FOILED?
PERHAPS IT'S A STATEMENT ON THE HOLLOWNESS OF AMBITION...
OR MERELY POINTING OUT THAT THE JOURNEY IS MORE IMPORTANT THAN THE DESTINATION.
DUNLAP
OR MAYBE IT'S JUST FUNNY TO SEE SOMEONE GET CREAMED.
THIS IS THE LAST TIME I HELP YOU WITH YOUR INTELLECTUAL EXERCISES...

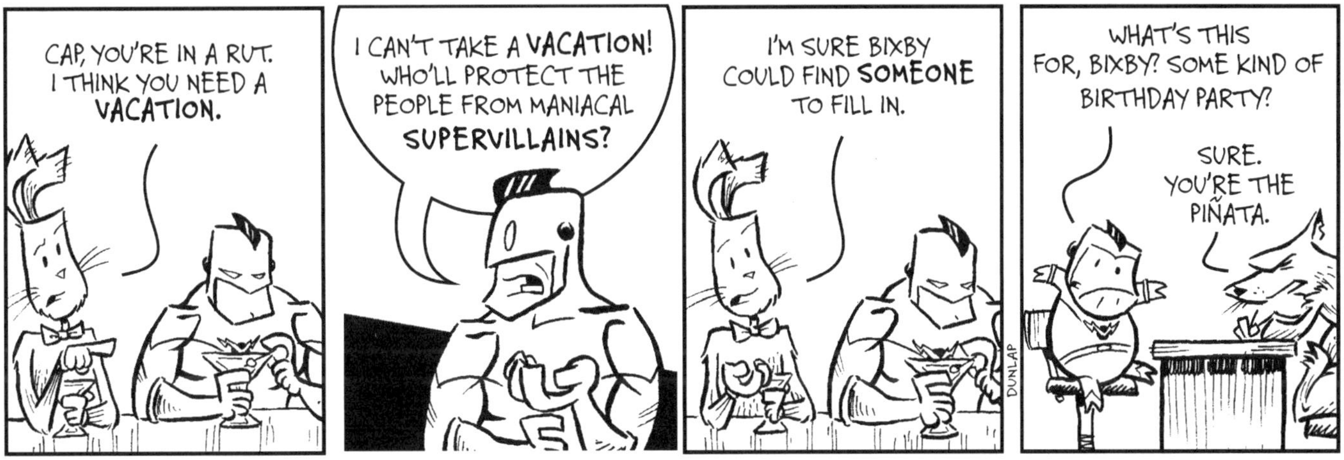
CAP, YOU'RE IN A RUT. I THINK YOU NEED A VACATION.
I CAN'T TAKE A VACATION! WHO'LL PROTECT THE PEOPLE FROM MANIACAL SUPERVILLAINS?
I'M SURE BIXBY COULD FIND SOMEONE TO FILL IN.
DUNLAP
WHAT'S THIS FOR, BIXBY? SOME KIND OF BIRTHDAY PARTY?
SURE. YOU'RE THE PIÑATA.

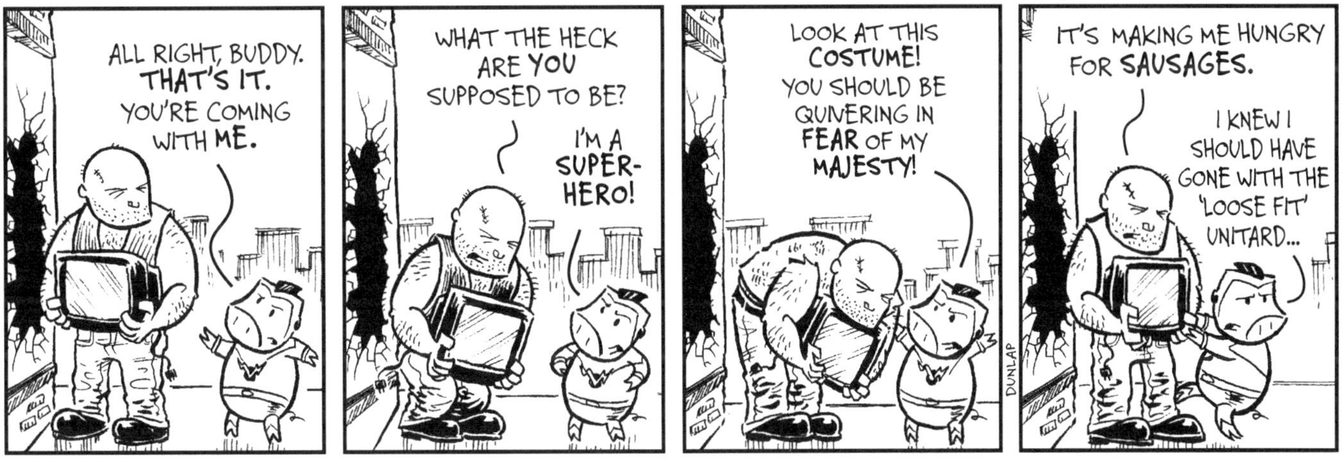
ALL RIGHT, BUDDY. THAT'S IT. YOU'RE COMING WITH ME.
WHAT THE HECK ARE YOU SUPPOSED TO BE?
I'M A SUPER-HERO!
LOOK AT THIS COSTUME! YOU SHOULD BE QUIVERING IN FEAR OF MY MAJESTY!
DUNLAP
IT'S MAKING ME HUNGRY FOR SAUSAGES.
I KNEW I SHOULD HAVE GONE WITH THE 'LOOSE FIT' UNITARD...

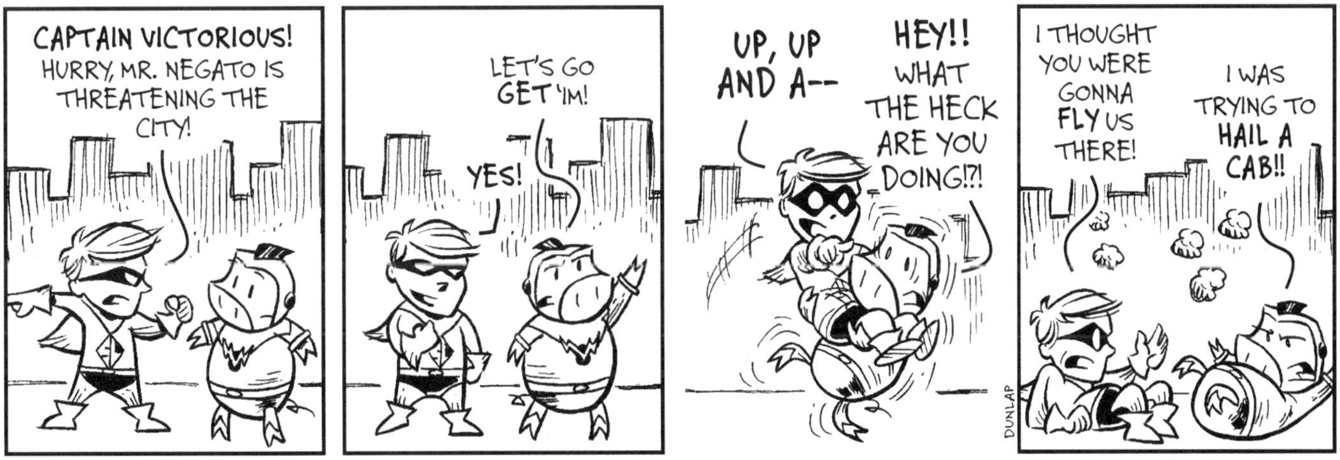
CAPTAIN VICTORIOUS! HURRY, MR. NEGATO IS THREATENING THE CITY!
LET'S GO GET 'IM!
YES!
UP, UP AND A--
HEY!! WHAT THE HECK ARE YOU DOING!?!
DUNLAP
I THOUGHT YOU WERE GONNA FLY US THERE!
I WAS TRYING TO HAIL A CAB!!

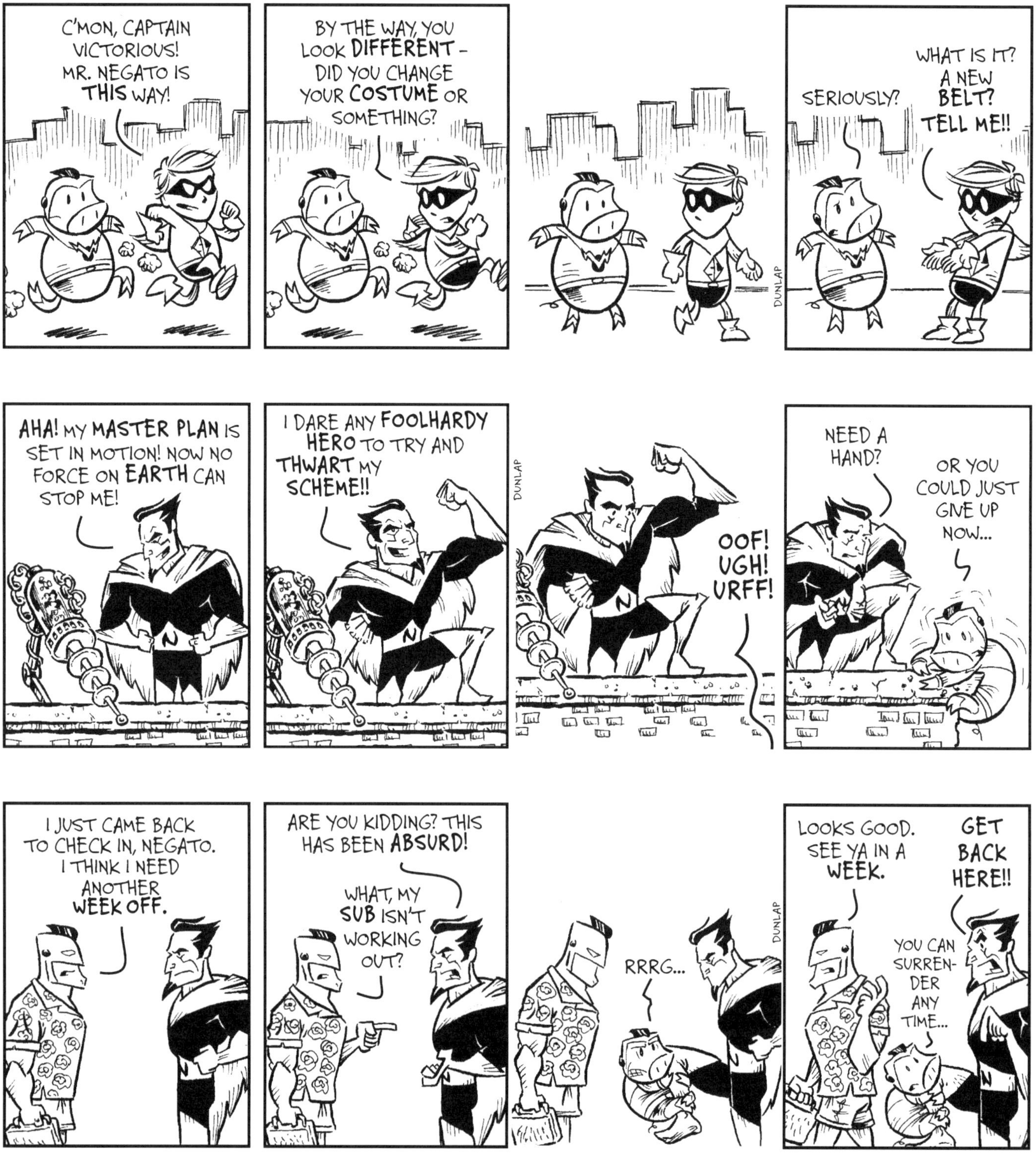
C'MON, CAPTAIN VICTORIOUS! MR. NEGATO IS THIS WAY!
BY THE WAY, YOU LOOK DIFFERENT - DID YOU CHANGE YOUR COSTUME OR SOMETHING?
SERIOUSLY?
WHAT IS IT? A NEW BELT? TELL ME!!
DUNLAP
AHA! MY MASTER PLAN IS SET IN MOTION! NOW NO FORCE ON EARTH CAN STOP ME!
I DARE ANY FOOLHARDY HERO TO TRY AND THWART MY SCHEME!!
DUNLAP
OOF! UGH! URFF!
NEED A HAND?
OR YOU COULD JUST GIVE UP NOW...
I JUST CAME BACK TO CHECK IN, NEGATO. I THINK I NEED ANOTHER WEEK OFF.
ARE YOU KIDDING? THIS HAS BEEN ABSURD!
WHAT, MY SUB ISN'T WORKING OUT?
RRRG...
DUNLAP
LOOKS GOOD. SEE YA IN A WEEK.
GET BACK HERE!!
YOU CAN SURREN-DER ANY TIME...

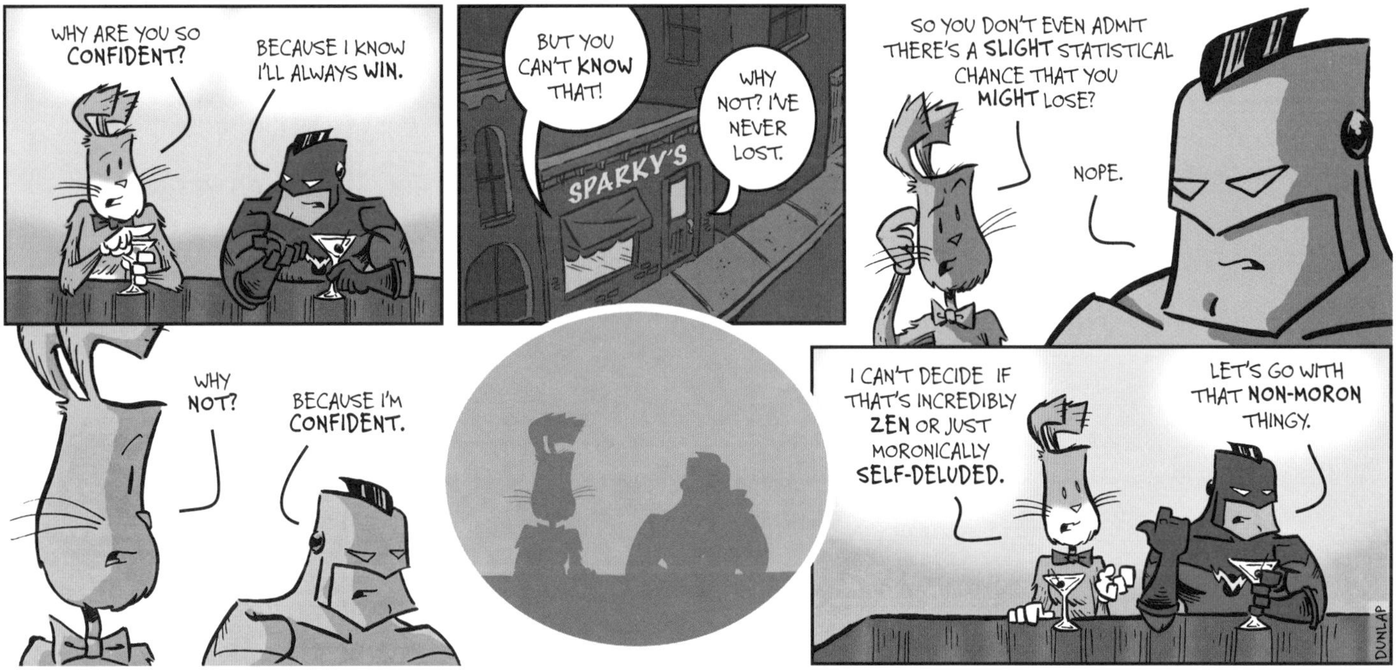

WHY ARE YOU SO CONFIDENT?
BECAUSE I KNOW I'LL ALWAYS WIN.
BUT YOU CAN'T KNOW THAT!
SPARKY'S
WHY NOT? I'VE NEVER LOST.
SO YOU DON'T EVEN ADMIT THERE'S A SLIGHT STATISTICAL CHANCE THAT YOU MIGHT LOSE?
NOPE.
WHY NOT?
BECAUSE I'M CONFIDENT.
I CAN'T DECIDE IF THAT'S INCREDIBLY ZEN OR JUST MORONICALLY SELF-DELUDED.
LET'S GO WITH THAT NON-MORON THINGY.
DUNLAP

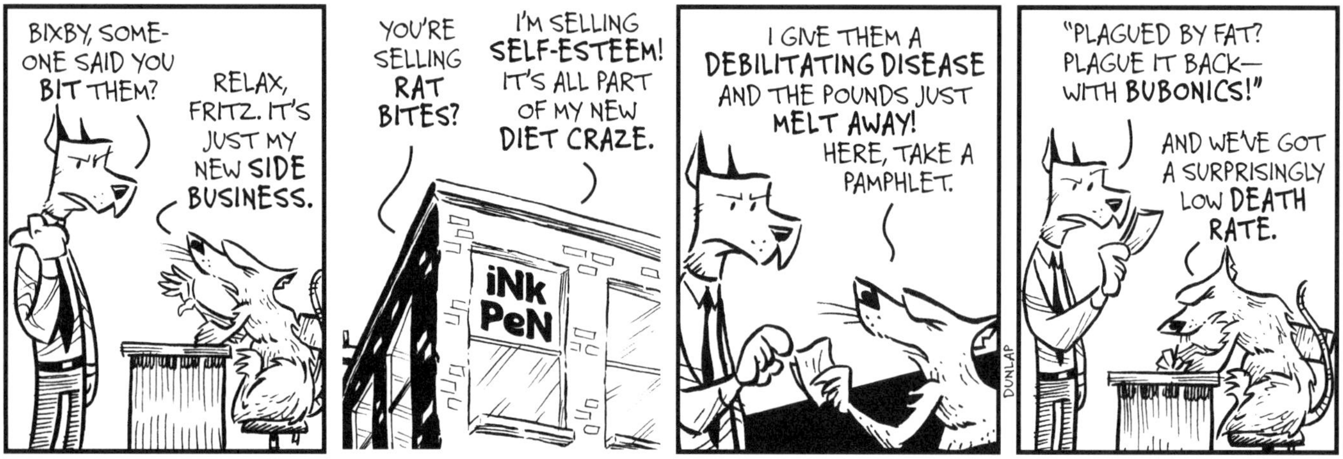
BIXBY, SOME-ONE SAID YOU BIT THEM?
RELAX, FRITZ. IT'S JUST MY NEW SIDE BUSINESS.
YOU'RE SELLING RAT BITES?
I'M SELLING SELF-ESTEEM! IT'S ALL PART OF MY NEW DIET CRAZE.
iNk PeN
I GIVE THEM A DEBILITATING DISEASE AND THE POUNDS JUST MELT AWAY!
HERE, TAKE A PAMPHLET.
DUNLAP
"PLAGUED BY FAT? PLAGUE IT BACK— WITH BUBONICS!"
AND WE'VE GOT A SURPRISINGLY LOW DEATH RATE.

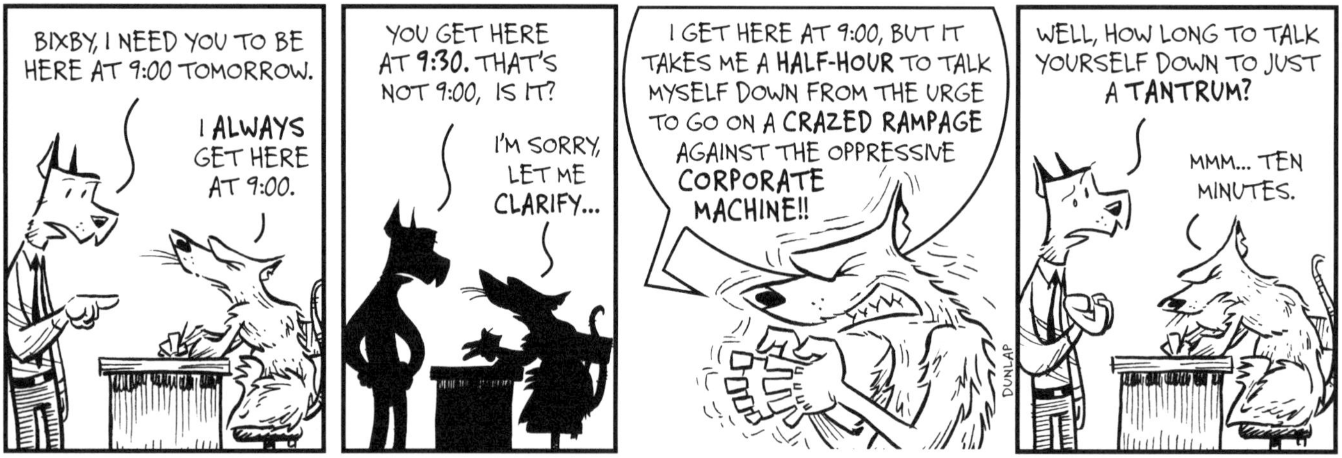
BIXBY, I NEED YOU TO BE HERE AT 9:00 TOMORROW.
I ALWAYS GET HERE AT 9:00.
YOU GET HERE AT 9:30. THAT'S NOT 9:00, IS IT?
I'M SORRY, LET ME CLARIFY...
I GET HERE AT 9:00, BUT IT TAKES ME A HALF-HOUR TO TALK MYSELF DOWN FROM THE URGE TO GO ON A CRAZED RAMPAGE AGAINST THE OPPRESSIVE CORPORATE MACHINE!!
DUNLAP
WELL, HOW LONG TO TALK YOURSELF DOWN TO JUST A TANTRUM?
MMM... TEN MINUTES.

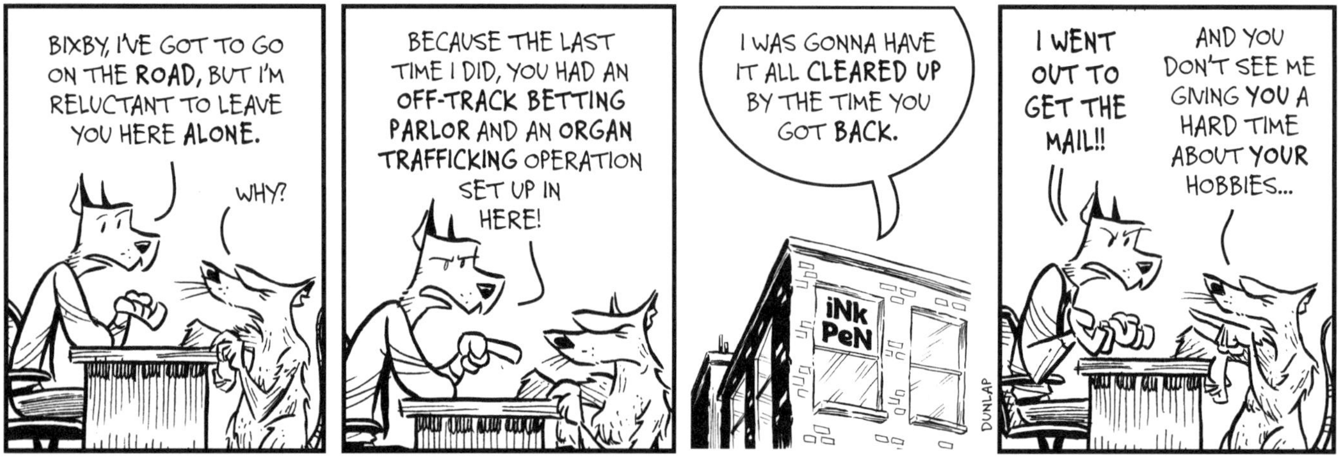
BIXBY, I'VE GOT TO GO ON THE ROAD, BUT I'M RELUCTANT TO LEAVE YOU HERE ALONE.
WHY?
BECAUSE THE LAST TIME I DID, YOU HAD AN OFF-TRACK BETTING PARLOR AND AN ORGAN TRAFFICKING OPERATION SET UP IN HERE!
I WAS GONNA HAVE IT ALL CLEARED UP BY THE TIME YOU GOT BACK.
iNk PeN
DUNLAP
I WENT OUT TO GET THE MAIL!!
AND YOU DON'T SEE ME GIVING YOU A HARD TIME ABOUT YOUR HOBBIES...

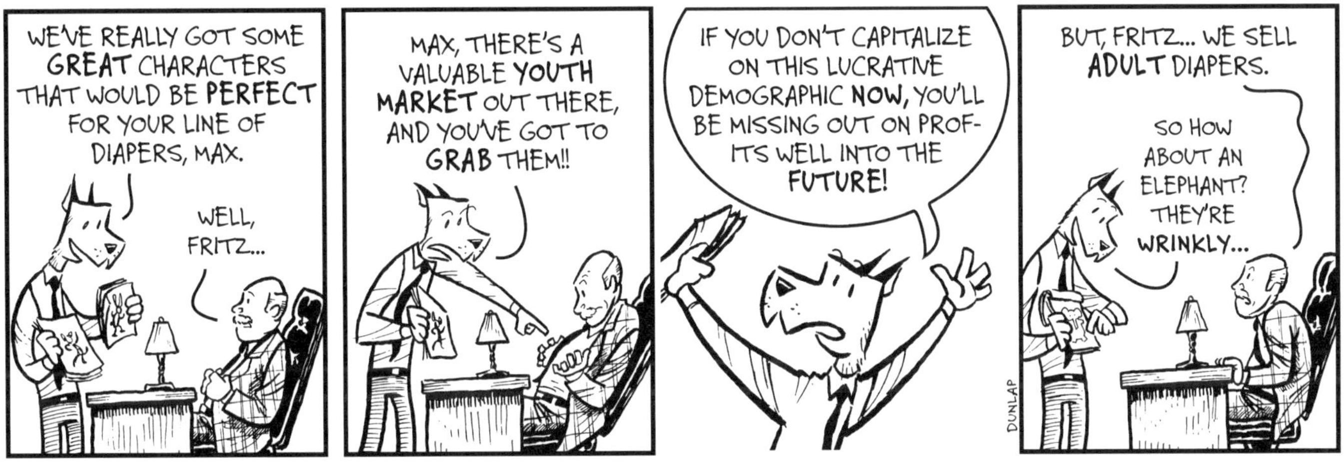
WE'VE REALLY GOT SOME GREAT CHARACTERS THAT WOULD BE PERFECT FOR YOUR LINE OF DIAPERS, MAX.
WELL, FRITZ...
MAX, THERE'S A VALUABLE YOUTH MARKET OUT THERE, AND YOU'VE GOT TO GRAB THEM!!
IF YOU DON'T CAPITALIZE ON THIS LUCRATIVE DEMOGRAPHIC NOW, YOU'LL BE MISSING OUT ON PROF-ITS WELL INTO THE FUTURE!
BUT, FRITZ... WE SELL ADULT DIAPERS.
SO HOW ABOUT AN ELEPHANT? THEY'RE WRINKLY...
DUNLAP

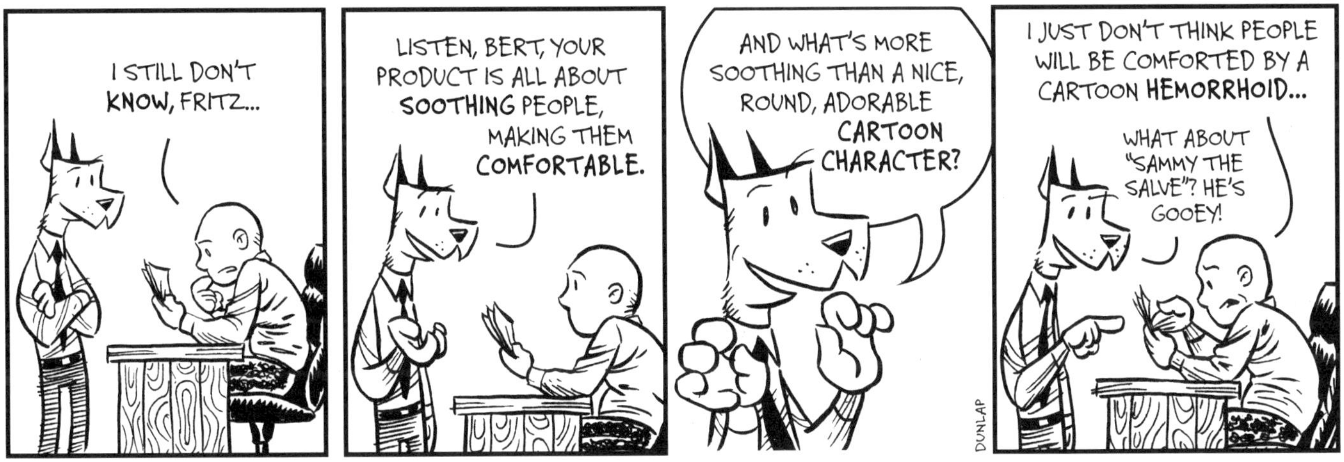
I STILL DON'T KNOW, FRITZ...
LISTEN, BERT, YOUR PRODUCT IS ALL ABOUT SOOTHING PEOPLE, MAKING THEM COMFORTABLE.
AND WHAT'S MORE SOOTHING THAN A NICE, ROUND, ADORABLE CARTOON CHARACTER?
I JUST DON'T THINK PEOPLE WILL BE COMFORTED BY A CARTOON HEMORRHOID...
WHAT ABOUT "SAMMY THE SALVE"? HE'S GOOEY!
DUNLAP

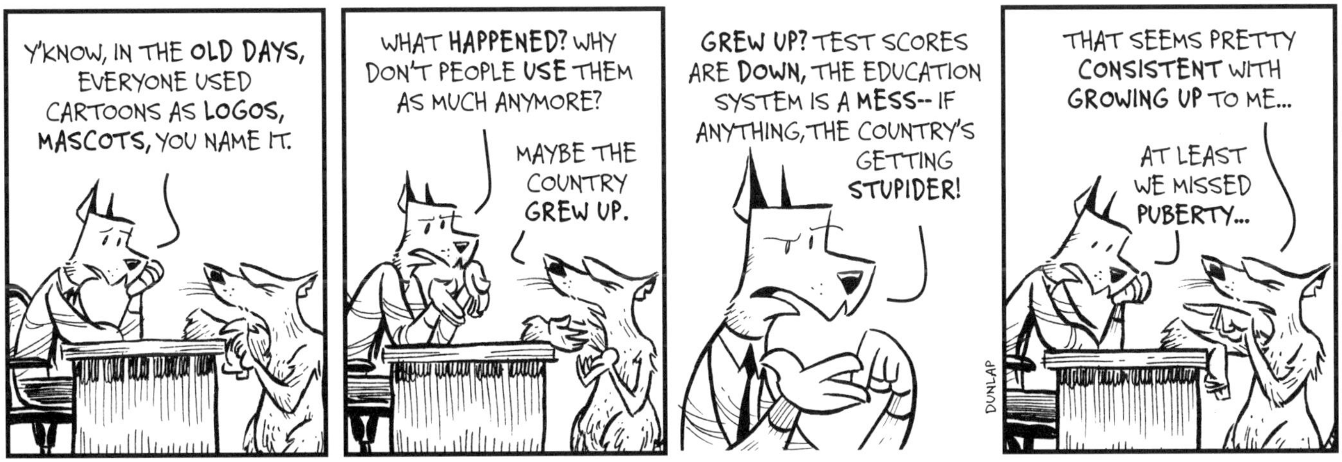
Y'KNOW, IN THE OLD DAYS, EVERYONE USED CARTOONS AS LOGOS, MASCOTS, YOU NAME IT.
WHAT HAPPENED? WHY DON'T PEOPLE USE THEM AS MUCH ANYMORE?
MAYBE THE COUNTRY GREW UP.
GREW UP? TEST SCORES ARE DOWN, THE EDUCATION SYSTEM IS A MESS-- IF ANYTHING, THE COUNTRY'S GETTING STUPIDER!
THAT SEEMS PRETTY CONSISTENT WITH GROWING UP TO ME...
AT LEAST WE MISSED PUBERTY...
DUNLAP

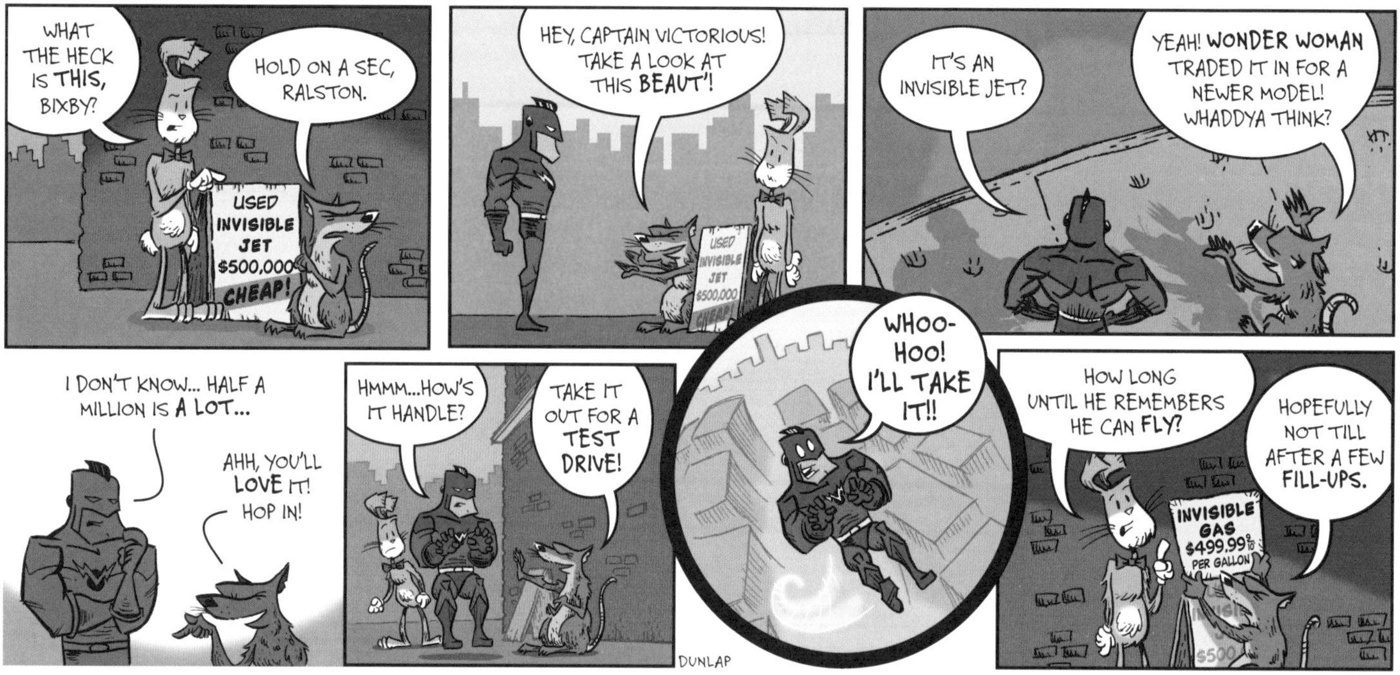
WHAT THE HECK IS THIS, BIXBY?
HOLD ON A SEC, RALSTON.
USED INVISIBLE JET $500,000 CHEAP!
HEY, CAPTAIN VICTORIOUS! TAKE A LOOK AT THIS BEAUT'!
IT'S AN INVISIBLE JET?
YEAH! WONDER WOMAN TRADED IT IN FOR A NEWER MODEL! WHADDYA THINK?
I DON'T KNOW... HALF A MILLION IS A LOT...
AHH, YOU'LL LOVE IT! HOP IN!
HMMM...HOW'S IT HANDLE?
TAKE IT OUT FOR A TEST DRIVE!
WHOO-HOO! I'LL TAKE IT!!
HOW LONG UNTIL HE REMEMBERS HE CAN FLY?
HOPEFULLY NOT TILL AFTER A FEW FILL-UPS.
INVISIBLE GAS $499.99 9/10 PER GALLON
DUNLAP

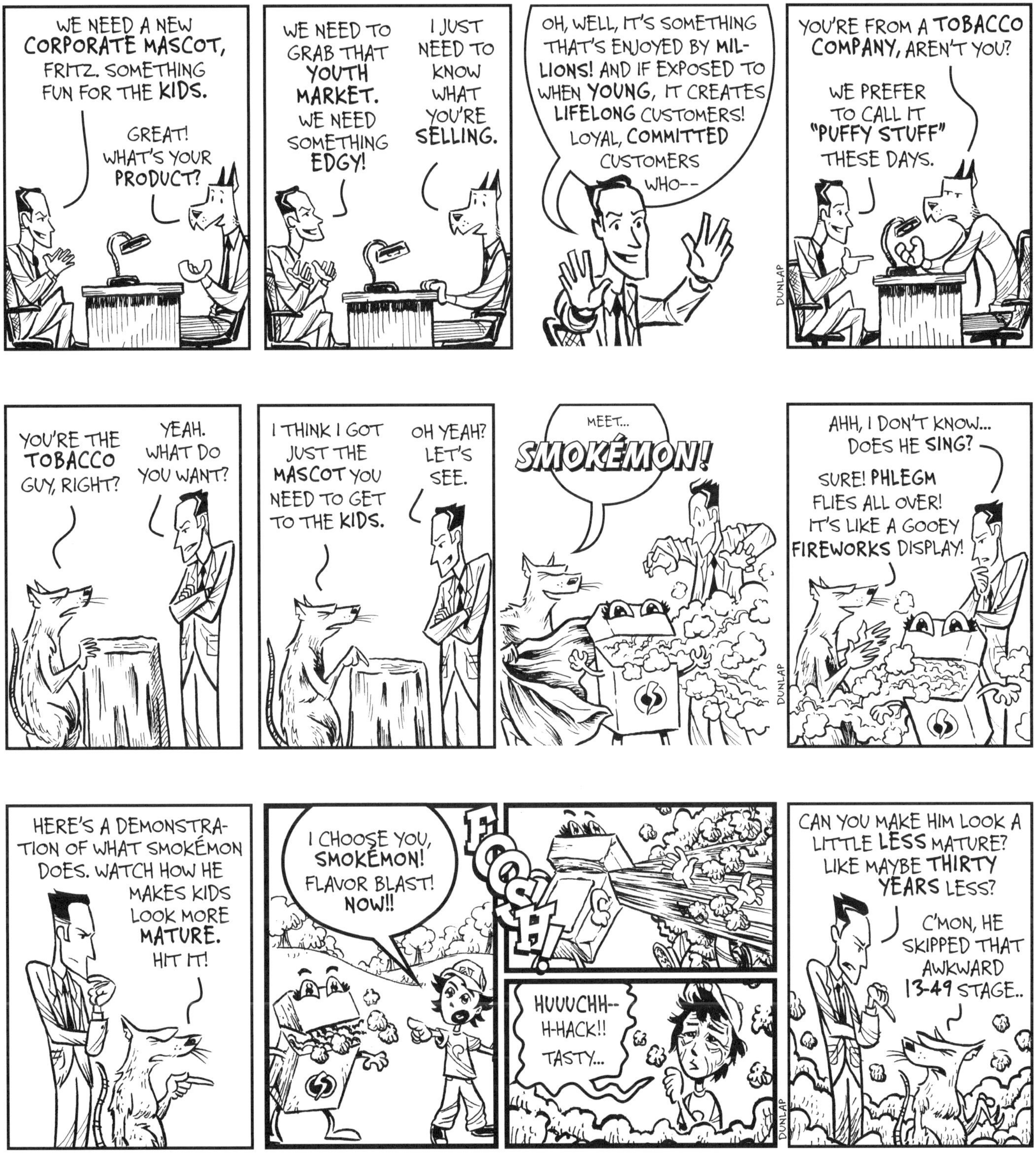

WE NEED A NEW CORPORATE MASCOT, FRITZ. SOMETHING FUN FOR THE KIDS.
GREAT! WHAT'S YOUR PRODUCT?
WE NEED TO GRAB THAT YOUTH MARKET. WE NEED SOMETHING EDGY!
I JUST NEED TO KNOW WHAT YOU'RE SELLING.
OH, WELL, IT'S SOMETHING THAT'S ENJOYED BY MILLIONS! AND IF EXPOSED TO WHEN YOUNG, IT CREATES LIFELONG CUSTOMERS! LOYAL, COMMITTED CUSTOMERS WHO--
YOU'RE FROM A TOBACCO COMPANY, AREN'T YOU?
WE PREFER TO CALL IT "PUFFY STUFF" THESE DAYS.
DUNLAP
YOU'RE THE TOBACCO GUY, RIGHT?
YEAH. WHAT DO YOU WANT?
I THINK I GOT JUST THE MASCOT YOU NEED TO GET TO THE KIDS.
OH YEAH? LET'S SEE.
MEET...
SMOKÉMON!
AHH, I DON'T KNOW... DOES HE SING?
SURE! PHLEGM FLIES ALL OVER! IT'S LIKE A GOOEY FIREWORKS DISPLAY!
DUNLAP
HERE'S A DEMONSTRATION OF WHAT SMOKÉMON DOES. WATCH HOW HE MAKES KIDS LOOK MORE MATURE. HIT IT!
I CHOOSE YOU, SMOKÉMON! FLAVOR BLAST! NOW!!
FOOSH!
HUUUCHH--H-HACK!! TASTY...
CAN YOU MAKE HIM LOOK A LITTLE LESS MATURE? LIKE MAYBE THIRTY YEARS LESS?
C'MON, HE SKIPPED THAT AWKWARD 13-49 STAGE..
DUNLAP

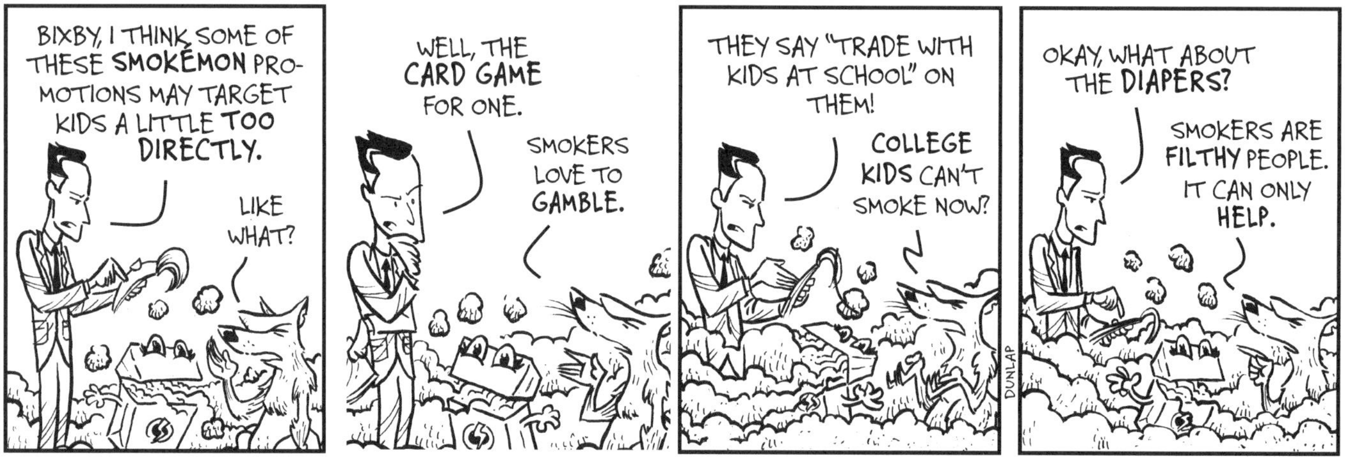
BIXBY, I THINK SOME OF THESE SMOKÉMON PROMOTIONS MAY TARGET KIDS A LITTLE TOO DIRECTLY.
LIKE WHAT?
WELL, THE CARD GAME FOR ONE.
SMOKERS LOVE TO GAMBLE.
THEY SAY "TRADE WITH KIDS AT SCHOOL" ON THEM!
COLLEGE KIDS CAN'T SMOKE NOW?
DUNLAP
OKAY, WHAT ABOUT THE DIAPERS?
SMOKERS ARE FILTHY PEOPLE. IT CAN ONLY HELP.

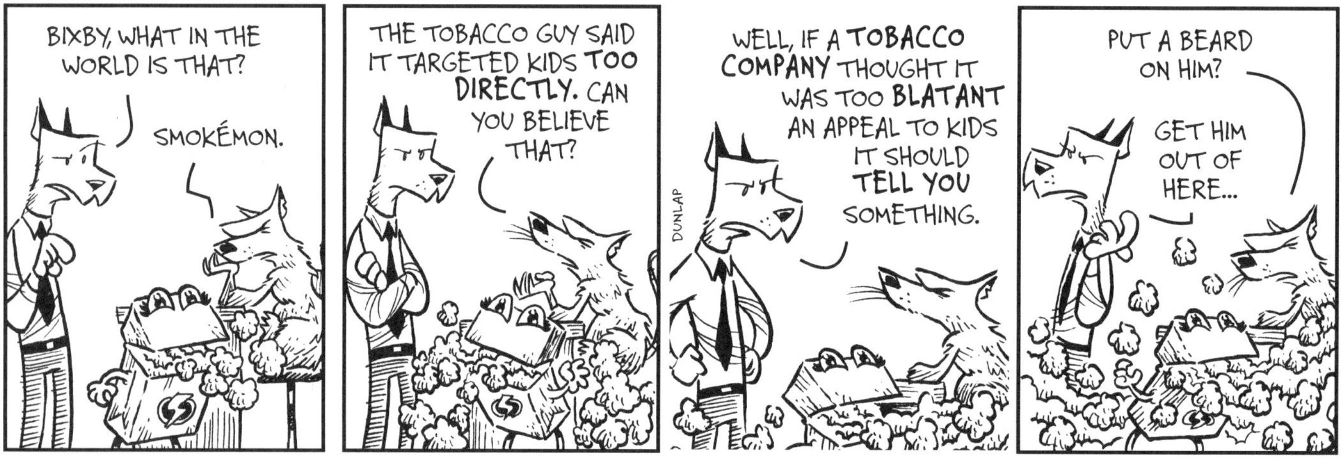
BIXBY, WHAT IN THE WORLD IS THAT?
SMOKÉMON.
THE TOBACCO GUY SAID IT TARGETED KIDS TOO DIRECTLY. CAN YOU BELIEVE THAT?
DUNLAP
WELL, IF A TOBACCO COMPANY THOUGHT IT WAS TOO BLATANT AN APPEAL TO KIDS IT SHOULD TELL YOU SOMETHING.
PUT A BEARD ON HIM?
GET HIM OUT OF HERE...

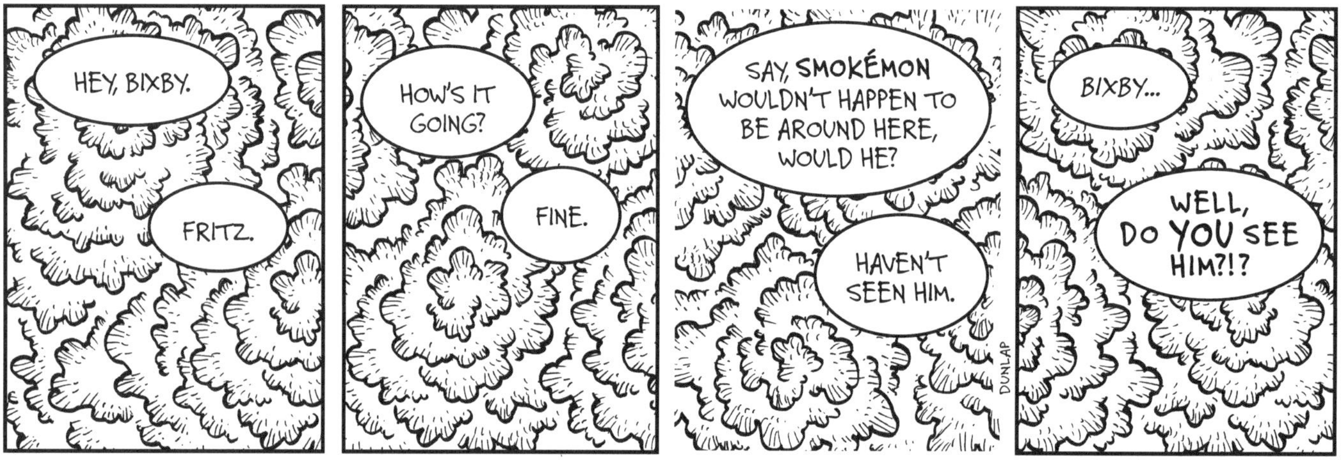
HEY, BIXBY.
FRITZ.
HOW'S IT GOING?
FINE.
SAY, SMOKÉMON WOULDN'T HAPPEN TO BE AROUND HERE, WOULD HE?
HAVEN'T SEEN HIM.
DUNLAP
BIXBY...
WELL, DO YOU SEE HIM?!?

HEY, CAP, HAVE A SEAT. DO YOU PLAY CHESS?
NO.
GOOD. I WANT TO TEST A HYPOTHESIS.
YOU NEVER LOSE AT ANYTHING, RIGHT?
SURE.
BUT YOU HAVE NO IDEA HOW TO PLAY CHESS, AND EVEN IF YOU DID, THERE'S NO WAY YOU COULD POSSIBLY OUTWIT ME.
SO I JUST WANT TO SEE WHAT WILL HAPPEN WHEN YOU FINALLY LOSE AT SOMETHING.
I MEAN, WILL THE WORLD END? WILL TIME STOP? WILL THE FABRIC OF REALITY REND ITSELF APART?
OF COURSE NOT! I JUST WANT TO SHOW THAT YOU CAN LOSE LIKE ANY OTHER-
DUNLAP
HOW DO YOU DO THAT!?
I DON'T KNOW. I WASN'T REALLY PAYING ATTENTION...

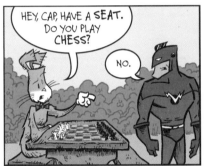

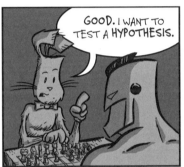

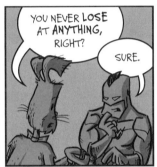

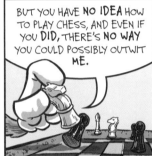

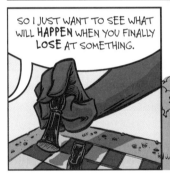

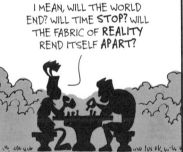

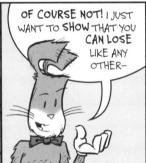

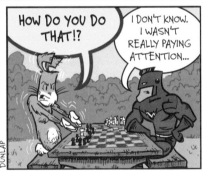

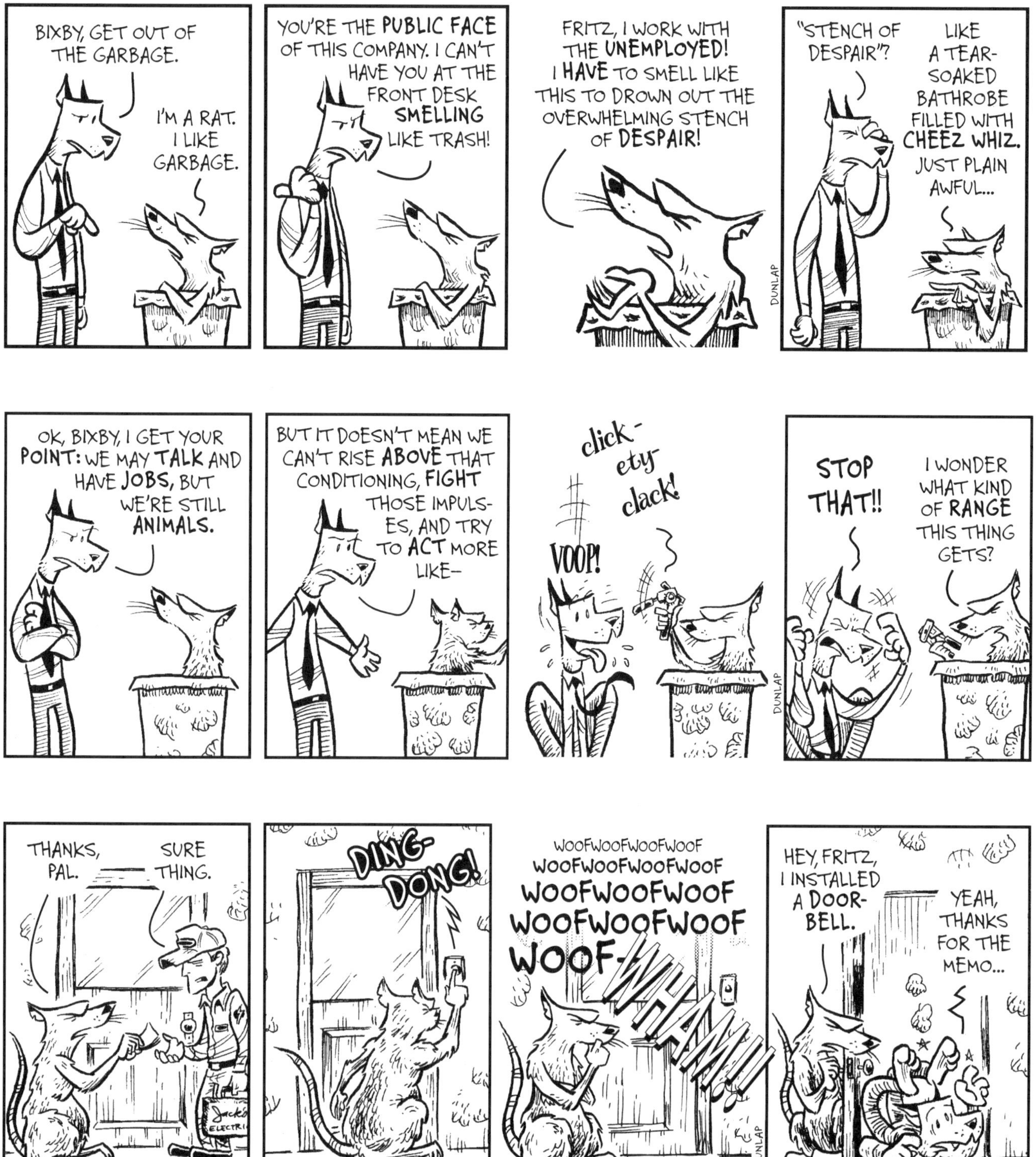
BIXBY, GET OUT OF THE GARBAGE.
I'M A RAT. I LIKE GARBAGE.
YOU'RE THE PUBLIC FACE OF THIS COMPANY. I CAN'T HAVE YOU AT THE FRONT DESK SMELLING LIKE TRASH!
FRITZ, I WORK WITH THE UNEMPLOYED! I HAVE TO SMELL LIKE THIS TO DROWN OUT THE OVERWHELMING STENCH OF DESPAIR!
DUNLAP
"STENCH OF DESPAIR"?
LIKE A TEAR-SOAKED BATHROBE FILLED WITH CHEEZ WHIZ. JUST PLAIN AWFUL...
OK, BIXBY, I GET YOUR POINT: WE MAY TALK AND HAVE JOBS, BUT WE'RE STILL ANIMALS.
BUT IT DOESN'T MEAN WE CAN'T RISE ABOVE THAT CONDITIONING, FIGHT THOSE IMPULSES, AND TRY TO ACT MORE LIKE–
click-ety-clack!
VOOP!
DUNLAP
STOP THAT!!
I WONDER WHAT KIND OF RANGE THIS THING GETS?
THANKS, PAL.
SURE THING.
DING-DONG!
WOOFWOOFWOOFWOOF
WOOFWOOFWOOFWOOF
WOOFWOOFWOOF
WOOFWOOFWOOF
WOOF-
WHAM!!
DUNLAP
HEY, FRITZ, I INSTALLED A DOOR-BELL.
YEAH, THANKS FOR THE MEMO...

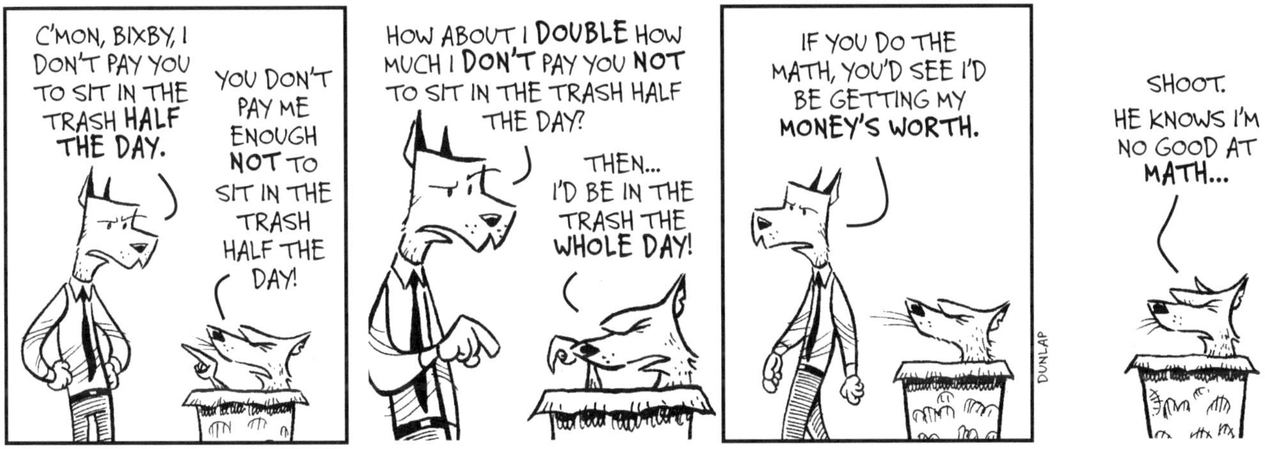
C'MON, BIXBY, I DON'T PAY YOU TO SIT IN THE TRASH HALF THE DAY.
YOU DON'T PAY ME ENOUGH NOT TO SIT IN THE TRASH HALF THE DAY!
HOW ABOUT I DOUBLE HOW MUCH I DON'T PAY YOU NOT TO SIT IN THE TRASH HALF THE DAY?
THEN... I'D BE IN THE TRASH THE WHOLE DAY!
IF YOU DO THE MATH, YOU'D SEE I'D BE GETTING MY MONEY'S WORTH.
DUNLAP
SHOOT.
HE KNOWS I'M NO GOOD AT MATH...

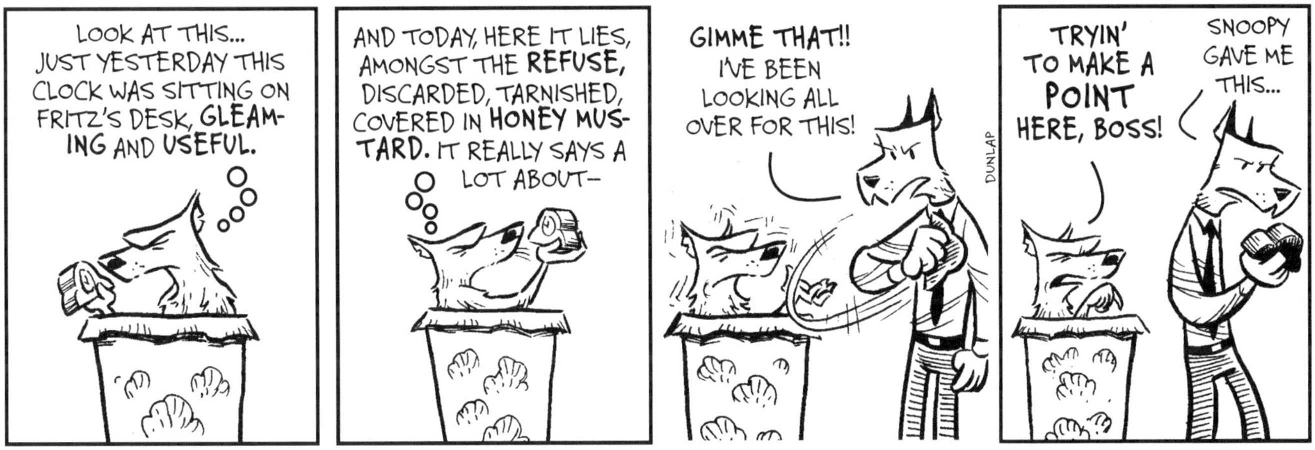
LOOK AT THIS... JUST YESTERDAY THIS CLOCK WAS SITTING ON FRITZ'S DESK, GLEAMING AND USEFUL.
AND TODAY, HERE IT LIES, AMONGST THE REFUSE, DISCARDED, TARNISHED, COVERED IN HONEY MUSTARD. IT REALLY SAYS A LOT ABOUT—
GIMME THAT!! I'VE BEEN LOOKING ALL OVER FOR THIS!
DUNLAP
TRYIN' TO MAKE A POINT HERE, BOSS!
SNOOPY GAVE ME THIS...

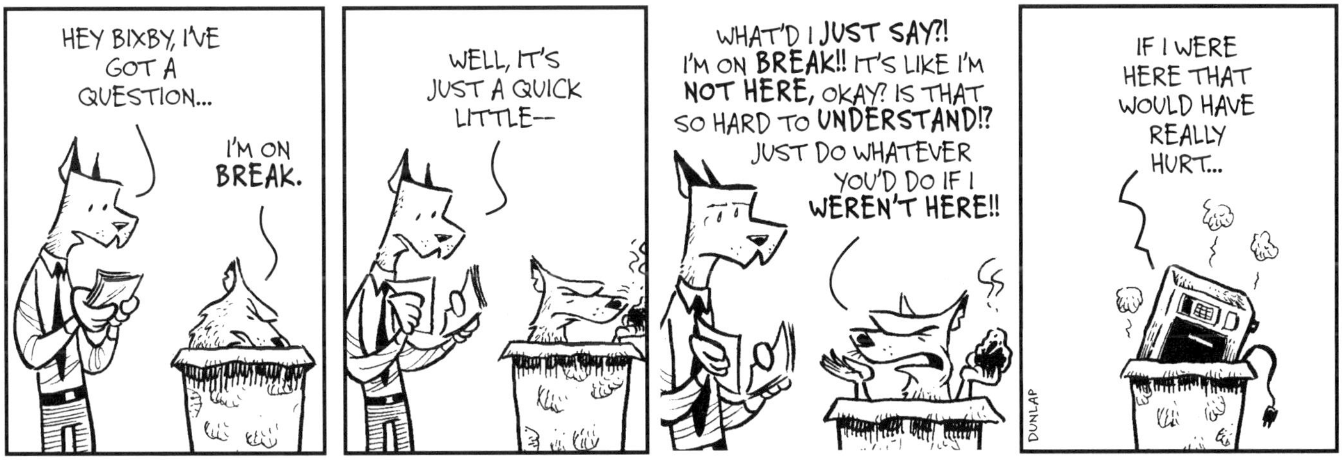
HEY BIXBY, I'VE GOT A QUESTION...
I'M ON BREAK.
WELL, IT'S JUST A QUICK LITTLE—
WHAT'D I JUST SAY?! I'M ON BREAK!! IT'S LIKE I'M NOT HERE, OKAY? IS THAT SO HARD TO UNDERSTAND!? JUST DO WHATEVER YOU'D DO IF I WEREN'T HERE!!
DUNLAP
IF I WERE HERE THAT WOULD HAVE REALLY HURT...

GET FIT WITH
KICK-FU!
ONE-ON-ONE SESSIONS!
ONLY $50/hr.
WHAT THE--?
"KICK-FU"? BIXBY, IS THIS ANOTHER ONE OF YOUR CHEAP SCHEMES TO FLEECE THE MASSES?
NO, NO, FRITZ, YOU GOT IT ALL WRONG!
THIS IS A PHYSICALLY EXERTING AND DEMANDING WAY FOR PEOPLE TO LOSE WEIGHT! I EVEN GOT RALSTON RABBIT INVOLVED, SO YOU KNOW IT'S ON THE LEVEL!
INK PEN
REALLY? WHAT KIND OF A WORKOUT IS IT?
WELL, THERE'S A LOT OF KICKING...
STOP EATING.
PUNT!
DUNLAP

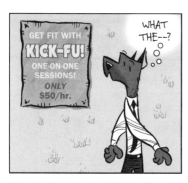

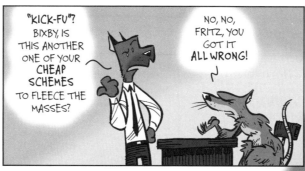

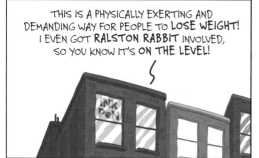

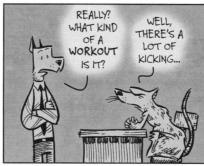

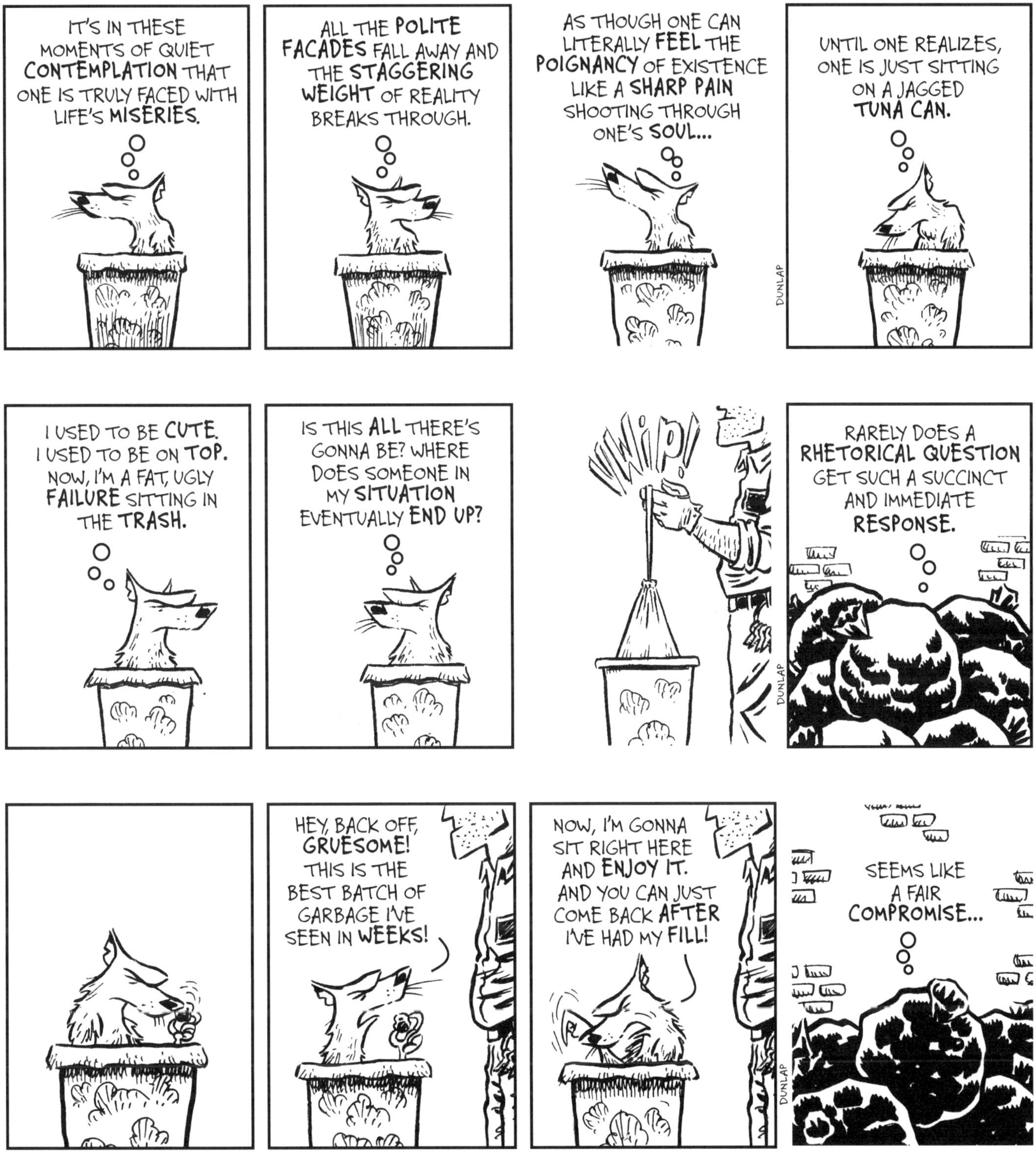
IT'S IN THESE MOMENTS OF QUIET CONTEMPLATION THAT ONE IS TRULY FACED WITH LIFE'S MISERIES.
ALL THE POLITE FACADES FALL AWAY AND THE STAGGERING WEIGHT OF REALITY BREAKS THROUGH.
AS THOUGH ONE CAN LITERALLY FEEL THE POIGNANCY OF EXISTENCE LIKE A SHARP PAIN SHOOTING THROUGH ONE'S SOUL...
DUNLAP
UNTIL ONE REALIZES, ONE IS JUST SITTING ON A JAGGED TUNA CAN.
I USED TO BE CUTE. I USED TO BE ON TOP. NOW, I'M A FAT, UGLY FAILURE SITTING IN THE TRASH.
IS THIS ALL THERE'S GONNA BE? WHERE DOES SOMEONE IN MY SITUATION EVENTUALLY END UP?
WIP!
DUNLAP
RARELY DOES A RHETORICAL QUESTION GET SUCH A SUCCINCT AND IMMEDIATE RESPONSE.
HEY, BACK OFF, GRUESOME! THIS IS THE BEST BATCH OF GARBAGE I'VE SEEN IN WEEKS!
NOW, I'M GONNA SIT RIGHT HERE AND ENJOY IT. AND YOU CAN JUST COME BACK AFTER I'VE HAD MY FILL!
DUNLAP
SEEMS LIKE A FAIR COMPROMISE...

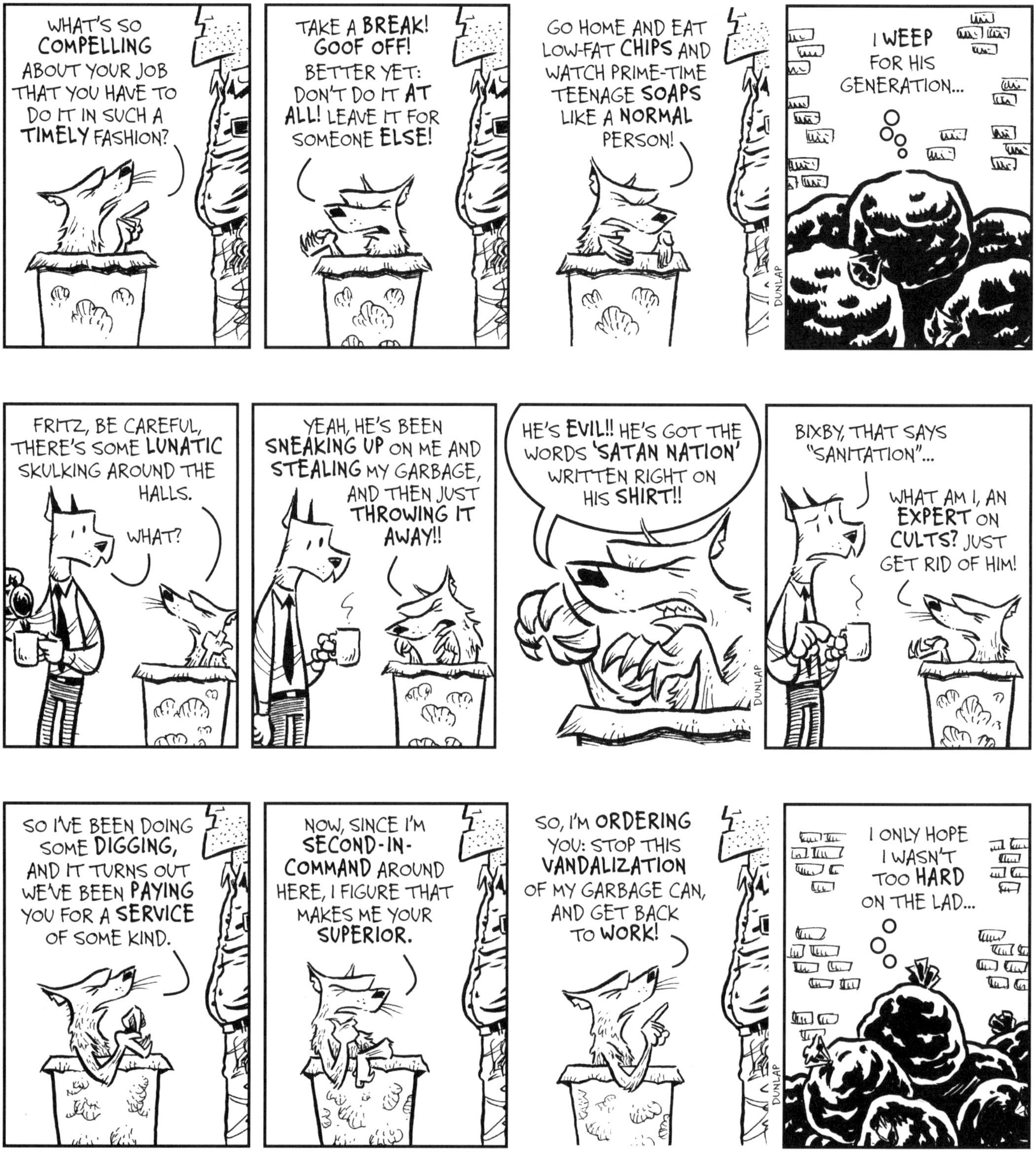
WHAT'S SO COMPELLING ABOUT YOUR JOB THAT YOU HAVE TO DO IT IN SUCH A TIMELY FASHION?
TAKE A BREAK! GOOF OFF! BETTER YET: DON'T DO IT AT ALL! LEAVE IT FOR SOMEONE ELSE!
GO HOME AND EAT LOW-FAT CHIPS AND WATCH PRIME-TIME TEENAGE SOAPS LIKE A NORMAL PERSON!
DUNLAP
I WEEP FOR HIS GENERATION...
FRITZ, BE CAREFUL, THERE'S SOME LUNATIC SKULKING AROUND THE HALLS.
WHAT?
YEAH, HE'S BEEN SNEAKING UP ON ME AND STEALING MY GARBAGE, AND THEN JUST THROWING IT AWAY!!
HE'S EVIL!! HE'S GOT THE WORDS 'SATAN NATION' WRITTEN RIGHT ON HIS SHIRT!!
DUNLAP
BIXBY, THAT SAYS "SANITATION"...
WHAT AM I, AN EXPERT ON CULTS? JUST GET RID OF HIM!
SO I'VE BEEN DOING SOME DIGGING, AND IT TURNS OUT WE'VE BEEN PAYING YOU FOR A SERVICE OF SOME KIND.
NOW, SINCE I'M SECOND-IN-COMMAND AROUND HERE, I FIGURE THAT MAKES ME YOUR SUPERIOR.
SO, I'M ORDERING YOU: STOP THIS VANDALIZATION OF MY GARBAGE CAN, AND GET BACK TO WORK!
DUNLAP
I ONLY HOPE I WASN'T TOO HARD ON THE LAD...

HAHAHAHAHAHAHAHA
NNNOOOOOO!
AAAAAAAA!!
HEY, CAP, YOUR SHOES ARE UNTIED!
YEAH, LIKE I'D EVER FALL FOR THAT ONE!
DUNLAP

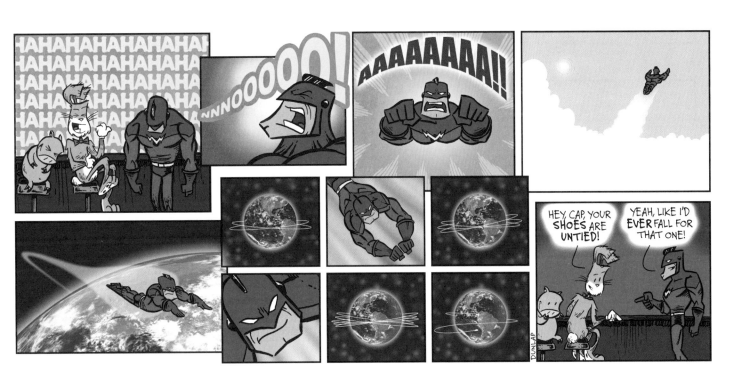

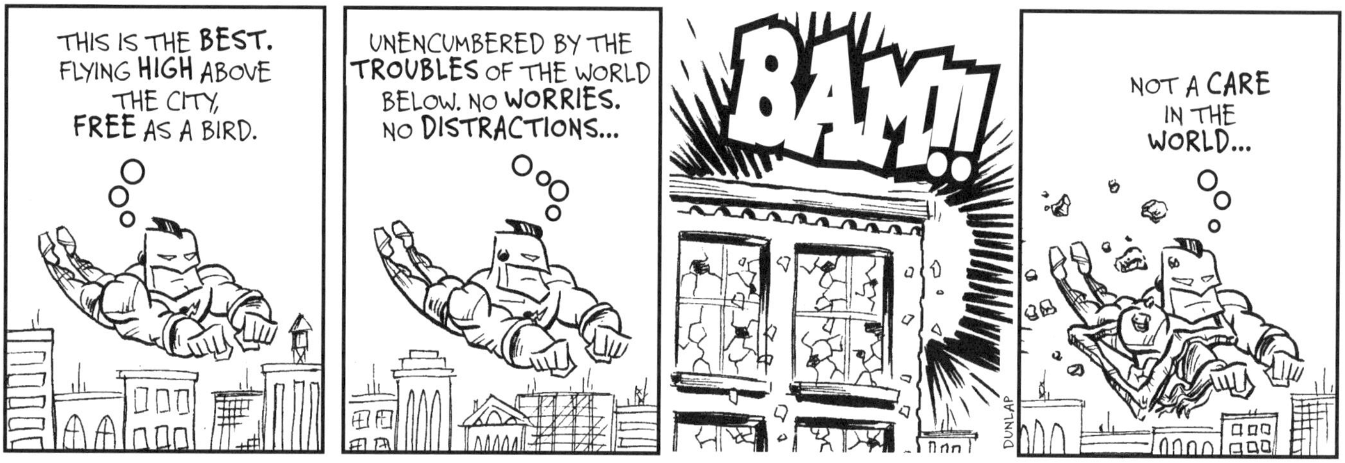
THIS IS THE BEST. FLYING HIGH ABOVE THE CITY, FREE AS A BIRD.
UNENCUMBERED BY THE TROUBLES OF THE WORLD BELOW. NO WORRIES. NO DISTRACTIONS...
BAM!!
NOT A CARE IN THE WORLD...
DUNLAP

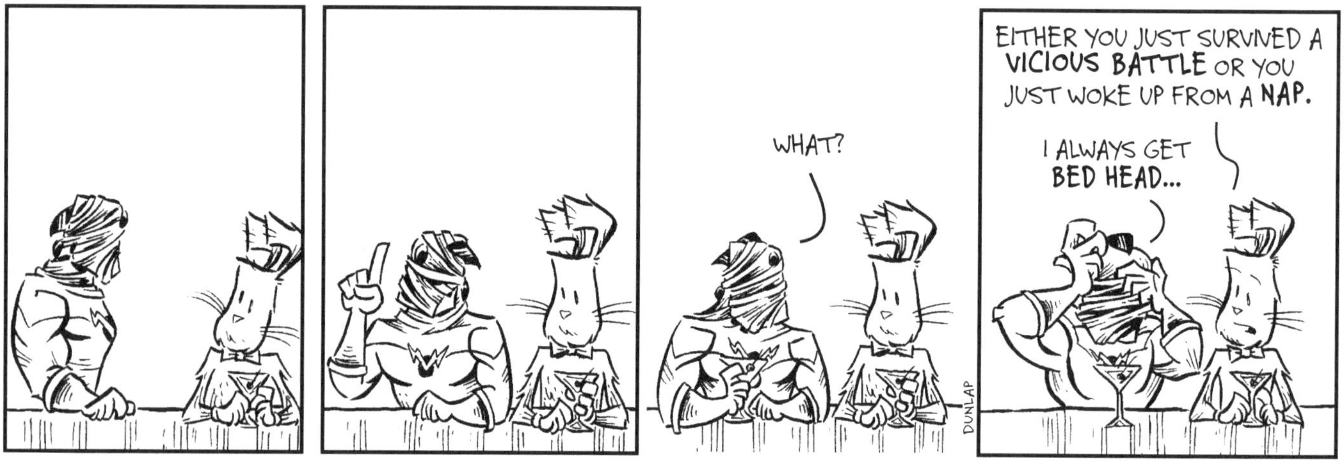
WHAT?
EITHER YOU JUST SURVIVED A VICIOUS BATTLE OR YOU JUST WOKE UP FROM A NAP.
I ALWAYS GET BED HEAD...
DUNLAP

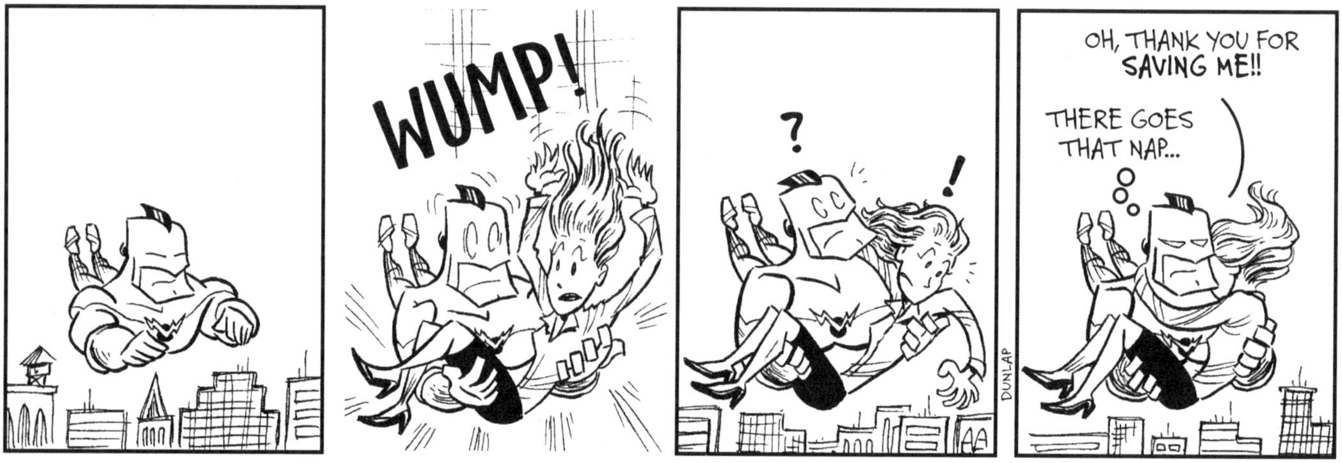
WUMP!
?
!
OH, THANK YOU FOR SAVING ME!!
THERE GOES THAT NAP...
DUNLAP

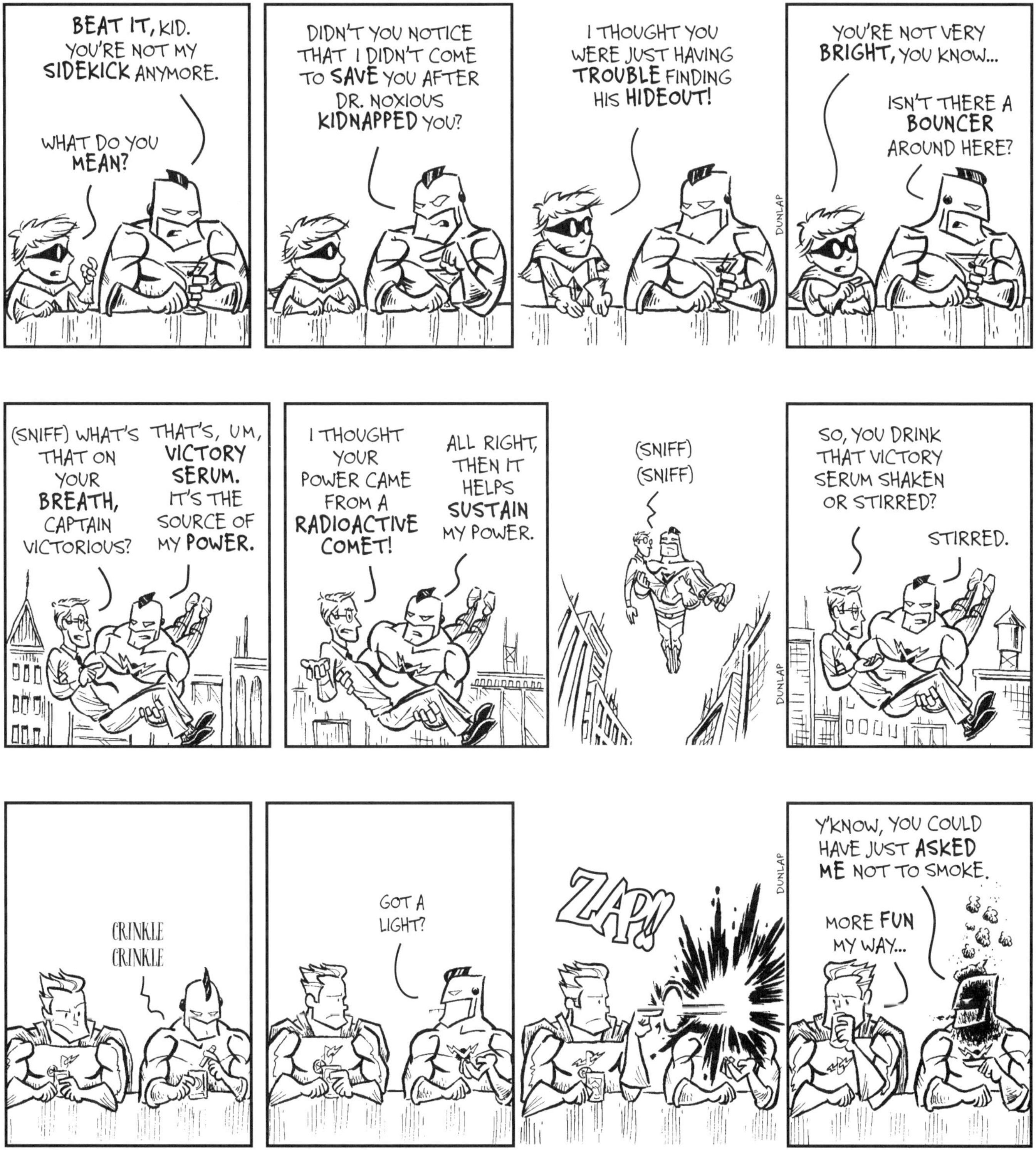
WHAT DO YOU MEAN?
BEAT IT, KID. YOU'RE NOT MY SIDEKICK ANYMORE.
DIDN'T YOU NOTICE THAT I DIDN'T COME TO SAVE YOU AFTER DR. NOXIOUS KIDNAPPED YOU?
I THOUGHT YOU WERE JUST HAVING TROUBLE FINDING HIS HIDEOUT!
DUNLAP
YOU'RE NOT VERY BRIGHT, YOU KNOW...
ISN'T THERE A BOUNCER AROUND HERE?
(SNIFF) WHAT'S THAT ON YOUR BREATH, CAPTAIN VICTORIOUS?
THAT'S, UM, VICTORY SERUM. IT'S THE SOURCE OF MY POWER.
I THOUGHT YOUR POWER CAME FROM A RADIOACTIVE COMET!
ALL RIGHT, THEN IT HELPS SUSTAIN MY POWER.
(SNIFF) (SNIFF)
DUNLAP
SO, YOU DRINK THAT VICTORY SERUM SHAKEN OR STIRRED?
STIRRED.
CRINKLE CRINKLE
GOT A LIGHT?
ZAP!!
DUNLAP
Y'KNOW, YOU COULD HAVE JUST ASKED ME NOT TO SMOKE.
MORE FUN MY WAY...

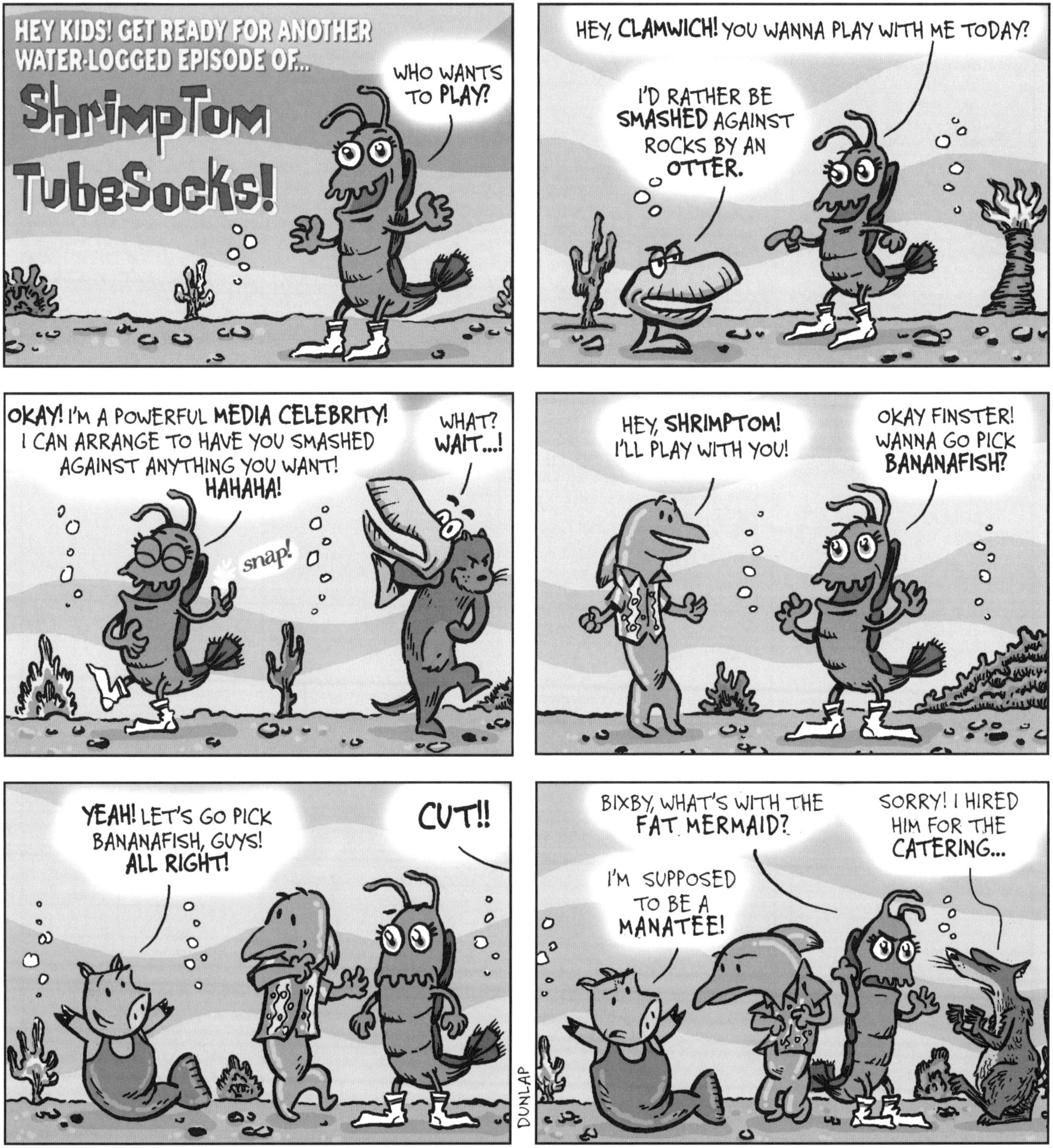
HEY KIDS! GET READY FOR ANOTHER WATER-LOGGED EPISODE OF...
ShrimpTom TubeSocks!
WHO WANTS TO PLAY?
HEY, CLAMWICH! YOU WANNA PLAY WITH ME TODAY?
I'D RATHER BE SMASHED AGAINST ROCKS BY AN OTTER.
OKAY! I'M A POWERFUL MEDIA CELEBRITY! I CAN ARRANGE TO HAVE YOU SMASHED AGAINST ANYTHING YOU WANT! HAHAHA!
snap!
WHAT? WAIT...!
HEY, SHRIMPTOM! I'LL PLAY WITH YOU!
OKAY FINSTER! WANNA GO PICK BANANAFISH?
YEAH! LET'S GO PICK BANANAFISH, GUYS! ALL RIGHT!
CUT!!
DUNLAP
BIXBY, WHAT'S WITH THE FAT MERMAID?
I'M SUPPOSED TO BE A MANATEE!
SORRY! I HIRED HIM FOR THE CATERING...

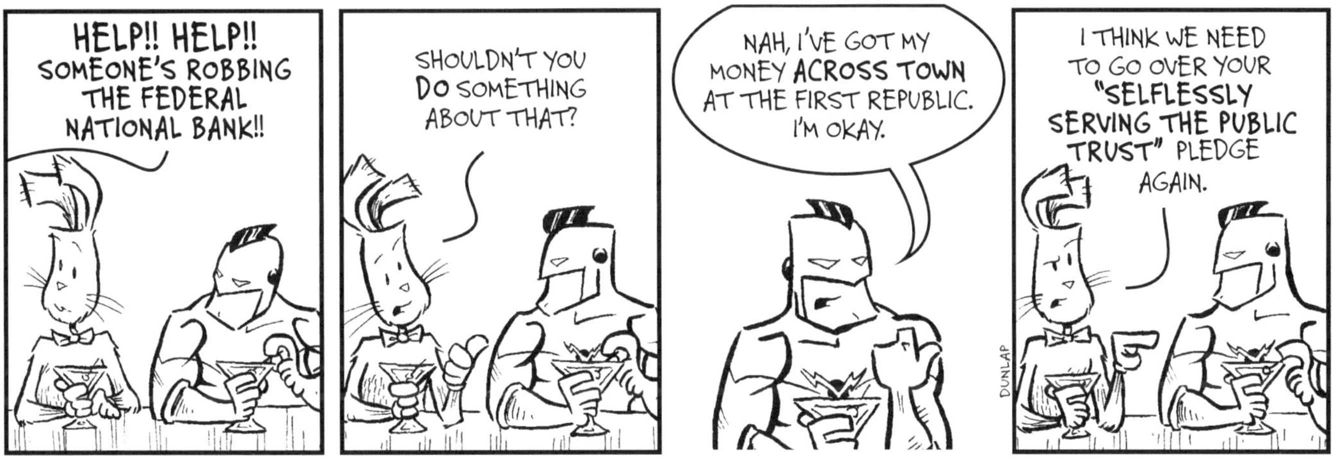
HELP!! HELP!! SOMEONE'S ROBBING THE FEDERAL NATIONAL BANK!!
SHOULDN'T YOU DO SOMETHING ABOUT THAT?
NAH, I'VE GOT MY MONEY ACROSS TOWN AT THE FIRST REPUBLIC. I'M OKAY.
I THINK WE NEED TO GO OVER YOUR "SELFLESSLY SERVING THE PUBLIC TRUST" PLEDGE AGAIN.
DUNLAP

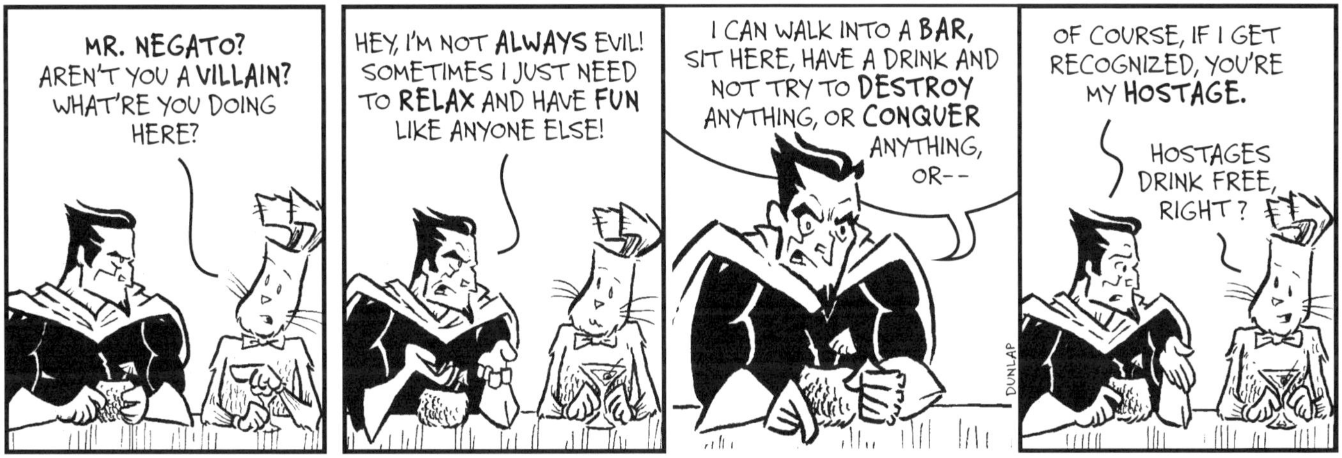
MR. NEGATO? AREN'T YOU A VILLAIN? WHAT'RE YOU DOING HERE?
HEY, I'M NOT ALWAYS EVIL! SOMETIMES I JUST NEED TO RELAX AND HAVE FUN LIKE ANYONE ELSE!
I CAN WALK INTO A BAR, SIT HERE, HAVE A DRINK AND NOT TRY TO DESTROY ANYTHING, OR CONQUER ANYTHING, OR--
OF COURSE, IF I GET RECOGNIZED, YOU'RE MY HOSTAGE.
HOSTAGES DRINK FREE, RIGHT?
DUNLAP

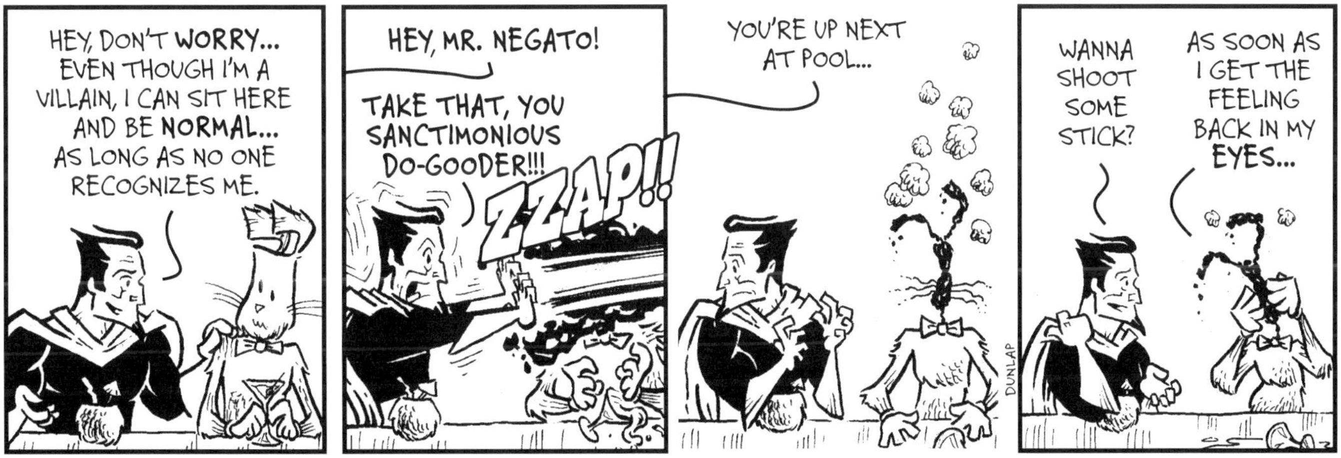
HEY, DON'T WORRY... EVEN THOUGH I'M A VILLAIN, I CAN SIT HERE AND BE NORMAL... AS LONG AS NO ONE RECOGNIZES ME.
HEY, MR. NEGATO!
TAKE THAT, YOU SANCTIMONIOUS DO-GOODER!!!
ZZAP!!
YOU'RE UP NEXT AT POOL...
WANNA SHOOT SOME STICK?
AS SOON AS I GET THE FEELING BACK IN MY EYES...
DUNLAP

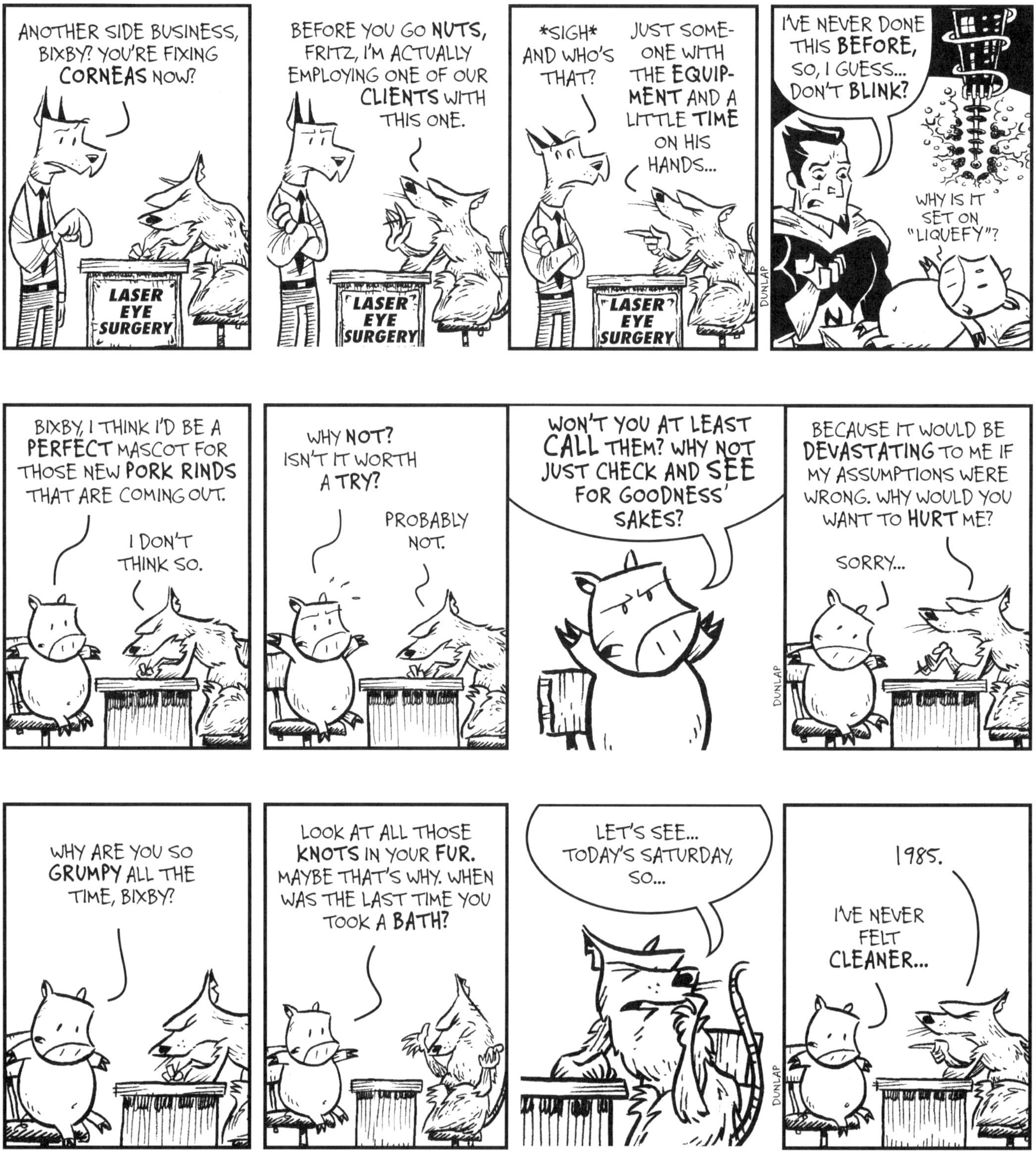
ANOTHER SIDE BUSINESS, BIXBY? YOU'RE FIXING CORNEAS NOW?
LASER EYE SURGERY
BEFORE YOU GO NUTS, FRITZ, I'M ACTUALLY EMPLOYING ONE OF OUR CLIENTS WITH THIS ONE.
LASER EYE SURGERY
*SIGH* AND WHO'S THAT?
JUST SOMEONE WITH THE EQUIPMENT AND A LITTLE TIME ON HIS HANDS...
LASER EYE SURGERY
DUNLAP
I'VE NEVER DONE THIS BEFORE, SO, I GUESS... DON'T BLINK?
WHY IS IT SET ON "LIQUEFY"?
BIXBY, I THINK I'D BE A PERFECT MASCOT FOR THOSE NEW PORK RINDS THAT ARE COMING OUT.
I DON'T THINK SO.
WHY NOT? ISN'T IT WORTH A TRY?
PROBABLY NOT.
WON'T YOU AT LEAST CALL THEM? WHY NOT JUST CHECK AND SEE FOR GOODNESS' SAKES?
DUNLAP
BECAUSE IT WOULD BE DEVASTATING TO ME IF MY ASSUMPTIONS WERE WRONG. WHY WOULD YOU WANT TO HURT ME?
SORRY...
WHY ARE YOU SO GRUMPY ALL THE TIME, BIXBY?
LOOK AT ALL THOSE KNOTS IN YOUR FUR. MAYBE THAT'S WHY. WHEN WAS THE LAST TIME YOU TOOK A BATH?
LET'S SEE... TODAY'S SATURDAY, SO...
DUNLAP
1985.
I'VE NEVER FELT CLEANER...

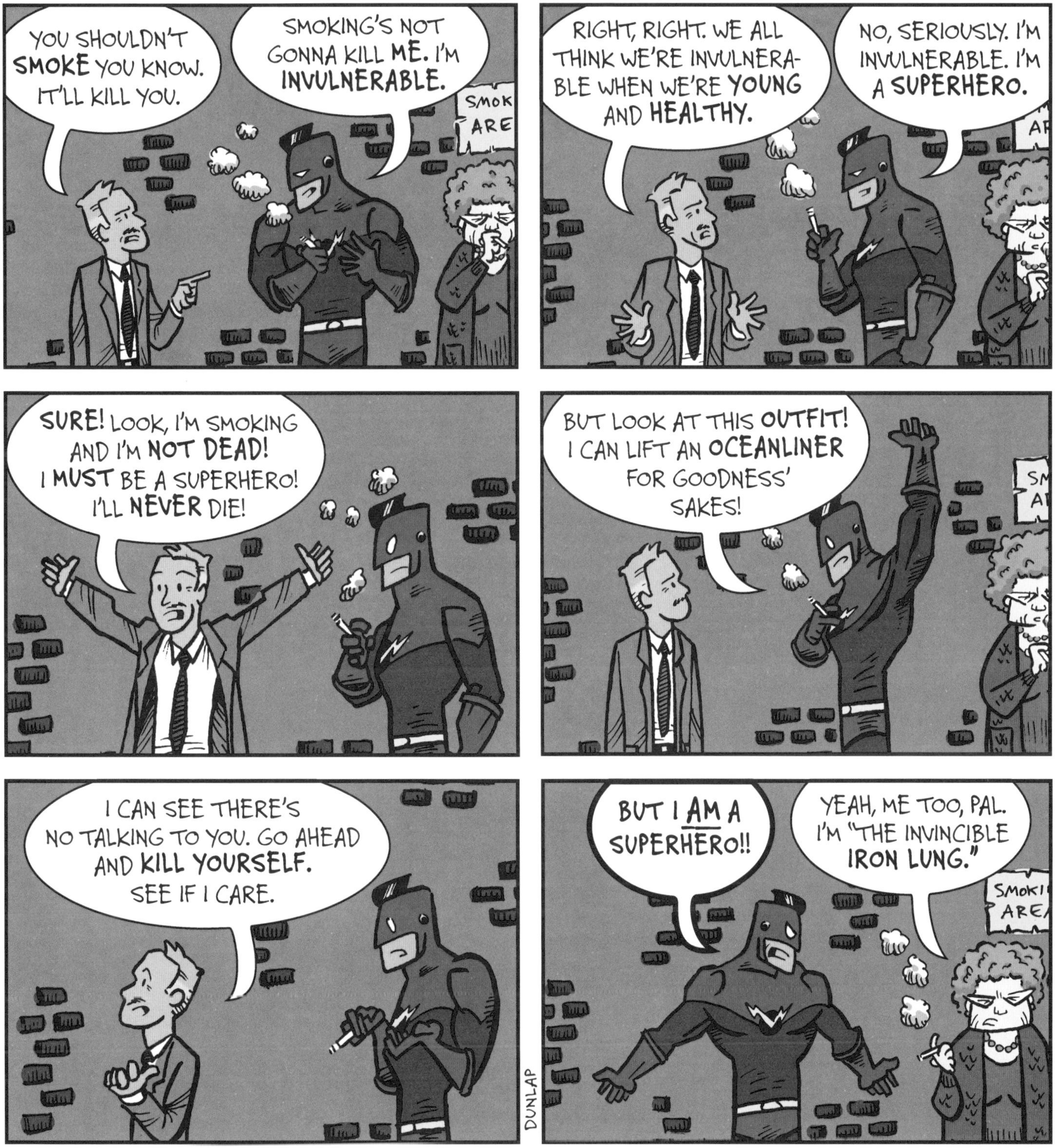
YOU SHOULDN'T SMOKE YOU KNOW. IT'LL KILL YOU.
SMOKING'S NOT GONNA KILL ME. I'M INVULNERABLE.
SMOK ARE
RIGHT, RIGHT. WE ALL THINK WE'RE INVULNERA-BLE WHEN WE'RE YOUNG AND HEALTHY.
NO, SERIOUSLY. I'M INVULNERABLE. I'M A SUPERHERO.
SURE! LOOK, I'M SMOKING AND I'M NOT DEAD! I MUST BE A SUPERHERO! I'LL NEVER DIE!
BUT LOOK AT THIS OUTFIT! I CAN LIFT AN OCEANLINER FOR GOODNESS' SAKES!
I CAN SEE THERE'S NO TALKING TO YOU. GO AHEAD AND KILL YOURSELF. SEE IF I CARE.
DUNLAP
BUT I AM A SUPERHERO!!
YEAH, ME TOO, PAL. I'M "THE INVINCIBLE IRON LUNG."
SMOKI AREA

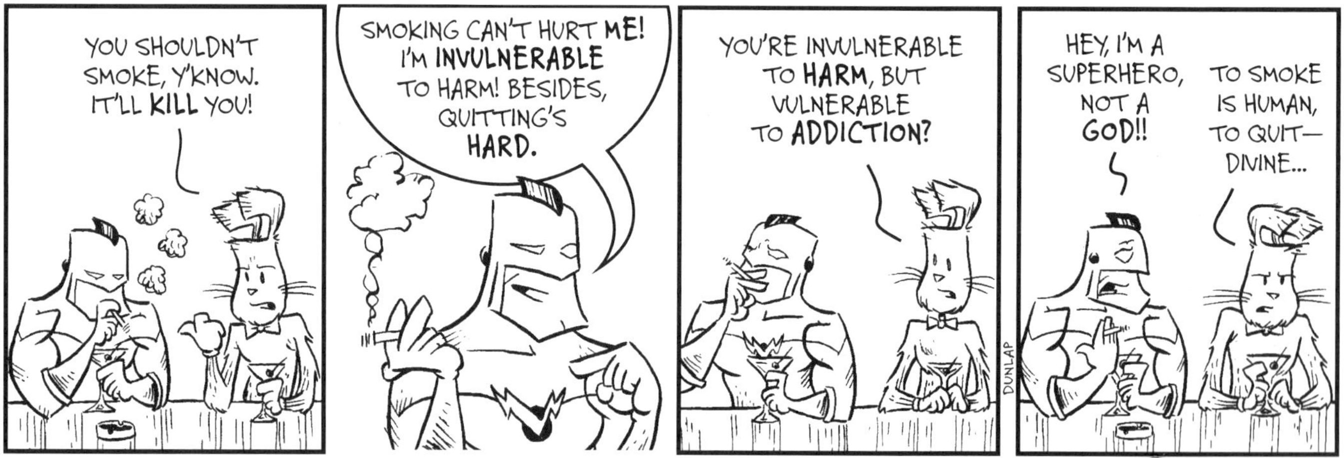
YOU SHOULDN'T SMOKE, Y'KNOW. IT'LL KILL YOU!
SMOKING CAN'T HURT ME! I'M INVULNERABLE TO HARM! BESIDES, QUITTING'S HARD.
YOU'RE INVULNERABLE TO HARM, BUT VULNERABLE TO ADDICTION?
HEY, I'M A SUPERHERO, NOT A GOD!!
TO SMOKE IS HUMAN, TO QUIT— DIVINE...
DUNLAP

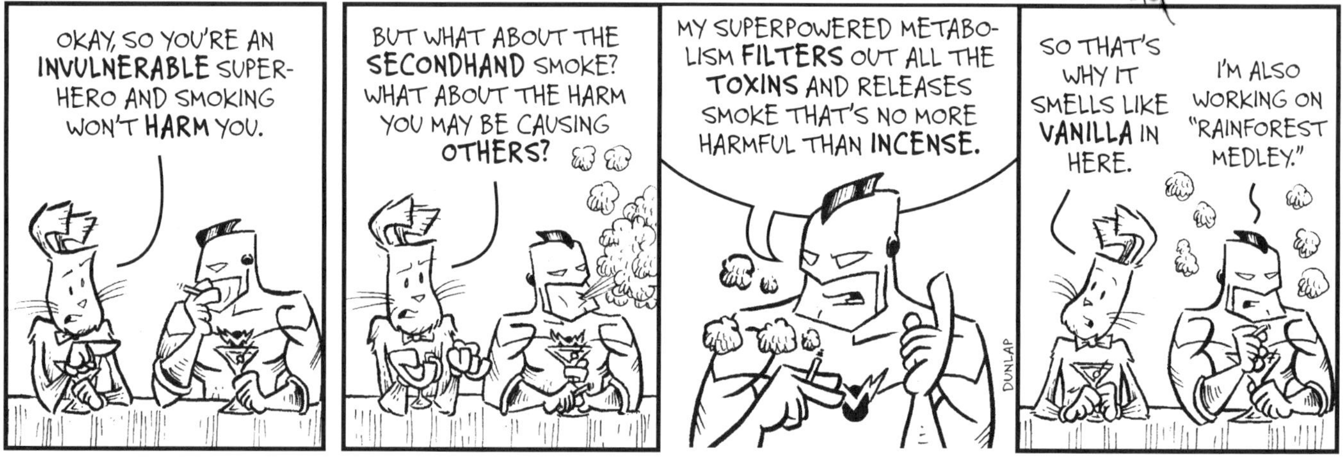
OKAY, SO YOU'RE AN INVULNERABLE SUPER-HERO AND SMOKING WON'T HARM YOU.
BUT WHAT ABOUT THE SECONDHAND SMOKE? WHAT ABOUT THE HARM YOU MAY BE CAUSING OTHERS?
MY SUPERPOWERED METABO-LISM FILTERS OUT ALL THE TOXINS AND RELEASES SMOKE THAT'S NO MORE HARMFUL THAN INCENSE.
SO THAT'S WHY IT SMELLS LIKE VANILLA IN HERE.
I'M ALSO WORKING ON "RAINFOREST MEDLEY."
DUNLAP

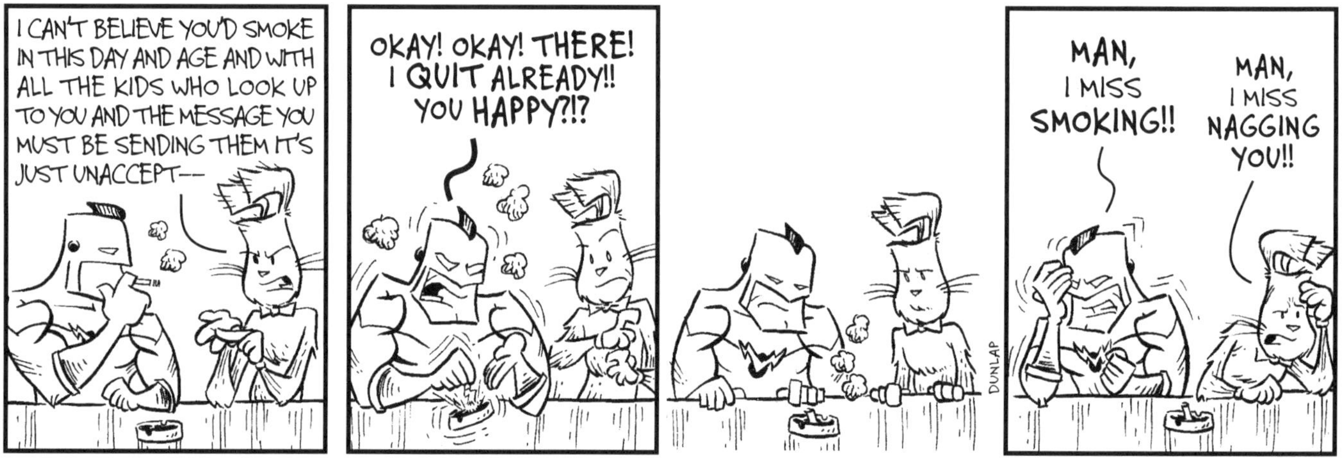
I CAN'T BELIEVE YOU'D SMOKE IN THIS DAY AND AGE AND WITH ALL THE KIDS WHO LOOK UP TO YOU AND THE MESSAGE YOU MUST BE SENDING THEM IT'S JUST UNACCEPT--
OKAY! OKAY! THERE! I QUIT ALREADY!! YOU HAPPY?!?
MAN, I MISS SMOKING!!
MAN, I MISS NAGGING YOU!!
DUNLAP

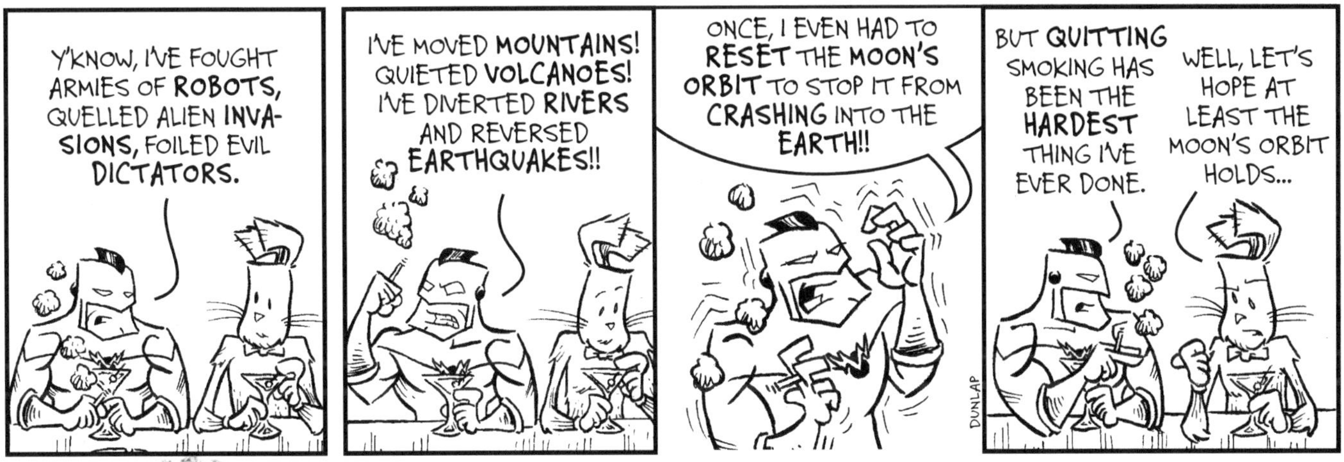
Y'KNOW, I'VE FOUGHT ARMIES OF ROBOTS, QUELLED ALIEN INVASIONS, FOILED EVIL DICTATORS.
I'VE MOVED MOUNTAINS! QUIETED VOLCANOES! I'VE DIVERTED RIVERS AND REVERSED EARTHQUAKES!!
ONCE, I EVEN HAD TO RESET THE MOON'S ORBIT TO STOP IT FROM CRASHING INTO THE EARTH!!
BUT QUITTING SMOKING HAS BEEN THE HARDEST THING I'VE EVER DONE.
WELL, LET'S HOPE AT LEAST THE MOON'S ORBIT HOLDS...
DUNLAP

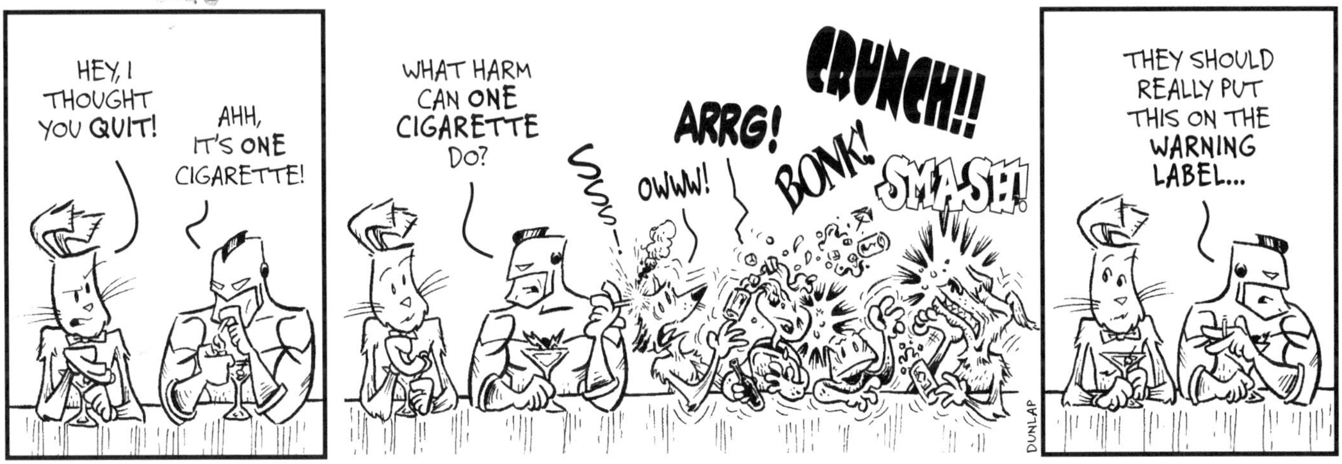
HEY, I THOUGHT YOU QUIT!
AHH, IT'S ONE CIGARETTE!
WHAT HARM CAN ONE CIGARETTE DO?
OWWW!
ARRG!
CRUNCH!!
BONK!
SMASH!
THEY SHOULD REALLY PUT THIS ON THE WARNING LABEL...
DUNLAP

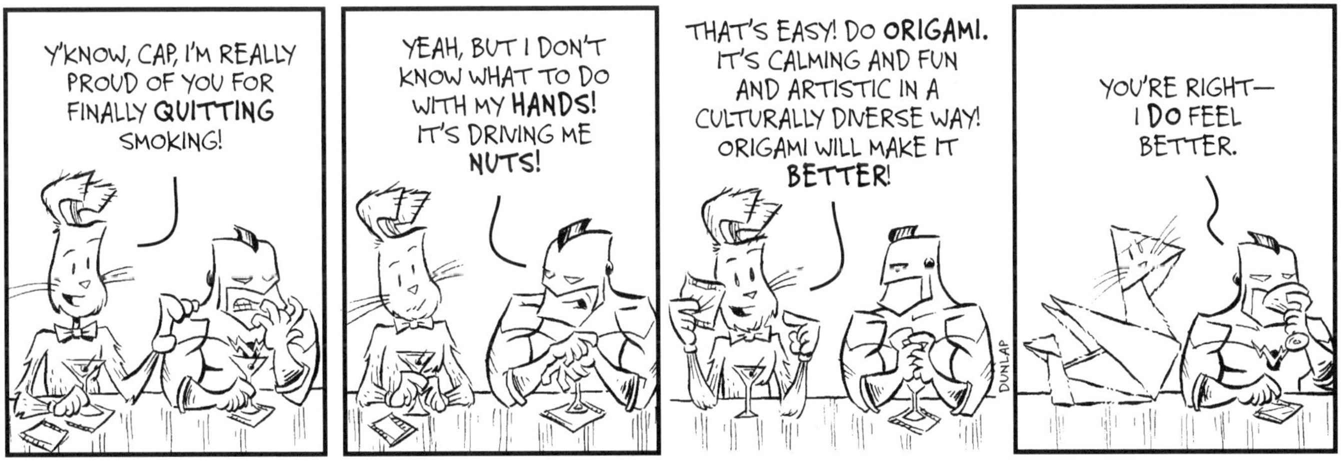
Y'KNOW, CAP, I'M REALLY PROUD OF YOU FOR FINALLY QUITTING SMOKING!
YEAH, BUT I DON'T KNOW WHAT TO DO WITH MY HANDS! IT'S DRIVING ME NUTS!
THAT'S EASY! DO ORIGAMI. IT'S CALMING AND FUN AND ARTISTIC IN A CULTURALLY DIVERSE WAY! ORIGAMI WILL MAKE IT BETTER!
YOU'RE RIGHT— I DO FEEL BETTER.
DUNLAP

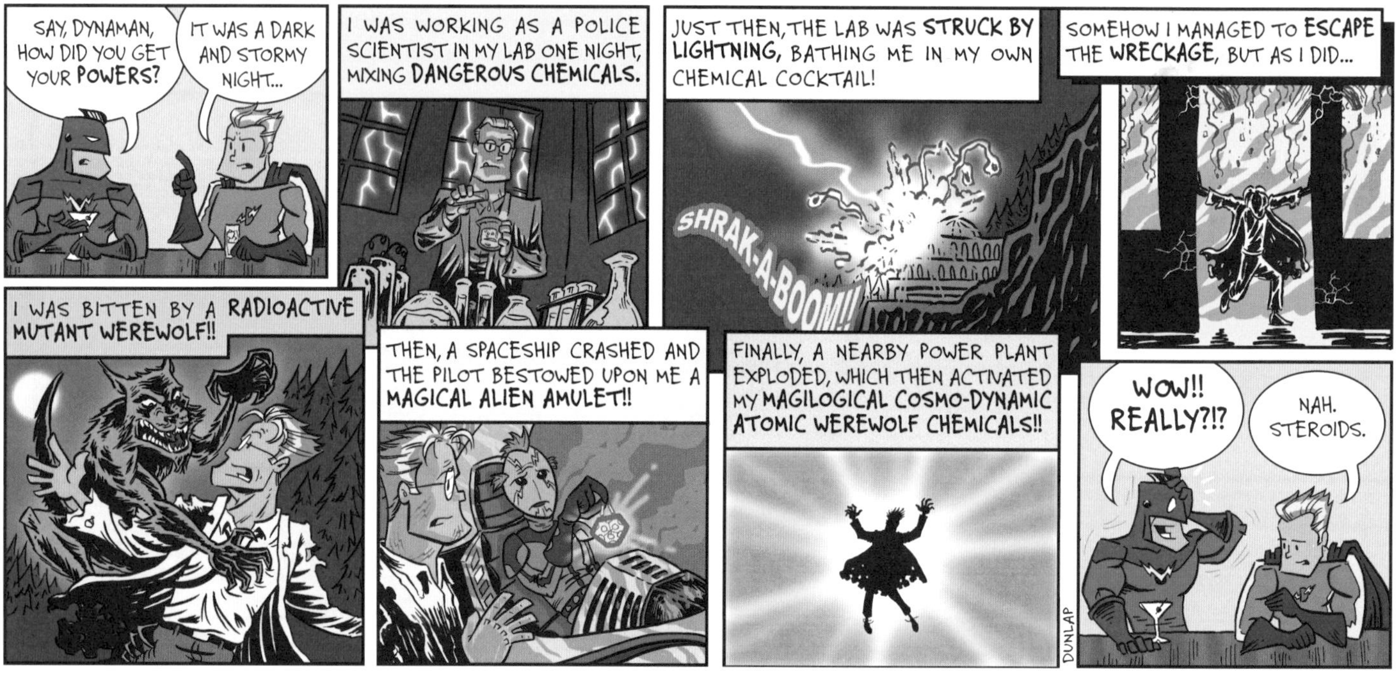
SAY, DYNAMAN, HOW DID YOU GET YOUR POWERS?
IT WAS A DARK AND STORMY NIGHT...
I WAS WORKING AS A POLICE SCIENTIST IN MY LAB ONE NIGHT, MIXING DANGEROUS CHEMICALS.
JUST THEN, THE LAB WAS STRUCK BY LIGHTNING, BATHING ME IN MY OWN CHEMICAL COCKTAIL!
SHRAK-A-BOOM!!
SOMEHOW I MANAGED TO ESCAPE THE WRECKAGE, BUT AS I DID...
I WAS BITTEN BY A RADIOACTIVE MUTANT WEREWOLF!!
THEN, A SPACESHIP CRASHED AND THE PILOT BESTOWED UPON ME A MAGICAL ALIEN AMULET!!
FINALLY, A NEARBY POWER PLANT EXPLODED, WHICH THEN ACTIVATED MY MAGILOGICAL COSMO-DYNAMIC ATOMIC WEREWOLF CHEMICALS!!
DUNLAP
WOW!! REALLY?!?
NAH. STEROIDS.

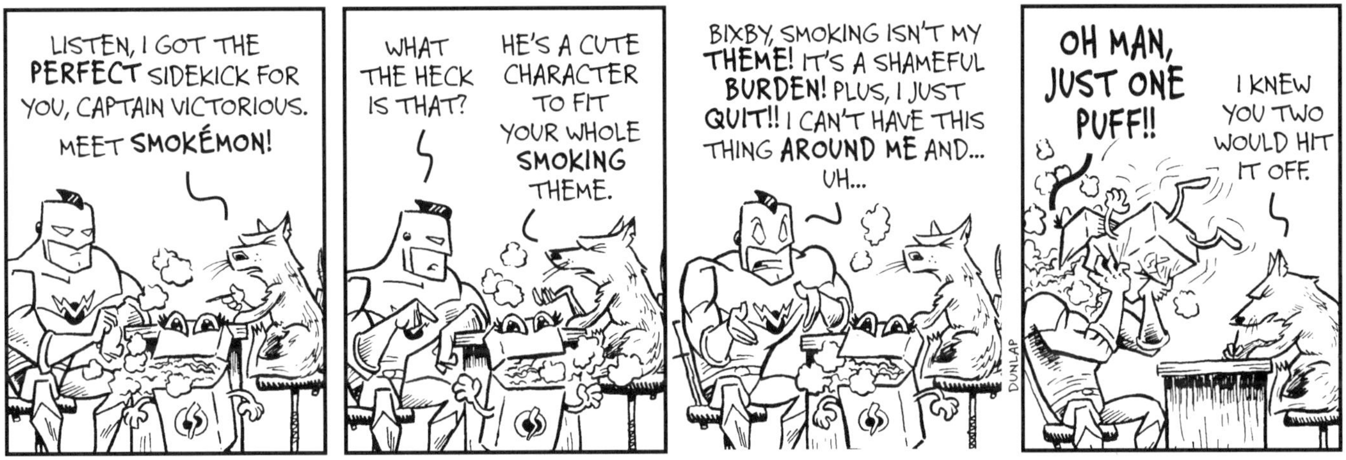
LISTEN, I GOT THE PERFECT SIDEKICK FOR YOU, CAPTAIN VICTORIOUS. MEET SMOKÉMON!
WHAT THE HECK IS THAT?
HE'S A CUTE CHARACTER TO FIT YOUR WHOLE SMOKING THEME.
BIXBY, SMOKING ISN'T MY THEME! IT'S A SHAMEFUL BURDEN! PLUS, I JUST QUIT!! I CAN'T HAVE THIS THING AROUND ME AND... UH...
DUNLAP
OH MAN, JUST ONE PUFF!!
I KNEW YOU TWO WOULD HIT IT OFF.

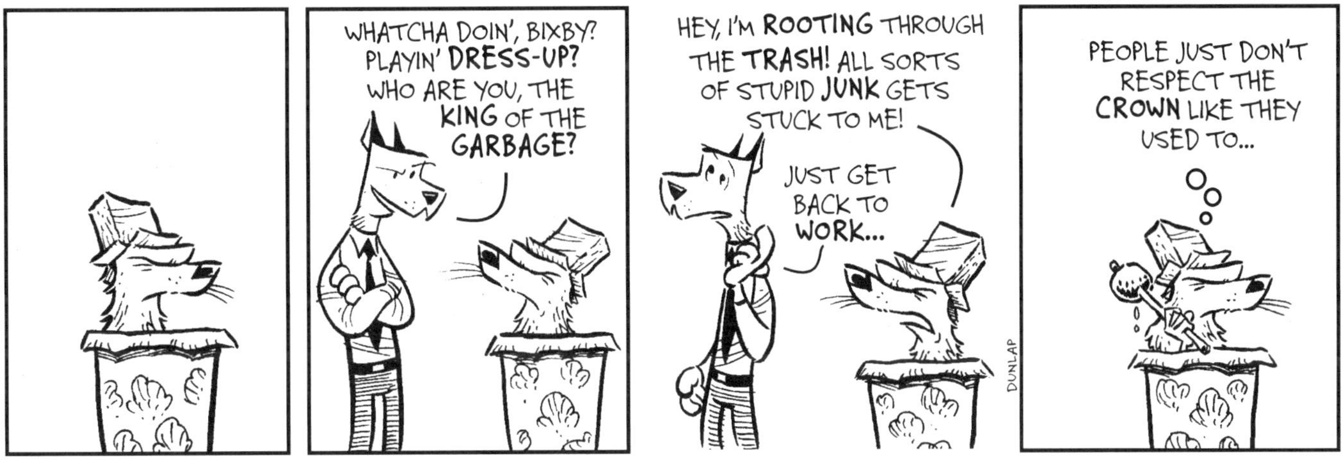
WHATCHA DOIN', BIXBY? PLAYIN' DRESS-UP? WHO ARE YOU, THE KING OF THE GARBAGE?
HEY, I'M ROOTING THROUGH THE TRASH! ALL SORTS OF STUPID JUNK GETS STUCK TO ME!
JUST GET BACK TO WORK...
DUNLAP
PEOPLE JUST DON'T RESPECT THE CROWN LIKE THEY USED TO...

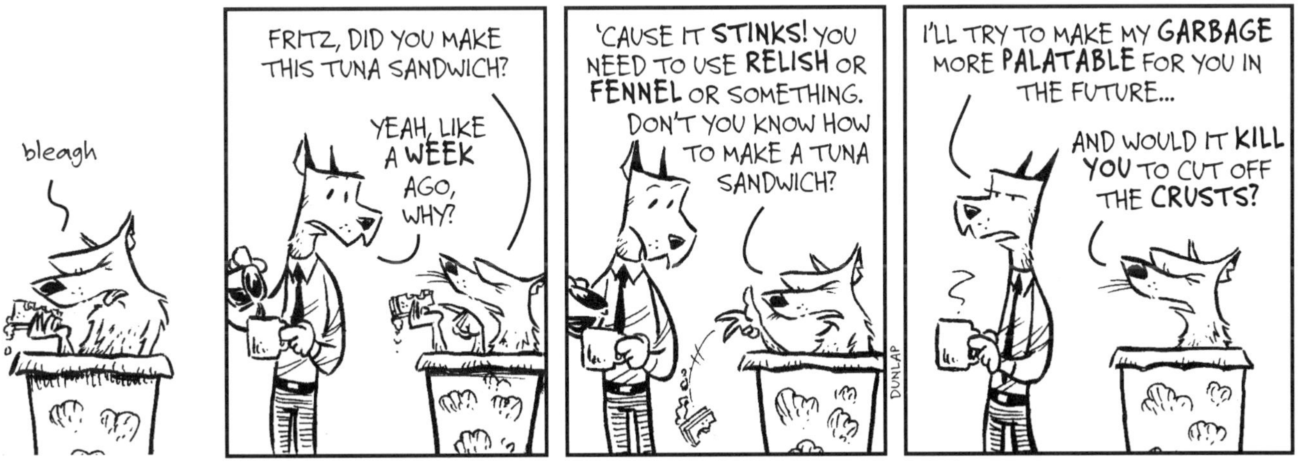
bleagh
FRITZ, DID YOU MAKE THIS TUNA SANDWICH?
YEAH, LIKE A WEEK AGO, WHY?
'CAUSE IT STINKS! YOU NEED TO USE RELISH OR FENNEL OR SOMETHING. DON'T YOU KNOW HOW TO MAKE A TUNA SANDWICH?
DUNLAP
I'LL TRY TO MAKE MY GARBAGE MORE PALATABLE FOR YOU IN THE FUTURE...
AND WOULD IT KILL YOU TO CUT OFF THE CRUSTS?

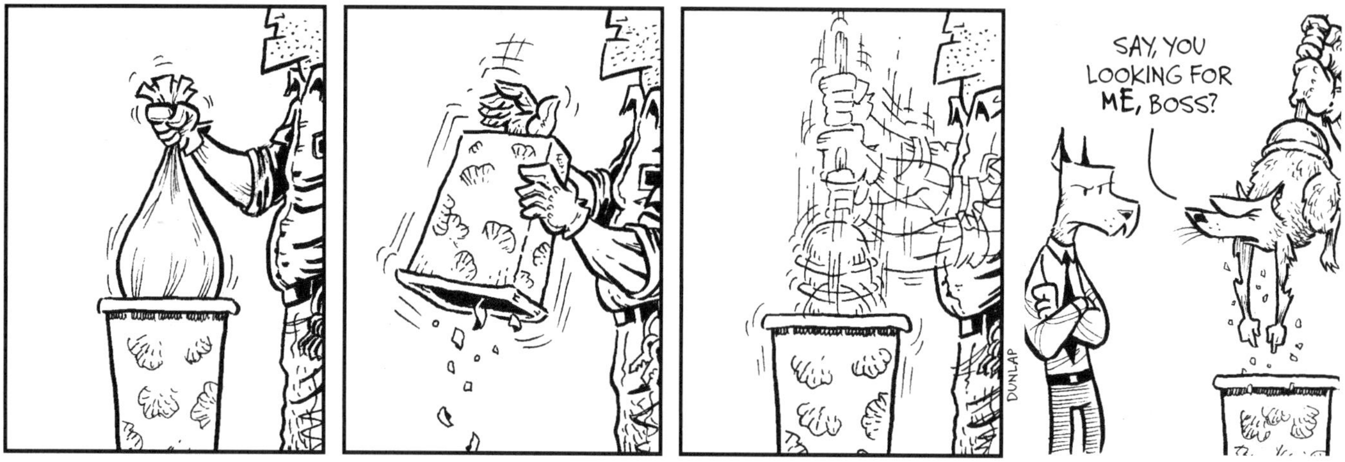

DUNLAP
SAY, YOU LOOKING FOR ME, BOSS?


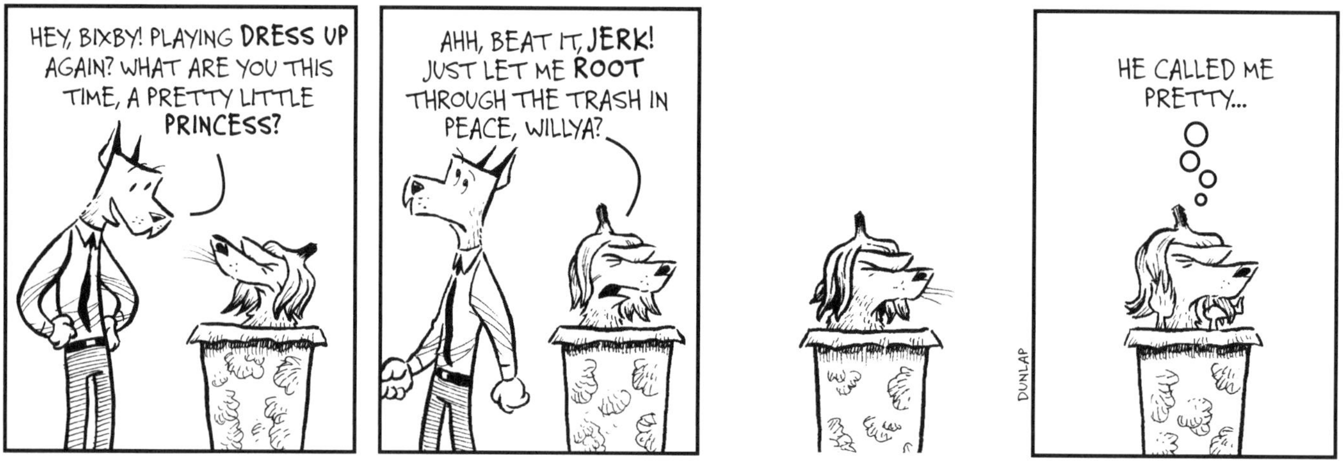

HEY, BIXBY! PLAYING DRESS UP AGAIN? WHAT ARE YOU THIS TIME, A PRETTY LITTLE PRINCESS?
AHH, BEAT IT, JERK! JUST LET ME ROOT THROUGH THE TRASH IN PEACE, WILLYA?
DUNLAP
HE CALLED ME PRETTY...


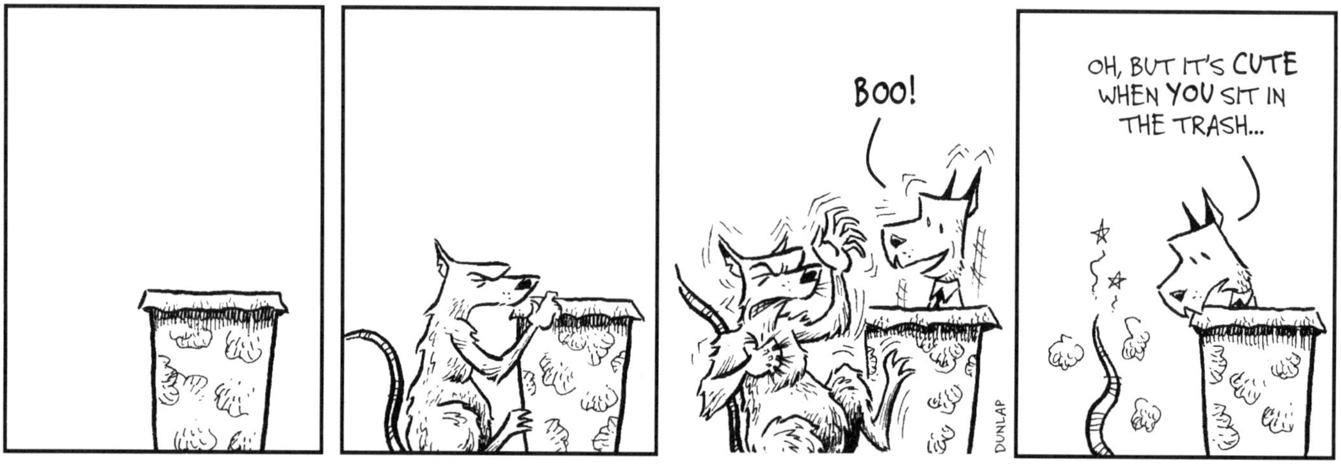

BOO!
DUNLAP
OH, BUT IT'S CUTE WHEN YOU SIT IN THE TRASH...

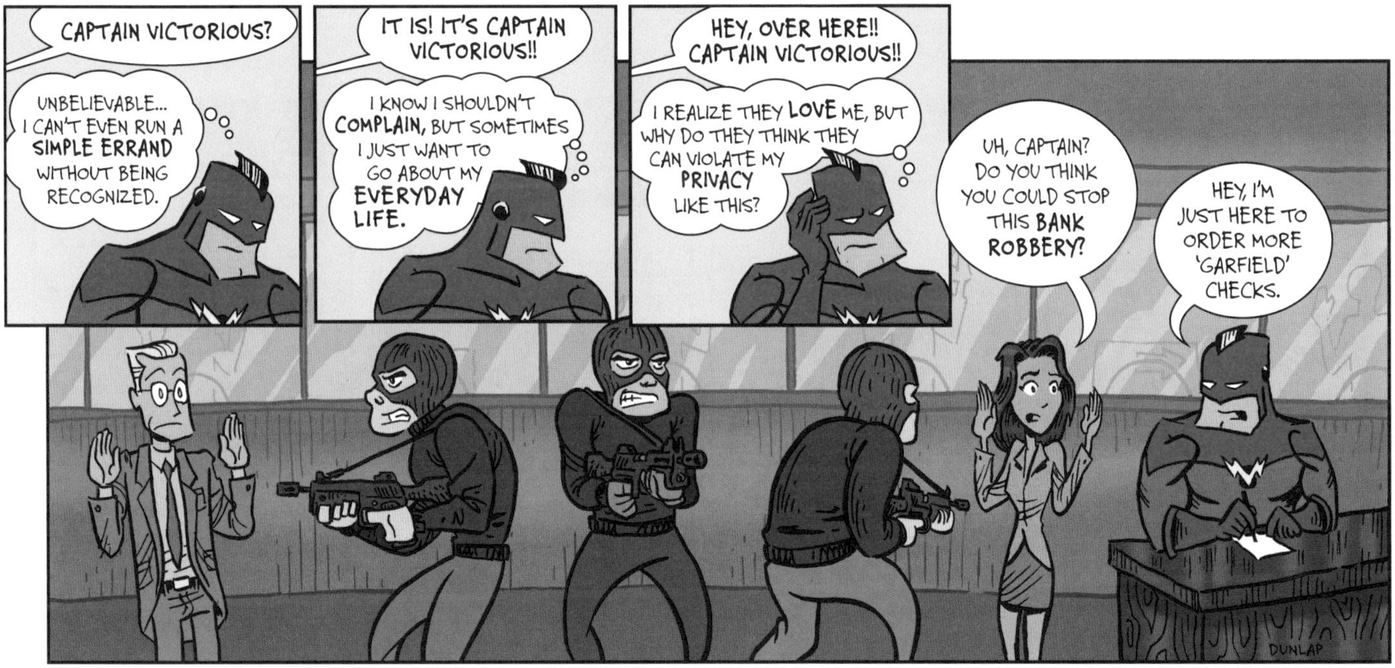
CAPTAIN VICTORIOUS?
UNBELIEVABLE... I CAN'T EVEN RUN A SIMPLE ERRAND WITHOUT BEING RECOGNIZED.
IT IS! IT'S CAPTAIN VICTORIOUS!!
I KNOW I SHOULDN'T COMPLAIN, BUT SOMETIMES I JUST WANT TO GO ABOUT MY EVERYDAY LIFE.
HEY, OVER HERE!! CAPTAIN VICTORIOUS!!
I REALIZE THEY LOVE ME, BUT WHY DO THEY THINK THEY CAN VIOLATE MY PRIVACY LIKE THIS?
UH, CAPTAIN? DO YOU THINK YOU COULD STOP THIS BANK ROBBERY?
HEY, I'M JUST HERE TO ORDER MORE 'GARFIELD' CHECKS.
DUNLAP

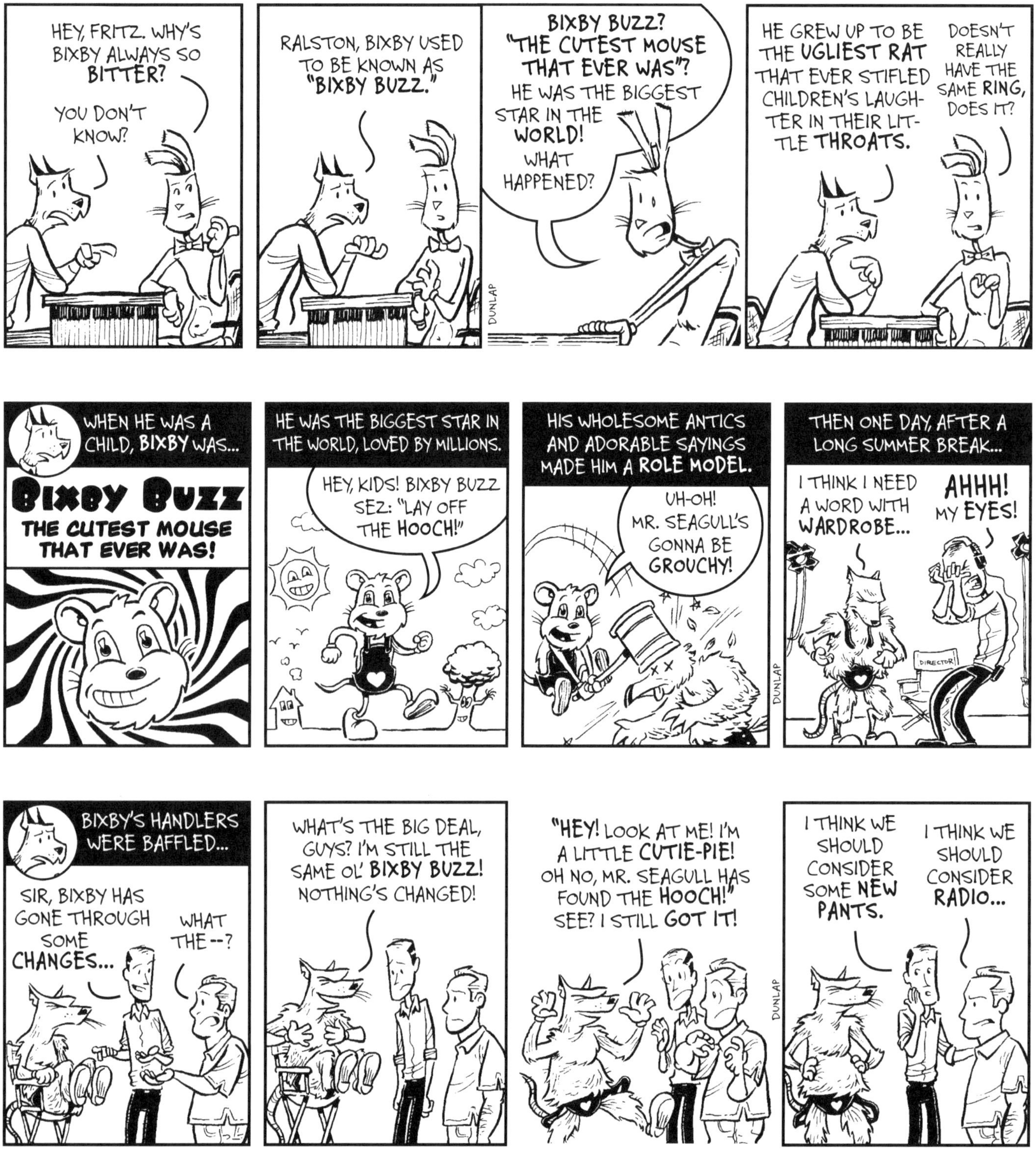
HEY, FRITZ. WHY'S BIXBY ALWAYS SO BITTER?
YOU DON'T KNOW?
RALSTON, BIXBY USED TO BE KNOWN AS "BIXBY BUZZ."
BIXBY BUZZ? "THE CUTEST MOUSE THAT EVER WAS"? HE WAS THE BIGGEST STAR IN THE WORLD! WHAT HAPPENED?
HE GREW UP TO BE THE UGLIEST RAT THAT EVER STIFLED CHILDREN'S LAUGHTER IN THEIR LITTLE THROATS.
DOESN'T REALLY HAVE THE SAME RING, DOES IT?
DUNLAP
WHEN HE WAS A CHILD, BIXBY WAS...
BIXBY BUZZ
THE CUTEST MOUSE THAT EVER WAS!
HE WAS THE BIGGEST STAR IN THE WORLD, LOVED BY MILLIONS.
HEY, KIDS! BIXBY BUZZ SEZ: "LAY OFF THE HOOCH!"
HIS WHOLESOME ANTICS AND ADORABLE SAYINGS MADE HIM A ROLE MODEL.
UH-OH! MR. SEAGULL'S GONNA BE GROUCHY!
DUNLAP
THEN ONE DAY, AFTER A LONG SUMMER BREAK...
I THINK I NEED A WORD WITH WARDROBE...
AHHH! MY EYES!
DIRECTOR
BIXBY'S HANDLERS WERE BAFFLED...
SIR, BIXBY HAS GONE THROUGH SOME CHANGES...
WHAT THE --?
WHAT'S THE BIG DEAL, GUYS? I'M STILL THE SAME OL' BIXBY BUZZ! NOTHING'S CHANGED!
"HEY! LOOK AT ME! I'M A LITTLE CUTIE-PIE! OH NO, MR. SEAGULL HAS FOUND THE HOOCH!" SEE? I STILL GOT IT!
DUNLAP
I THINK WE SHOULD CONSIDER SOME NEW PANTS.
I THINK WE SHOULD CONSIDER RADIO...

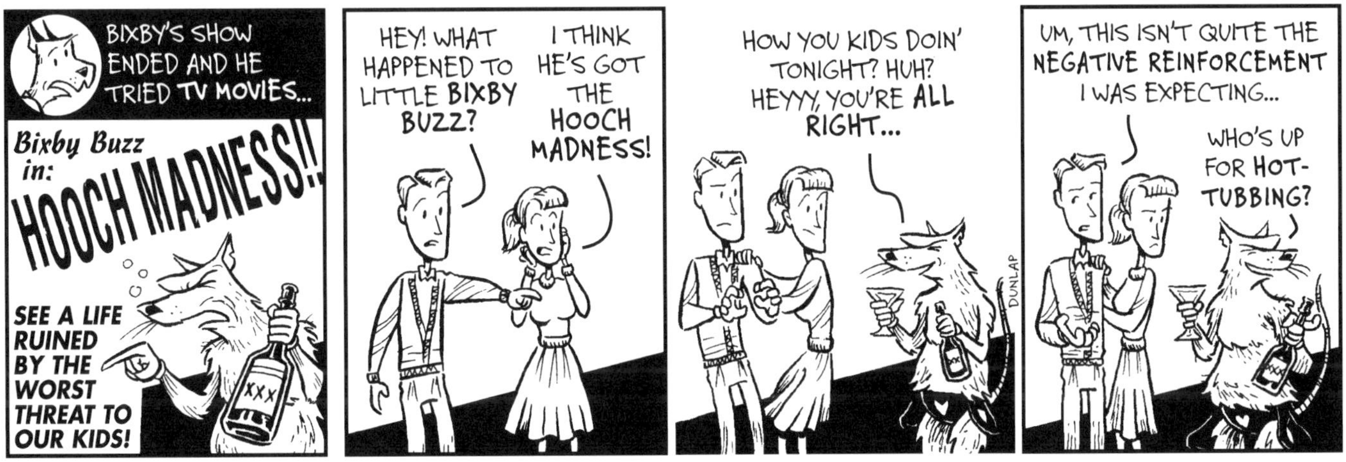
BIXBY'S SHOW ENDED AND HE TRIED TV MOVIES...
Bixby Buzz in:
HOOCH MADNESS!!
SEE A LIFE RUINED BY THE WORST THREAT TO OUR KIDS!
XXX
HEY! WHAT HAPPENED TO LITTLE BIXBY BUZZ?
I THINK HE'S GOT THE HOOCH MADNESS!
HOW YOU KIDS DOIN' TONIGHT? HUH? HEYYY, YOU'RE ALL RIGHT...
DUNLAP
UM, THIS ISN'T QUITE THE NEGATIVE REINFORCEMENT I WAS EXPECTING...
WHO'S UP FOR HOT-TUBBING?

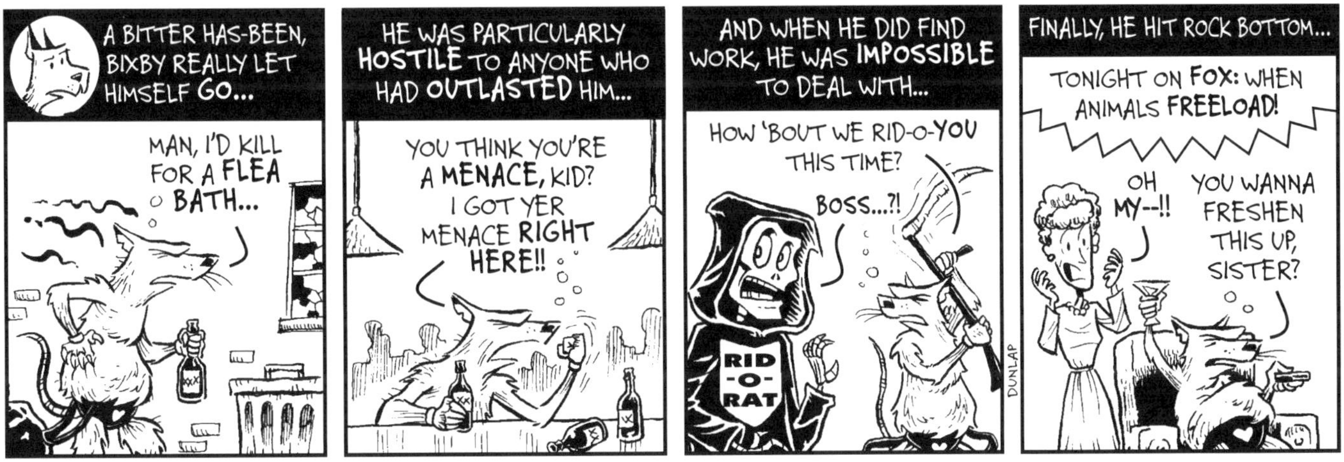
A BITTER HAS-BEEN, BIXBY REALLY LET HIMSELF GO...
MAN, I'D KILL FOR A FLEA BATH...
HE WAS PARTICULARLY HOSTILE TO ANYONE WHO HAD OUTLASTED HIM...
YOU THINK YOU'RE A MENACE, KID? I GOT YER MENACE RIGHT HERE!!
AND WHEN HE DID FIND WORK, HE WAS IMPOSSIBLE TO DEAL WITH...
HOW 'BOUT WE RID-O-YOU THIS TIME?
BOSS...?!
RID-O-RAT
DUNLAP
FINALLY, HE HIT ROCK BOTTOM...
TONIGHT ON FOX: WHEN ANIMALS FREELOAD!
OH MY--!!
YOU WANNA FRESHEN THIS UP, SISTER?

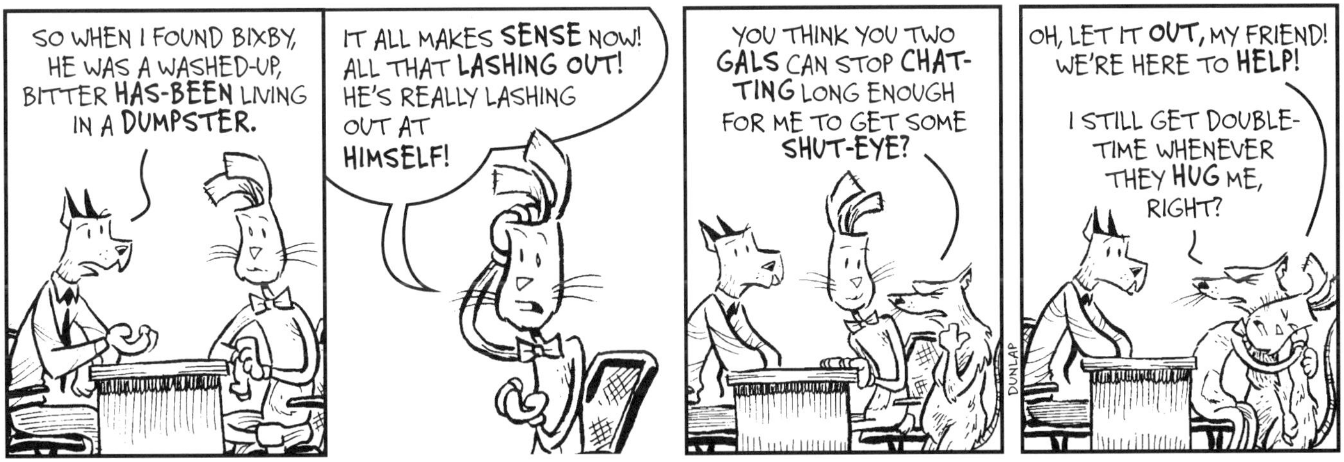
SO WHEN I FOUND BIXBY, HE WAS A WASHED-UP, BITTER HAS-BEEN LIVING IN A DUMPSTER.
IT ALL MAKES SENSE NOW! ALL THAT LASHING OUT! HE'S REALLY LASHING OUT AT HIMSELF!
YOU THINK YOU TWO GALS CAN STOP CHAT-TING LONG ENOUGH FOR ME TO GET SOME SHUT-EYE?
DUNLAP
OH, LET IT OUT, MY FRIEND! WE'RE HERE TO HELP!
I STILL GET DOUBLE-TIME WHENEVER THEY HUG ME, RIGHT?

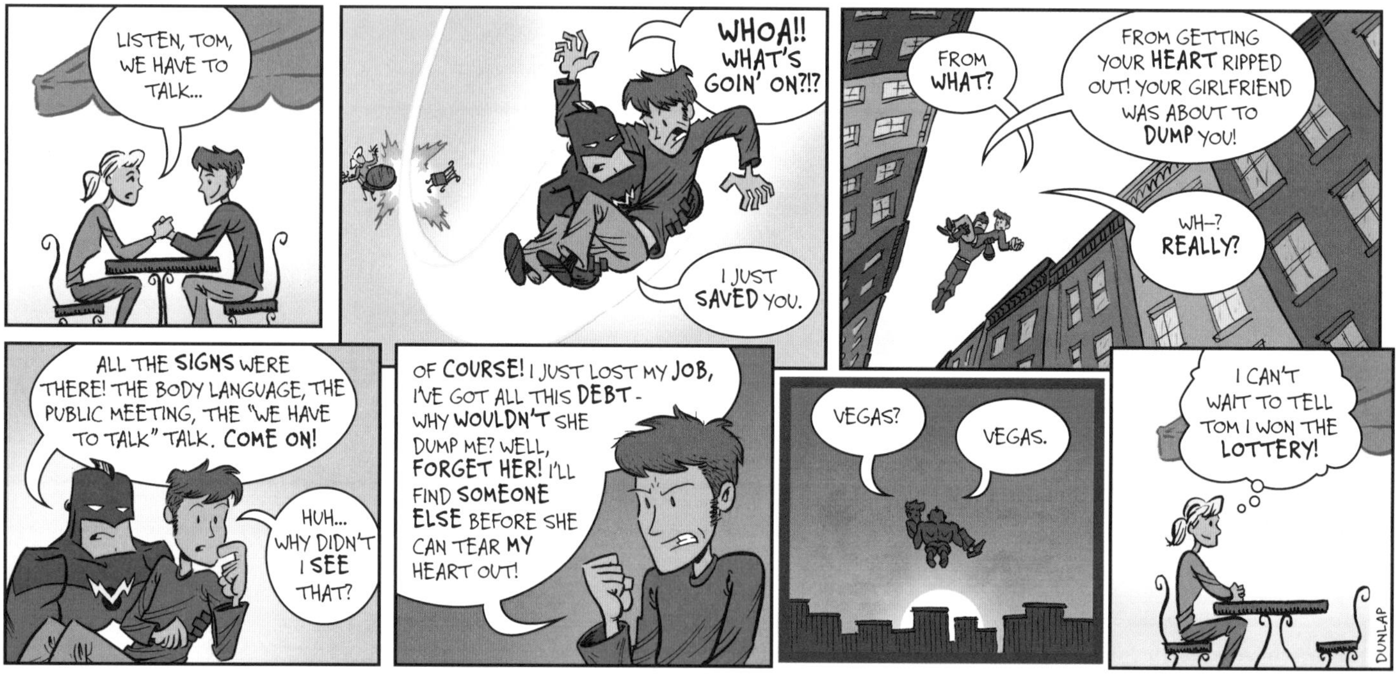
LISTEN, TOM, WE HAVE TO TALK...
WHOA!! WHAT'S GOIN' ON?!?
I JUST SAVED YOU.
FROM WHAT?
FROM GETTING YOUR HEART RIPPED OUT! YOUR GIRLFRIEND WAS ABOUT TO DUMP YOU!
WH–? REALLY?
ALL THE SIGNS WERE THERE! THE BODY LANGUAGE, THE PUBLIC MEETING, THE "WE HAVE TO TALK" TALK. COME ON!
HUH... WHY DIDN'T I SEE THAT?
OF COURSE! I JUST LOST MY JOB, I'VE GOT ALL THIS DEBT - WHY WOULDN'T SHE DUMP ME? WELL, FORGET HER! I'LL FIND SOMEONE ELSE BEFORE SHE CAN TEAR MY HEART OUT!
VEGAS?
VEGAS.
I CAN'T WAIT TO TELL TOM I WON THE LOTTERY!
DUNLAP

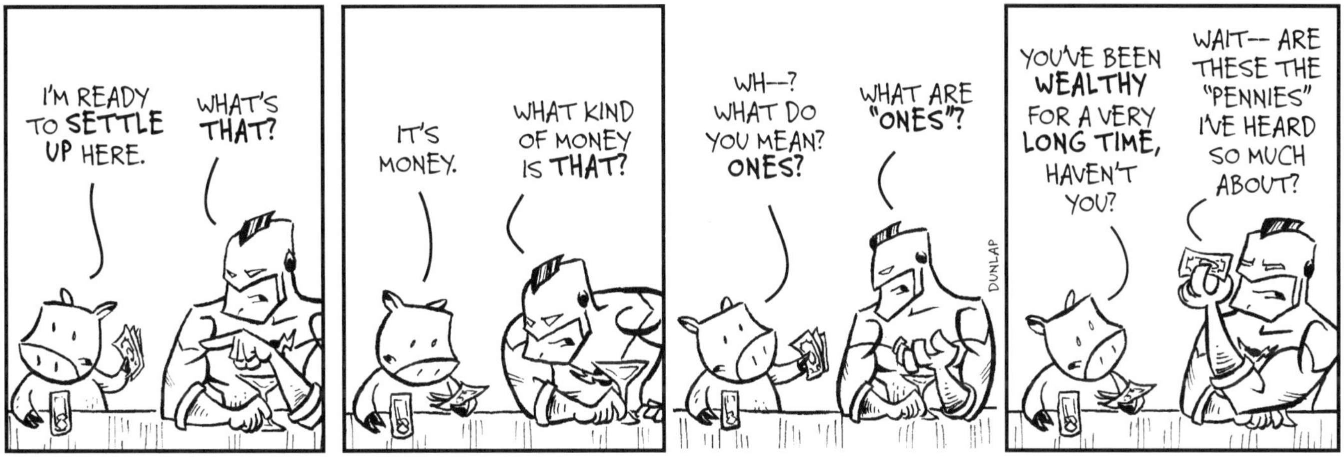
I'M READY TO SETTLE UP HERE.
WHAT'S THAT?
IT'S MONEY.
WHAT KIND OF MONEY IS THAT?
WH--? WHAT DO YOU MEAN? ONES?
WHAT ARE "ONES"?
DUNLAP
YOU'VE BEEN WEALTHY FOR A VERY LONG TIME, HAVEN'T YOU?
WAIT-- ARE THESE THE "PENNIES" I'VE HEARD SO MUCH ABOUT?

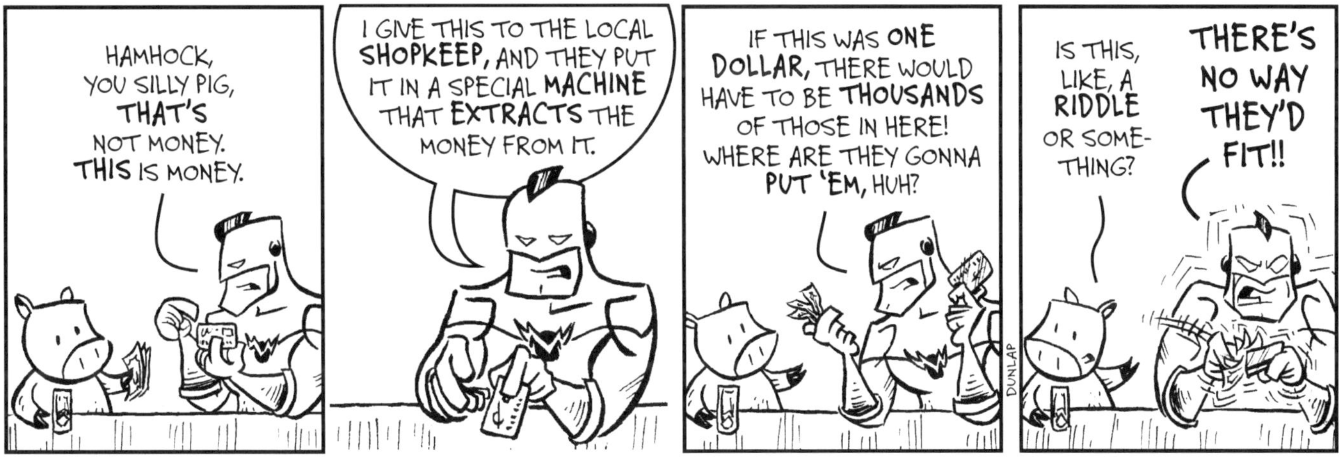
HAMHOCK, YOU SILLY PIG, THAT'S NOT MONEY. THIS IS MONEY.
I GIVE THIS TO THE LOCAL SHOPKEEP, AND THEY PUT IT IN A SPECIAL MACHINE THAT EXTRACTS THE MONEY FROM IT.
IF THIS WAS ONE DOLLAR, THERE WOULD HAVE TO BE THOUSANDS OF THOSE IN HERE! WHERE ARE THEY GONNA PUT 'EM, HUH?
DUNLAP
IS THIS, LIKE, A RIDDLE OR SOME-THING?
THERE'S NO WAY THEY'D FIT!!

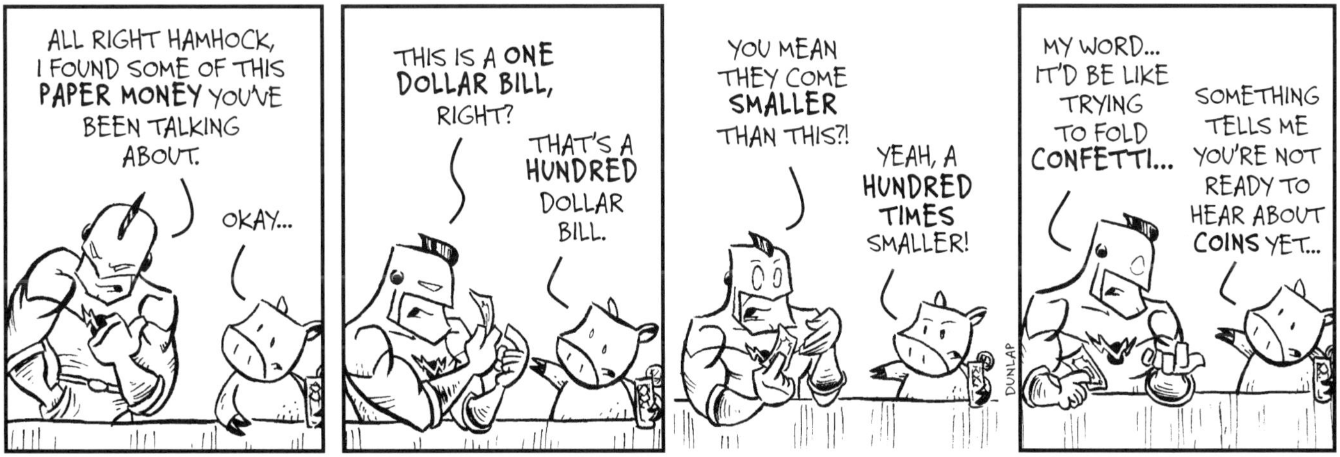
ALL RIGHT HAMHOCK, I FOUND SOME OF THIS PAPER MONEY YOU'VE BEEN TALKING ABOUT.
OKAY...
THIS IS A ONE DOLLAR BILL, RIGHT?
THAT'S A HUNDRED DOLLAR BILL.
YOU MEAN THEY COME SMALLER THAN THIS?!
YEAH, A HUNDRED TIMES SMALLER!
DUNLAP
MY WORD... IT'D BE LIKE TRYING TO FOLD CONFETTI...
SOMETHING TELLS ME YOU'RE NOT READY TO HEAR ABOUT COINS YET...

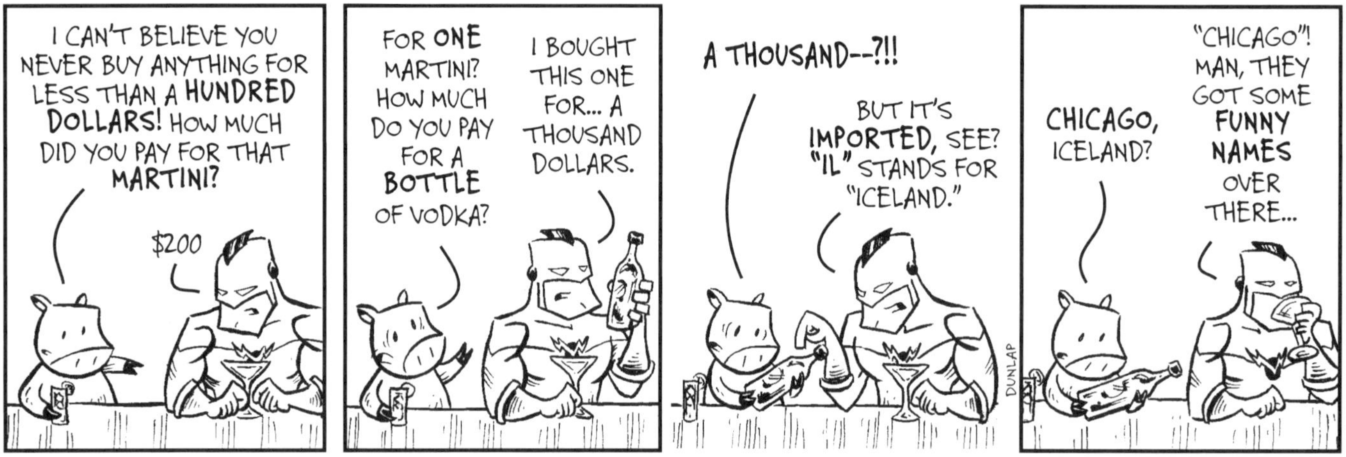
I CAN'T BELIEVE YOU NEVER BUY ANYTHING FOR LESS THAN A HUNDRED DOLLARS! HOW MUCH DID YOU PAY FOR THAT MARTINI?
$200
FOR ONE MARTINI? HOW MUCH DO YOU PAY FOR A BOTTLE OF VODKA?
I BOUGHT THIS ONE FOR... A THOUSAND DOLLARS.
A THOUSAND--?!!
BUT IT'S IMPORTED, SEE? "IL" STANDS FOR "ICELAND."
DUNLAP
CHICAGO, ICELAND?
"CHICAGO"! MAN, THEY GOT SOME FUNNY NAMES OVER THERE...

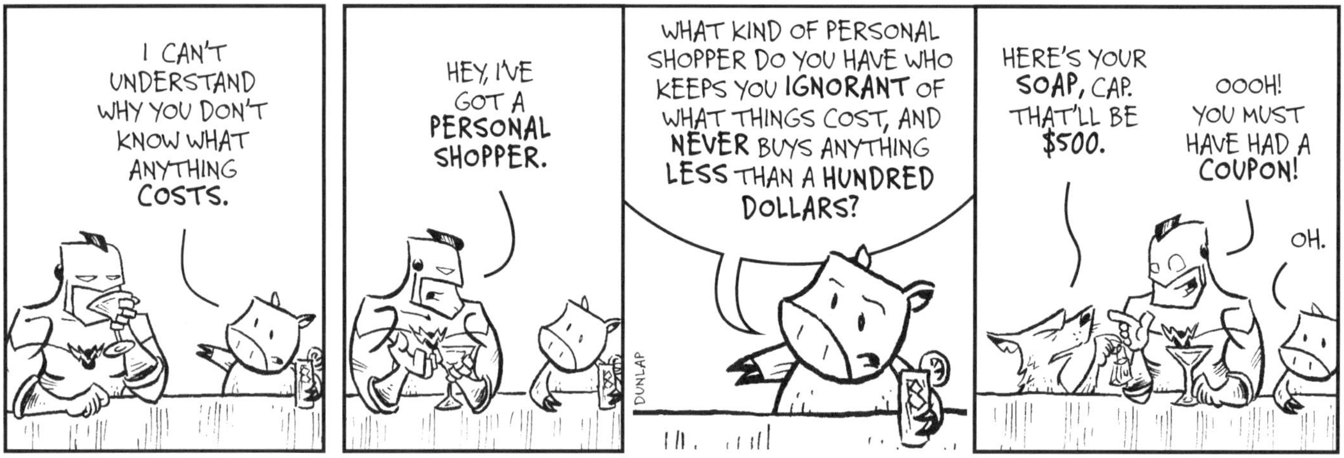
I CAN'T UNDERSTAND WHY YOU DON'T KNOW WHAT ANYTHING COSTS.
HEY, I'VE GOT A PERSONAL SHOPPER.
DUNLAP
WHAT KIND OF PERSONAL SHOPPER DO YOU HAVE WHO KEEPS YOU IGNORANT OF WHAT THINGS COST, AND NEVER BUYS ANYTHING LESS THAN A HUNDRED DOLLARS?
HERE'S YOUR SOAP, CAP. THAT'LL BE $500.
OOOH! YOU MUST HAVE HAD A COUPON!
OH.

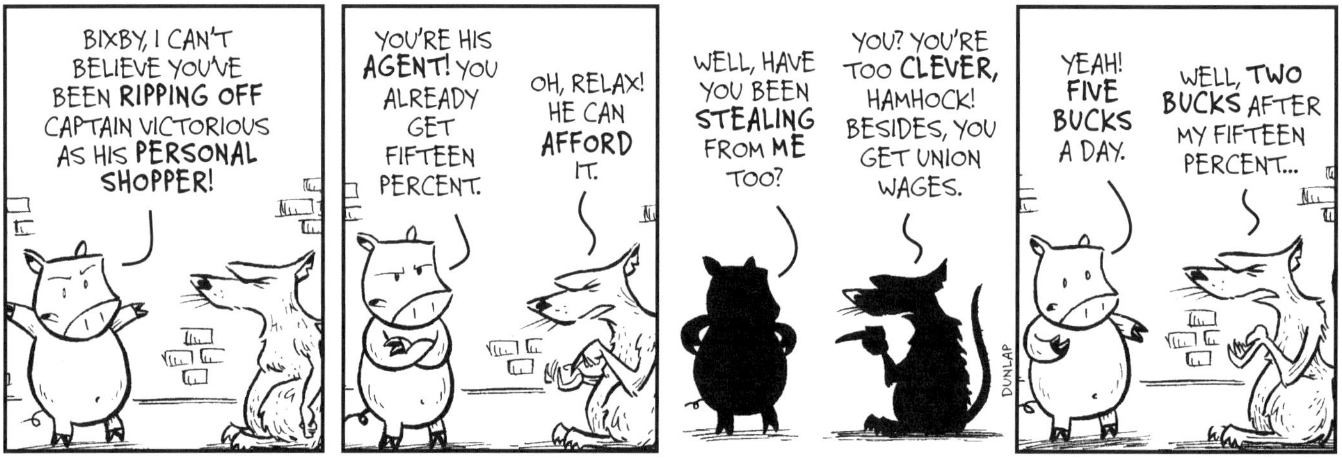
BIXBY, I CAN'T BELIEVE YOU'VE BEEN RIPPING OFF CAPTAIN VICTORIOUS AS HIS PERSONAL SHOPPER!
YOU'RE HIS AGENT! YOU ALREADY GET FIFTEEN PERCENT.
OH, RELAX! HE CAN AFFORD IT.
WELL, HAVE YOU BEEN STEALING FROM ME TOO?
YOU? YOU'RE TOO CLEVER, HAMHOCK! BESIDES, YOU GET UNION WAGES.
DUNLAP
YEAH! FIVE BUCKS A DAY.
WELL, TWO BUCKS AFTER MY FIFTEEN PERCENT...

I'LL TAKE A MEGA TITAN BURGER, AND OBSCENE SIZE IT.
MMM... I'LL HAVE THE GARDEN SALAD.
GARDEN SALAD? THAT'S RABBIT FOOD! EAT SOME REAL FOOD!
TITAN BURGER
YOU KNOW, PIG SLOP IS A HIGH-PROTEIN GRUEL MADE FROM GRAINS, MEAT AND BONE MEAL.
SO?
SO IT'S ALL LEFTOVER PARTS MASHED TOGETHER AND IT'S STILL MORE NUTRITIOUS THAN WHAT YOU ORDERED!
IF I'M EATING RABBIT FOOD, THEN WHAT YOU'RE EATING DOESN'T EVEN REACH THE QUALITY OF PIG FOOD.
DUNLAP
YEAH. PIGS CAN BE SUCH HEALTH FREAKS.
SLOP BURGER WITH CHEESE. EXTRA BONE MEAL.

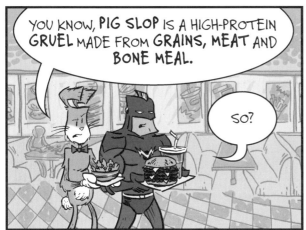

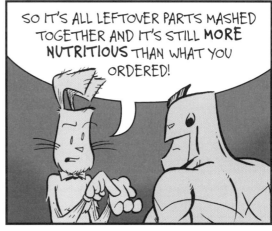

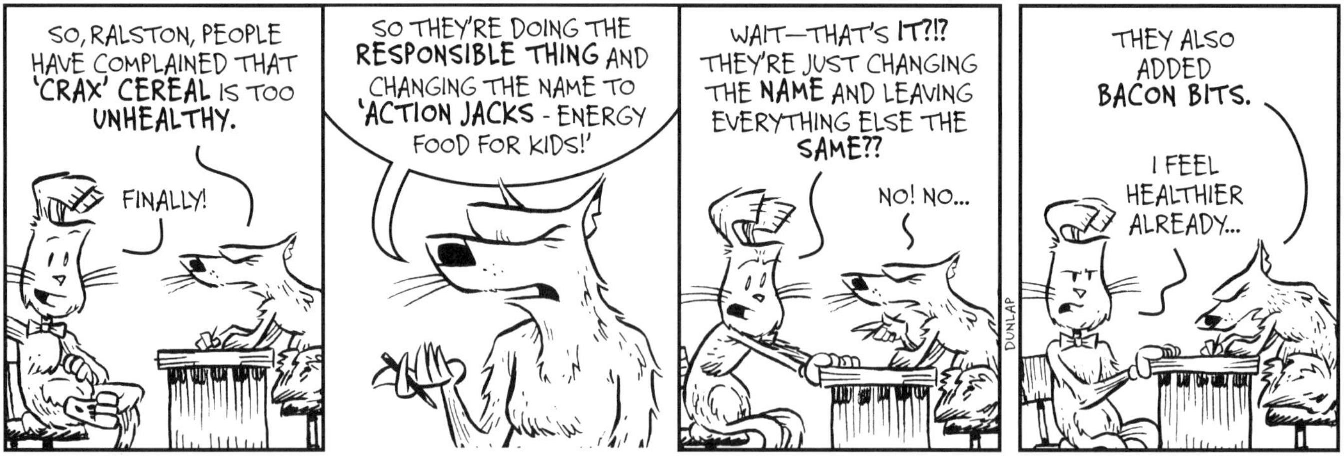
SO, RALSTON, PEOPLE HAVE COMPLAINED THAT 'CRAX' CEREAL IS TOO UNHEALTHY.
FINALLY!
SO THEY'RE DOING THE RESPONSIBLE THING AND CHANGING THE NAME TO 'ACTION JACKS - ENERGY FOOD FOR KIDS!'
WAIT—THAT'S IT?!? THEY'RE JUST CHANGING THE NAME AND LEAVING EVERYTHING ELSE THE SAME??
NO! NO...
THEY ALSO ADDED BACON BITS.
I FEEL HEALTHIER ALREADY...
DUNLAP

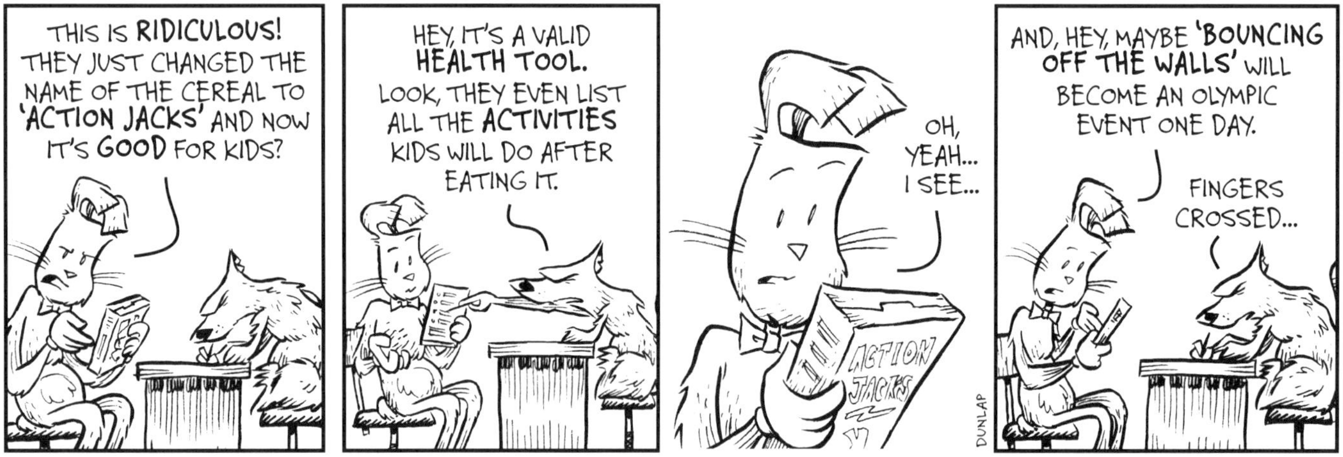
THIS IS RIDICULOUS! THEY JUST CHANGED THE NAME OF THE CEREAL TO 'ACTION JACKS' AND NOW IT'S GOOD FOR KIDS?
HEY, IT'S A VALID HEALTH TOOL. LOOK, THEY EVEN LIST ALL THE ACTIVITIES KIDS WILL DO AFTER EATING IT.
OH, YEAH... I SEE...
ACTION JACKS
AND, HEY, MAYBE 'BOUNCING OFF THE WALLS' WILL BECOME AN OLYMPIC EVENT ONE DAY.
FINGERS CROSSED...
DUNLAP

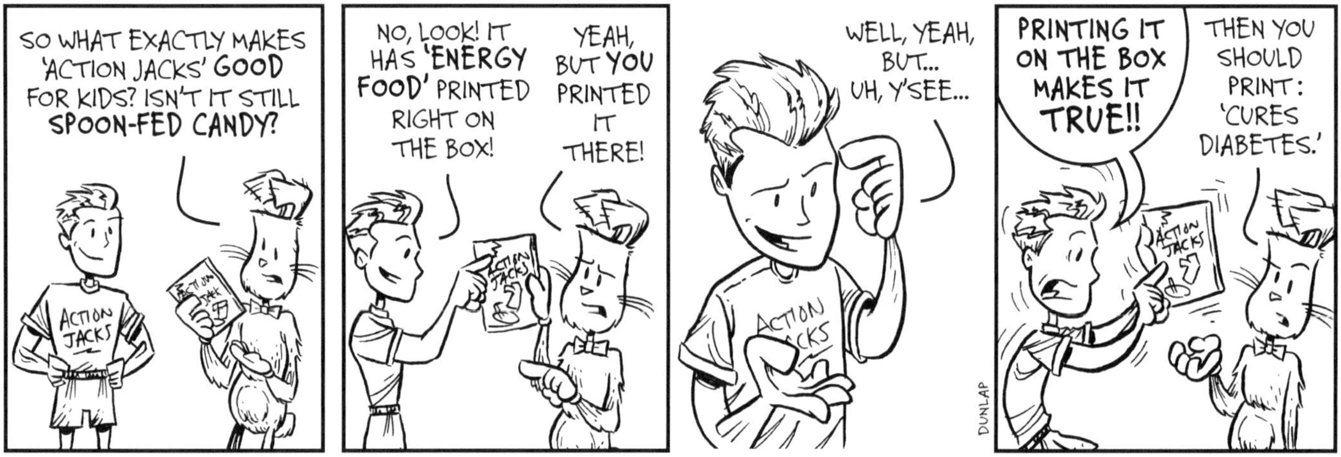
SO WHAT EXACTLY MAKES 'ACTION JACKS' GOOD FOR KIDS? ISN'T IT STILL SPOON-FED CANDY?
ACTION JACKS
NO, LOOK! IT HAS 'ENERGY FOOD' PRINTED RIGHT ON THE BOX!
YEAH, BUT YOU PRINTED IT THERE!
WELL, YEAH, BUT... UH, Y'SEE...
PRINTING IT ON THE BOX MAKES IT TRUE!!
THEN YOU SHOULD PRINT: 'CURES DIABETES.'
ACTION JACKS
DUNLAP

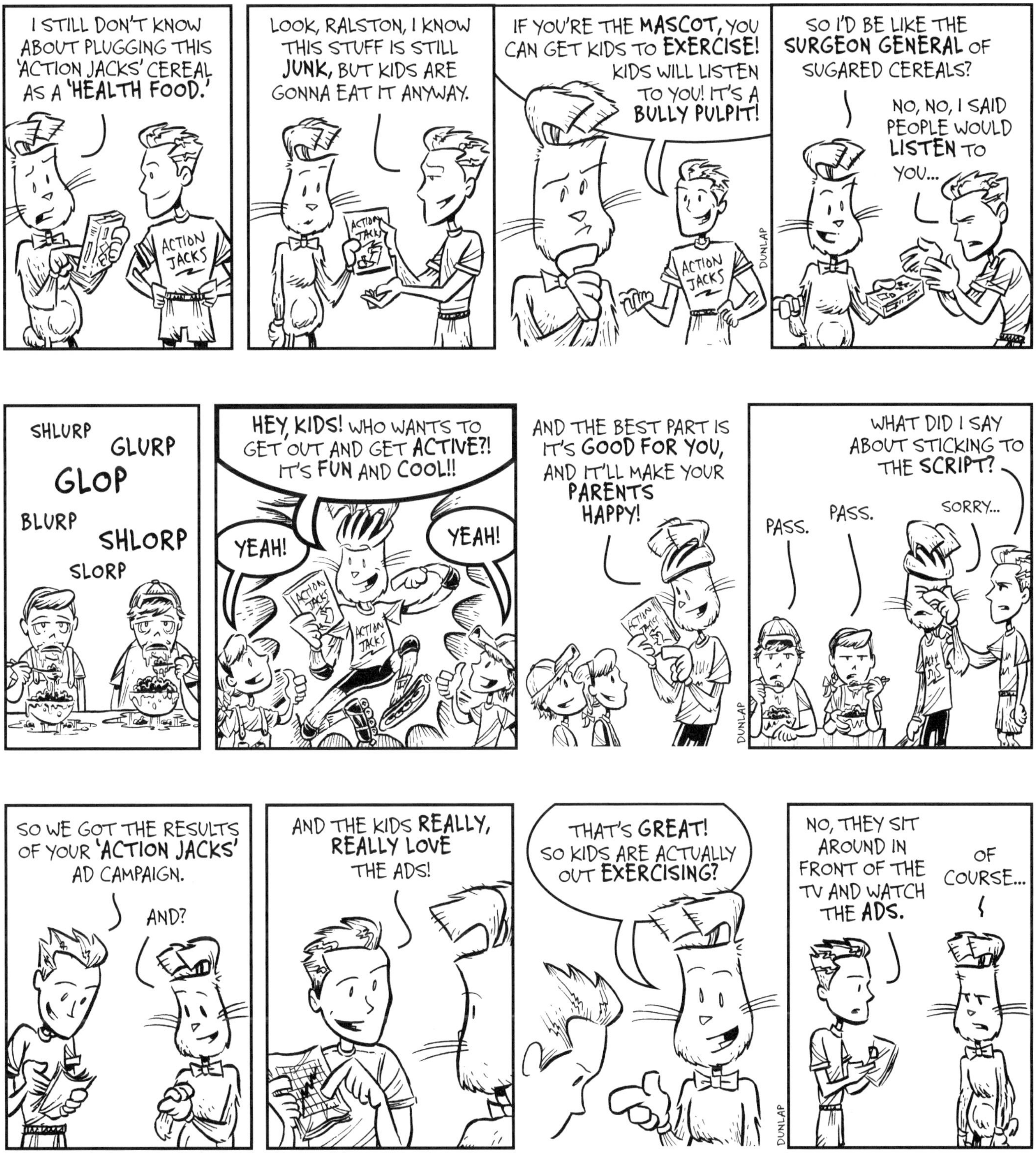
I STILL DON'T KNOW ABOUT PLUGGING THIS 'ACTION JACKS' CEREAL AS A 'HEALTH FOOD.'
ACTION JACKS
LOOK, RALSTON, I KNOW THIS STUFF IS STILL JUNK, BUT KIDS ARE GONNA EAT IT ANYWAY.
IF YOU'RE THE MASCOT, YOU CAN GET KIDS TO EXERCISE! KIDS WILL LISTEN TO YOU! IT'S A BULLY PULPIT!
ACTION JACKS
DUNLAP
SO I'D BE LIKE THE SURGEON GENERAL OF SUGARED CEREALS?
NO, NO, I SAID PEOPLE WOULD LISTEN TO YOU...
SHLURP
GLURP
GLOP
BLURP
SHLORP
SLORP
HEY, KIDS! WHO WANTS TO GET OUT AND GET ACTIVE?! IT'S FUN AND COOL!!
YEAH!
YEAH!
ACTION JACKS
AND THE BEST PART IS IT'S GOOD FOR YOU, AND IT'LL MAKE YOUR PARENTS HAPPY!
DUNLAP
WHAT DID I SAY ABOUT STICKING TO THE SCRIPT?
PASS.
PASS.
SORRY...
SO WE GOT THE RESULTS OF YOUR 'ACTION JACKS' AD CAMPAIGN.
AND?
AND THE KIDS REALLY, REALLY LOVE THE ADS!
THAT'S GREAT! SO KIDS ARE ACTUALLY OUT EXERCISING?
DUNLAP
NO, THEY SIT AROUND IN FRONT OF THE TV AND WATCH THE ADS.
OF COURSE...

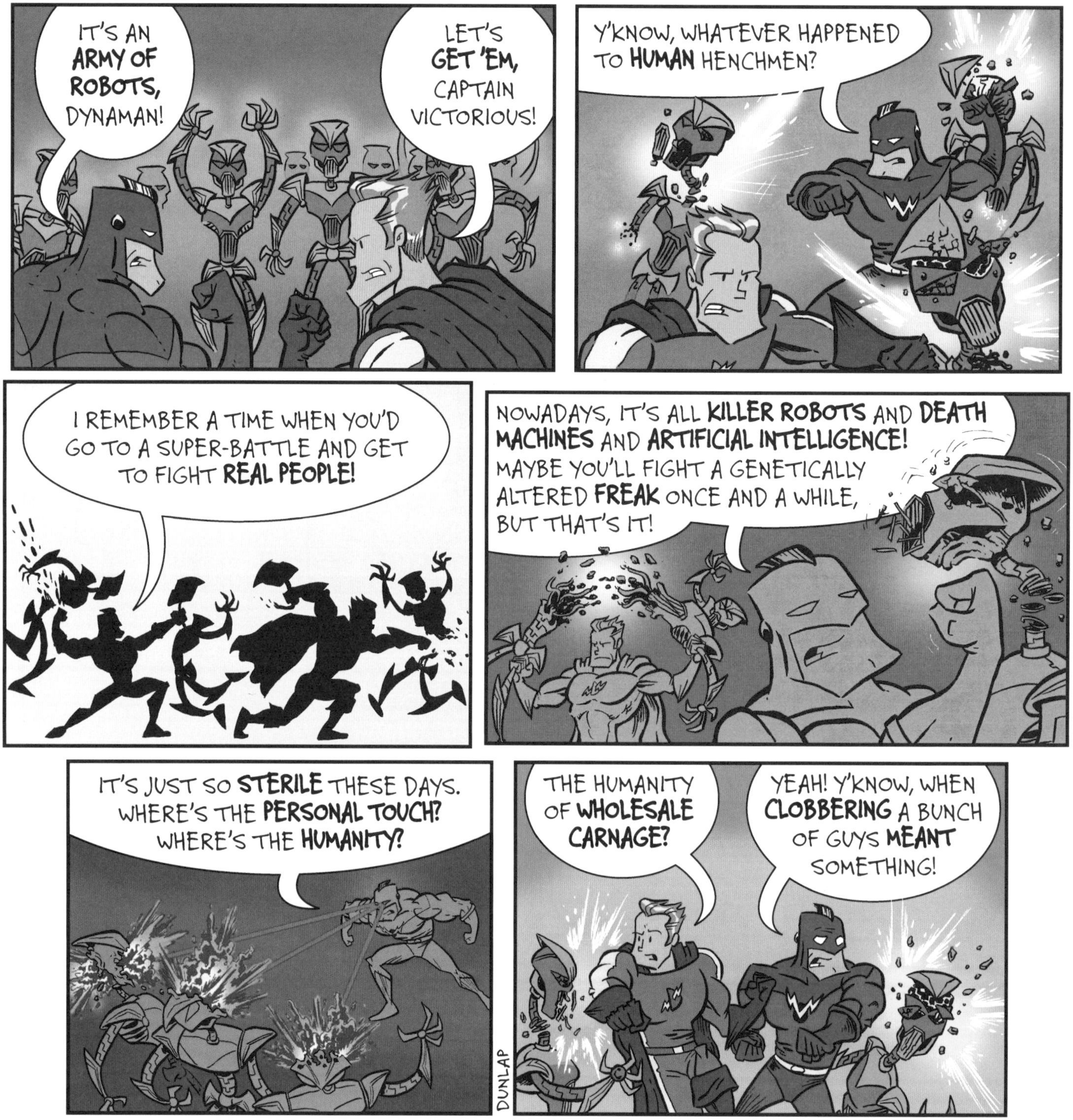
IT'S AN ARMY OF ROBOTS, DYNAMAN!
LET'S GET 'EM, CAPTAIN VICTORIOUS!
Y'KNOW, WHATEVER HAPPENED TO HUMAN HENCHMEN?
I REMEMBER A TIME WHEN YOU'D GO TO A SUPER-BATTLE AND GET TO FIGHT REAL PEOPLE!
NOWADAYS, IT'S ALL KILLER ROBOTS AND DEATH MACHINES AND ARTIFICIAL INTELLIGENCE! MAYBE YOU'LL FIGHT A GENETICALLY ALTERED FREAK ONCE AND A WHILE, BUT THAT'S IT!
IT'S JUST SO STERILE THESE DAYS. WHERE'S THE PERSONAL TOUCH? WHERE'S THE HUMANITY?
THE HUMANITY OF WHOLESALE CARNAGE?
YEAH! Y'KNOW, WHEN CLOBBERING A BUNCH OF GUYS MEANT SOMETHING!
DUNLAP

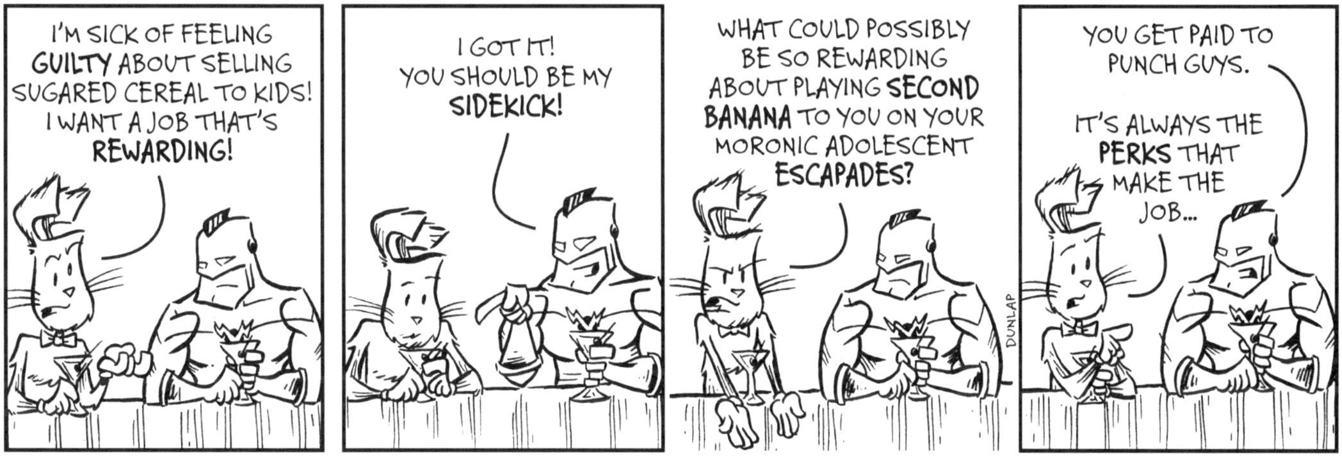
I'M SICK OF FEELING GUILTY ABOUT SELLING SUGARED CEREAL TO KIDS! I WANT A JOB THAT'S REWARDING!
I GOT IT! YOU SHOULD BE MY SIDEKICK!
WHAT COULD POSSIBLY BE SO REWARDING ABOUT PLAYING SECOND BANANA TO YOU ON YOUR MORONIC ADOLESCENT ESCAPADES?
DUNLAP
YOU GET PAID TO PUNCH GUYS.
IT'S ALWAYS THE PERKS THAT MAKE THE JOB...

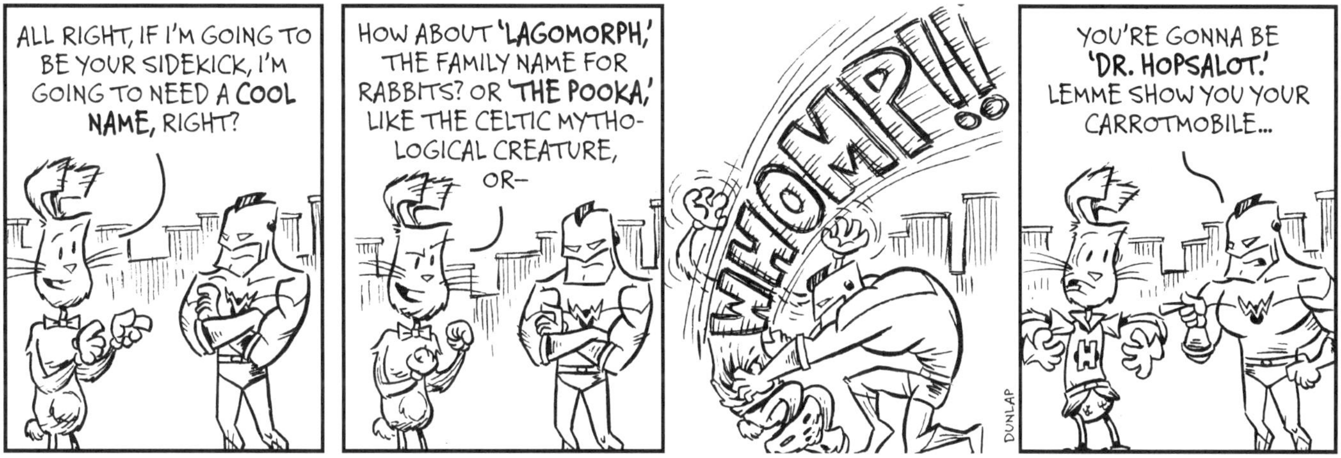
ALL RIGHT, IF I'M GOING TO BE YOUR SIDEKICK, I'M GOING TO NEED A COOL NAME, RIGHT?
HOW ABOUT 'LAGOMORPH,' THE FAMILY NAME FOR RABBITS? OR 'THE POOKA,' LIKE THE CELTIC MYTHOLOGICAL CREATURE, OR–
WHOMP!!
DUNLAP
YOU'RE GONNA BE 'DR. HOPSALOT.' LEMME SHOW YOU YOUR CARROTMOBILE...

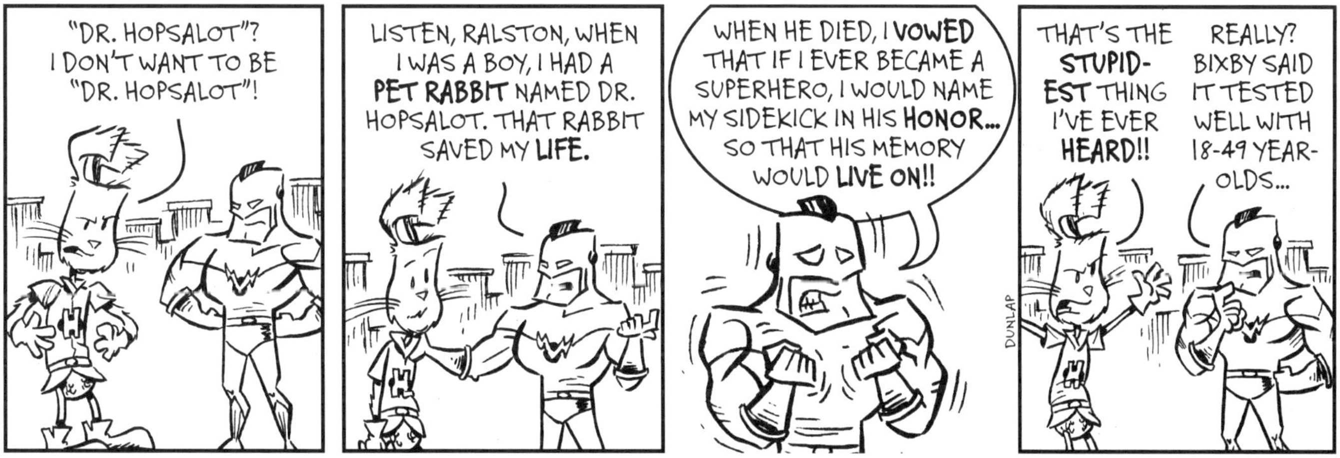
"DR. HOPSALOT"? I DON'T WANT TO BE "DR. HOPSALOT"!
LISTEN, RALSTON, WHEN I WAS A BOY, I HAD A PET RABBIT NAMED DR. HOPSALOT. THAT RABBIT SAVED MY LIFE.
WHEN HE DIED, I VOWED THAT IF I EVER BECAME A SUPERHERO, I WOULD NAME MY SIDEKICK IN HIS HONOR... SO THAT HIS MEMORY WOULD LIVE ON!!
DUNLAP
THAT'S THE STUPIDEST THING I'VE EVER HEARD!!
REALLY? BIXBY SAID IT TESTED WELL WITH 18-49 YEAR-OLDS...

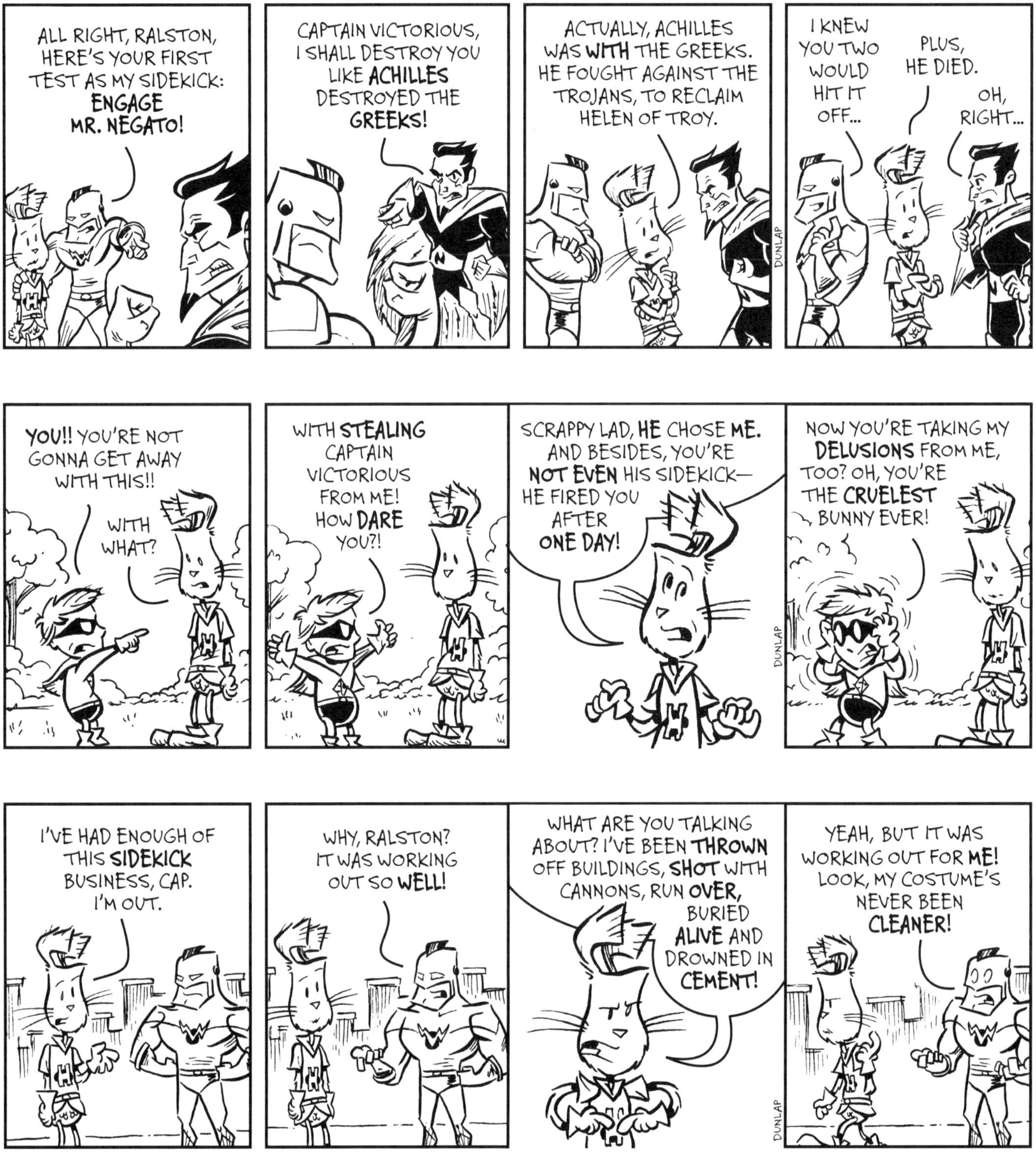
ALL RIGHT, RALSTON, HERE'S YOUR FIRST TEST AS MY SIDEKICK: **ENGAGE MR. NEGATO!**
CAPTAIN VICTORIOUS, I SHALL DESTROY YOU LIKE **ACHILLES** DESTROYED THE **GREEKS!**
ACTUALLY, ACHILLES WAS **WITH** THE GREEKS. HE FOUGHT AGAINST THE TROJANS, TO RECLAIM HELEN OF TROY.
DUNLAP
I KNEW YOU TWO WOULD HIT IT OFF...
PLUS, HE DIED.
OH, RIGHT...
**YOU!!** YOU'RE NOT GONNA GET AWAY WITH THIS!!
WITH WHAT?
WITH **STEALING** CAPTAIN VICTORIOUS FROM ME! HOW **DARE** YOU?!
SCRAPPY LAD, **HE** CHOSE **ME.** AND BESIDES, YOU'RE **NOT EVEN** HIS SIDEKICK— HE FIRED YOU AFTER **ONE DAY!**
DUNLAP
NOW YOU'RE TAKING MY **DELUSIONS** FROM ME, TOO? OH, YOU'RE THE **CRUELEST** BUNNY EVER!
I'VE HAD ENOUGH OF THIS **SIDEKICK** BUSINESS, CAP. I'M OUT.
WHY, RALSTON? IT WAS WORKING OUT SO **WELL!**
WHAT ARE YOU TALKING ABOUT? I'VE BEEN **THROWN** OFF BUILDINGS, **SHOT** WITH CANNONS, RUN **OVER,** BURIED **ALIVE** AND DROWNED IN **CEMENT!**
DUNLAP
YEAH, BUT IT WAS WORKING OUT FOR **ME!** LOOK, MY COSTUME'S NEVER BEEN **CLEANER!**

DUNLAP

CAN'T YOU BOYS PLAY OUTSIDE?
BUT HE'S GOT THE LAST ROLO!!
I CALLED IT!!

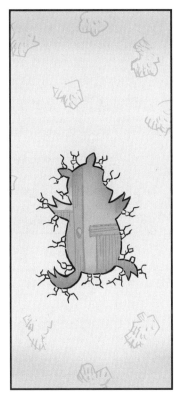

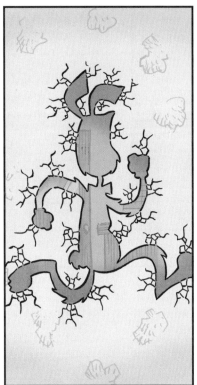

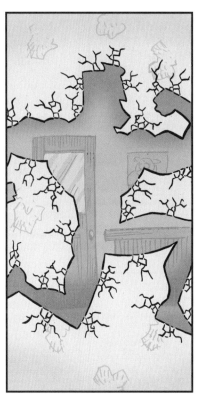

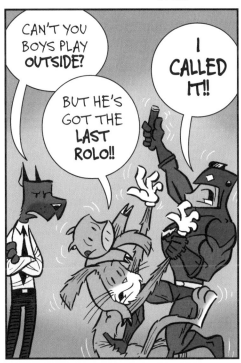

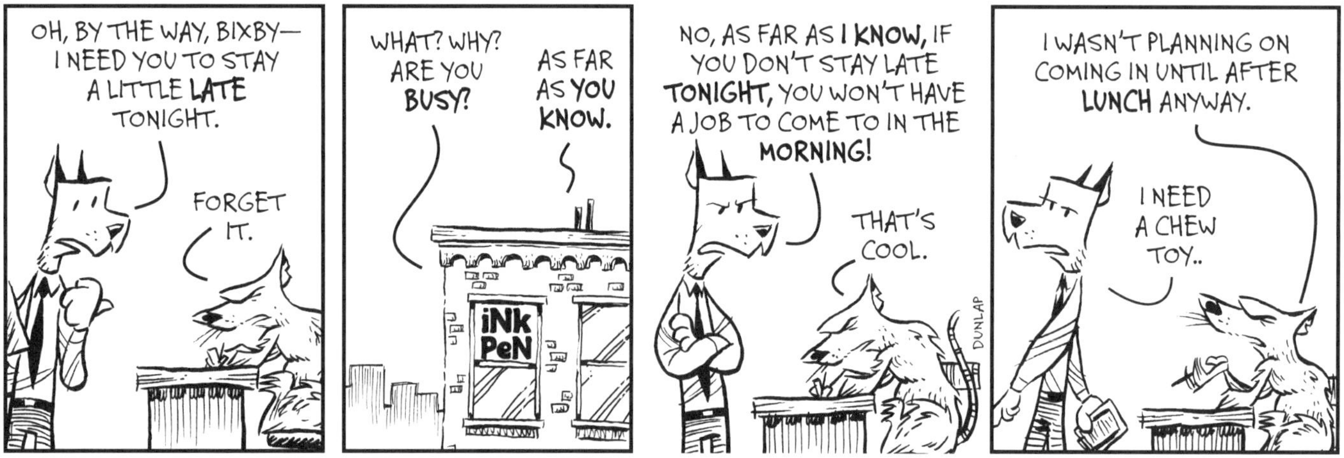
OH, BY THE WAY, BIXBY— I NEED YOU TO STAY A LITTLE LATE TONIGHT.
FORGET IT.
WHAT? WHY? ARE YOU BUSY?
AS FAR AS YOU KNOW.
iNk PeN
NO, AS FAR AS I KNOW, IF YOU DON'T STAY LATE TONIGHT, YOU WON'T HAVE A JOB TO COME TO IN THE MORNING!
THAT'S COOL.
DUNLAP
I WASN'T PLANNING ON COMING IN UNTIL AFTER LUNCH ANYWAY.
I NEED A CHEW TOY..

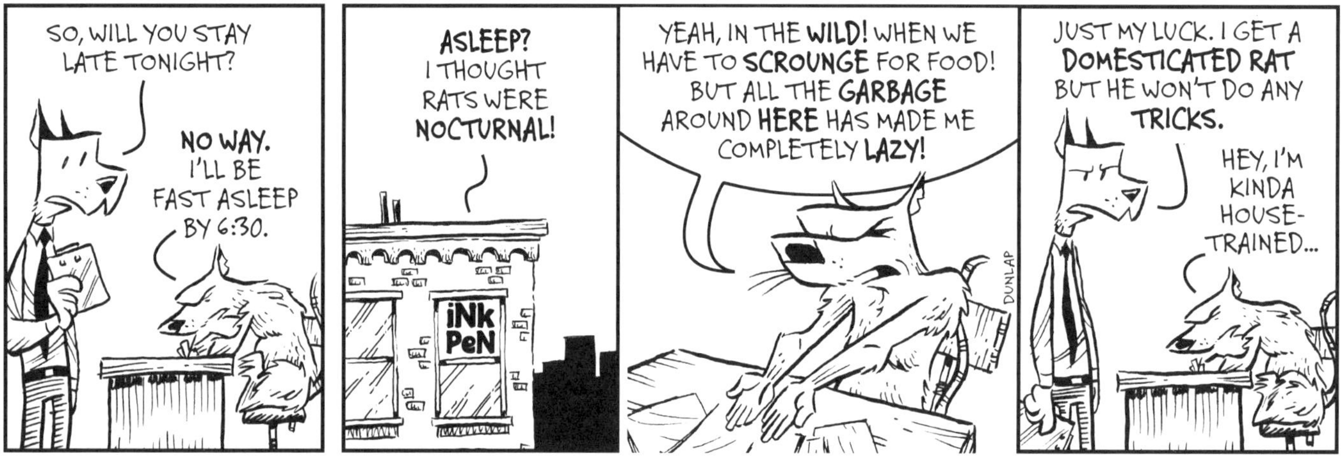
SO, WILL YOU STAY LATE TONIGHT?
NO WAY. I'LL BE FAST ASLEEP BY 6:30.
ASLEEP? I THOUGHT RATS WERE NOCTURNAL!
iNk PeN
YEAH, IN THE WILD! WHEN WE HAVE TO SCROUNGE FOR FOOD! BUT ALL THE GARBAGE AROUND HERE HAS MADE ME COMPLETELY LAZY!
DUNLAP
JUST MY LUCK. I GET A DOMESTICATED RAT BUT HE WON'T DO ANY TRICKS.
HEY, I'M KINDA HOUSE-TRAINED...

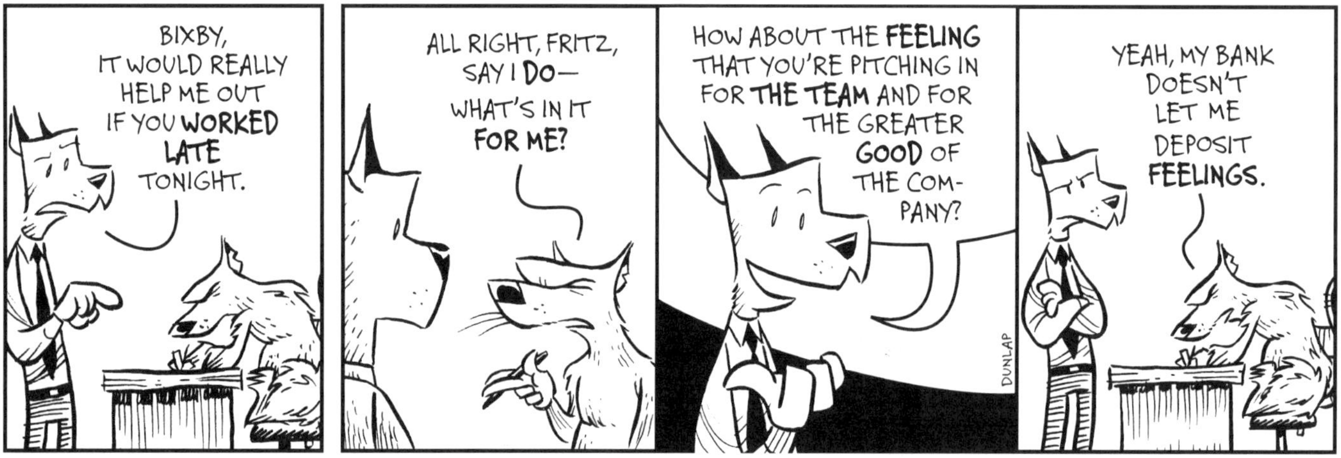
BIXBY, IT WOULD REALLY HELP ME OUT IF YOU WORKED LATE TONIGHT.
ALL RIGHT, FRITZ, SAY I DO— WHAT'S IN IT FOR ME?
HOW ABOUT THE FEELING THAT YOU'RE PITCHING IN FOR THE TEAM AND FOR THE GREATER GOOD OF THE COM-PANY?
DUNLAP
YEAH, MY BANK DOESN'T LET ME DEPOSIT FEELINGS.

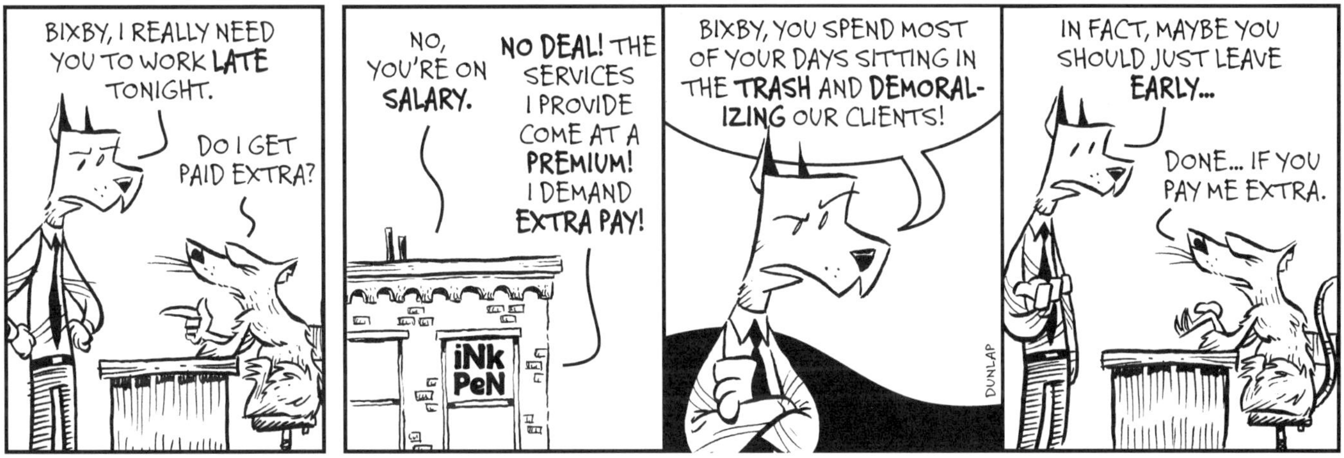
BIXBY, I REALLY NEED YOU TO WORK **LATE** TONIGHT.
DO I GET PAID EXTRA?
NO, YOU'RE ON **SALARY.**
**NO DEAL!** THE SERVICES I PROVIDE COME AT A **PREMIUM!** I DEMAND **EXTRA PAY!**
iNk PeN
BIXBY, YOU SPEND MOST OF YOUR DAYS SITTING IN THE **TRASH** AND **DEMORALIZING** OUR CLIENTS!
DUNLAP
IN FACT, MAYBE YOU SHOULD JUST LEAVE **EARLY...**
DONE... IF YOU PAY ME EXTRA.

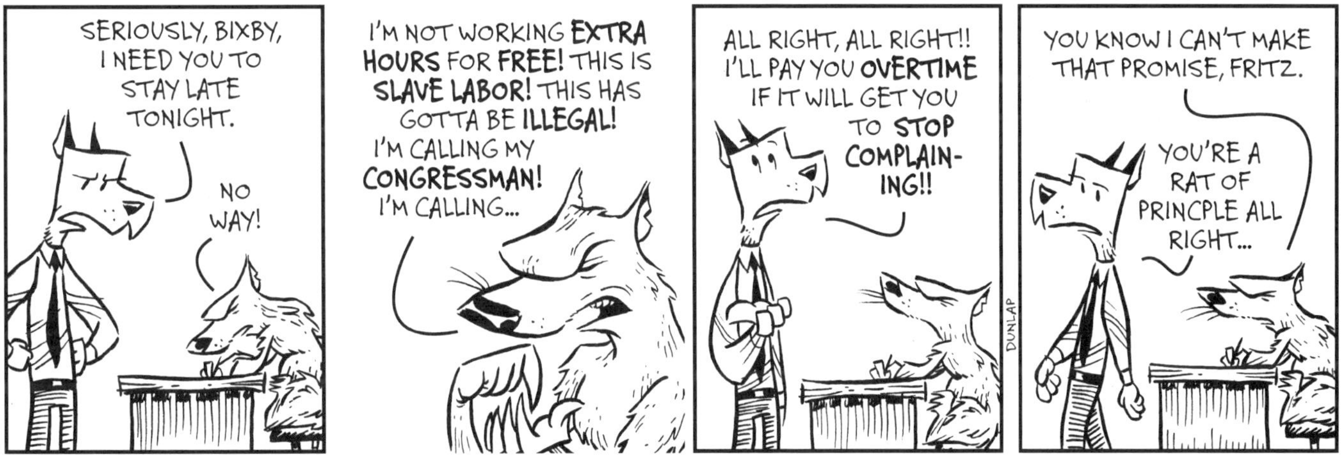
SERIOUSLY, BIXBY, I NEED YOU TO STAY LATE TONIGHT.
NO WAY!
I'M NOT WORKING **EXTRA HOURS** FOR **FREE!** THIS IS **SLAVE LABOR!** THIS HAS GOTTA BE **ILLEGAL!** I'M CALLING MY **CONGRESSMAN!** I'M CALLING...
ALL RIGHT, ALL RIGHT!! I'LL PAY YOU **OVERTIME** IF IT WILL GET YOU TO **STOP COMPLAINING!!**
DUNLAP
YOU KNOW I CAN'T MAKE THAT PROMISE, FRITZ.
YOU'RE A RAT OF PRINCPLE ALL RIGHT...

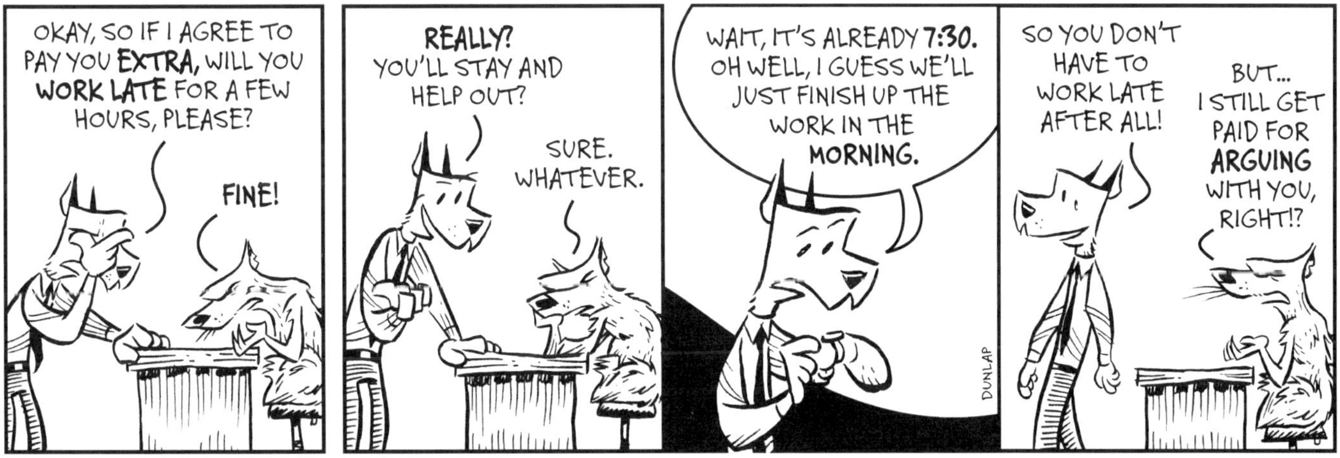
OKAY, SO IF I AGREE TO PAY YOU **EXTRA,** WILL YOU **WORK LATE** FOR A FEW HOURS, PLEASE?
**FINE!**
**REALLY?** YOU'LL STAY AND HELP OUT?
SURE. WHATEVER.
WAIT, IT'S ALREADY **7:30.** OH WELL, I GUESS WE'LL JUST FINISH UP THE WORK IN THE **MORNING.**
DUNLAP
SO YOU DON'T HAVE TO WORK LATE AFTER ALL!
BUT... I STILL GET PAID FOR **ARGUING** WITH YOU, RIGHT!?

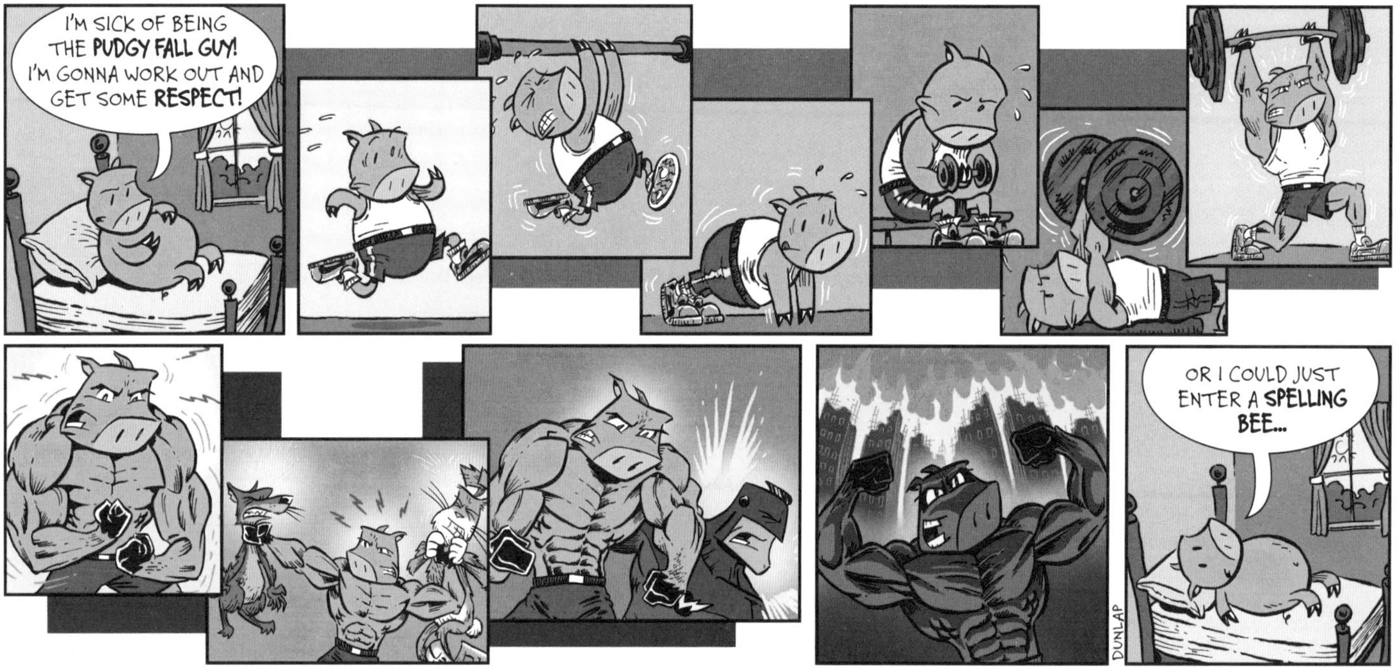
I'M SICK OF BEING THE **PUDGY FALL GUY!** I'M GONNA WORK OUT AND GET SOME **RESPECT!**
OR I COULD JUST ENTER A **SPELLING BEE...**
DUNLAP

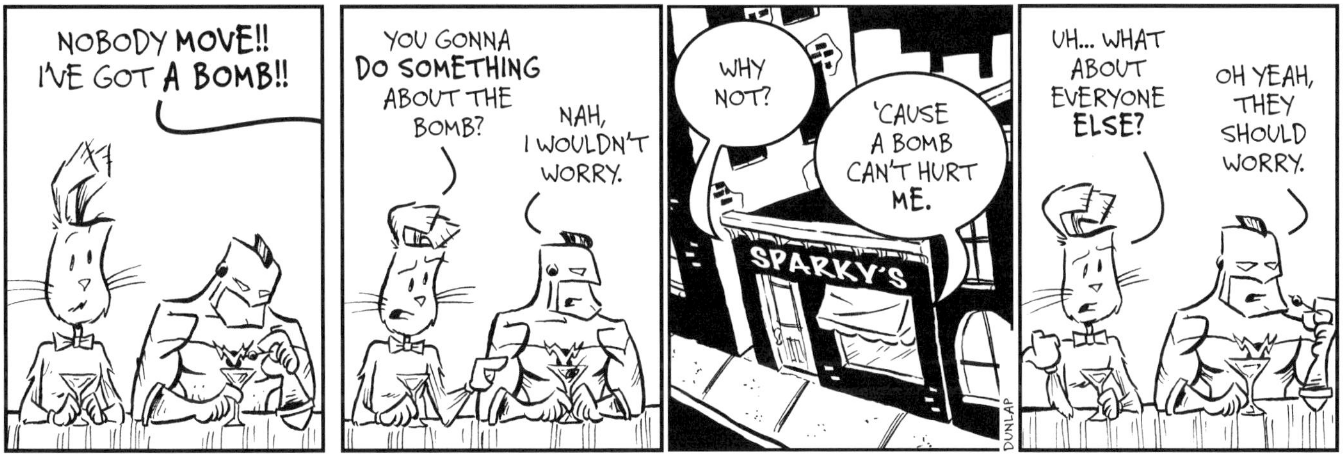
NOBODY MOVE!! I'VE GOT A BOMB!!
YOU GONNA DO SOMETHING ABOUT THE BOMB?
NAH, I WOULDN'T WORRY.
WHY NOT?
'CAUSE A BOMB CAN'T HURT ME.
SPARKY'S
UH... WHAT ABOUT EVERYONE ELSE?
OH YEAH, THEY SHOULD WORRY.
DUNLAP

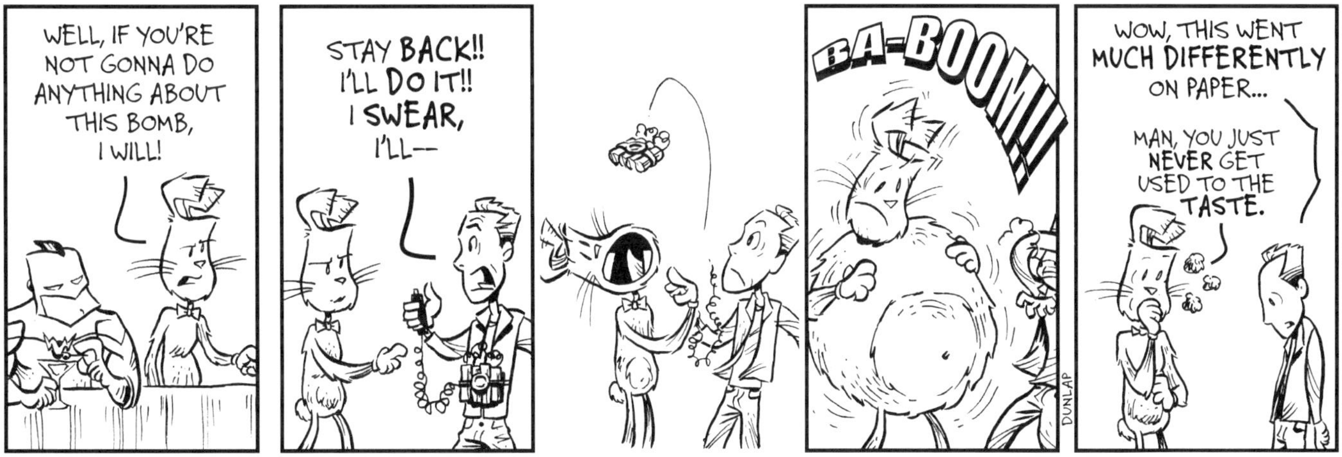
WELL, IF YOU'RE NOT GONNA DO ANYTHING ABOUT THIS BOMB, I WILL!
STAY BACK!! I'LL DO IT!! I SWEAR, I'LL--
BA-BOOM!!
WOW, THIS WENT MUCH DIFFERENTLY ON PAPER...
MAN, YOU JUST NEVER GET USED TO THE TASTE.
DUNLAP

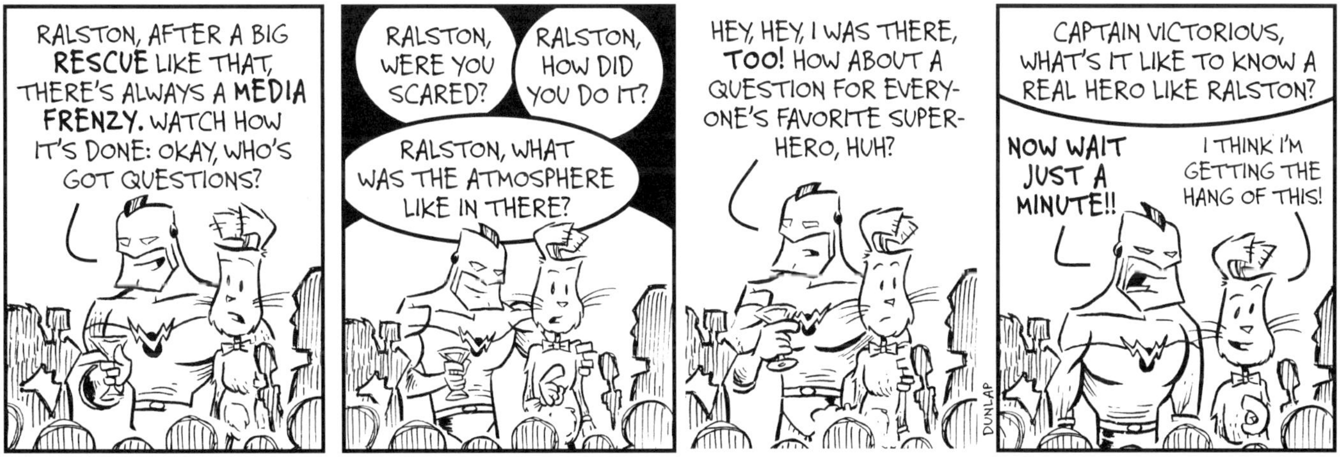
RALSTON, AFTER A BIG RESCUE LIKE THAT, THERE'S ALWAYS A MEDIA FRENZY. WATCH HOW IT'S DONE: OKAY, WHO'S GOT QUESTIONS?
RALSTON, WERE YOU SCARED?
RALSTON, HOW DID YOU DO IT?
RALSTON, WHAT WAS THE ATMOSPHERE LIKE IN THERE?
HEY, HEY, I WAS THERE, TOO! HOW ABOUT A QUESTION FOR EVERY-ONE'S FAVORITE SUPER-HERO, HUH?
CAPTAIN VICTORIOUS, WHAT'S IT LIKE TO KNOW A REAL HERO LIKE RALSTON?
NOW WAIT JUST A MINUTE!!
I THINK I'M GETTING THE HANG OF THIS!
DUNLAP

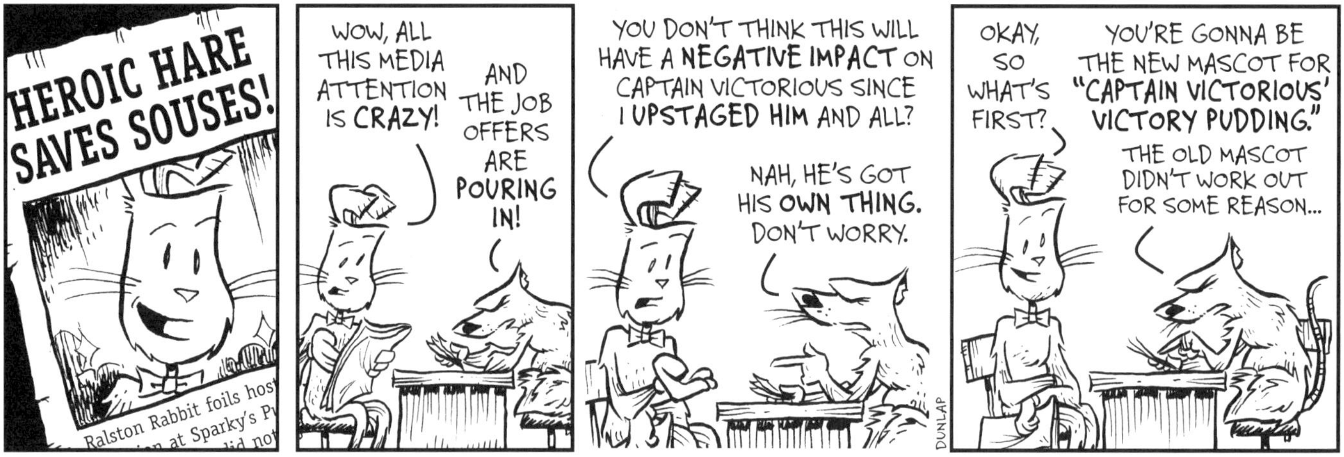
HEROIC HARE SAVES SOUSES!
Ralston Rabbit foils
WOW, ALL THIS MEDIA ATTENTION IS CRAZY!
AND THE JOB OFFERS ARE POURING IN!
YOU DON'T THINK THIS WILL HAVE A NEGATIVE IMPACT ON CAPTAIN VICTORIOUS SINCE I UPSTAGED HIM AND ALL?
NAH, HE'S GOT HIS OWN THING. DON'T WORRY.
DUNLAP
OKAY, SO WHAT'S FIRST?
YOU'RE GONNA BE THE NEW MASCOT FOR "CAPTAIN VICTORIOUS' VICTORY PUDDING."
THE OLD MASCOT DIDN'T WORK OUT FOR SOME REASON...

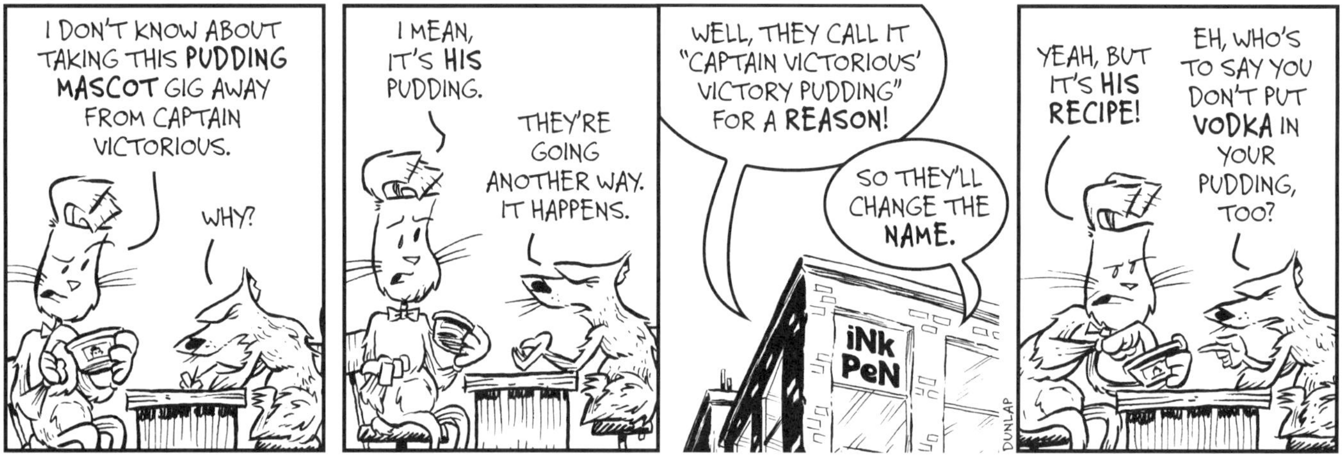
I DON'T KNOW ABOUT TAKING THIS PUDDING MASCOT GIG AWAY FROM CAPTAIN VICTORIOUS.
WHY?
I MEAN, IT'S HIS PUDDING.
THEY'RE GOING ANOTHER WAY. IT HAPPENS.
WELL, THEY CALL IT "CAPTAIN VICTORIOUS' VICTORY PUDDING" FOR A REASON!
SO THEY'LL CHANGE THE NAME.
iNk PeN
DUNLAP
YEAH, BUT IT'S HIS RECIPE!
EH, WHO'S TO SAY YOU DON'T PUT VODKA IN YOUR PUDDING, TOO?

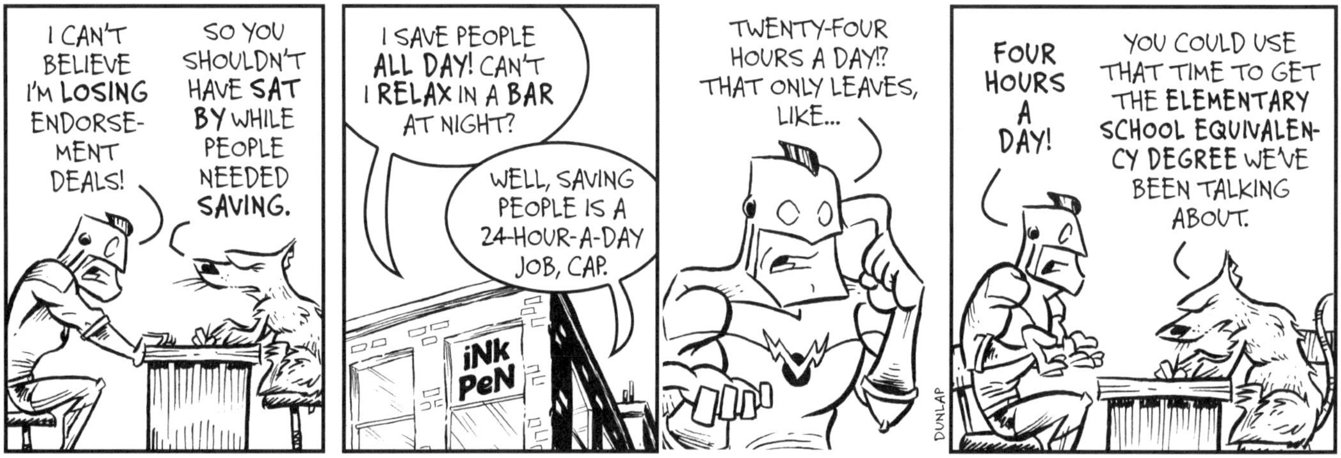
I CAN'T BELIEVE I'M LOSING ENDORSE-MENT DEALS!
SO YOU SHOULDN'T HAVE SAT BY WHILE PEOPLE NEEDED SAVING.
I SAVE PEOPLE ALL DAY! CAN'T I RELAX IN A BAR AT NIGHT?
WELL, SAVING PEOPLE IS A 24-HOUR-A-DAY JOB, CAP.
iNk PeN
TWENTY-FOUR HOURS A DAY!? THAT ONLY LEAVES, LIKE...
DUNLAP
FOUR HOURS A DAY!
YOU COULD USE THAT TIME TO GET THE ELEMENTARY SCHOOL EQUIVALEN-CY DEGREE WE'VE BEEN TALKING ABOUT.

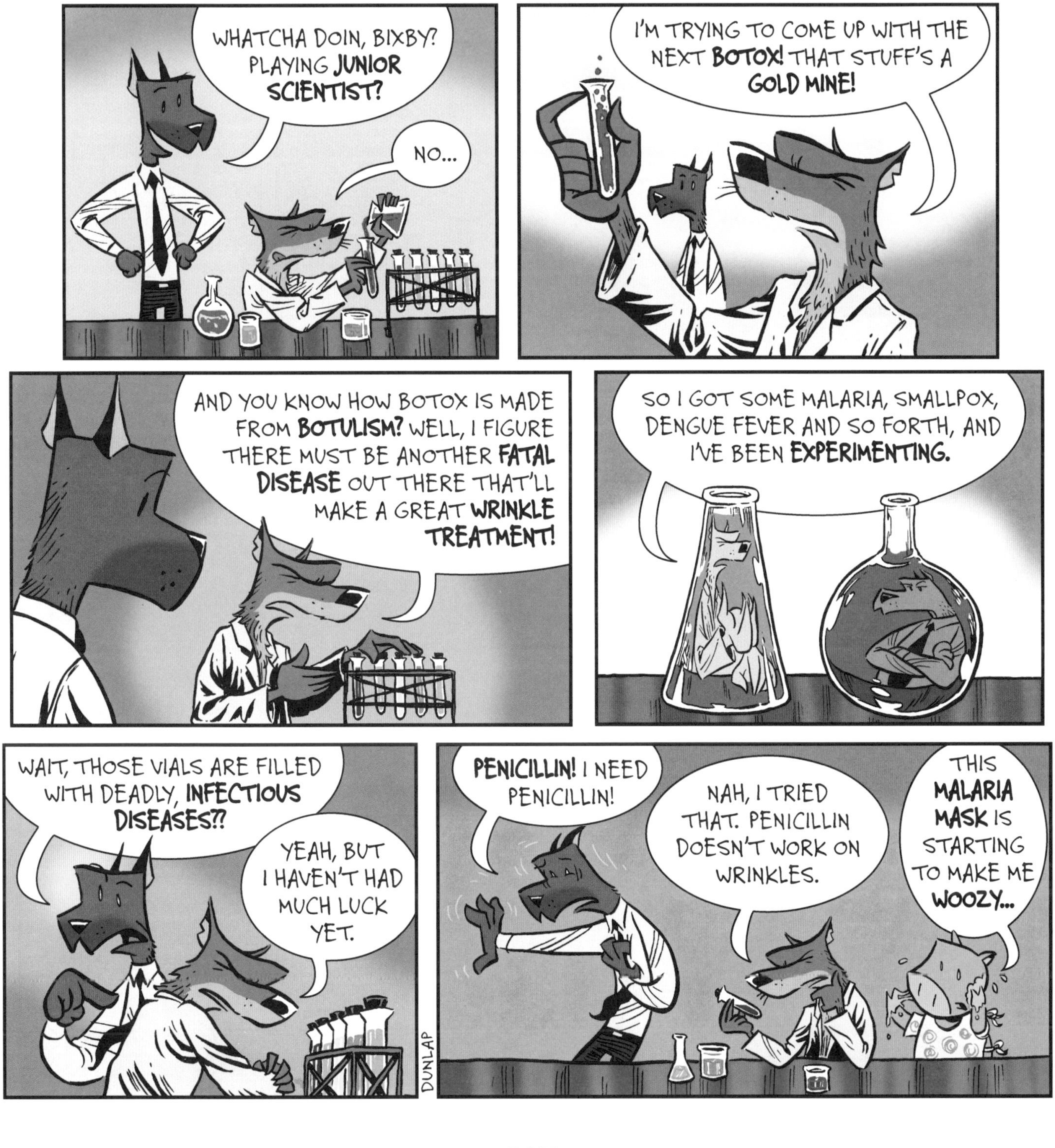
WHATCHA DOIN, BIXBY? PLAYING **JUNIOR SCIENTIST?**
NO...
I'M TRYING TO COME UP WITH THE NEXT **BOTOX!** THAT STUFF'S A **GOLD MINE!**
AND YOU KNOW HOW BOTOX IS MADE FROM **BOTULISM?** WELL, I FIGURE THERE MUST BE ANOTHER **FATAL DISEASE** OUT THERE THAT'LL MAKE A GREAT **WRINKLE TREATMENT!**
SO I GOT SOME MALARIA, SMALLPOX, DENGUE FEVER AND SO FORTH, AND I'VE BEEN **EXPERIMENTING.**
WAIT, THOSE VIALS ARE FILLED WITH DEADLY, **INFECTIOUS DISEASES?!**
YEAH, BUT I HAVEN'T HAD MUCH LUCK YET.
DUNLAP
**PENICILLIN!** I NEED PENICILLIN!
NAH, I TRIED THAT. PENICILLIN DOESN'T WORK ON WRINKLES.
THIS **MALARIA MASK** IS STARTING TO MAKE ME **WOOZY...**

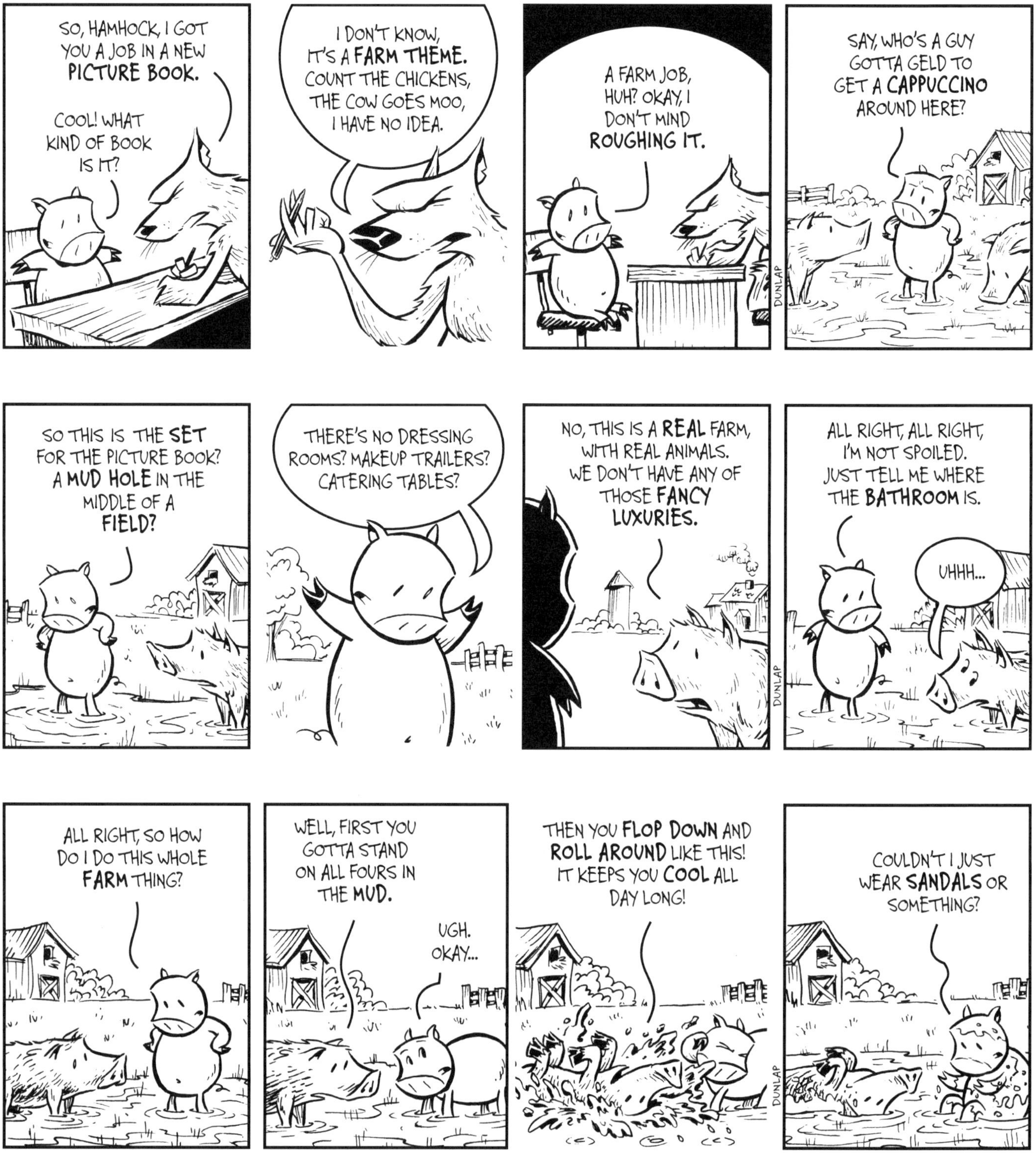
SO, HAMHOCK, I GOT YOU A JOB IN A NEW PICTURE BOOK.
COOL! WHAT KIND OF BOOK IS IT?
I DON'T KNOW, IT'S A FARM THEME. COUNT THE CHICKENS, THE COW GOES MOO, I HAVE NO IDEA.
A FARM JOB, HUH? OKAY, I DON'T MIND ROUGHING IT.
DUNLAP
SAY, WHO'S A GUY GOTTA GELD TO GET A CAPPUCCINO AROUND HERE?
SO THIS IS THE SET FOR THE PICTURE BOOK? A MUD HOLE IN THE MIDDLE OF A FIELD?
THERE'S NO DRESSING ROOMS? MAKEUP TRAILERS? CATERING TABLES?
NO, THIS IS A REAL FARM, WITH REAL ANIMALS. WE DON'T HAVE ANY OF THOSE FANCY LUXURIES.
DUNLAP
ALL RIGHT, ALL RIGHT, I'M NOT SPOILED. JUST TELL ME WHERE THE BATHROOM IS.
UHHH...
ALL RIGHT, SO HOW DO I DO THIS WHOLE FARM THING?
WELL, FIRST YOU GOTTA STAND ON ALL FOURS IN THE MUD.
UGH. OKAY...
THEN YOU FLOP DOWN AND ROLL AROUND LIKE THIS! IT KEEPS YOU COOL ALL DAY LONG!
DUNLAP
COULDN'T I JUST WEAR SANDALS OR SOMETHING?

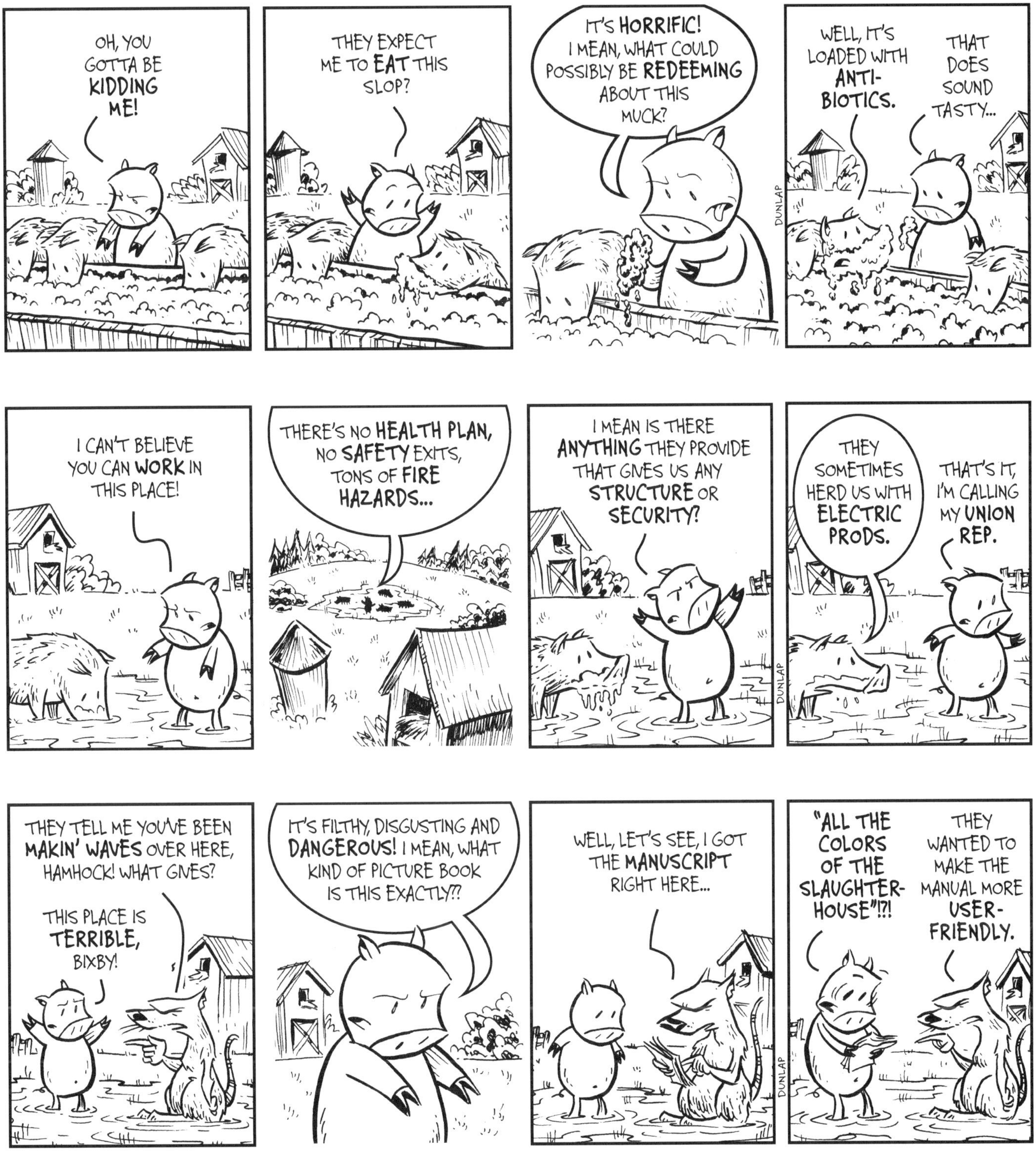

OH, YOU GOTTA BE KIDDING ME!
THEY EXPECT ME TO EAT THIS SLOP?
IT'S HORRIFIC! I MEAN, WHAT COULD POSSIBLY BE REDEEMING ABOUT THIS MUCK?
DUNLAP
WELL, IT'S LOADED WITH ANTI-BIOTICS.
THAT DOES SOUND TASTY...
I CAN'T BELIEVE YOU CAN WORK IN THIS PLACE!
THERE'S NO HEALTH PLAN, NO SAFETY EXITS, TONS OF FIRE HAZARDS...
I MEAN IS THERE ANYTHING THEY PROVIDE THAT GIVES US ANY STRUCTURE OR SECURITY?
DUNLAP
THEY SOMETIMES HERD US WITH ELECTRIC PRODS.
THAT'S IT, I'M CALLING MY UNION REP.
THEY TELL ME YOU'VE BEEN MAKIN' WAVES OVER HERE, HAMHOCK! WHAT GIVES?
THIS PLACE IS TERRIBLE, BIXBY!
IT'S FILTHY, DISGUSTING AND DANGEROUS! I MEAN, WHAT KIND OF PICTURE BOOK IS THIS EXACTLY?!?
WELL, LET'S SEE, I GOT THE MANUSCRIPT RIGHT HERE...
DUNLAP
"ALL THE COLORS OF THE SLAUGHTER-HOUSE"!?!
THEY WANTED TO MAKE THE MANUAL MORE USER-FRIENDLY.

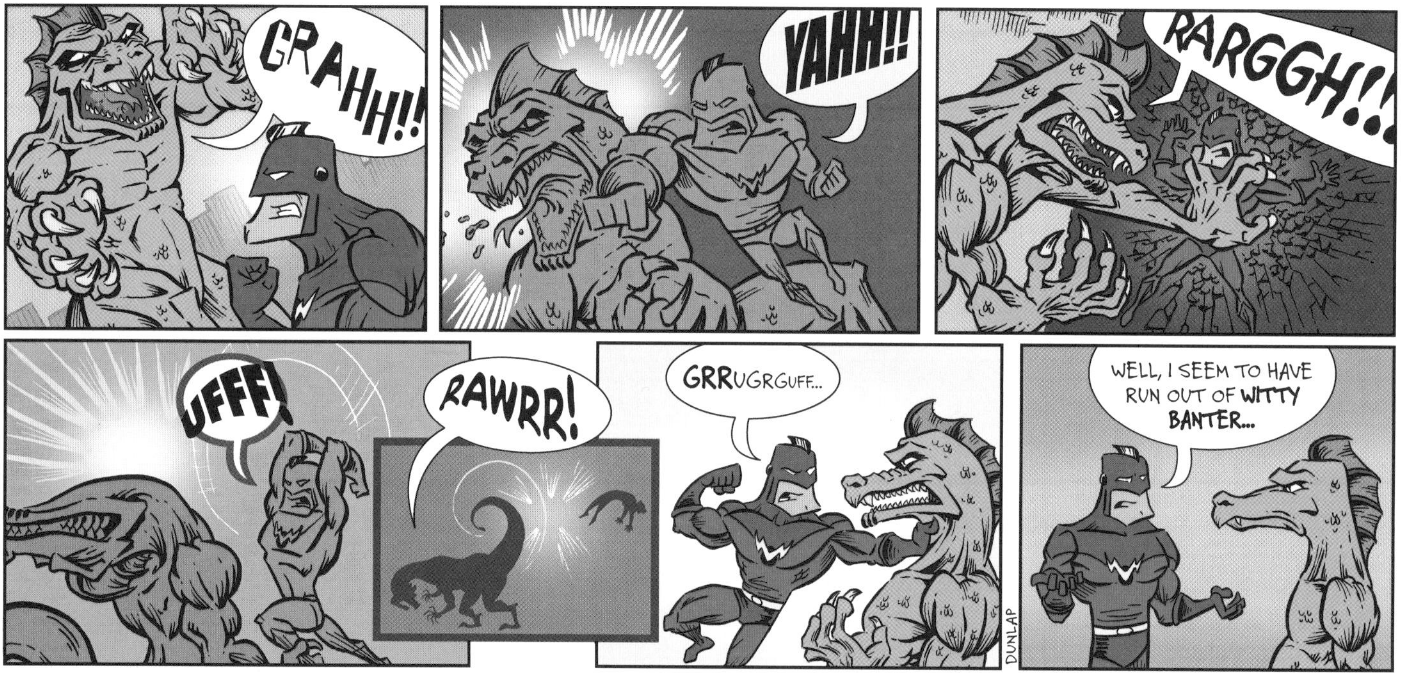
GRAHH!!
YAHH!!
RARGGH!!!
UFFF!
RAWRR!
GRRUGRGUFF...
DUNLAP
WELL, I SEEM TO HAVE RUN OUT OF WITTY BANTER...

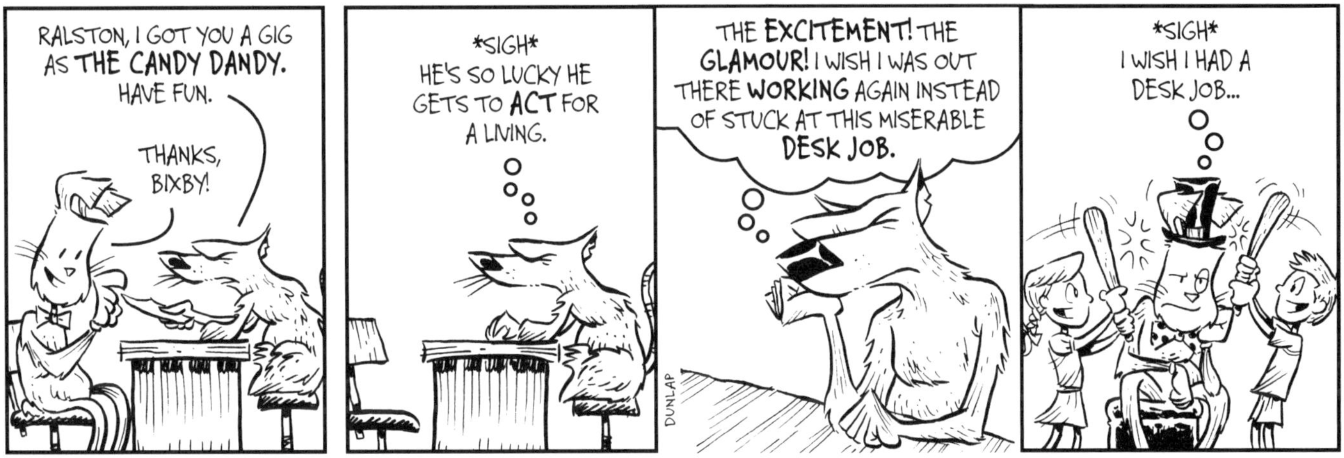
RALSTON, I GOT YOU A GIG AS THE CANDY DANDY. HAVE FUN.
THANKS, BIXBY!
*SIGH* HE'S SO LUCKY HE GETS TO ACT FOR A LIVING.
THE EXCITEMENT! THE GLAMOUR! I WISH I WAS OUT THERE WORKING AGAIN INSTEAD OF STUCK AT THIS MISERABLE DESK JOB.
DUNLAP
*SIGH* I WISH I HAD A DESK JOB...

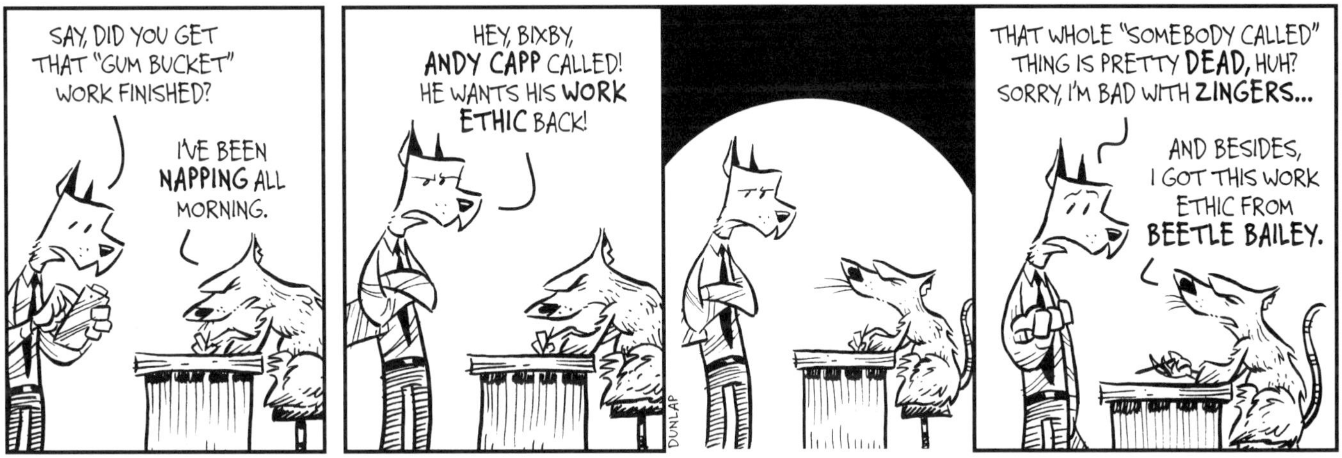
SAY, DID YOU GET THAT "GUM BUCKET" WORK FINISHED?
I'VE BEEN NAPPING ALL MORNING.
HEY, BIXBY, ANDY CAPP CALLED! HE WANTS HIS WORK ETHIC BACK!
DUNLAP
THAT WHOLE "SOMEBODY CALLED" THING IS PRETTY DEAD, HUH? SORRY, I'M BAD WITH ZINGERS...
AND BESIDES, I GOT THIS WORK ETHIC FROM BEETLE BAILEY.

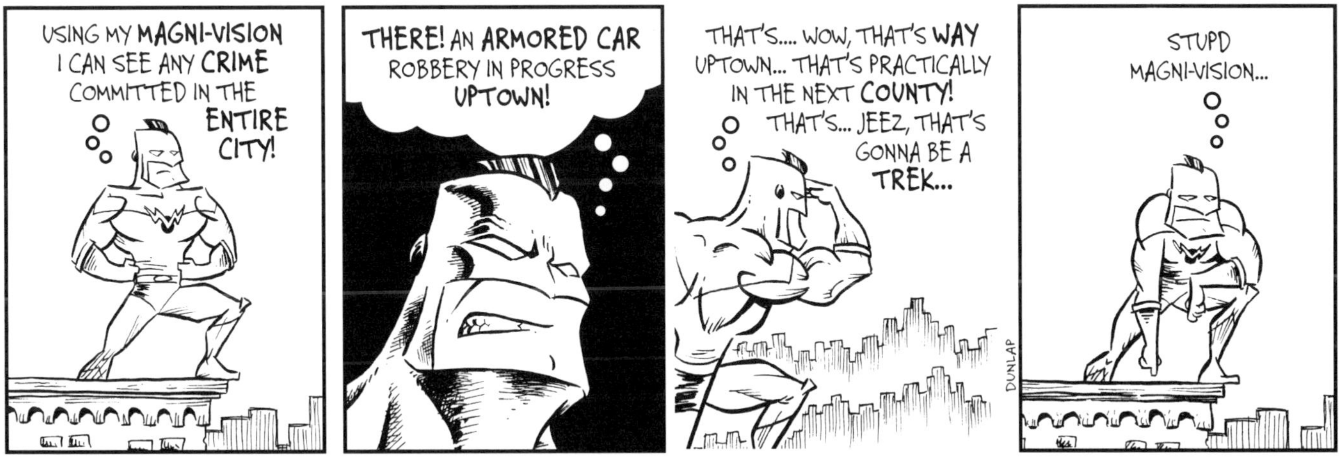
USING MY MAGNI-VISION I CAN SEE ANY CRIME COMMITTED IN THE ENTIRE CITY!
THERE! AN ARMORED CAR ROBBERY IN PROGRESS UPTOWN!
THAT'S.... WOW, THAT'S WAY UPTOWN... THAT'S PRACTICALLY IN THE NEXT COUNTY!
THAT'S... JEEZ, THAT'S GONNA BE A TREK...
DUNLAP
STUPD MAGNI-VISION...

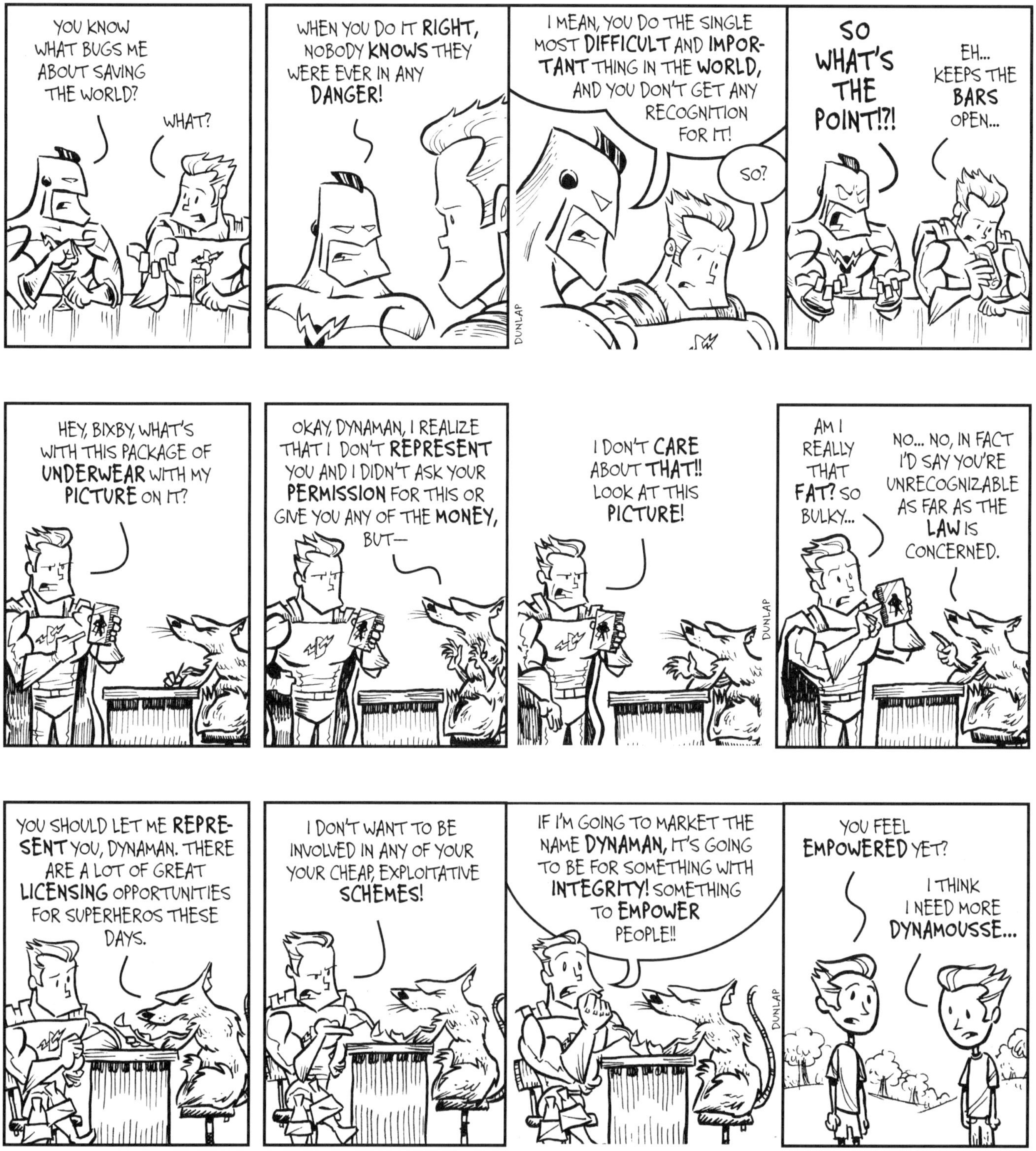
YOU KNOW WHAT BUGS ME ABOUT SAVING THE WORLD?
WHAT?
WHEN YOU DO IT RIGHT, NOBODY KNOWS THEY WERE EVER IN ANY DANGER!
I MEAN, YOU DO THE SINGLE MOST DIFFICULT AND IMPORTANT THING IN THE WORLD, AND YOU DON'T GET ANY RECOGNITION FOR IT!
SO?
SO WHAT'S THE POINT!?!
EH... KEEPS THE BARS OPEN...
DUNLAP
HEY, BIXBY, WHAT'S WITH THIS PACKAGE OF UNDERWEAR WITH MY PICTURE ON IT?
OKAY, DYNAMAN, I REALIZE THAT I DON'T REPRESENT YOU AND I DIDN'T ASK YOUR PERMISSION FOR THIS OR GIVE YOU ANY OF THE MONEY, BUT—
I DON'T CARE ABOUT THAT!! LOOK AT THIS PICTURE!
AM I REALLY THAT FAT? SO BULKY...
NO... NO, IN FACT I'D SAY YOU'RE UNRECOGNIZABLE AS FAR AS THE LAW IS CONCERNED.
DUNLAP
YOU SHOULD LET ME REPRESENT YOU, DYNAMAN. THERE ARE A LOT OF GREAT LICENSING OPPORTUNITIES FOR SUPERHEROS THESE DAYS.
I DON'T WANT TO BE INVOLVED IN ANY OF YOUR YOUR CHEAP, EXPLOITATIVE SCHEMES!
IF I'M GOING TO MARKET THE NAME DYNAMAN, IT'S GOING TO BE FOR SOMETHING WITH INTEGRITY! SOMETHING TO EMPOWER PEOPLE!!
YOU FEEL EMPOWERED YET?
I THINK I NEED MORE DYNAMOUSSE...
DUNLAP

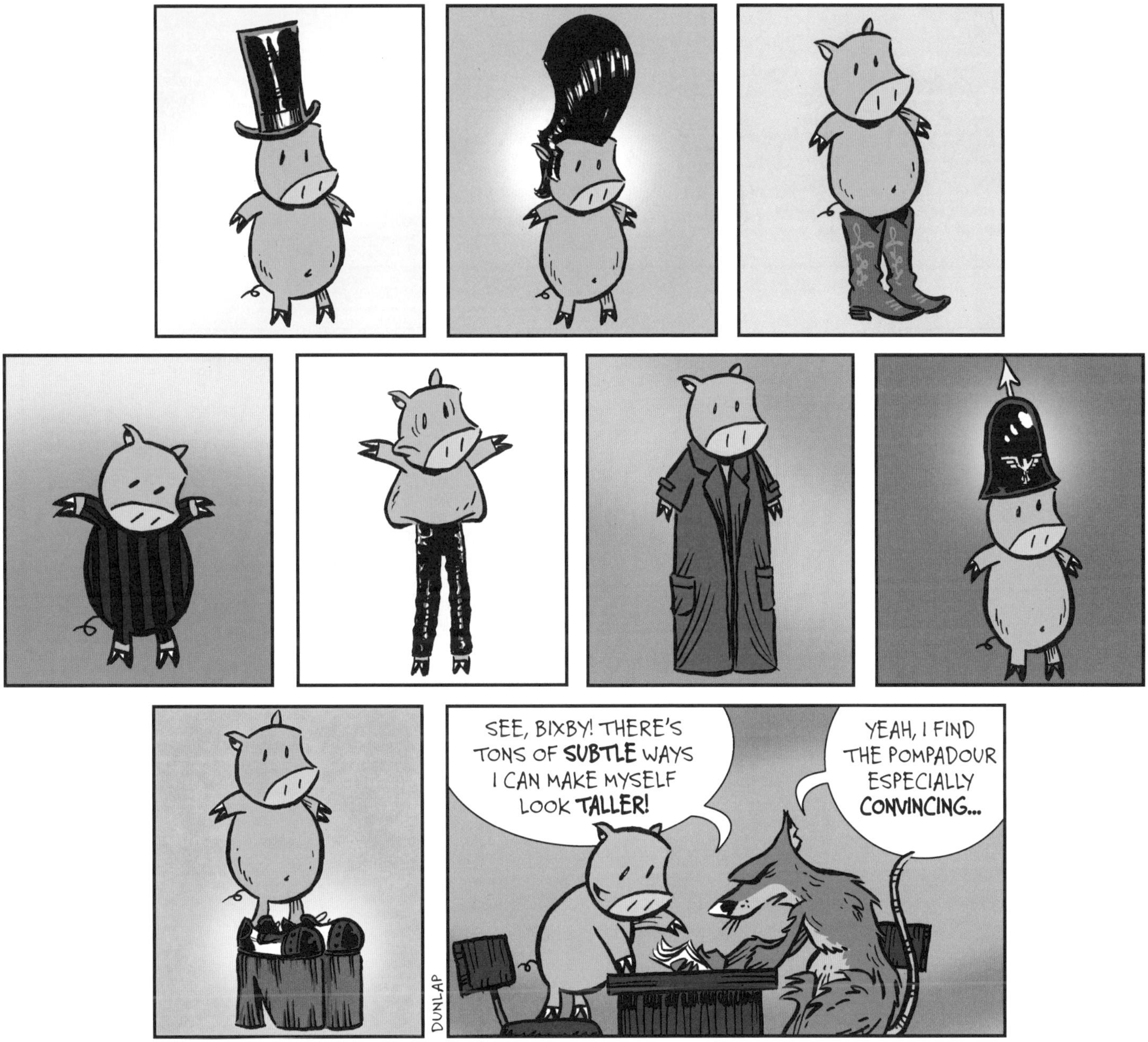
SEE, BIXBY! THERE'S TONS OF **SUBTLE** WAYS I CAN MAKE MYSELF LOOK **TALLER!**
YEAH, I FIND THE POMPADOUR ESPECIALLY **CONVINCING...**
DUNLAP

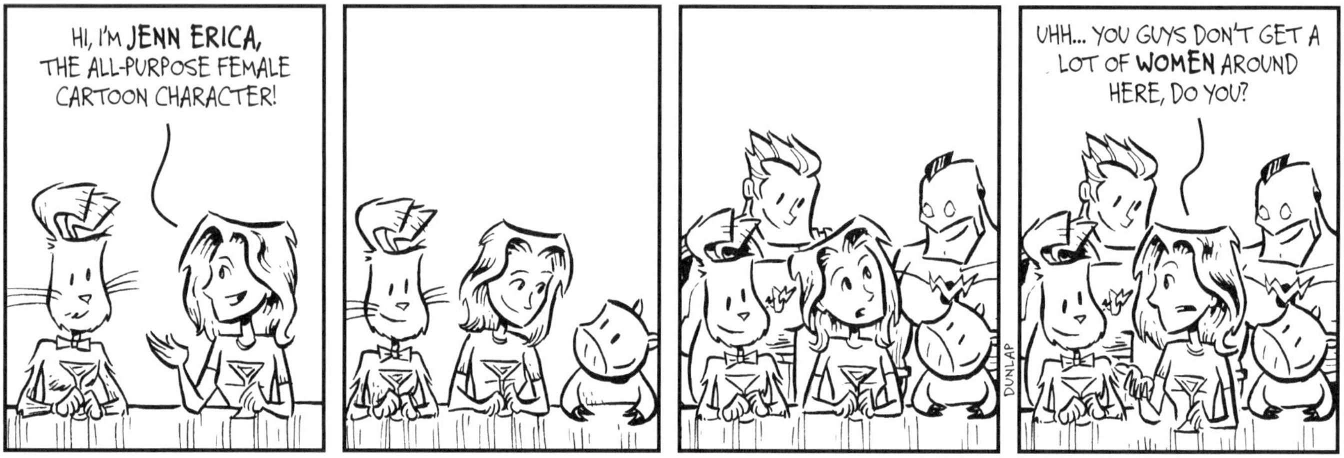
HI, I'M JENN ERICA, THE ALL-PURPOSE FEMALE CARTOON CHARACTER!
DUNLAP
UHH... YOU GUYS DON'T GET A LOT OF WOMEN AROUND HERE, DO YOU?

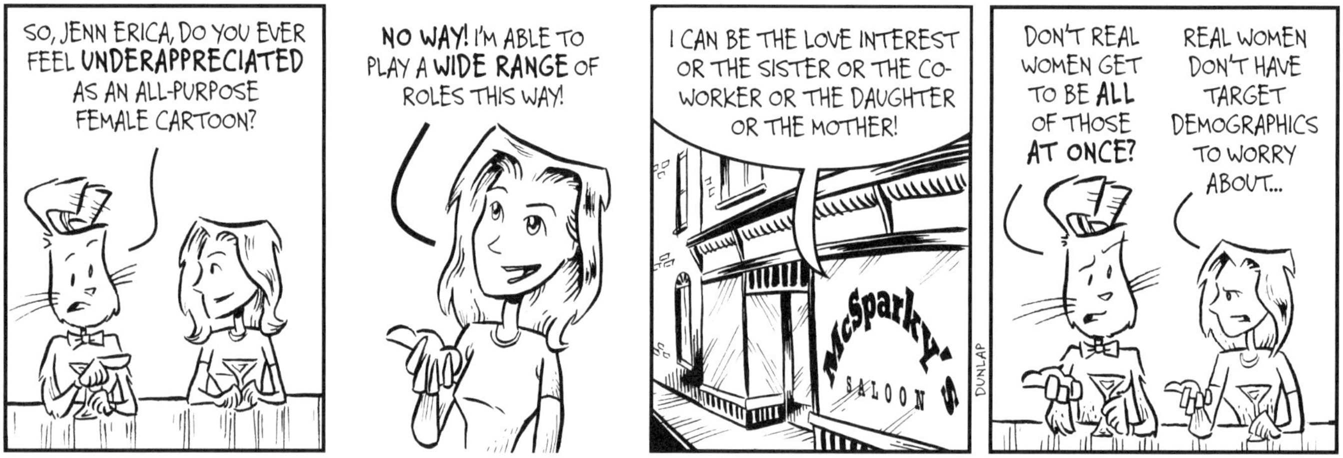
SO, JENN ERICA, DO YOU EVER FEEL UNDERAPPRECIATED AS AN ALL-PURPOSE FEMALE CARTOON?
NO WAY! I'M ABLE TO PLAY A WIDE RANGE OF ROLES THIS WAY!
I CAN BE THE LOVE INTEREST OR THE SISTER OR THE CO-WORKER OR THE DAUGHTER OR THE MOTHER!
McSparky's
SALOON
DUNLAP
DON'T REAL WOMEN GET TO BE ALL OF THOSE AT ONCE?
REAL WOMEN DON'T HAVE TARGET DEMOGRAPHICS TO WORRY ABOUT...

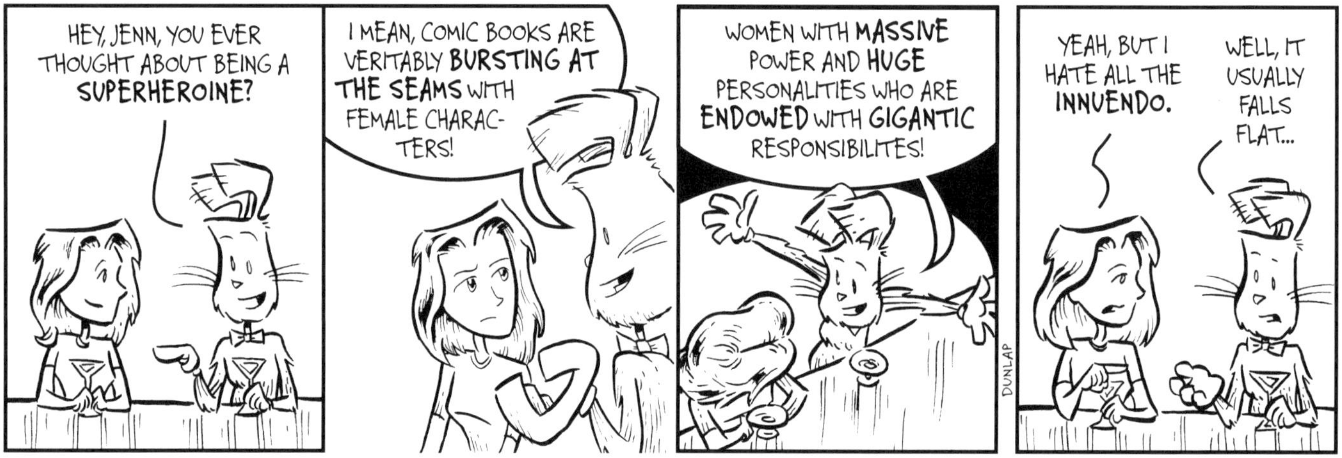
HEY, JENN, YOU EVER THOUGHT ABOUT BEING A SUPERHEROINE?
I MEAN, COMIC BOOKS ARE VERITABLY BURSTING AT THE SEAMS WITH FEMALE CHARAC-TERS!
WOMEN WITH MASSIVE POWER AND HUGE PERSONALITIES WHO ARE ENDOWED WITH GIGANTIC RESPONSIBILITES!
DUNLAP
YEAH, BUT I HATE ALL THE INNUENDO.
WELL, IT USUALLY FALLS FLAT...

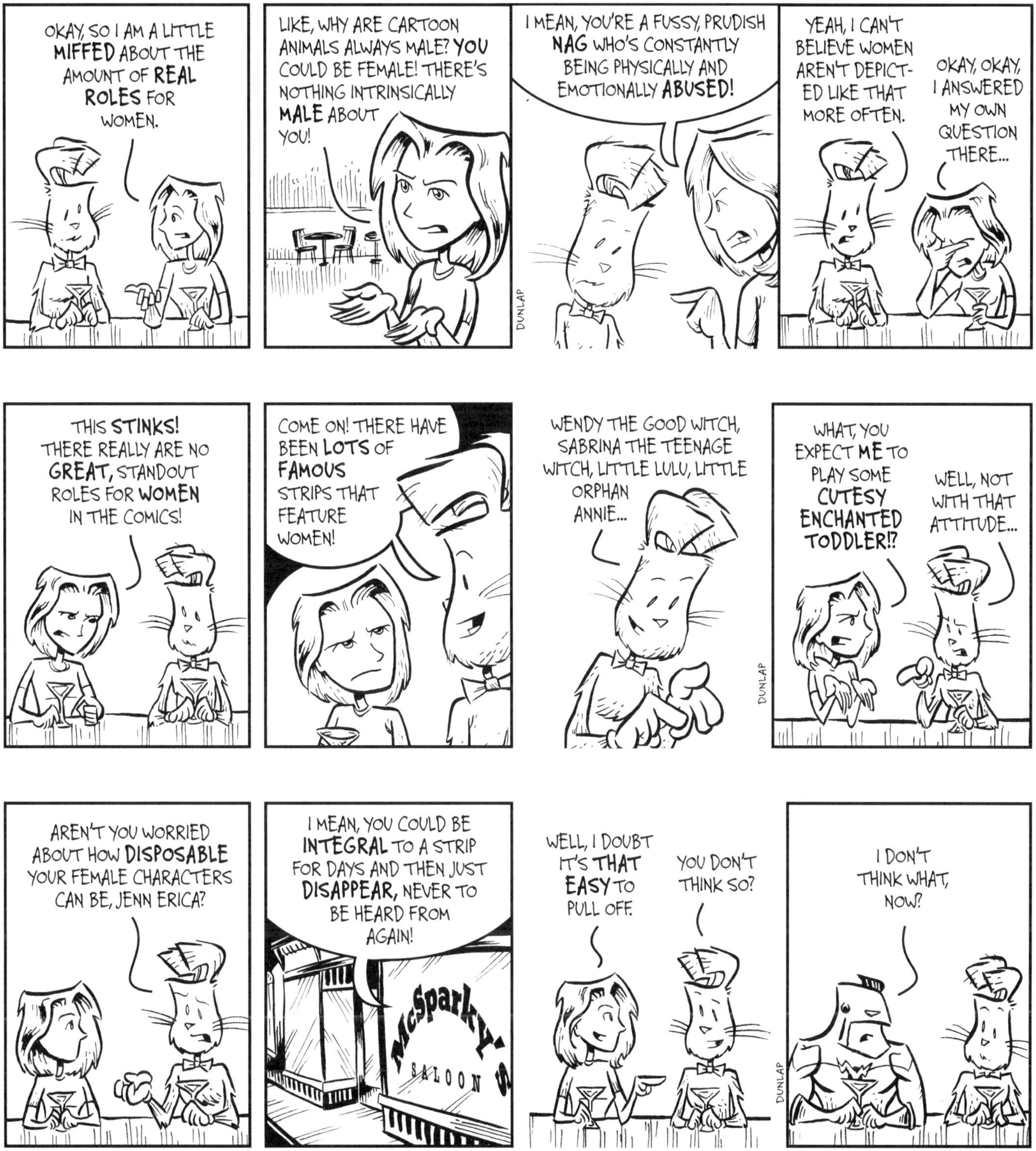
OKAY, SO I AM A LITTLE MIFFED ABOUT THE AMOUNT OF REAL ROLES FOR WOMEN.
LIKE, WHY ARE CARTOON ANIMALS ALWAYS MALE? YOU COULD BE FEMALE! THERE'S NOTHING INTRINSICALLY MALE ABOUT YOU!
I MEAN, YOU'RE A FUSSY, PRUDISH NAG WHO'S CONSTANTLY BEING PHYSICALLY AND EMOTIONALLY ABUSED!
DUNLAP
YEAH, I CAN'T BELIEVE WOMEN AREN'T DEPICTED LIKE THAT MORE OFTEN.
OKAY, OKAY, I ANSWERED MY OWN QUESTION THERE...
THIS STINKS! THERE REALLY ARE NO GREAT, STANDOUT ROLES FOR WOMEN IN THE COMICS!
COME ON! THERE HAVE BEEN LOTS OF FAMOUS STRIPS THAT FEATURE WOMEN!
WENDY THE GOOD WITCH, SABRINA THE TEENAGE WITCH, LITTLE LULU, LITTLE ORPHAN ANNIE...
DUNLAP
WHAT, YOU EXPECT ME TO PLAY SOME CUTESY ENCHANTED TODDLER!?
WELL, NOT WITH THAT ATTITUDE...
AREN'T YOU WORRIED ABOUT HOW DISPOSABLE YOUR FEMALE CHARACTERS CAN BE, JENN ERICA?
I MEAN, YOU COULD BE INTEGRAL TO A STRIP FOR DAYS AND THEN JUST DISAPPEAR, NEVER TO BE HEARD FROM AGAIN!
McSparky's
SALOON
WELL, I DOUBT IT'S THAT EASY TO PULL OFF.
YOU DON'T THINK SO?
DUNLAP
I DON'T THINK WHAT, NOW?

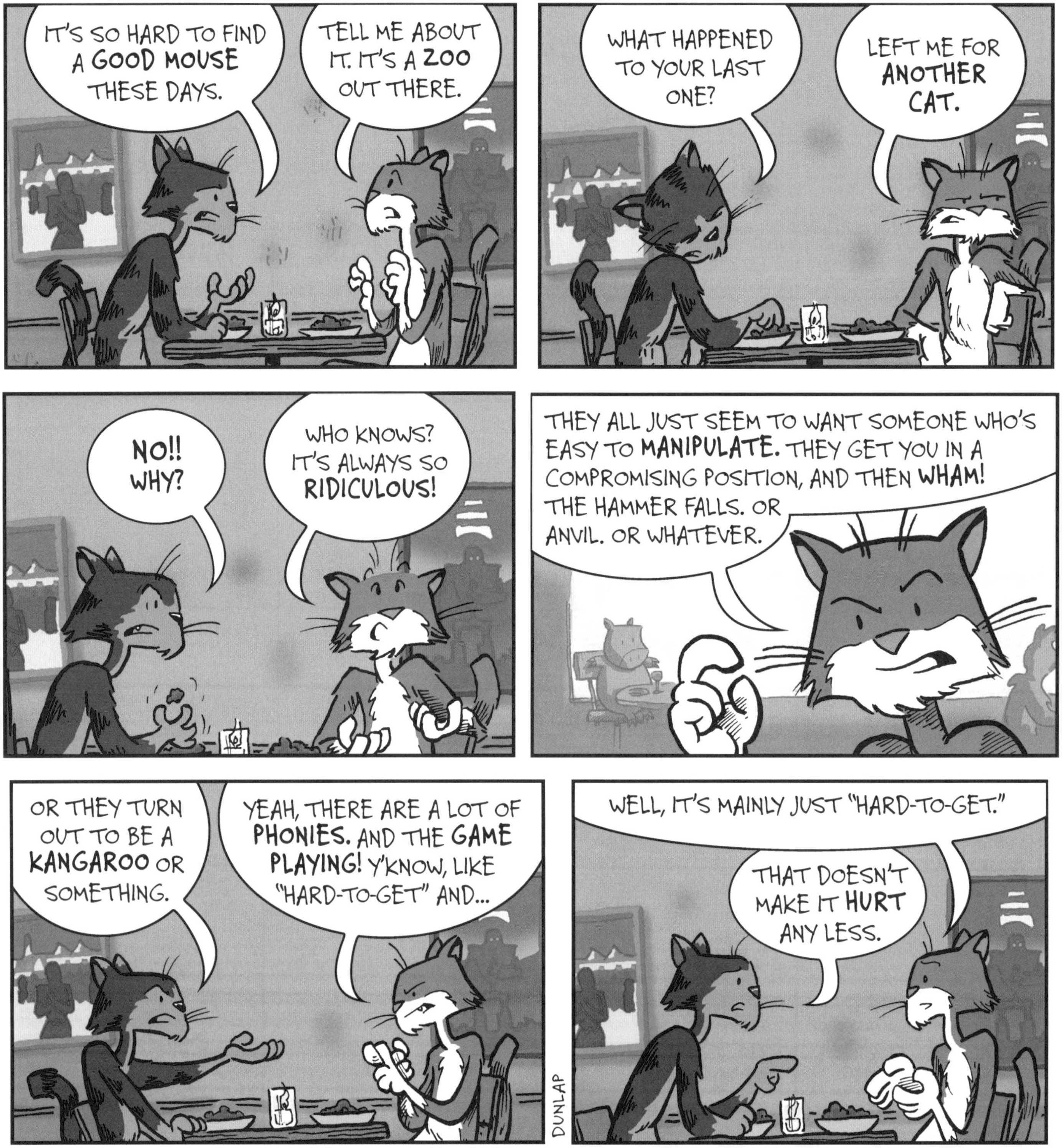
IT'S SO HARD TO FIND A GOOD MOUSE THESE DAYS.
TELL ME ABOUT IT. IT'S A ZOO OUT THERE.
WHAT HAPPENED TO YOUR LAST ONE?
LEFT ME FOR ANOTHER CAT.
NO!! WHY?
WHO KNOWS? IT'S ALWAYS SO RIDICULOUS!
THEY ALL JUST SEEM TO WANT SOMEONE WHO'S EASY TO MANIPULATE. THEY GET YOU IN A COMPROMISING POSITION, AND THEN WHAM! THE HAMMER FALLS. OR ANVIL. OR WHATEVER.
OR THEY TURN OUT TO BE A KANGAROO OR SOMETHING.
YEAH, THERE ARE A LOT OF PHONIES. AND THE GAME PLAYING! Y'KNOW, LIKE "HARD-TO-GET" AND...
DUNLAP
WELL, IT'S MAINLY JUST "HARD-TO-GET."
THAT DOESN'T MAKE IT HURT ANY LESS.

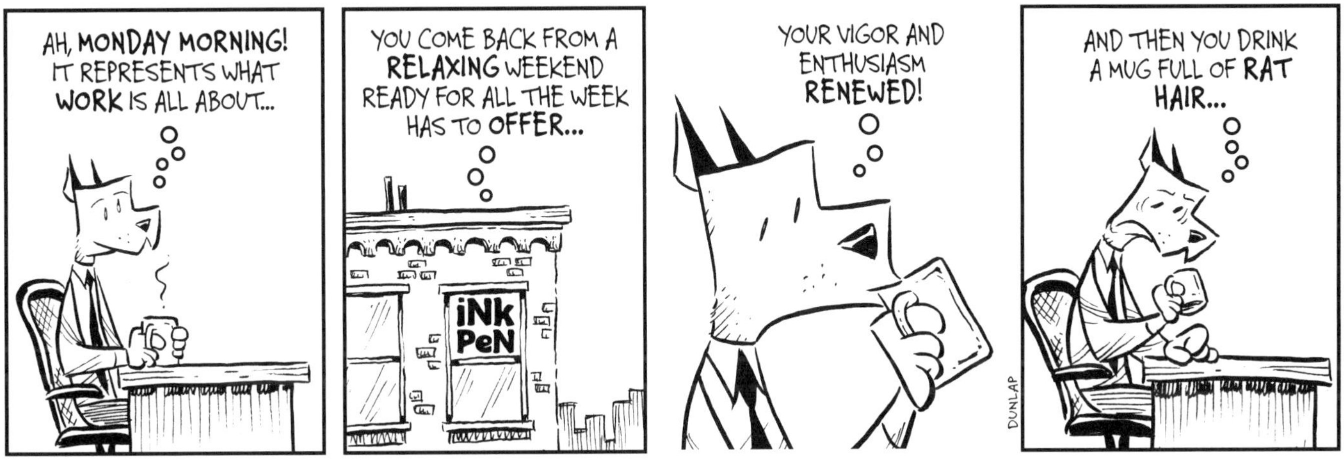
AH, MONDAY MORNING! IT REPRESENTS WHAT WORK IS ALL ABOUT...
YOU COME BACK FROM A RELAXING WEEKEND READY FOR ALL THE WEEK HAS TO OFFER...
iNk PeN
YOUR VIGOR AND ENTHUSIASM RENEWED!
DUNLAP
AND THEN YOU DRINK A MUG FULL OF RAT HAIR...

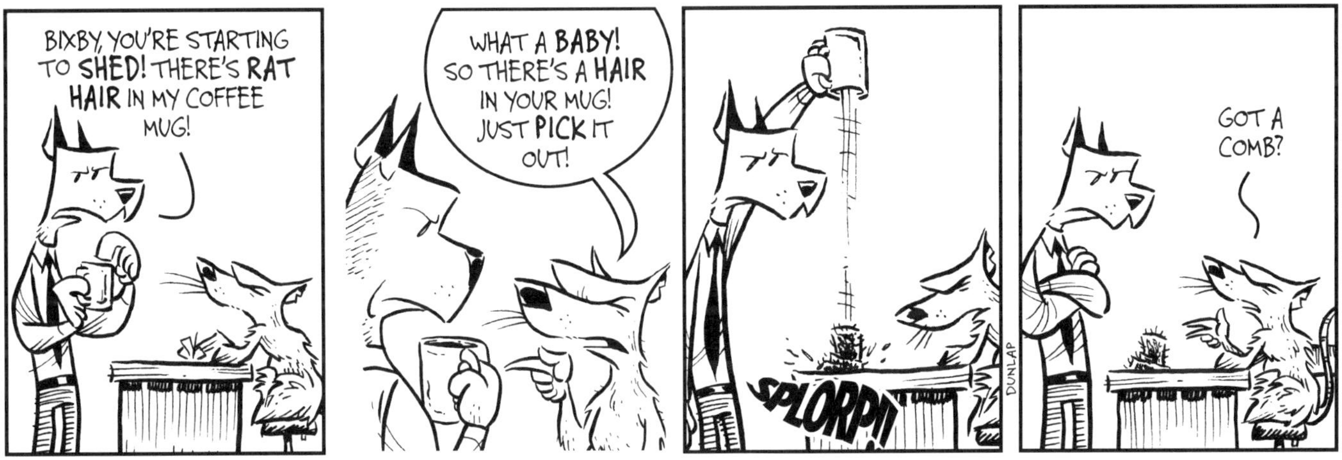
BIXBY, YOU'RE STARTING TO SHED! THERE'S RAT HAIR IN MY COFFEE MUG!
WHAT A BABY! SO THERE'S A HAIR IN YOUR MUG! JUST PICK IT OUT!
SPLORP!!
DUNLAP
GOT A COMB?

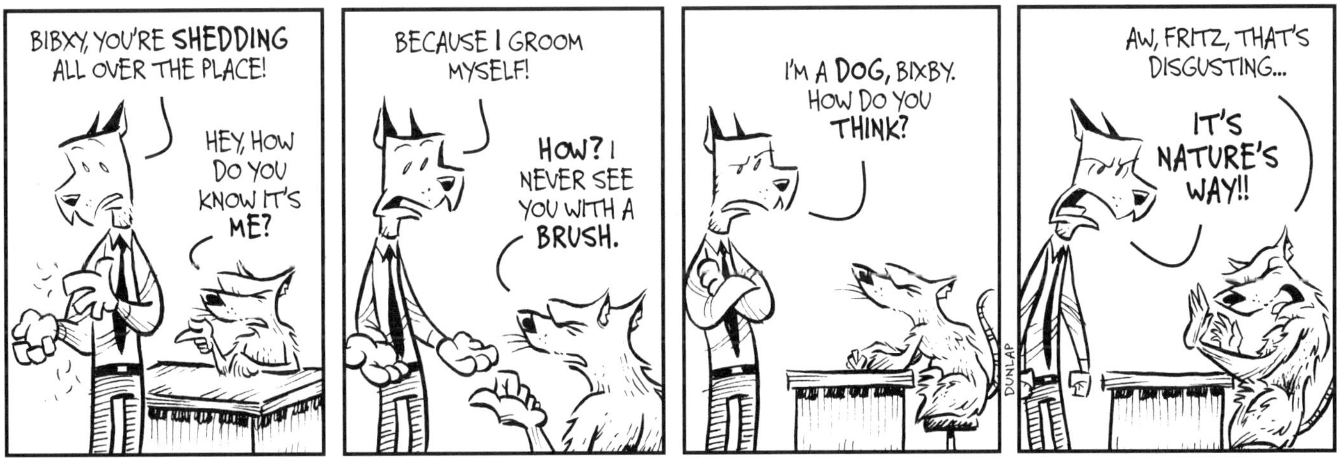
BIBXY, YOU'RE SHEDDING ALL OVER THE PLACE!
HEY, HOW DO YOU KNOW IT'S ME?
BECAUSE I GROOM MYSELF!
HOW? I NEVER SEE YOU WITH A BRUSH.
I'M A DOG, BIXBY. HOW DO YOU THINK?
DUNLAP
AW, FRITZ, THAT'S DISGUSTING...
IT'S NATURE'S WAY!!

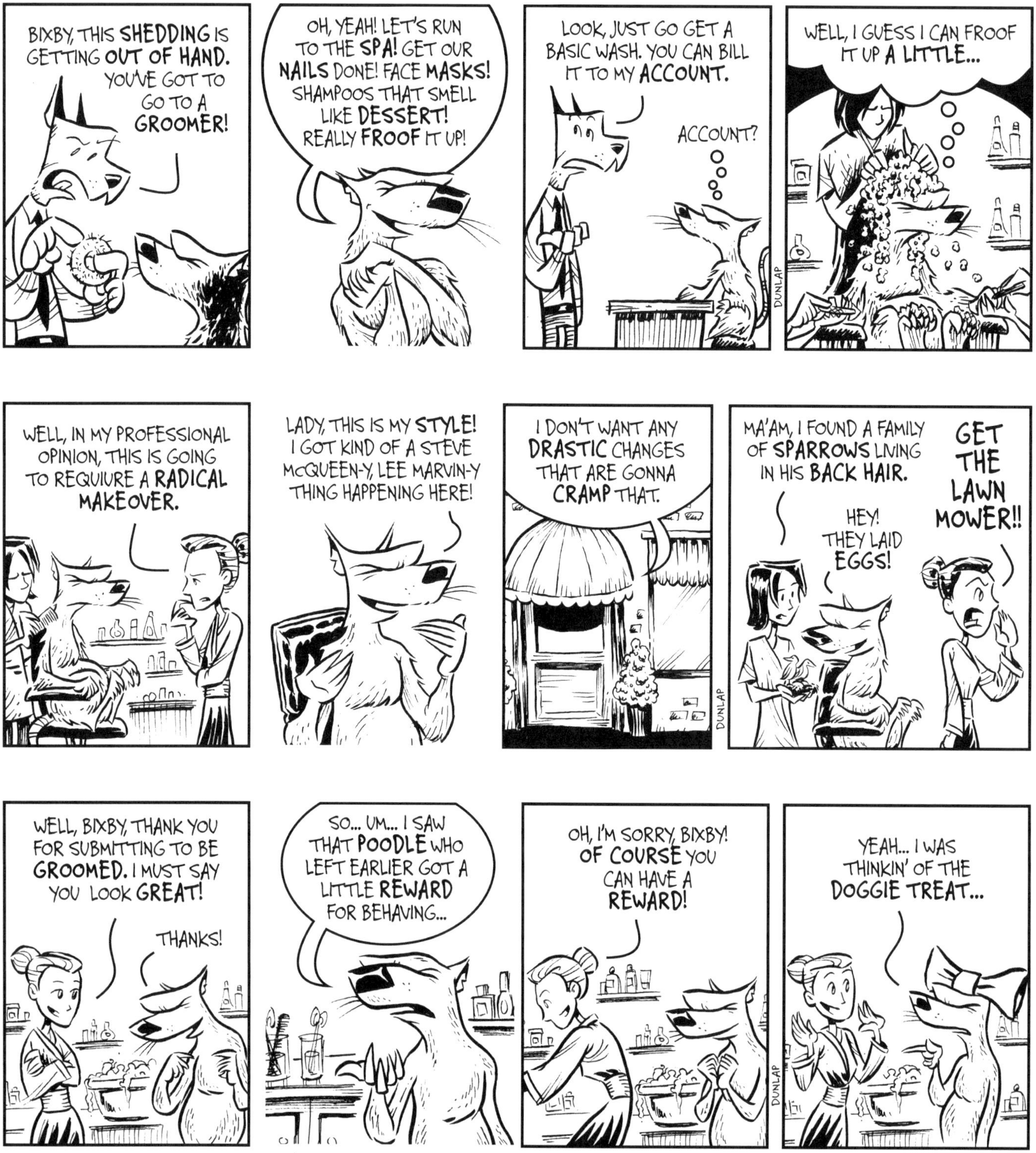
BIXBY, THIS SHEDDING IS GETTING OUT OF HAND. YOU'VE GOT TO GO TO A GROOMER!
OH, YEAH! LET'S RUN TO THE SPA! GET OUR NAILS DONE! FACE MASKS! SHAMPOOS THAT SMELL LIKE DESSERT! REALLY FROOF IT UP!
LOOK, JUST GO GET A BASIC WASH. YOU CAN BILL IT TO MY ACCOUNT.
ACCOUNT?
DUNLAP
WELL, I GUESS I CAN FROOF IT UP A LITTLE...
WELL, IN MY PROFESSIONAL OPINION, THIS IS GOING TO REQUIURE A RADICAL MAKEOVER.
LADY, THIS IS MY STYLE! I GOT KIND OF A STEVE McQUEEN-Y, LEE MARVIN-Y THING HAPPENING HERE!
I DON'T WANT ANY DRASTIC CHANGES THAT ARE GONNA CRAMP THAT.
DUNLAP
MA'AM, I FOUND A FAMILY OF SPARROWS LIVING IN HIS BACK HAIR.
HEY! THEY LAID EGGS!
GET THE LAWN MOWER!!
WELL, BIXBY, THANK YOU FOR SUBMITTING TO BE GROOMED. I MUST SAY YOU LOOK GREAT!
THANKS!
SO... UM... I SAW THAT POODLE WHO LEFT EARLIER GOT A LITTLE REWARD FOR BEHAVING...
OH, I'M SORRY, BIXBY! OF COURSE YOU CAN HAVE A REWARD!
DUNLAP
YEAH... I WAS THINKIN' OF THE DOGGIE TREAT...

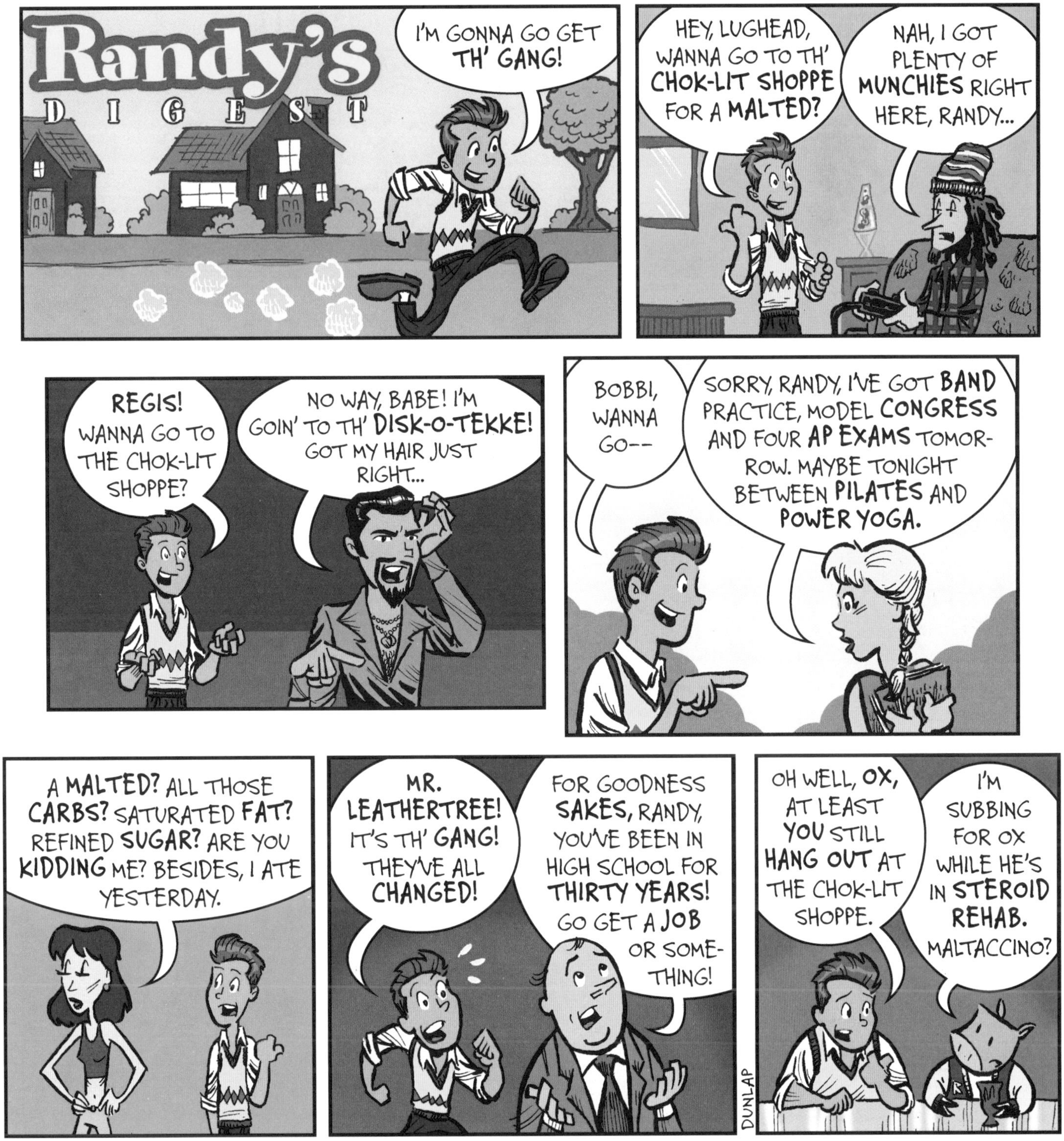
Randy's DIGEST
I'M GONNA GO GET TH' GANG!
HEY, LUGHEAD, WANNA GO TO TH' CHOK-LIT SHOPPE FOR A MALTED?
NAH, I GOT PLENTY OF MUNCHIES RIGHT HERE, RANDY...
REGIS! WANNA GO TO THE CHOK-LIT SHOPPE?
NO WAY, BABE! I'M GOIN' TO TH' DISK-O-TEKKE! GOT MY HAIR JUST RIGHT...
BOBBI, WANNA GO--
SORRY, RANDY, I'VE GOT BAND PRACTICE, MODEL CONGRESS AND FOUR AP EXAMS TOMOR-ROW. MAYBE TONIGHT BETWEEN PILATES AND POWER YOGA.
A MALTED? ALL THOSE CARBS? SATURATED FAT? REFINED SUGAR? ARE YOU KIDDING ME? BESIDES, I ATE YESTERDAY.
MR. LEATHERTREE! IT'S TH' GANG! THEY'VE ALL CHANGED!
FOR GOODNESS SAKES, RANDY, YOU'VE BEEN IN HIGH SCHOOL FOR THIRTY YEARS! GO GET A JOB OR SOME-THING!
OH WELL, OX, AT LEAST YOU STILL HANG OUT AT THE CHOK-LIT SHOPPE.
I'M SUBBING FOR OX WHILE HE'S IN STEROID REHAB. MALTACCINO?
DUNLAP

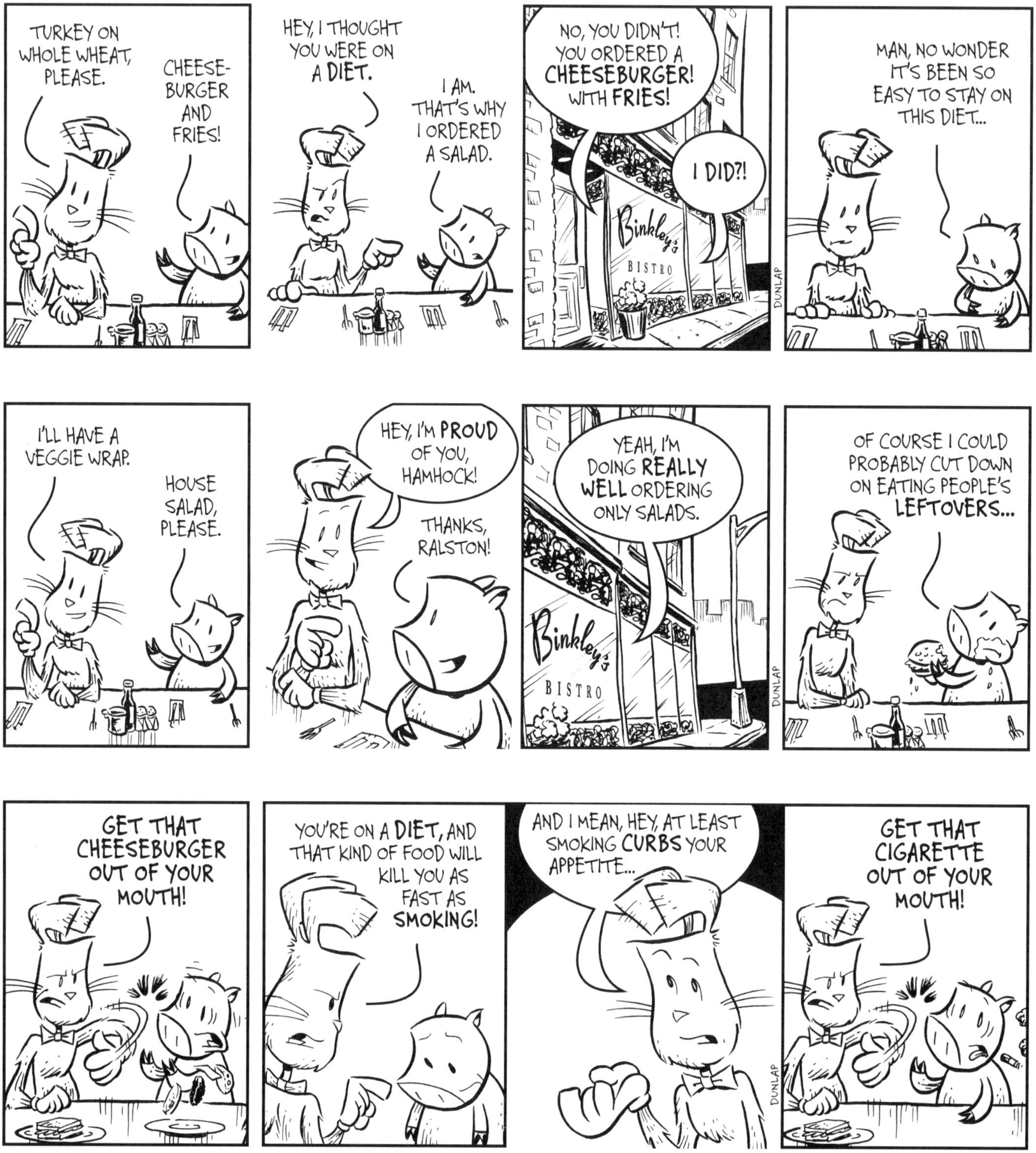

TURKEY ON WHOLE WHEAT, PLEASE.
CHEESE-BURGER AND FRIES!
HEY, I THOUGHT YOU WERE ON A DIET.
I AM. THAT'S WHY I ORDERED A SALAD.
NO, YOU DIDN'T! YOU ORDERED A CHEESEBURGER! WITH FRIES!
I DID?!
Binkley's BISTRO
DUNLAP
MAN, NO WONDER IT'S BEEN SO EASY TO STAY ON THIS DIET...
I'LL HAVE A VEGGIE WRAP.
HOUSE SALAD, PLEASE.
HEY, I'M PROUD OF YOU, HAMHOCK!
THANKS, RALSTON!
YEAH, I'M DOING REALLY WELL ORDERING ONLY SALADS.
Binkley's BISTRO
DUNLAP
OF COURSE I COULD PROBABLY CUT DOWN ON EATING PEOPLE'S LEFTOVERS...
GET THAT CHEESEBURGER OUT OF YOUR MOUTH!
YOU'RE ON A DIET, AND THAT KIND OF FOOD WILL KILL YOU AS FAST AS SMOKING!
AND I MEAN, HEY, AT LEAST SMOKING CURBS YOUR APPETITE...
DUNLAP
GET THAT CIGARETTE OUT OF YOUR MOUTH!

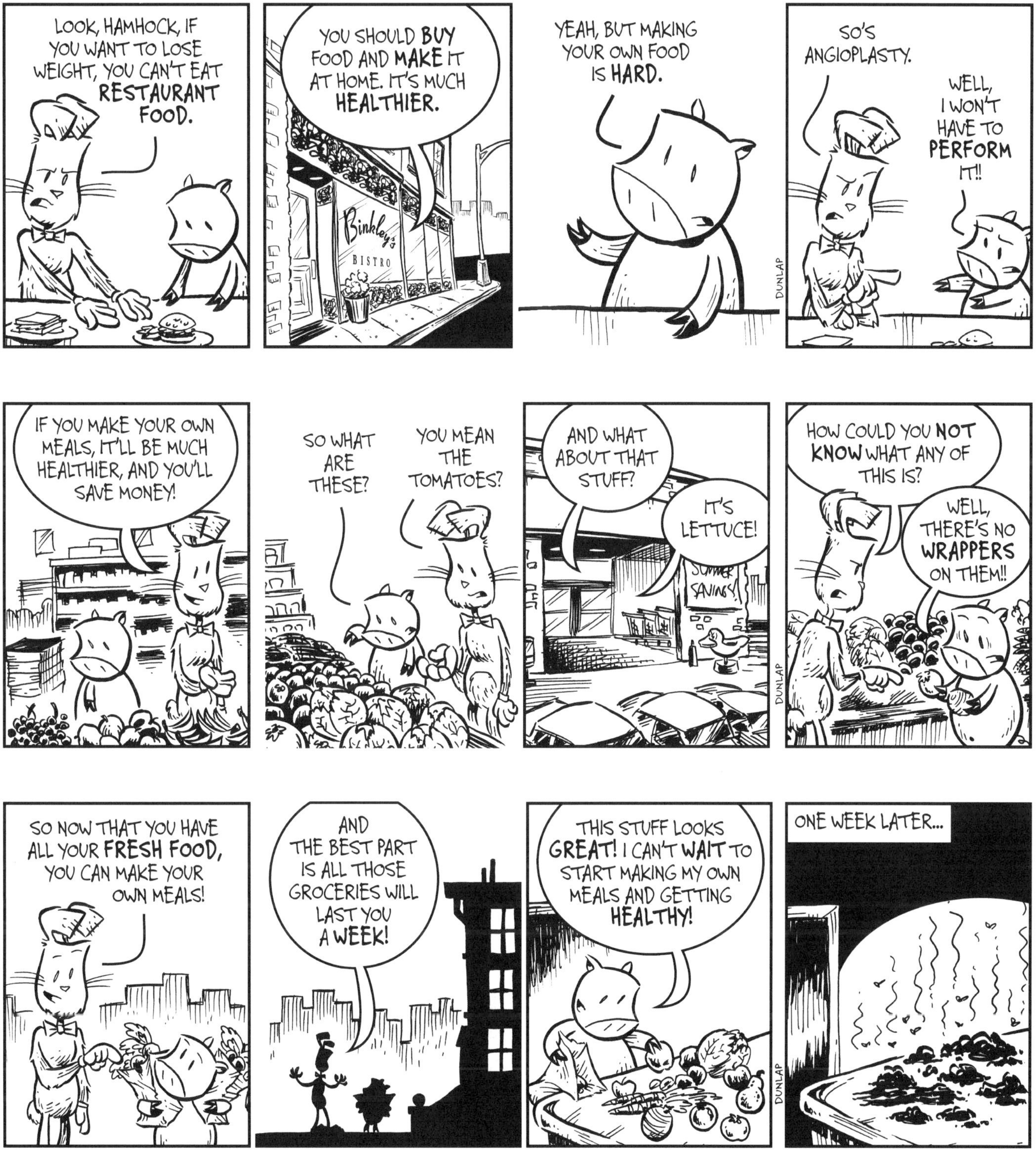
LOOK, HAMHOCK, IF YOU WANT TO LOSE WEIGHT, YOU CAN'T EAT **RESTAURANT FOOD.**
YOU SHOULD **BUY** FOOD AND **MAKE** IT AT HOME. IT'S MUCH **HEALTHIER.**
Binkley's BISTRO
YEAH, BUT MAKING YOUR OWN FOOD IS **HARD.**
DUNLAP
SO'S ANGIOPLASTY.
WELL, I WON'T HAVE TO **PERFORM** IT!!
IF YOU MAKE YOUR OWN MEALS, IT'LL BE MUCH HEALTHIER, AND YOU'LL SAVE MONEY!
SO WHAT ARE THESE?
YOU MEAN THE TOMATOES?
AND WHAT ABOUT THAT STUFF?
IT'S LETTUCE!
SUMMER SAVINGS
DUNLAP
HOW COULD YOU **NOT KNOW** WHAT ANY OF THIS IS?
WELL, THERE'S NO **WRAPPERS** ON THEM!!
SO NOW THAT YOU HAVE ALL YOUR **FRESH FOOD,** YOU CAN MAKE YOUR OWN MEALS!
AND THE BEST PART IS ALL THOSE GROCERIES WILL LAST YOU A **WEEK!**
THIS STUFF LOOKS **GREAT!** I CAN'T **WAIT** TO START MAKING MY OWN MEALS AND GETTING **HEALTHY!**
DUNLAP
ONE WEEK LATER...

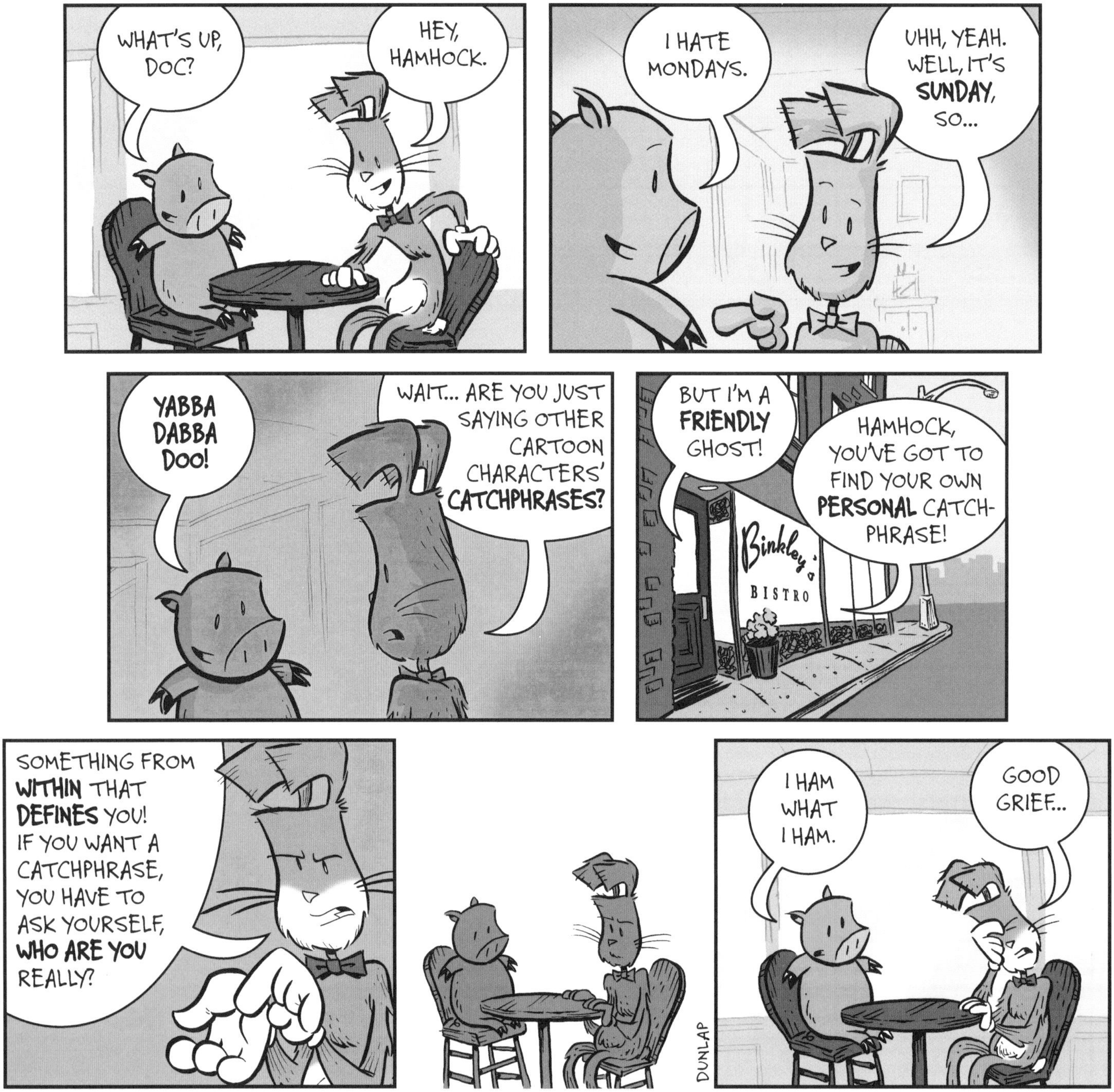
WHAT'S UP, DOC?
HEY, HAMHOCK.
I HATE MONDAYS.
UHH, YEAH. WELL, IT'S SUNDAY, SO...
YABBA DABBA DOO!
WAIT... ARE YOU JUST SAYING OTHER CARTOON CHARACTERS' CATCHPHRASES?
BUT I'M A FRIENDLY GHOST!
Binkley's BISTRO
HAMHOCK, YOU'VE GOT TO FIND YOUR OWN PERSONAL CATCH-PHRASE!
SOMETHING FROM WITHIN THAT DEFINES YOU! IF YOU WANT A CATCHPHRASE, YOU HAVE TO ASK YOURSELF, WHO ARE YOU REALLY?
DUNLAP
I HAM WHAT I HAM.
GOOD GRIEF...

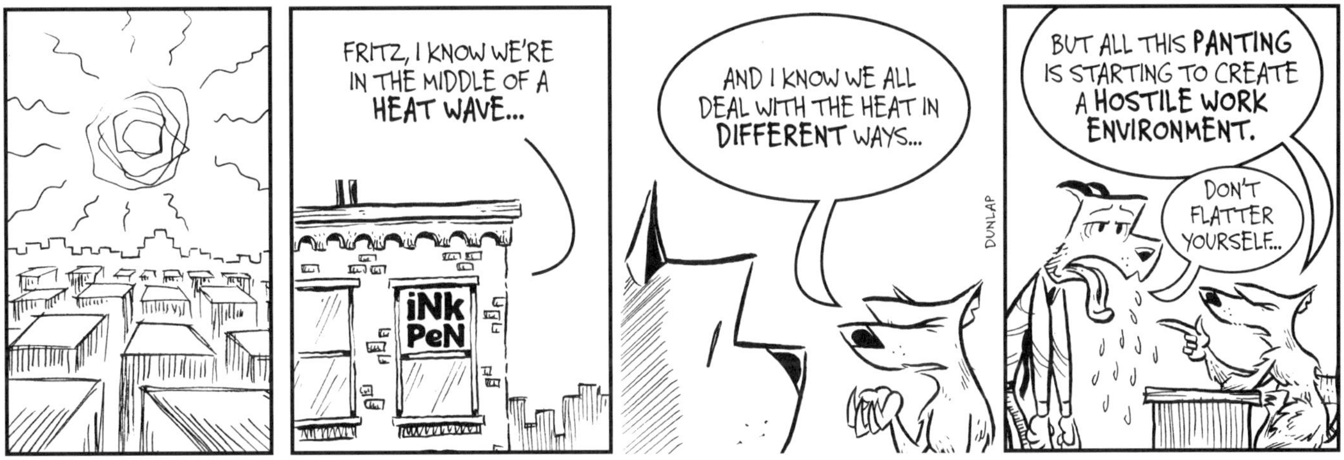
FRITZ, I KNOW WE'RE IN THE MIDDLE OF A HEAT WAVE...
AND I KNOW WE ALL DEAL WITH THE HEAT IN DIFFERENT WAYS...
BUT ALL THIS PANTING IS STARTING TO CREATE A HOSTILE WORK ENVIRONMENT.
DON'T FLATTER YOURSELF...
iNk PeN
DUNLAP

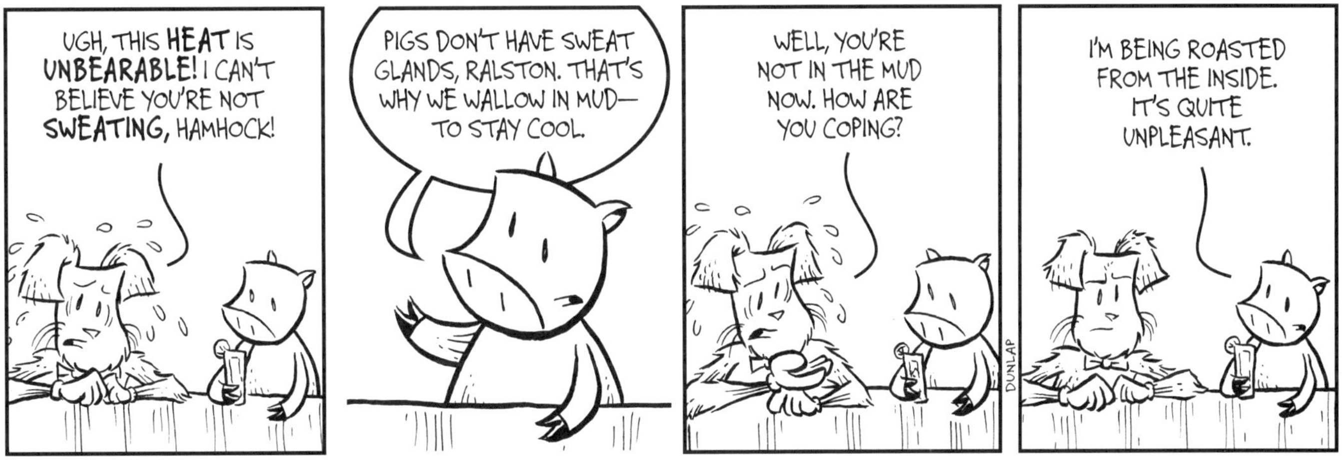
UGH, THIS HEAT IS UNBEARABLE! I CAN'T BELIEVE YOU'RE NOT SWEATING, HAMHOCK!
PIGS DON'T HAVE SWEAT GLANDS, RALSTON. THAT'S WHY WE WALLOW IN MUD— TO STAY COOL.
WELL, YOU'RE NOT IN THE MUD NOW. HOW ARE YOU COPING?
I'M BEING ROASTED FROM THE INSIDE. IT'S QUITE UNPLEASANT.
DUNLAP

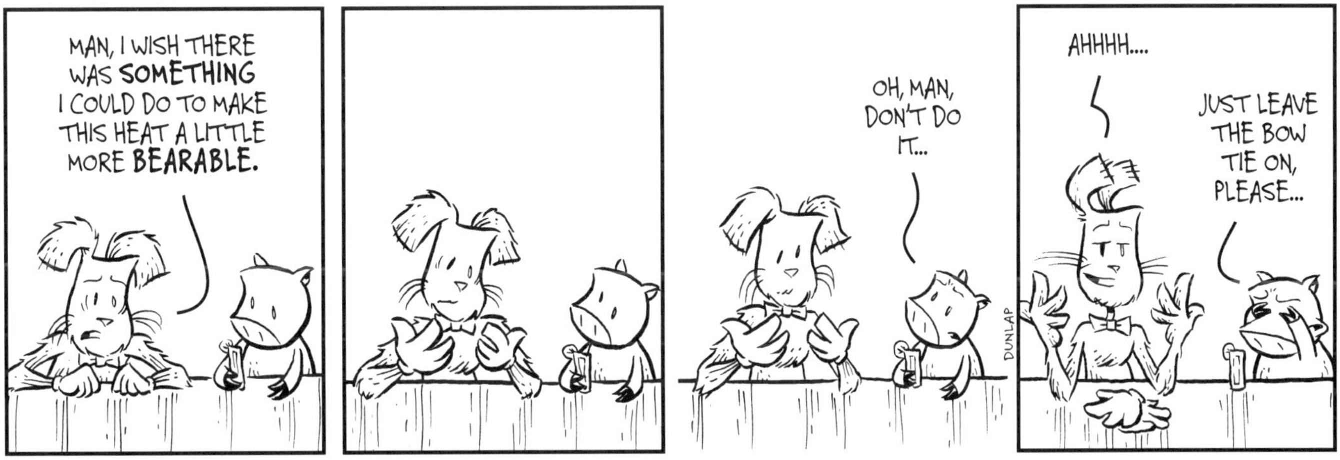
MAN, I WISH THERE WAS SOMETHING I COULD DO TO MAKE THIS HEAT A LITTLE MORE BEARABLE.
OH, MAN, DON'T DO IT...
AHHHH....
JUST LEAVE THE BOW TIE ON, PLEASE...
DUNLAP

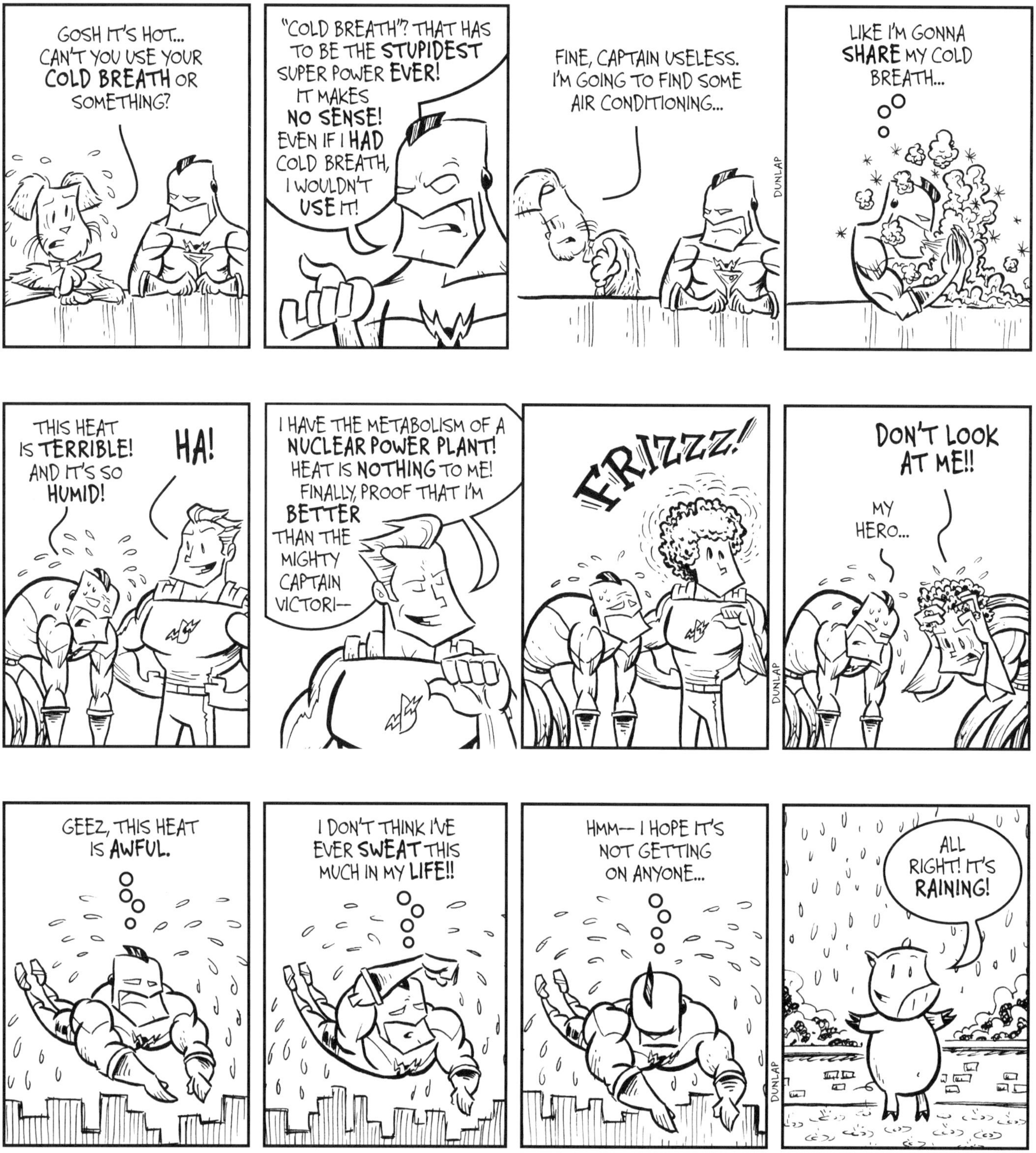

GOSH IT'S HOT... CAN'T YOU USE YOUR COLD BREATH OR SOMETHING?
"COLD BREATH"? THAT HAS TO BE THE STUPIDEST SUPER POWER EVER! IT MAKES NO SENSE! EVEN IF I HAD COLD BREATH, I WOULDN'T USE IT!
FINE, CAPTAIN USELESS. I'M GOING TO FIND SOME AIR CONDITIONING...
DUNLAP
LIKE I'M GONNA SHARE MY COLD BREATH...
THIS HEAT IS TERRIBLE! AND IT'S SO HUMID!
HA!
I HAVE THE METABOLISM OF A NUCLEAR POWER PLANT! HEAT IS NOTHING TO ME! FINALLY, PROOF THAT I'M BETTER THAN THE MIGHTY CAPTAIN VICTORI—
FRIZZZ!
DUNLAP
MY HERO...
DON'T LOOK AT ME!!
GEEZ, THIS HEAT IS AWFUL.
I DON'T THINK I'VE EVER SWEAT THIS MUCH IN MY LIFE!!
HMM— I HOPE IT'S NOT GETTING ON ANYONE...
DUNLAP
ALL RIGHT! IT'S RAINING!

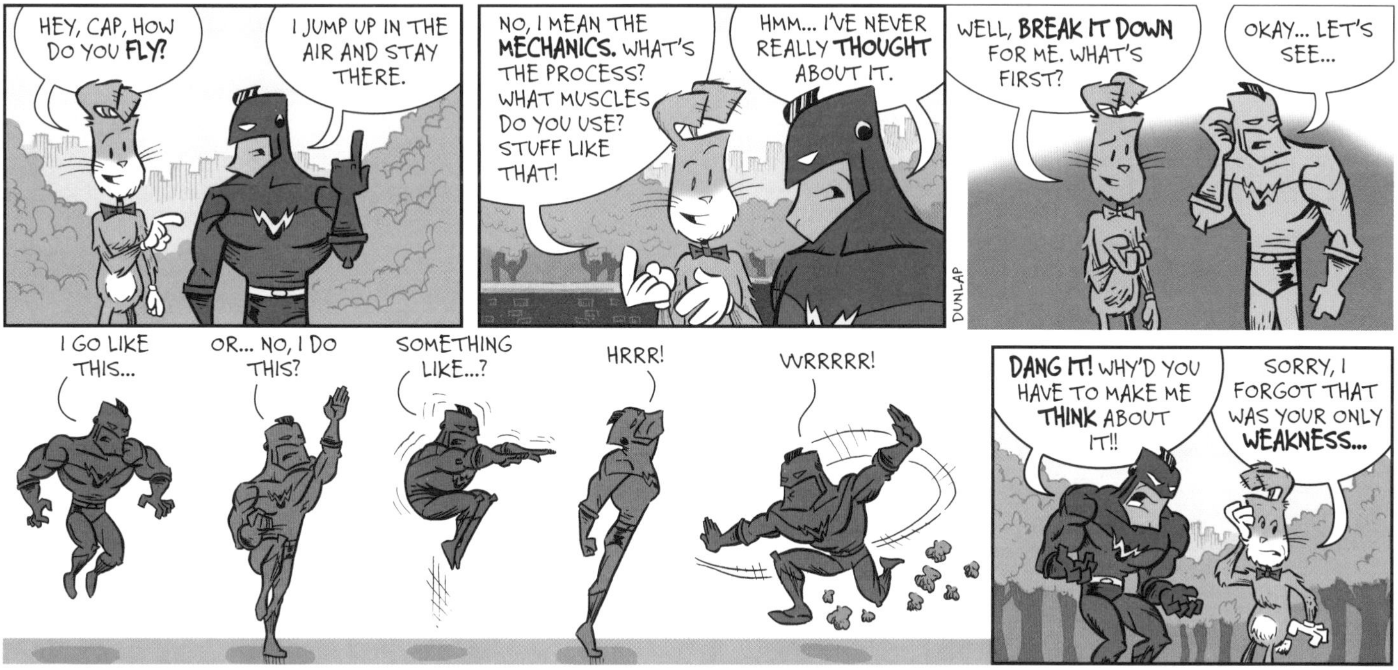
HEY, CAP, HOW DO YOU **FLY?**
I JUMP UP IN THE AIR AND STAY THERE.
NO, I MEAN THE **MECHANICS.** WHAT'S THE PROCESS? WHAT MUSCLES DO YOU USE? STUFF LIKE THAT!
HMM... I'VE NEVER REALLY **THOUGHT** ABOUT IT.
DUNLAP
WELL, **BREAK IT DOWN** FOR ME. WHAT'S FIRST?
OKAY... LET'S SEE...
I GO LIKE THIS...
OR... NO, I DO THIS?
SOMETHING LIKE...?
HRRR!
WRRRRR!
**DANG IT!** WHY'D YOU HAVE TO MAKE ME **THINK** ABOUT IT!!
SORRY, I FORGOT THAT WAS YOUR ONLY **WEAKNESS...**

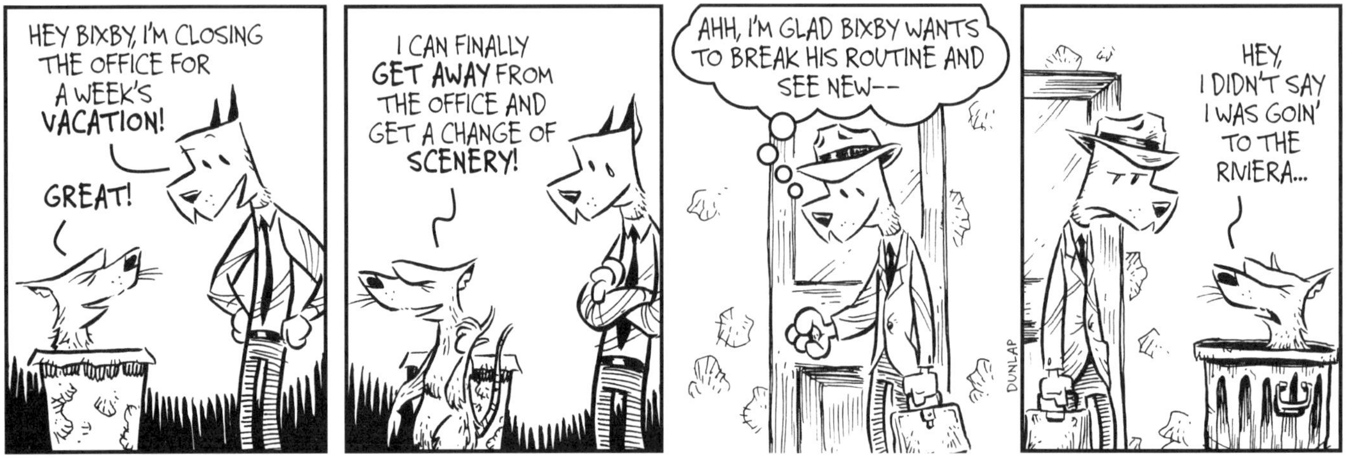
HEY BIXBY, I'M CLOSING THE OFFICE FOR A WEEK'S **VACATION**!
**GREAT!**
I CAN FINALLY **GET AWAY** FROM THE OFFICE AND GET A CHANGE OF **SCENERY**!
AHH, I'M GLAD BIXBY WANTS TO BREAK HIS ROUTINE AND SEE NEW--
DUNLAP
HEY, I DIDN'T SAY I WAS GOIN' TO THE RIVIERA...

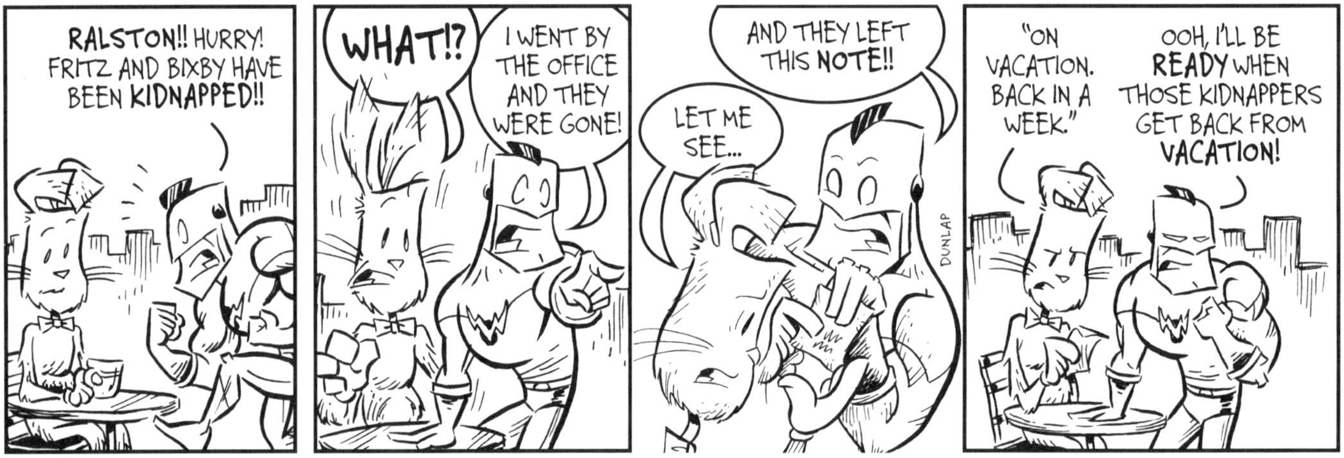
**RALSTON!!** HURRY! FRITZ AND BIXBY HAVE BEEN **KIDNAPPED!!**
**WHAT!?**
I WENT BY THE OFFICE AND THEY WERE GONE!
AND THEY LEFT THIS **NOTE!!**
LET ME SEE...
DUNLAP
"ON VACATION. BACK IN A WEEK."
OOH, I'LL BE **READY** WHEN THOSE KIDNAPPERS GET BACK FROM **VACATION!**

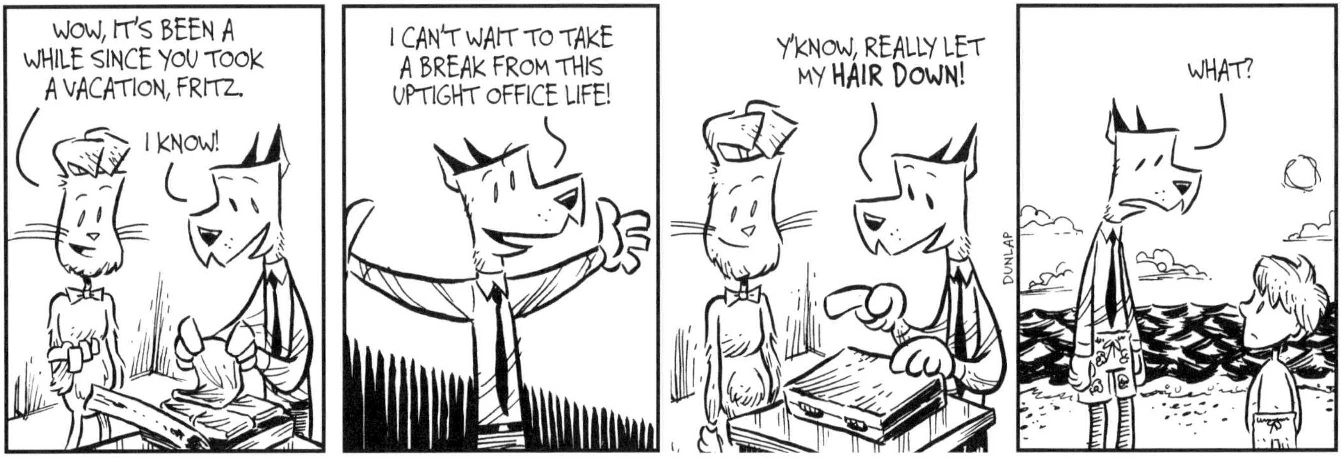
WOW, IT'S BEEN A WHILE SINCE YOU TOOK A VACATION, FRITZ.
I KNOW!
I CAN'T WAIT TO TAKE A BREAK FROM THIS UPTIGHT OFFICE LIFE!
Y'KNOW, REALLY LET MY **HAIR DOWN!**
DUNLAP
WHAT?

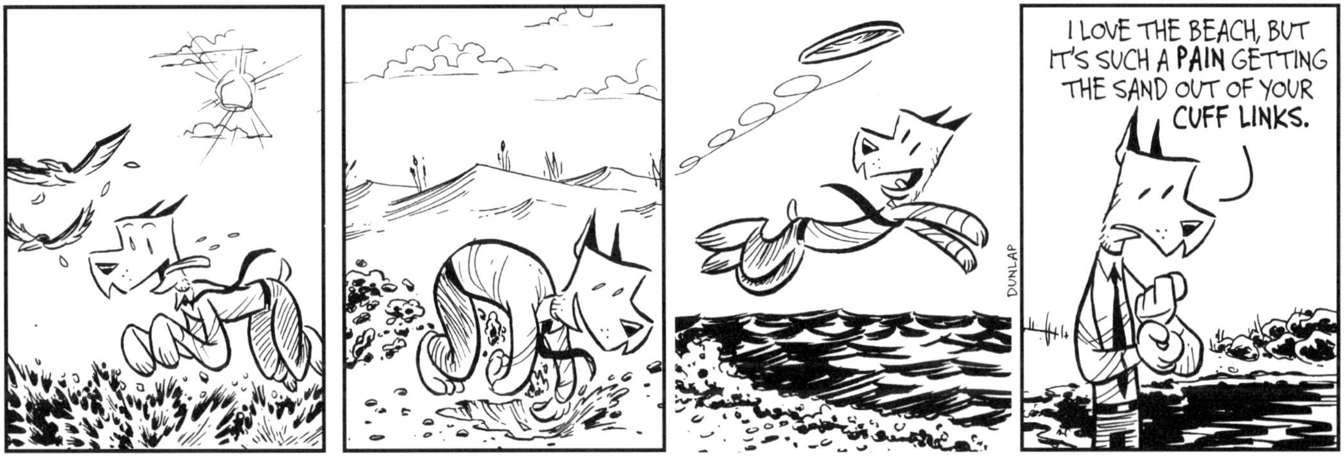
DUNLAP
I LOVE THE BEACH, BUT IT'S SUCH A **PAIN** GETTING THE SAND OUT OF YOUR **CUFF LINKS.**

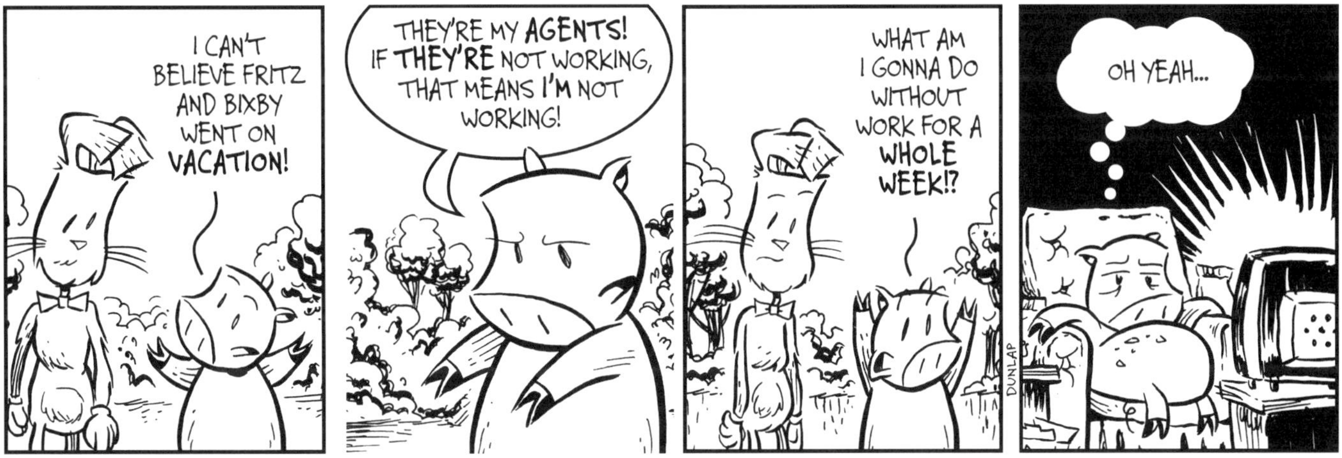
I CAN'T BELIEVE FRITZ AND BIXBY WENT ON **VACATION**!
THEY'RE MY **AGENTS**! IF **THEY'RE** NOT WORKING, THAT MEANS **I'M** NOT WORKING!
WHAT AM I GONNA DO WITHOUT WORK FOR A **WHOLE WEEK**!?
DUNLAP
OH YEAH...

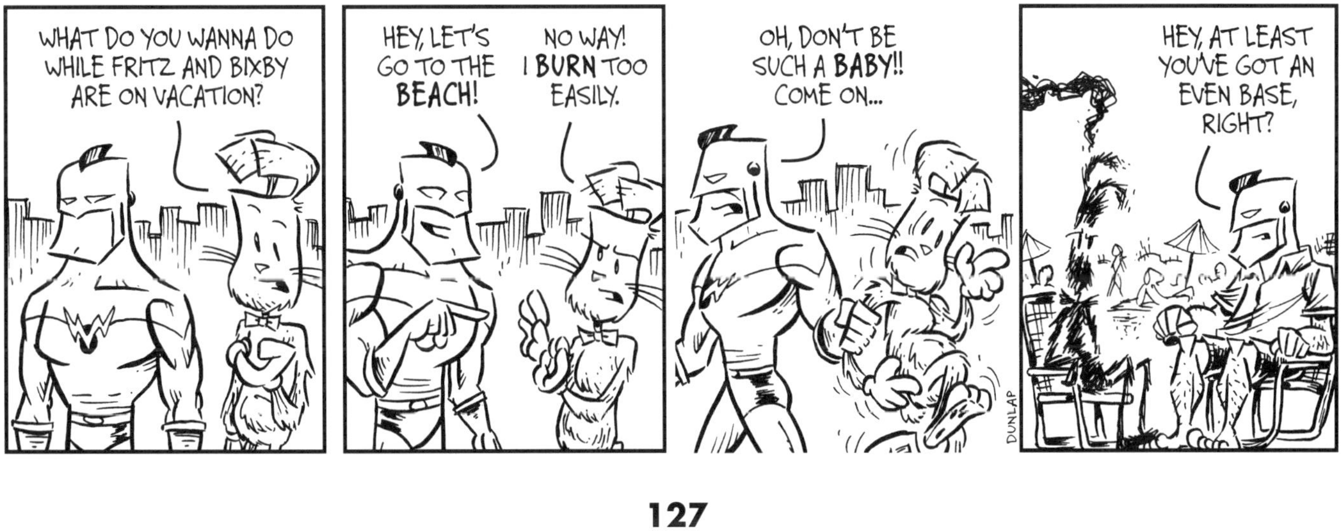
WHAT DO YOU WANNA DO WHILE FRITZ AND BIXBY ARE ON VACATION?
HEY, LET'S GO TO THE **BEACH**!
NO WAY! I **BURN** TOO EASILY.
OH, DON'T BE SUCH A **BABY**!! COME ON...
DUNLAP
HEY, AT LEAST YOU'VE GOT AN EVEN BASE, RIGHT?

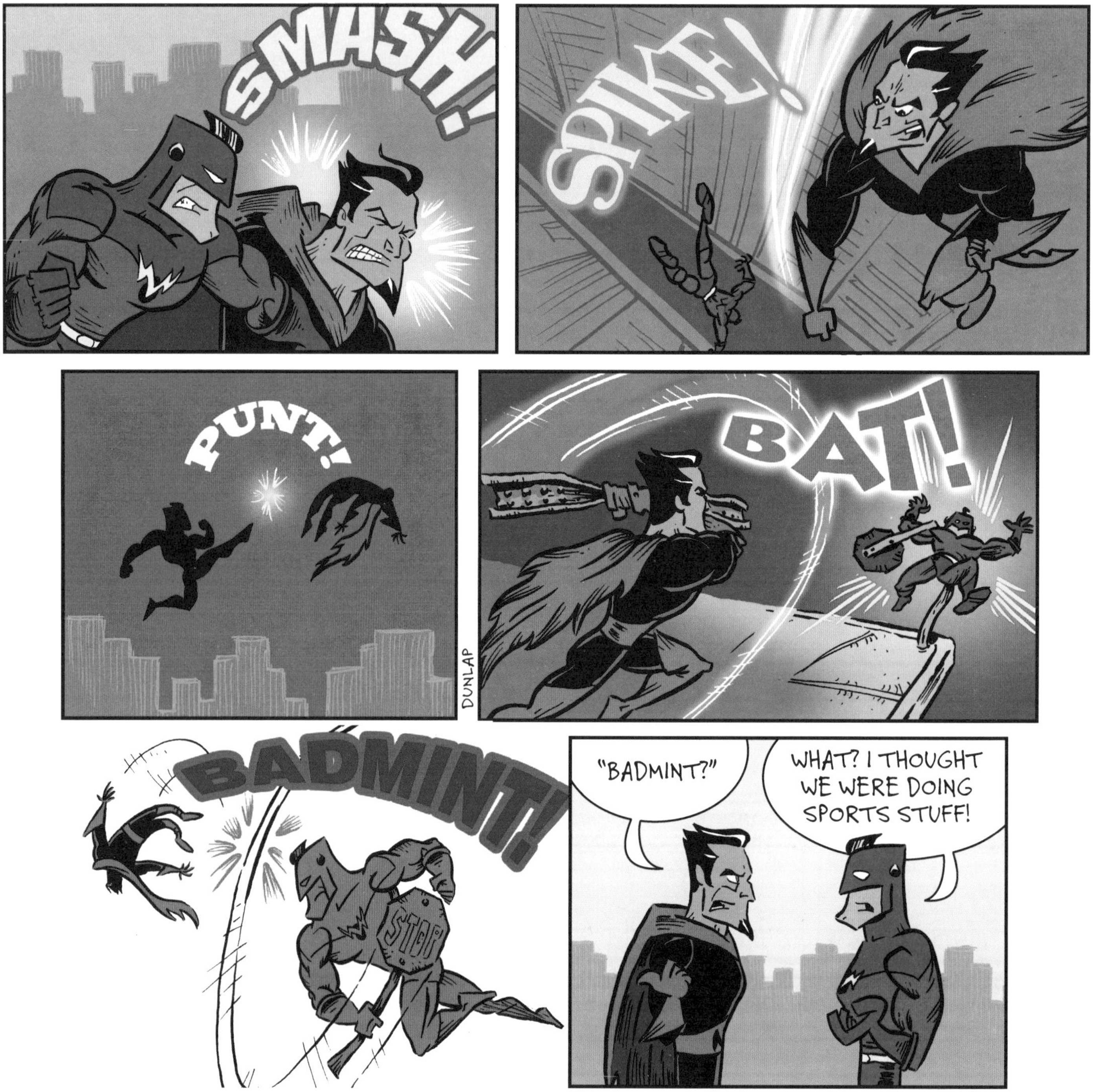
SMASH!
SPIKE!
PUNT!
BAT!
DUNLAP
BADMINT!
STOP
"BADMINT?"
WHAT? I THOUGHT WE WERE DOING SPORTS STUFF!